MEDIEVAL DUBLIN XIII

D0913708

This volume is dedicated
to the memory of

James Lydon

MA (Dubl, NUI), PhD (Lond), DLitt (*h.c.* NUI), MRIA, FTCD (1965)
Lecky Professor of Medieval History (1980)
(1928–2013)

Medieval Dublin XIII

Proceedings of the Friends of Medieval Dublin
Symposium 2011

Seán Duffy

EDITOR

FOUR COURTS PRESS

Typeset in 10.5 pt on 12.5 pt Ehrhardt by
Carrigboy Typesetting Services for
FOUR COURTS PRESS LTD
7 Malpas Street, Dublin 8, Ireland
www.fourcourtspress.ie
and in North America for
FOUR COURTS PRESS
c/o ISBS, 920 NE 58th Avenue, Suite 300, Portland, OR 97213.

A catalogue record for this title is available
from the British Library.

ISBN 978–1–84682–389–3 hbk
ISBN 978–1–84682–390–9 pbk

This book is published with the active support of
Dublin City Council/Comhairle Chathair Átha Cliath.

Printed in England
by CPI Group (UK) Ltd, Croydon, CR0 4YY

Contents

Abbreviations

AFM	*Annala rioghachta Eireann: annals of the kingdom of Ireland by the Four Masters, from the earliest period to the year 1616*, ed. John O'Donovan (7 vols, Dublin, 1851)
AI	*The annals of Inisfallen (MS Rawlinson B503)*, ed. Seán Mac Airt (Dublin, 1951)
Alen	*Calendar of Archbishop Alen's register, c.1172–1534*, ed. Charles McNeill (Dublin, 1950)
ATig.	'Annals of Tigernach', ed. Whitley Stokes, in *Revue Celtique*, 16 (1895), 374–419; 17 (1896), 6–33, 119–263, 337–420; 18 (1897), 9–59, 150–97, 267–303 (repr. in 2 vols, Felinfach, 1993)
AU	*The annals of Ulster (to AD1131)*, ed. Seán Mac Airt and Gearóid Mac Niocaill (Dublin, 1983)
BL	British Library [formerly British Museum], London
CARD	*Calendar of ancient records of Dublin, in the possession of the municipal corporation of that city*, 1, ed. J.T. Gilbert (Dublin, 1889)
CCD	*Christ Church deeds*, ed. M.J. McEnery and Raymond Refaussé (Dublin, 2001)
CDI	*Calendar of documents relating to Ireland*, ed. H.S. Sweetman (5 vols, London, 1875–86)
CGR	*Calendar of the Gormanston register, c.1175–1397, from the original in the possession of the Right Honourable the Viscount of Gormanston*, ed. James Mills and M.J. McEnery (Dublin, 1916)
Chronicles	Raphael Holinshed, *The historie of Irelande from the first inhabitation thereof, unto the yeare 1509* within his *Chronicles of England, Scotland and Ireland*
CIRCLE	*A calendar of Irish chancery letters, c.1244–1509*, ed. Peter Crooks
CS	*Chronicon Scotorum*, ed. W.M. Hennessy (London, 1866)
CSMA	*Chartularies of St Mary's Abbey Dublin*, ed. J.T. Gilbert (2 vols, London, 1884)
DCLA	Dublin City Library and Archives
DGMR	*The Dublin guild merchant roll, c.1190–1265*, ed. Philonema Connolly and Geoffrey Martin (Dublin, 1992)
DIL	*Dictionary of the Irish language* and *Contributions to a dictionary of the Irish language* (Dublin, 1913–76; compact ed., 1983)
FA	*Fragmentary annals of Ireland*, ed. Joan Newlon Radner (Dublin, 1978)
HSJB	*Register of the hospital of St John the Baptist, without the New Gate, Dublin*, ed. Eric St John Brooks (Dublin, 1936)

JRSAI	*Journal of the Royal Society of Antiquaries of Ireland*
LL	*The Book of Leinster*, ed. R.I. Best, Osbern Bergin, M.A. O'Brien and Anne O'Sullivan (6 vols, Dublin, 1954–83)
O'Heyne, *Irish Dominicans*	John O'Heyne, *Epilogus chronologicus exponens succinte conventus et fundationes sacriordinis praedicatorum in regno Hyberniae* (Louvain, 1760); ed. and trans. Ambrose Coleman as *The Irish Dominicans of the seventeenth century*, together with Ambrose Coleman, *Ancient Dominican foundations in Ireland* (Dundalk, 1902)
OS	Ordnance Survey
Otway-Ruthven, 'Church lands'	A.J. Otway-Ruthven, 'The mediaeval church lands of County Dublin' in J.A. Watt, J.B. Morrall and F.X. Martin (eds), *Medieval studies presented to Aubrey Gwynn SJ* (Dublin, 1961)
PR	Patent Rolls
PRIA	*Proceedings of the Royal Irish Academy*
RAST	*The register of the abbey of St Thomas, Dublin*, ed. J.T. Gilbert (London, 1889)
VMH	*Vetera monumenta Hibernorum et Scotorum historiam illustantia quae ex Vaticani, Neapolis ac Florentiae tabularis depromsit et ordine chronologico diposuit, 1216–1547*, ed. Augustinus Theiner (Rome, 1864)
WSC	Wide Streets Commission

Contributors

DENIS CASEY is an independent scholar and holds a PhD from the University of Cambridge.

SEÁN DUFFY is chairman of the Friends of Medieval Dublin and a fellow of Trinity College Dublin.

LENORE FISCHER is an independent scholar and holds an MA in medieval history from the University of Limerick.

DECLAN JOHNSTON graduated in 2013 with a BA (Mod.) in history and Russian from Trinity College Dublin.

PAUL MacCOTTER holds a PhD in history from University College Cork.

NIALL McCULLOUGH is a partner with McCullough Mulvin Architects, Dublin.

JOHN MONTAGUE is an architectural historian and holds a PhD in history of art and architecture from Trinity College Dublin.

EOIN O'FLYNN holds a PhD in medieval history from Trinity College Dublin.

GRACE O'KEEFFE holds a PhD in medieval history from Trinity College Dublin.

NIALL Ó SÚILLEABHÁIN graduated in 2013 with a BA (Mod.) in history from Trinity College Dublin and is currently a postgraduate student at Oriel College, Oxford.

LINZI SIMPSON is an archaeological consultant and project manager.

CAOIMHE WHELAN holds the Irish Research Council's Daniel O'Connell Award in Irish history and is a postgraduate scholar based at the Department of History, Trinity College Dublin.

BERNADETTE WILLIAMS is an independent scholar and holds a PhD in medieval history from Trinity College Dublin.

ANDREW WOODS is curator of numismatics for York Museums Trust.

Editor's preface

This volume of essays arises from the thirteenth Medieval Dublin Symposium, which took place in Trinity College Dublin on Saturday 11 May 2011. The costs of the symposium, principally hire of the lecture theatre, were borne by the Department of History, TCD, for which the editor is very grateful. Bringing the essays to publication – by Four Courts Press, where Michael Potterton's eye for detail has again proved invaluable – is an altogether more expensive business and is only possible thanks to the support of Dublin City Council: the Friends of Medieval Dublin are therefore grateful to the Heritage Officer, Charles Duggan, and the City Archaeologist, Ruth Johnson, for their ongoing support for the *Medieval Dublin* series, of which this is the thirteenth volume to appear.

We trust it is worth the investment. This volume alone, for instance, contains four new essays shedding light on the subject of Viking Age Dublin, including one on the Battle of Clontarf, the commemorations of whose millennium are now upon us. It contains the first detailed attempt to reconstruct the lands of the medieval diocese of Dublin since the pioneering efforts of the late Professor Otway-Ruthven over fifty years ago. Another essay develops a theme first highlighted by Aubrey Gwynn back in 1947 by forensically examining the link between Dublin and Bristol in the Middle Ages. Dublin today is a city famous for its writers, and this volume contains a discussion of its first great writer in the English language, the little-known James Yonge. Neither is it well known that beneath the Front Square of Trinity College lie the remains of the original All Hallows, a medieval priory founded by no less a figure than Dermot McMurrough, and the archaeological excavations that uncovered the priory walls and that have helped piece together the location of the earliest college buildings, dating from the 1590s, are detailed below.

One might mention also that another essay in this volume traces the origins of Dublin's municipal government from the days of the Viking Thingmoot through to the City Assembly of the later Middles Ages, developing the theme of an essay published in *Medieval Dublin II* (2001). The latter was written by James Lydon, emeritus Lecky Professor of Medieval History at Trinity College, who sadly passed away on 25 June 2013. Best known for his vivid narrative, *The lordship of Ireland in the Middle Ages* (1972; 2nd ed., 2003), one of his abiding interests was the history of Dublin. For many years, he taught a sophister special subject on medieval Dublin in Trinity and as the Wood Quay controversy raged in the mid-1970s he was involved in the moves to found what would become the Friends of Medieval Dublin. The latter therefore wish to dedicate this volume of essays to the memory of a man who was the proverbial scholar and gentleman, whose passionate enthusiasm and ceaseless encouragement were greatly appreciated and will be much missed. *I measc na naomh go raibh sé go deo.*

Seán Duffy
Chairman
Friends of Medieval Dublin

The Dublin Vikings and the Clann Cholmáin kings of the Southern Uí Néill

EOIN O'FLYNN

Of the southern branches of the Uí Néill, Clann Cholmáin emerged as the most powerful about the middle of the eighth century. The dynasty was based in Mide, with its main royal complex at Lough Ennell in present-day Co. Westmeath. This period saw Clann Cholmáin overtake the previously dominant Síl nÁedo Sláine branch of the Southern Uí Néill, which was based farther to the east in Brega. This growth in Clann Cholmáin power also saw the dynasty emerge as a claimant to the kingship of Tara and therefore to primacy among the wider Uí Néill grouping, both northern and southern branches.[1] By the dawn of the Viking Age then, Clann Cholmáin was one of the most important political forces on the island.

The dynasty had little recorded contact or interaction with Vikings before 841 and the establishment of Dublin. As has often been repeated, the first generation of Viking attacks on Ireland generally saw only hit-and-run raids targeting coastal areas with little penetration into the interior. By the 820s, the rate and ambition of Viking attacks had increased markedly, but even then Clann Cholmáin does not seem to have been involved.[2] One Clann Cholmáin king of Tara from this period, Conchobor (d. 833), is brought into contact with the Vikings in *Ríg Uisnig*, a midland kinglist found in the Book of Leinster: 'Conchob*or* m*ac* Don*dchada* .xii. a bádud i n-usci i C*luain* Iraird la ríg Gall (Conchobor son of Donnchad [reigned for] twelve years; he was drowned in water at Clonard by the king of the Foreigners)'.[3] But this is a false alarm. It seems that these details have been misplaced in the text and actually refer to a

---

1 For a consideration of the various factors that brought about these changes, see Thomas Charles-Edwards, 'The Uí Néill, 695–743: the rise and fall of dynasties', *Peritia*, 16 (2002), 396–418.   2 Kings and dynasties more readily accessible from the sea continued to bear the brunt of Viking aggression. In the year 828, for example, the Dál nAraide in northeast Ulster routed a Viking force, the king of Ard Cíannachtae further south in Co. Louth was fatally wounded in a clash with Vikings, while the king of Uí Chennselaig, in southern Leinster, routed another force: see *The annals of Ulster (to AD1131)*, ed. Seán Mac Airt and Gearóid Mac Niocaill (Dublin, 1983) (hereafter *AU*) 828.5, 828.4, 828.6. At this point, we should note that there is a significant lacuna in the Clonmacnoise annal texts ('Annals of Tigernach', ed. Whitley Stokes, in *Revue Celtique*, 16 (1895), 374–419; 17 (1896), 6–33, 119–263, 337–420; 18 (1897), 9–59, 150–97, 267–303 (repr. in 2 vols, Felinfach, 1993) (hereafter *ATig.*), 766–974; *Chronicon Scotorum*, ed. W.M. Hennessy (London, 1866) (hereafter *CS*), 722–804) for the period under discussion.   3 *The Book of Leinster*, ed. R.I. Best, Osbern Bergin, M.A. O'Brien and Anne O'Sullivan (6 vols, Dublin, 1954–83)

later ninth-century Clann Cholmáin king also called Conchobor. The Annals of Ulster record for 864 that 'Concobur m. Donncadha, leithri Mide, do marb*ad* i n-uisciu oc Cluain Irairdd la Amlaiph, ri Gall (Conchobor son of Donnchad, one of two kings of Mide, was put to death in water at Cluain Iraird by Amláib, king of the Foreigners)'.

The Vikings *were* becoming increasing visible on the Irish political scene during the earlier Conchobor's lifetime, something that is made clear in *Baile in Scáil* or the 'Phantom's Frenzy', a text believed to contain a later ninth-century core. In this text, time is divided by the reigns of kings of Tara and under the section on Conchobor (d. 833) we find the following: 'Túaruscbáil tíchtan geinti (Tidings of the coming of the Norse)'.[4] But this must be taken as a rather general comment on the situation in the earlier ninth century. There is not, it seems, strong evidence for direct contact between Vikings and Clann Cholmáin at this point.

By the later 830s in particular, the Vikings were appearing in greater strength, pushing farther into the interior and staying for longer. As well as two huge fleets on the Boyne and the Liffey, the year 837 also saw Vikings on the Shannon.[5] Mide was starting to look more vulnerable and Clann Cholmáin could now add the Viking threat to the problems of pressure from Northern Uí Néill rivals and Munster aggression, all of which was exacerbated by the dynasty's own internal feuding.[6] Of course a crucial date was 841, which saw the establishment of the *longphort* at Dublin. Máel Sechnaill I, a crucial figure in what follows and one of Clann Cholmáin's most successful kings, first appears in the record about the same time.[7] An attack was immediately launched from newly established Dublin on the Midlands. Clonard, a church closely linked to Clann Cholmáin, was a target.[8] However the Viking camp established on Lough Ree during the 840s probably posed as much as if not more of an immediate threat to Clann Cholmáin interests than the *longphuirt* on the east coast. Máel Sechnaill moved quickly on this front. He drowned the famous Tuirgéis, a method of execution he was to employ again later.[9]

The year 848 saw several major defeats for the Vikings in Ireland, including one at the hands of Máel Sechnaill, by now king of Tara, who prevailed in a

(hereafter *LL*), i, p. 197 (l.5950).   4 Kevin Murray (ed.), *Baile in Scáil: The phantom's frenzy* (Dublin, 2004), pp 45, 63 (§48).   5 *AU* 837; *CS* 837.   6 For example, see *AU* 835.3; *AU* 840.4; *CS* 840; *AU* 841.1.   7 *AU* 841.4; *CS* 841; *AU* 839.6.   8 For example, the Ruaidrí whose death is recorded at *CS* 838 and who held posts at both Clonard and Clonmacnoise was probably a member of Clann Cholmáin. While perhaps a long shot, among the many grave-slabs at Clonmacnoise is one bearing this name that has been tentatively matched (by Lionard) with the Ruaidrí of the annal entry: see R.A.S. Macalister, *Corpus inscriptionum Insularum Celticarum*, ii (Dublin, 1945; repr. Dublin, 1996), p. 48, pl. xv; Pádraig Lionard, 'Early Irish grave-slabs', *Proceedings of the Royal Irish Academy* (hereafter *PRIA*), 61(C) (1961–2), 160. Over the next few years, further attacks were launched from Dublin targeting the Midlands: see *AU* 842.2; *AU* 842.7 and possibly *AU* 845.2.   9 *AU* 844.4; *CS* 844; *AU* 845; *CS* 845.

battle fought deep in the Midlands in which seven hundred *gennti* ('heathens') fell.[10] Though we are not told where this defeated Viking force had originated, it is tempting to argue for Dublin because in the following year Máel Sechnaill launched the first recorded Irish attack on the settlement, probably in retaliation.[11] Máel Sechnaill was supported in this attack on Dublin by Tigernach, a king who belonged to the Uí Chernaig dynasty based at Lagore (*Loch nGabor*).[12] Close cousins but fierce rivals of this dynasty were the Uí Chonaing based further north at Knowth (*Cnodbae*). In the following year, 850, the king of this dynasty Cináed 'rebelled against Máel Sechnaill with the support of the Foreigners'. Lagore and its associated church, Trevet (*Treóit*), bore the brunt of Cináed's aggression.[13] Retaliation followed quickly as Máel Sechnaill and Tigernach responded by drowning Cináed.[14] It may be that his

10 *AU* 848.4; *CS* 848. The battle was fought at 'Forach'. O'Donovan, followed by Hennessy, put it in Co. Meath, 'near Skreen': *Annala rioghachta Eireann: annals of the kingdom of Ireland by the Four Masters, from the earliest period to the year 1616*, ed. John O'Donovan (7 vols, Dublin, 1851) (hereafter *AFM*), i, p. 474, n. z; *Annala Uladh ('Annals of Ulster'), otherwise Annala Senait ('Annals of Senat'): a chronicle of Irish Affairs, AD431 to AD1540*, ed. W.M. Hennessy and B. Mac Carthy (4 vols, Dublin, 1887–1901), i, p. 355, n. 8. But Hogan later argued that the site was 'rather, Farrow tl. near Mullingar': Edmund Hogan, *Onomasticon Goedelicum: locorum et tribuum Hiberniae et Scotiae* (Dublin, 1910; repr. 1993), *s.v. Forrach*. This more westerly location in the Westmeath lakelands finds some confirmation in the text *Do Fhlaithesaib Hérend Iar creitim* in the Book of Leinster, where 'Cath Farcha' is accompanied by the marginal note '.i. tilach i n-iarthur Mide' (*LL*, i, p. 97, l.3114). See Paul Walsh, *The place-names of Westmeath* (Dublin, 1957), pp 96–7, 131 ff. The battle is also mentioned in *Baile in Scáil*: Murray (ed.), *Baile in Scáil*, pp 45, 63 (§50). 11 *CS* 849. Clarke has it that Donnchad Donn's attack in 936 was the first: Howard Clarke, 'Gaelic, Viking and Hiberno-Norse Dublin' in Art Cosgrave (ed.), *Dublin through the ages* (Dublin, 1988), p. 18. 12 Tigernach had also defeated a Viking force the previous year, probably in Brega and probably from Dublin, in which 1,200 fell: *AU* 848.6; *CS* 848. As a useful illustration of how quickly political allegiances and alliances could change, we should note that Tigernach had clashed with and defeated Máel Sechnaill just a few years before: *AU* 846.7. 13 *AU* 850.3; *CS* 850. The number of casualties given at Trevet in the *AU* translation is mistaken: '[…] *coro* loscad leis derthach Treoit 7 tri .xx.it dec di doinibh ann.' *Fichit* is the substantive giving 13x20=260, i.e. the same figure as found in *CS*, which reads '[…] ocus ra loisccedh leis durtech Treoite cum .cc.lx. hominibus': see *Dictionary of the Irish language* and *contributions to a dictionary of the Irish language* (Dublin, 1913–76; compact ed. 1983), *s.v. deec*, Ib. Though Cináed is described as king of the Cíannachta, that kingship had been held by the Uí Chonaing branch of Síl nÁedo Sláine since the early eighth century: see Donnchadh Ó Corráin, 'High-kings, Vikings and other kings', *Irish Historical Studies*, 22 (83) (1979), 306; Thomas Charles-Edwards, *The chronicle of Ireland* (2 vols, Liverpool, 2006), i, p. 214, n. 3. Indeed, his father who died the previous year is described as *rex bregh* in his obit, while his brother Flann is later described as 'rig Bregh n-uile': *AU* 849.1; *CS* 849; *AU* 868.4; *CS* 868. 14 *AU* 851.2; *CS* 851 (Hennessy mistranslated one clause: see F.J. Byrne, *Irish kings and high kings* (London, 1973; repr. Dublin, 2001), p. 263). Also, Charles-Edwards argues that we should re-translate the section that reads that Cináed 'was cruelly drowned in a pool (*demersus est in lacu crudeli*)' and instead regard the drowning as taking place 'in a cruel lake' and that 'there was something

Viking allies could not offer Cináed much practical support when he faced the backlash from Máel Sechnaill and Tigernach, since these years saw a great deal of upheaval and conflict between various Viking groups.[15] Taken together, however, the events of 848–51 seem to show clearly that an alliance between Clann Cholmáin and Uí Chernaig on the one hand was faced by one between the Dublin Vikings and Uí Chonaing on the other.

By this period, we can start to put some names to the Viking leaders at Dublin. The duo of Amlaíb and Ímar were the dominant Dublin Vikings until the early 870s, though we should remember that Dublin was but one of their interests and they both spent plenty of time campaigning in Britain during this period too.[16] In 856, Máel Sechnaill was involved in 'great warfare' (*cocadh mór*) with unidentified *gennti*.[17] We cannot be sure whether these were the Dublin Vikings, but it seems quite possible. Máel Sechnaill was supported against these Vikings by a force of *Gall-Goídil*, literally 'Foreign-Irish'. These may have been mercenaries of mixed ethnic background who perhaps originated in Viking Scotland.[18] Two years later, the *Gall-Goídil* of *Leth Cuinn* appear, this time supporting Cenél Fíachach, another Southern Uí Néill branch based around the Hill of Uisnech in Mide.[19] This force was heavily defeated by Ímar of Dublin and Cerball king of Osraige when they clashed in the Munster client-kingdom of Araid Tíre. These victors, though they did not meet Máel Sechnaill directly in this battle, were clearly intent on challenging

---

entitled "the cruel lake", namely a lake or pool used for executions'. Charles-Edwards, *Chronicle of Ireland*, i, p. 307, n. 3. The *AU* entry is also accompanied by a marginal Irish verse with the slightly different detail that Cináed had been taken bound to a pit. According to the legal evidence, a condemned person could be left to die from starvation and/or exposure in a pit: Fergus Kelly, *Guide to early Irish law* (Dublin, 1988), pp 218–19. But the marginal verse is found only in TCD MS H.1.8. and not in its sister manuscript, Rawl. B489, suggesting that it is 'extraneous material and a dubious source': Ó Corráin, 'High-kings, Vikings and other kings', 309. Byrne argues that drowning as a method of execution was 'probably borrowed from the Norse': Byrne, *Irish kings and high-kings*, p. 263. But an annal entry from 734 suggests that this was also a method practiced by the Picts: *AU* 734.5. **15** *AU* 849.6; *AU* 851.3; *AU* 852.3. **16** *AU* 853.2. **17** According to Byrne, 'previously the word *cocad* "war" had been rare in the annals, which use the Latin *bellum* as the equivalent of Irish *cath* – a mere battle. The Vikings were upsetting the ritual norms of Irish warfare': Byrne, *Irish kings and high-kings*, p. 264. **18** *AU* 856.3; *CS* 856: see Donnchadh Ó Corráin, 'Vikings in Ireland and Scotland in the ninth century', *Peritia*, 12 (1998), 326. Máire Herbert also suggests that the use of *Gall-Goídil* by Máel Sechnaill in 856 and his hosting *co feraib Érenn* in 858 hint at changes in both the operation of kingship and political identity in ninth-century Ireland. Máel Sechnaill was projecting his power far beyond the boundaries of his own Midland territories and using military forces of diverse origins to make real his claim to island-wide political dominance. For Herbert, 'association with the island of Ireland bonded a heterogeneous royal following, and geography supplanted genealogy as a common identifier': Máire Herbert, '*Rí Éirenn, Rí Alban*, kingship and identity in the ninth and tenth centuries' in Simon Taylor (ed.), *Kings, clerics and chronicles in Scotland, 500–1297* (Dublin, 2000), p. 64. **19** *CS* 858.

his position in the Midlands. The following year, Ímar, this time along with Amlaíb as well as Cerball of Osraige, led a large force into Mide.[20]

The threat posed by this alliance was one of the reasons Máel Sechnaill I convened a royal conference (*rígdál*) in the same year, at which he very firmly reasserted himself.[21] Osraige, traditionally under Munster's wing, now found itself bound closely to Máel Sechnaill, whose marriage to King Cerball's sister may date to this period.[22] While we must place these events in the wider context of Máel Sechnaill's determination to dominate Munster, one dimension was certainly a response to the alliance of Cerball and the Dublin Vikings that had developed against him. The high-king also faced continuing opposition from the Northern Uí Néill in the final years of his life, specifically from Áed Findliath, who would ultimately succeed him.[23] Áed invaded Mide twice, supported on one occasion by Uí Chonaing, now led by Flann, a brother of the king that Máel Sechnaill had earlier drowned. On both occasions, Áed also had Viking support. The Annals of the Four Masters are explicit in naming Amlaíb as one of Áed's allies and also provide the detail that Máel Sechnaill was now able to call on the support of the recently chastened Cerball.[24] A separate victory for Máel Sechnaill over the Dublin Vikings (*galloibh Átha Clíath*) in 861, deep in the Midlands, is also recorded and the combined evidence suggests that he faced a range of hostile alliances.[25] Máel Sechnaill I died in 862, and his description as 'king of Ireland' was both written into the annals and inscribed on high crosses and was claimed with some accuracy.[26] He did

---

20 *AU* 859.2. *The annals of Inisfallen (MS Rawlinson B503)*, ed. Seán Mac Airt (Dublin, 1951) (hereafter *AI*) is faulty here: see Charles-Edwards, *Chronicle of Ireland*, i, p. 313, n. 1. **21** It was held at Ráith Áedo maic Bricc (Rahugh) in Cenél Fíachach territory. **22** *AU* 859.3; *CS* 859: see *AFM* 857 [=859], which suggests further raiding into Mide by Cerball and the Vikings. Máel Sechnaill married Land, Cerball's sister and the daughter of the previous king of Osraige, Dúngal (d. 842). She was to be Flann Sinna's mother. See the *Banshenchus* (Metrical), in Margaret Dobbs (ed.), 'The Ban-Shenchus', *Revue Celtique*, 47 (1930), 311, 335; Muireann Ní Bhrolcháin, 'An Banshenchas Filíochta' (MA NUI (UCG), 1977), pp 134, 202 (§216); the *Banshenchus* (Prose), in Margaret Dobbs (ed.), 'The Ban-Shenchus', *Revue Celtique*, 48 (1931), 186; Muireann Ní Bhrolcháin, 'The Prose Bansenchas' (PhD NUI (UCG), 1980), pp 265–6, 383 (§392). **23** When Máel Sechnaill led a grand alliance of Leinstermen, Munstermen, the Connachta and Southern Uí Néill north to Armagh in 860, he was unsuccessfully attacked by Áed of Cenél nEógain and Flann of Uí Chonaing: *AU* 860.1; *CS* 860. **24** *AU* 861.1; *CS* 861; *AFM* 859 [=861]; *AU* 862.2; *CS* 862. **25** The battle was won at *Druim-da-mhaighe*, variously identified as Drumcaw or Drumomuy, Co. Offaly: Hogan, *Onomasticon*, p. 362. The Fragmentary Annals tell us that Amlaíb's wife was Áed Findliath's daughter: *Fragmentary annals of Ireland*, ed. Joan Newlon Radner (Dublin, 1978) (hereafter *FA*), pp 112–13 (§292) [=862]. We are also told that another of Amlaíb's wives was the daughter of Cináed, presumably from Uí Chonaing, and also that Flann of Uí Chonaing was a son of Áed Finliath's sister: *FA*, pp 106–7 (§269) [=862]. **26** *AU* 862.5; Liam de Paor, 'The high crosses of Tech Theille (Tihilly), Kinnitty, and related sculpture' in Etienne Rynne (ed.), *Figures from the past: studies on figurative art in Christian Ireland in honour of Helen M. Roe* (Dublin, 1987), p. 140; Domhnall Ó Murchadha

extend his influence throughout more of the island than any previous high-king and one important aspect of his career was his general success in seeing off the Dublin Vikings, whether they were allied with Uí Chonaing, Osraige or the Northern Uí Néill.

Máel Sechnaill's death was followed by a period of considerable upheaval for Clann Cholmáin, and outside forces took advantage. The new situation saw the Dublin Vikings turn on their former allies, the Uí Chonaing, as Amlaíb and Ímar led a raid that took in the royal site at Knowth.[27] In quite a turnaround, they were accompanied in this by the 'king of Mide', one Lorcán. Despite his title, Lorcán did not belong to Clann Cholmáin but rather the Luigni, a minor non-Uí Néill grouping in Mide.[28] There are at least two possibilities in considering Lorcán. It may be that before his death Máel Sechnaill had delegated the kingship of Mide to Lorcán, allowing him to hold it as a prize or honour. There are other examples of Clann Cholmáin doing this with local supporters.[29] Or perhaps Lorcán had simply taken advantage of the upheaval following Máel Sechnaill's death to seize the position. Either way, his decision to ally himself with Amlaíb and Ímar ultimately proved costly. He was blinded in 864 by the new high-king from the north, Áed Findliath.[30] As we saw, Áed had already been active in the Midlands in the final years of Máel Sechnaill's life. However, the Dublin Vikings clearly sought to contest his claims to influence in the Midlands: 'Concobur m. Donncadha, leithri Mide, do marb*ad* i n-uisciu oc Cluain Irairdd la Amlaiph, ri Gall (Conchobor son of Donnchad, one of two kings of Mide, was put to death in water at Cluain Iraird by Amlaíb, king of the Foreigners'.[31] We have seen this annal entry before, the record of this Conchobor's demise at the hands of the Dublin Vikings being mistakenly attributed to a Clann Cholmáin ancestor and namesake in the Book of Leinster text *Ríg Uisnig* introduced at the outset.[32] The year 864 then saw Lorcán, the

and Giollamuire Ó Murchú, 'Fragmentary inscriptions from the West Cross at Durrow, the South Cross at Clonmacnois, and the Cross of Kinnitty', *Journal of the Royal Society of Antiquaries of Ireland* (hereafter *JRSAI*), 118 (1998), 58. **27** *AU* 863.4. **28** Charles-Edwards, *The chronicle of Ireland*, i, p. 316, n. 3. This identification is based on the appearance of Lorcán's son at *AU* 901, where he is clearly regarded as belonging to the Luigni: see also *CS* 901; *AI* 901; *AFM* 896 [=901]. It has, however, been argued that a chronologically plausible position for Lorcán can be found in the Clann Cholmáin family tree: see Ailbhe MacShamhráin's contribution on Máel Sechnaill for the *Dictionary of Irish biography* (http://dib.cambridge.org) and Bart Jaski, *Early Irish kingship and succession* (Dublin, 2000), p. 308. But, overall, the evidence suggests that he belonged to the Luigni. **29** Thomas Charles-Edwards, *Early Christian Ireland* (Cambridge, 2000), pp 479–80. **30** *AU* 864.1; *CS* 864. This is hardly surprising, considering that Lorcán had plundered the land of Flann son of Conaing, one of Áed's own allies. As we have seen, Áed and Flann had together attacked Máel Sechnaill outside Armagh in 860 and both also plundered Mide in 862: *AU* 860.1; *AU* 862.2. **31** *AU* 864.2; also *CS* 864. **32** This Conchobor was probably a son of Donnchad (d. 845) son of Fallomon (d. 830). His title, literally 'half-king', suggests a division of political power in Mide at this time. We have already seen that the recently

Dublin Vikings' man in Mide, blinded by Áed while Amlaíb in turn drowned Conchobor of Clann Cholmáin at Clonard.[33] Clearly, these outside forces were competing for control and influence in Mide in the turbulent years following Máel Sechnaill's death.

This period saw Áed enjoy some success against the Vikings along the northern coast, while Amlaíb and Ímar returned to Dublin in 871 following successful campaigning in Britain 'with two hundred ships' and 'a great prey of Angles and Britons and Picts'.[34] It is not until the later 870s and the emergence of Máel Sechnaill's son Flann Sinna that Clann Cholmáin properly reappears in the record.[35] Áed died in 879 and Flann succeeded him as high-king, throwing himself into action, attacking Leinster, Munster and in 882 marching north to Armagh with an army 'both of Foreigners and Irish' as the annals put it. Again, unfortunately no further details are forthcoming on where exactly these 'Foreigners' were from.[36] *Baile in Scáil* also notes this event but provides the added detail that the Foreigners involved were sons of Ímar (*maic Ímair*). There is a single copy of this section of *Baile in Scail*, contained in the fifteenth-century MS Rawlinson B512. The specific identification of the sons of Ímar does not appear in the main text but rather as an interlinear gloss above the section describing Flann's hosting with 'Foreigners' (*co nechtrandaib*).[37] Ímar's two recorded sons, Sichfrith and Sitriucc, are obscure figures killed by other Vikings in 888 and 896 respectively.[38] While therefore alive at the time of Flann's raid north in 882, it is difficult to know how much weight to give this piece of evidence. Flann may have welcomed any support on a hosting to Armagh early in his reign but, as we will see, if this was the case, the usual antipathy between Clann Cholmáin and Dublin was restored soon after. One problem in considering this issue is our almost complete lack of information about Dublin at this time. As noted, Sichfrith and Sitriucc are obscure, as are a series of other Vikings who appear fleetingly in the record.[39] That said, in 888

blinded Lorcán was another king of Mide. **33** *AU* 859.2. **34** *AU* 871.2; *AU* 866.4; *AU* 868.4. **35** His first appearance is at *AU* 877.2. **36** *AU* 882.1; *CS* 882. **37** Murray (ed.), *Baile in Scáil*, pp 45–6, 63–4 (§52). For a manuscript image, see http://image.ox.ac.uk/show?collection=bodleian&manuscript=msrawlb512 [fo. 104vb]. According to Ó Cuív, 'Apart from some later additions, ff. 5–36 and 101–22 seem to be the work of one unnamed scribe whose hand varies greatly both in quality and in size, with large and small script at times alternating in the one column, citations in Latin being generally in large script' (Brian Ó Cuív, *Catalogue of Irish language manuscripts in the Bodleian Library at Oxford and Oxford College Libraries* (Dublin, 2001), p. 231); 'According to the heading in Rawl., BS was copied from the book of Dub dá Leithe (†1064) who was appointed *fer léiginn* of Armagh in 1046' (Murray (ed.), *Baile in Scáil*, p. 5). **38** *AU* 888.9; *AU* 896.3. **39** For example, Barith (obit at *AU* 881.3) or the son of Auisle ('Mors m. Ausli o m. Iergni 7 o ingain Mael Sechnaill (Death of Auisle's son at the hands of Iergne's son and the daughter of Mael Sechnaill) (*AU* 883.4; also *CS* 883)). It seems that Flann Sinna's sister was married to a Viking, although her husband appears to have belonged to a faction opposed to the Dublin Vikings. If the son of Auisle was, like his father, attached to the Dublin Vikings, this would

Flann was defeated by the Vikings, identified specifically as Dublin Vikings in some annal texts (*CS* and *AFM*), at an unrecorded location.[40] *Baile in Scáil* refers to this battle too, providing the extra detail that the clash, a 'slaughter of the Goídil', took place at Dublin.[41] In this case, the information is part of the main text of *Baile in Scáil*. While the Dublin Vikings seem then to have successfully resisted Flann, their internal upheaval saw Sichfrith son of Ímar 'deceitfully killed by his kinsman', quite possibly his brother Sitriuc, in the same year.[42]

Another possible sign of cooperation between the Dublin Vikings and Clann Cholmáin from this period is the notice that sons of Ímar fought alongside Flann Sinna's son Máel Ruanaid in 895. Sitriuc (d. 896) may have been involved, but we should note that this information is found only in the Annals of the Four Masters, which tells us that they were defeated in Osraige.[43] Flann faced recurring rebellion from many of his sons including Máel Ruanaid; indeed, war broke out between them soon after, and one possibility is that it was one rebellious section of Clann Cholmáin that had allied with the Dublin Vikings in this instance.[44] But Sitriuc was killed the next year, 896, 'by other Norsemen' and, as we know, the next few years of Dublin weakness culminated in the abandonment of the *longphort*, by the aristocratic rulers at least, following an Irish attack.[45] For the remainder of his life, Dublin was not a concern for Flann Sinna, although when he died in 916 it was during a huge upsurge in Viking activity in the south and south-east, the prelude to Dublin's reestablishment or reoccupation.

At this point, we should introduce another important body of evidence that suggests considerable complexity in the relationship between Clann Cholmáin and the Dublin Vikings. A huge quantity of Viking silver has been found in and around Lough Ennell near the Clann Cholmáin royal complex made up of Dún na Sciath, a ringfort on the south-western shore of the lake, and Cró Inis, the crannóg facing it.[46] It has been suggested that much of this silver – hack, ingots and coins – was deposited in the opening decades of the tenth century.[47]

fit into the longstanding pattern of antipathy between Clann Cholmáin and the Dublin Vikings: see *AU* 852.3; *CS* 852; *AU* 863.4; *AU* 867.6; *AU* 886.1; *CS* 886. Was it then this other faction of 'Foreigners' who accompanied Flann to Armagh in 882? **40** *AU* 888.5; *CS* 888; *AFM* 885 [=888]. **41** Murray (ed.), *Baile in Scáil*, pp 45–6, 63–4 (§52). **42** *AU* 888.9. Flann's failure at Dublin was quickly followed by renewed pressure on Southern Uí Néill territory from the north. There was Viking involvement in this squeeze too, perhaps from Dublin, but the use of the terms *gallaib* and *gennti* without further precision leaves us guessing: *AU* 889.1; *CS* 889; *CS* 890 [=891]. **43** *AFM* 890 [=895]; several other Midland kings also fell in a battle perhaps won by Diarmait mac Cerbaill, king of Osraige (894–905). **44** *CS* 897 [=898]. **45** *AU* 902.2; was Dublin ruled 896–902 by Ímar grandson of Ímar (d. 873)? His death in Pictland is recorded at *AU* 904.4. **46** Indeed, this falls into a general pattern in which discovered material is concentrated in areas of Clann Cholmáin control: see Michael Kenny, 'The geographical distribution of Irish Viking-Age coin hoards', *PRIA*, 87C (1987), 508–13. **47** Michael Ryan, Raghnall Ó Floinn, Nicholas Lowick, Michael

The size and weight of individual hoards varies hugely and it seems unlikely that a single explanation or interpretation will account for them all. While some of the recovered silver ingots weigh tens of grams or less (quite typical small units), more are found in massive units.[48] Five complete ingots found just north of Cró Inis had an average weight of over five hundred grams, while two more weighed over three kilos each. This was clearly a huge stockpile of silver kept by Clann Cholmáin. While it may be that some of this material was acquired through raiding or attacks on the Vikings, this can hardly be the whole story. It seems probable that at least some of the Lough Ennell silver reflects more 'ordinary' economic links with Dublin, whether through trade or tribute, and that the material was accumulated over time.[49] The concentration of this material around Lough Ennell reflects Clann Cholmáin's decision to keep tight control over the material necessary for interaction with the Vikings. One obvious puzzle is of course that Dublin had been abandoned, by the Viking aristocracy at least, in 902, just about the time the material was hoarded.[50]

The return of the Vikings to Dublin led by Sitriuc grandson of Ímar in 917 was the problem of Niall Glúndub, Flann Sinna's northern successor as high-king. But there was some Clann Cholmáin involvement in the famous Battle of Dublin fought in 919, which saw a resounding Viking victory and claimed the new high-king's life. Among the host of other Irish kings who fell alongside Niall was Conchobor son of Flann Sinna.[51] Another of Flann's sons, Donnchad, now assumed the high-kingship and would reign for twenty-five years. He began by inflicting a heavy defeat on an unidentified Viking force.[52] Sitriuc left for York the same year to be replaced by his brother Gothfrith.[53] We might be forgiven for thinking he came to some sort of arrangement with Donnchad because the high-king left Dublin alone while the Dublin Vikings stayed out of the Irish Midlands, concentrating instead on the north. Gothfrith attacked Armagh in 921, eventually driven off by Muirchertach of the Northern Uí Néill.[54] It was this northern king who was regularly in conflict with Vikings during this period, even being captured by them at one stage

Kenny and Peter Cazalet, 'Six silver finds of the Viking period from the vicinity of Lough Ennell, Co. Westmeath', *Peritia*, 3 (1984), 334–81.   **48** Ryan et al., 'Six silver finds', 336–41. **49** Kenny, 'The geographical distribution of Irish Viking-Age coin hoards', 517; Michael Kenny, 'Coins and coinage in the Irish Midlands during the Viking Age' in Catherine Karkov and Robert Farrell (eds), *Studies in Insular art and archaeology* (Oxford, OH, 1991), p. 115.   **50** Some of the other Midland coin hoards have suggested deposition dates from the 950s and early 960s, a period when Dublin was not attacked by the Irish, though it was a period of intense conflict between competing Uí Néill branches. Perhaps we had better view the deposition of these hoards in that context. Taken together, a simple 'war booty' explanation is clearly unsatisfactory: Kenny, 'Coins and coinage in the Irish Midlands during the Viking Age', pp 114–15.   **51** *AU* 919.3; *CS* 918 [=919].   **52** *AU* 920.2; *CS* 919 [=920]; *AFM* 918 [=920] is a similar account with extra detail that the battle took place: 'i cCiannachtaibh Bregh, .i. occ Tigh mic nEathach'.   **53** *AU* 920.5; *AU* 921.5.   **54** *AU* 921.8.

before ransoming himself.[55] There were also several instances in the 920s and 30s where Donnchad and Muirchertach clashed, but the death of Gothfrith in 934 led to a change.[56] His son and successor Amlaíb began by attacking the royal sites of Knowth and Lagore in 935 but it was the Dublin attack on Clonmacnoise in 936 that provoked a reaction.[57] This was, after all, where the Cross of the Scriptures stood, a monument erected at some expense by Donnchad's father and an impressive symbol of the close ties between Clann Cholmáin and Clonmacnoise. The Dubliners not only plundered but stayed at the site for two nights.[58] Donnchad responded by burning Dublin.[59] He returned two years later with Muirchertach and besieged the inhabitants and ravaged the southern hinterland.[60] It may be that Dublin was left in a weakened state at times during this period, since Amlaíb was also involved in great struggles, with varying success, with various Anglo-Saxon kings. Donnchad and his sometime rival Muirchertach appear to have put their rivalry aside at this point and are also recorded working together in exerting control over Leinster and Munster.[61] But, appropriately enough considering their respective careers, while Muirchertach died in battle against the Dublin Vikings in 943, the high-king Donnchad died peacefully the following year.[62]

The mid-tenth century is a period of considerable obscurity when it comes to Clann Cholmáin. The death of Donnchad was swiftly followed by those of two of his sons.[63] The dynasty was then beset by internal feuding and Mide was also subject to assault from outside forces, including from the Dublin Vikings.[64] In 946, Clonmacnoise was attacked by them again, along with 'the churches of the men of Mide'. In 951, using Kells as a base, they raided several other churches 'and three thousand men or more were taken captive and a great spoil of cattle and horses and gold and silver was taken away'.[65] But in truth this aggression was directed against the new Southern Uí Néill force, a revitalized Uí Chonaing under Congalach Cnogba (d. 956).[66] He was heavily involved with the Dublin Vikings, both in alliance and in opposition, who were led through most of this period by Amlaíb Cuarán. Although Congalach was succeeded as high-king by a northern king, Clann Cholmáin revival in the Midlands was still a long way off. Right through this period the dynasty only appears fleetingly in the record and appears to have been beset once more by internal feuding. This was but one problem. The new northern high-king

---

55 *AU* 939.3.   56 *AU* 927.4; *AU* 929.4; *AU* 938.4; *AU* 934.1.   57 *AU* 935.4.   58 *AU* 936.2.   59 *CS* 935 [=936].   60 *AU* 938.6; we are also told that Amlaíb plundered Cell Cuilind (Old Kilcullen, Co. Kildare) in the same year.   61 *AU* 940.1; *CS* 939 [=940]; *AU* 940.4 records the death of Donnchad's daughter, 'queen of Ailech', while *AU* 941.3 tells us Muirchertach brought the king of Cashel in submission to Donnchad showing at least some signs of cooperation.   62 *AU* 943.2; *AU* 944.4; *CS* 943 [=944].   63 *AU* 944.3; *CS* 944 [=945]; *AI* 944: the death of Gormlaith daughter of Flann is recorded at *AU* 948.5.   64 *AU* 946.1; *CS* 947 [=948]; *CS* 949 [=950]; *CS* 949 [=950]; *CS* 951 [=952]; *AI* 952.   65 *AU* 951.3; *CS* 950 [=951].   66 *AU* 956.3; he was killed by a force of Dublin Vikings and

Domnall spent a great deal of time trying to dominate Mide, even using sub-kings to rule his home territories while he concentrated his energies farther south. As well as Domnall, the other major player aiming for dominance in the Midlands at this time was Dublin's Amlaíb Cuarán. Particularly after he abandoned his ambitions in York, Amlaíb had considerable success in extending his influence far beyond Dublin and its hinterland, perhaps even into the neighbourhood of Tara itself.[67] Though an obscure period for Clann Cholmáin, one member of the dynasty, Carlus, does appear in 960 in Dublin, where he was killed by Amlaíb Cuarán.[68] But in truth it is not until the emergence of Máel Sechnaill son of Domnall in the later 970s that the picture becomes somewhat clearer.[69]

Máel Sechnaill II's first appearance in the record sees him attacking Dublin in 975.[70] At this stage, he may still have been only a contender for leadership

Leinstermen.   **67** *AU* 980.1; *ATig.* 979 [=980]; *AI* 980.4. Despite longstanding ties between Clann Cholmáin and the Columban church, Máel Sechnaill son of Domnall would 'profane' the church of Scrín in 988 and it is surely significant that his church had been patronized by Amlaíb Cúarán: see *CS* 986 [=988]. A *Dindshenchas* poem on Achall, that is, the Hill of Skreen, appears to have been written for Amlaíb by Cináed ua hArtacain: see Edward Gwynn (ed.), *The Metrical Dindshenchas* (5 vols, Dublin, 1903–35; repr. Dublin, 1991), i, pp 52–3; Edel Bhreathnach, 'Columban churches in Brega and Leinster: relations with the Norse and the Anglo-Normans', *JRSAI*, 129 (1999), 5–18.   **68** *AU* 960.2; and by Murchad Find according to *Rig Uisnig*: *LL* i, p. 198 (l.5969).   **69** Indeed, it seems possible that Clann Cholmáin was removed from the kingship of Mide for some or all of the later 960s and early 970s. According to a near contemporary poem attributed to Flann Mainistrech (d. 1056), Muirchertach ruled Mide for 'four years by four' at this time: Peter J. Smith, 'Mide Maigen Clainne Cuind: a medieval poem on the kings of Mide', *Peritia*, 15 (2001), 120, 132 (§45). Muirchertach was not a Clann Cholmáin dynast but rather the son of Domnall, the high-king. With his son installed as ruler of Mide, Domnall was active against his two great rivals, the king of Brega and Amlaíb Cúarán, king of Dublin.   **70** The interpretation of the annal entries for this attack is problematic and requires some consideration: 'Cetna toisc MaelSechnaill Moir, maic Domnaill, o Ath cliath, dar' briss 7 dar' theasc in caill (The first expedition of MaelSechnaill the Great, son of Domnall, from Dublin, when he broke and cut down the wood' (*ATig.* 974 [=975]); 'Cedna feacht Maoilsechlainn mic Domnaill o Ath cliath dar'bris cois an gaill (First expedition of Maelsechlainn, son of Domhnall, from Ath-cliath, on which occasion he broke the Foreigner's leg (*CS* 973 [=975])'. If Máel Sechnaill actually launched an attack *from* Dublin, perhaps he had found refuge there with Amlaíb Cúarán during a low ebb for Clann Cholmáin. As we will see, Amlaíb was after all his step-father and Muirchertach, the northern-imposed king of Mide, was still alive in 975. A much later poem involving the poet MacCoise suggests Máel Sechnaill had a residence or was based in Dublin: see Osborn Bergin, 'A dialogue between Donnchad son of Brian and Mac Coisse', *Ériu*, 9 (1921–3), 179. But this is certainly not a contemporary composition and does not carry much weight as evidence for tenth-century events. If Máel Sechnaill did find refuge with Amlaíb, this friendly relationship did not last long as they clashed violently soon afterwards. To make the case that Máel Sechnaill actually attacked Dublin, we must assume a scribal error. Hennessy suggested that we should read 'do Ath cliath' or 'co Ath cliath' rather than 'o Ath cliath', hence giving us 'to Dublin' (*CS*, p. 223, n. 8). This is possible, although it should be said

within Clann Cholmáin. Much more was at stake in 980 at the Battle of Tara. The northern high-king Domnall had just died and Máel Sechnaill had his sights set on succession, while Amlaíb Cuarán may have had equally ambitious plans. At this stage, we should note that Amlaíb was in fact Máel Sechnaill's step-father. Prior to this, Clann Cholmáin had not sought marriage alliance with the Dublin Vikings, even preferring to look to Uí Chonaing in the mid-tenth century. But after the death of Máel Sechnaill's father, his mother went on to marry Amlaíb. While these were the family links, Máel Sechnaill won a huge victory at Tara in 980.[71] He followed it up by moving against Dublin itself and from the loot, hostages and concessions he extracted it is clear just how successful Amlaíb had been in building up Dublin's position over the preceding period.[72]

Now defeated and in old age, he retired to Iona and died soon after. His death signalled the end of an era for Dublin.[73] His son, Glún Iairn, Máel Sechnaill's half-brother, was king of Dublin between 980 and his death in 989 but seems to have been cooperative, submissive even to the Clann Cholmáin king. For example, in 983 Máel Sechnaill and Glún Iairn together defeated the king of Leinster and Ímar, the Viking leader of Waterford.[74] As an indicator of Dublin's growing significance for those with eyes on the high-kingship, the

---

that both manuscripts very clearly read 'o Ath cliath' and there is no evidence to suggest a character has been lost through wear or damage in either case: see 'The Annals of Tigernach' (Ox. Bodl., Rawl. B488, fo. 15r); 'Chronicon Scotorum' (TCD MS 1292, fo. 197v). But the *CS* entry is also internally contradictory: Máel Sechnaill would hardly be coming from Dublin if intent on breaking 'the Foreigner's leg'. Overall, it is likely that Máel Sechnaill attacked the settlement and perhaps deliberately destroyed, in Lucas' words, 'a sacred grove in the neighbourhood of Viking Dublin': A.T. Lucas, 'The sacred trees of Ireland', *Journal of the Cork Historical and Archaeological Society*, 68 (1963), 21. As we shall see, Máel Sechnaill was fond of destroying or slighting the sacred places and objects of his political rivals, and it seems that the Dublin Vikings were the first to experience this: see Eoin O'Flynn, 'Máel Sechnaill Mór, Mide and the high-kingship of Ireland' in William Nolan (ed.), *Meath: history and society* (forthcoming).   **71** While Amlaíb Cúarán was king of Dublin at the time, he is not explicitly named as having led the Norse force into battle and perhaps played no personal role due to his advanced age: *AU* 980; *ATig.* 979 [=980]; *CS* 978 [=980]; *AI* 980.4; *AFM* 978 [=979]. Some of these entries suggest that his sons led the force. For a consideration of the possible identity of the Islesmen involved in the Battle of Tara, see Colmán Etchingham, 'North Wales, Ireland and the Isles: the Insular Viking zone', *Peritia*, 15 (2001), 173–5: see also Alex Woolf, 'Amlaíb Cúarán and the Gael, 941–81' in Seán Duffy (ed.), *Medieval Dublin III* (Dublin, 2002), pp 34–44.   **72** *ATig.* 979 [=980]. The follow-up attack on Dublin, where Máel Sechnaill was supported by the king of the Ulaid, is not included in *AU*. Regarding the *Crích Gall*, or territory of the Foreigners, see Mary Valante, 'Dublin's economic relations with hinterland and periphery in the later Viking Age' in Seán Duffy (ed.), *Medieval Dublin I* (Dublin, 2000), pp 69–84.   **73** T.M. Charles-Edwards, 'Irish warfare before 1100' in Thomas Bartlett and Keith Jeffery (eds), *A military history of Ireland* (Cambridge, 1996), p. 45; Alfred P. Smyth, *Scandinavian York and Dublin* (2 vols, Dublin, 1979), ii, p. 108.   **74** *AU* 983.2; *ATig.* 982 [=983]; *CS* 981 [=983];

following year Brian Boru and the Waterford Vikings exchanged hostages and plotted a move against the settlement.[75]

When Glún Iairn died in 989, however, Máel Sechnaill moved immediately to confirm *his* influence over Dublin.[76] He laid siege to it for twenty nights, cutting off the water supply and ultimately extracting a huge tribute, perhaps assessed on the basis of Dublin's plot divisions.[77] A few years later, in 995, Máel Sechnaill attacked Dublin again, seizing two ancient heirlooms, the ring of Tomar and the sword of Carlus.[78] He evidently had an eye for the grand and symbolic gesture and this seizure from Dublin must be regarded as a measured affront.[79]

Máel Sechnaill was gradually losing his grip on the bigger prize, however: the high-kingship. Brian Boru took the hostages of Dublin in 997 and although he campaigned along with Máel Sechnaill over the next few years, it was an uneasy alliance.[80] In 999, Brian won an important battle at Glenn Máma near Dublin against Sitriuc and Leinster forces.[81] It is unclear if Máel Sechnaill took part, although perhaps that is unlikely.[82] Following the battle, Brian Boru entered Dublin, stayed for a week before leaving laden down with gold and silver. The settlement was now very much under his control. Indeed, over the next few years as the uneasy alliance between Brian Boru and Máel Sechnaill broke down, the Munster king at times added the forces of Dublin to his own in fighting for and ultimately securing Máel Sechnaill's submission. As for the

AFM 982 [=983].   **75** *AI* 984.2.   **76** *ATig.* 988 [=989]; *CS* 987 [=989].   **77** *ATig.* 988 [=989]; *CS* 987 [=989]; *AFM* 988 [=989]. Also see *AFM* 942 for Dublin's plot divisions. According to *AFM*, the year 990 saw the Dublin Vikings and Leinstermen attack Mide so that they plundered 'as far as Loch Ainninn': *AFM* 989 [=990]. If we assume that an attack by Máel Sechnaill on the church of Domnach Pátraic in 993 had secured its obedience, then a combined attack against that church by the Dublin Vikings and Uí Chonaing a few years later makes sense: *AU* 993.4; *ATig.* 992 [=993]; *AFM* 992 [=993]; *AU* 995.2; *ATig.* 994 [=995]; *CS* 993[=995]; *AFM* 994 [=995]. The Vikings may also have found added motivation in Máel Sechnaill's recent attack on the Columban church of Swords, located within their sphere of influence: *AU* 994.3. Clonard and Kells were also targeted by the Vikings during this period: *AU* 997.3; *AFM* 996 [=997].   **78** *ATig.* 994 [=995]; *CS* 993 [=995]; *AFM* 994 [=995]. This may also have been in response to the recent attack on Domnach Pátraic: *AU* 995.2.   **79** Another example of this trait includes his destruction of the tree of Mag Adair, a sacred symbol of Dál Cais kingship most likely located at their inauguration site: see *ATig.* 981 [=982]; *CS* 980 [=982]; *AI* 982.4; *AFM* 981 [=982]. And his desecration of the *Lia Ailbi*, an ancient stone monument in Brega that he had made into millstones: see *AU* 999.4; *CS* 997 [=999]; *AFM* 998 [=999].   **80** *AI* 997.2.   **81** *AU* 999.8; *ATig.* 997 [=999]; *CS* 997 [=999]; *AI* 999.4; *AFM* 998 [=999]: see Ailbhe MacShamhráin, 'The Battle of Glenn Máma, Dublin, and the high-kingship of Ireland: a millennial commemoration' in Seán Duffy (ed.), *Medieval Dublin II* (Dublin, 2001), pp 53–64. **82** Having fled north after the defeat, Sitriuc 'returned to Áth Cliath and gave hostages to Brian Boru': *AU* 1000.4; *ATig.* 999 [=1000]; *CS* 998 [=1000]; *AI* 1000.2; *AFM* 999 [=1000]. In exchange, Brian Boru 'gave the fort to the Foreigners'. For an example of how Brian Boru used the forces of Dublin against Máel Sechnaill, see *AU* 1000.7; *ATig.* 999 [=1000].

famous Battle of Clontarf, there is some confusion as to whether Máel
Sechnaill participated and if so what role he played.[83] In fact, Máel Sechnaill
gained considerably from the outcome of the battle. The death of Brian Boru
and the subsequent infighting in Munster allowed him once more to assume
the high-kingship until his death in 1022.[84]

As we know, control over Dublin was a crucial objective for any aspiring
high-king between Clontarf and the English Invasion. While in life and
certainly in later legend Máel Sechnaill was thoroughly overshadowed by Brian
Boru, we should not underestimate his achievements, particularly when it
comes to Dublin. It was arguably during Máel Sechnaill's reign that Dublin
was reduced to and confirmed as a prize to be fought over by contending
outside forces. Following his great victory at Tara in 980 over Amlaíb Cuarán,
and his subsequent attack on Dublin, Máel Sechnaill effectively removed it as
a major threat to Mide. Following the death of Glún Iairn, his submissive half-
brother, Máel Sechnaill attacked Dublin successfully on several occasions. He
regularly exploited the settlement as a source of wealth and tribute. Dublin's
significance was just as clear to Máel Sechnaill II as it was to Brian Boru and
no previous Irish king had exerted such influence over it. His ancestor and
namesake in the mid-ninth century was the first Clann Cholmáin king to
encounter and take on the Dublin Vikings. Of course Dublin changed hugely
over this period, but the relationship between the settlement and the Southern
Uí Néill more generally, and Clann Cholmáin specifically, was significant
throughout most of the period examined above. Indeed, it was certainly one of
the most important relationships, or rather series of relationships, of the
Viking Age in Ireland.

---

83 The somewhat later *Cogadh Gáedhel re Gallaibh* claims that Máel Sechnaill, having
arrived, then deserted Brian Boru before the battle started: see J.H. Todd (ed.), *Cogadh
Gaedhel re Gallaibh. The war of the Gaedhil with the Gall* (London, 1867), pp 153–69. Of the
annals, those of *Inisfallen* make no mention of Máel Sechnaill whatsoever, while the *Annals
of Ulster*, *Loch Cé* and the *Chronicon Scotorum* place him at the battle fighting alongside
Brian Boru: see *AI* 1014.2; *AU* 1014.2; *ALC* 1014; *CS* 1012 [=1014]. It does seem
suspicious that the extensive list of the slain in these sources includes not one noble from
Mide. Máel Sechnaill's bravery is, however, strikingly described at *AFM* 1013 [=1014]. A
Norse account of the battle preserved in *Njal's Saga* makes no mention of Máel Sechnaill:
see Magnus Magnusson and Hermann Palsson (eds), *Njal's Saga* (London, 1960), pp 341ff.
See Máire Ní Mhaonaigh, *Brian Boru: Ireland's greatest king?* (Stroud, 2007), pp 53–100;
Seán Duffy, *Brian Boru and the Battle of Contarf* (Dublin, 2013), pp 185, 191, 201–2.
84 Máel Sechnaill was back at Dublin the year after Clontarf, burning 'the fortress and all
the houses that were from the fortress outwards', which, as an aside, is important evidence
for the development of the suburbs. Flaithbertach had arrived into Mide from the north in
1015 to 'assist' Máel Sechnaill in his attacks on Leinster, Dublin and Osraige: *AU* 1015.2;
CS 1013 [=1015]; *AFM* 1014 [=1015].

Norse, Gaelic or Hiberno-Scandinavian? The *airlabraid* of tenth-century Dublin[1]

DENIS CASEY

INTRODUCTION

Medieval and modern scholarly perceptions of the political and cultural character of mid-tenth-century Dublin, during the zenith of its power under Óláfr Sigtryggsson (known in Gaelic as Amlaíb Cúarán, d. 981), are strongly influenced by interpretations of that king's long reign. Óláfr's/Amlaíb's recorded career spans over forty years, during which time he was twice king of Northumbria, before being permanently ejected from Britain in 952. The remainder of his career was spent in Ireland, where he was an important political and military figure. By 980, he was one of the most powerful rulers in Ireland, but in that year his forces were heavily defeated at the Battle of Tara, by Máel Sechnaill mac Domnaill (king of Tara), and Amlaíb's abdication and death (in religious retirement in Iona) followed swiftly. Given the peripatetic nature of his career, it is interesting to ask what kind of kingdom Óláfr/Amlaíb ruled after his expulsion from Britain. Was it Norse, Gaelic or Hiberno-Scandinavian/Hiberno-Norse?

Modern scholars have generally seen Amlaíb's long reign as a period of increased gaelicization in Dublin. For example, Charles Doherty has suggested that the late tenth century was a transitional period and viewed Amlaíb in pragmatic terms, proposing that he was 'a man who had the genius to use the political ambiguities of his times – Christian and pagan, Irish and Norse – to rise in the political world of the tenth century'.[2] Howard Clarke has suggested that Amlaíb's rule saw the end of Viking Dublin, his 'principal achievement being the creation of the Hiberno-Norse town'.[3] Alex Woolf has gone further than Doherty or Clarke, hypothesizing that the Battle of Tara might have been precipitated by an attempt to seize the kingship of Tara, and that 'perhaps

1 I would like to thank *An Foras Feasa* (NUI Maynooth), for a visiting fellowship in 2012, during which time much of the research for this essay was undertaken. I am also grateful to Thomas Owen Clancy (University of Glasgow) and Kaarina Hollo (University of Sheffield), for making materials available to me, and to the attendees of the Medieval Dublin Symposium, for their comments on the presentation upon which this essay is based. 2 Charles Doherty, 'The Vikings in Ireland: a review' in H.B. Clarke, Raghnall Ó Floinn and Máire Ní Mhaonaigh (eds), *Ireland and Scandinavia in the early Viking Age* (Dublin, 1998), pp 288–330 at p. 305. 3 H.B. Clarke, 'Proto-towns and towns in Ireland and Britain in the ninth and tenth centuries' in Clarke et al. (eds), *Ireland and Scandinavia in the early Viking Age*, pp 331–80 at p. 334.

Amlaíb Cuarán was the first Irishman to rule in Dublin'.[4] This is by no means an exhaustive catalogue of opinions.

Assessments of Amlaíb's 'Irishness' have been based on a number of sources. Firstly, although his given name in Gaelic texts (Amlaíb) is simply a Gaelic pronunciation of the Old Norse name Óláfr, his epithet (*cúarán*) appears to be of Gaelic origin, though its exact meaning is disputed.[5] That this epithet is recorded in one of the manuscripts of the 'northern recension' of the Anglo-Saxon Chronicle suggests it was used in a non-Gaelic context, possibly by Amlaíb himself.[6] Further 'Gaelic' credentials may be detected in his patronage of the poet Cináed ua hArtacáin (d. 975), apparently a member of the Uí Chernaig branch of Síl nÁedo Sláine, whose territory lay adjacent to that of Amlaíb's kingdom. Cináed's poem *Achall ar aicce Temair* ('Achall over against Temair') refers to Amlaíb's kingship in relation to Bend Étair (Howth, Co. Dublin) and contains an unambiguous reference to his patronage:

> *Amlaib Átha Cliath cétaig*
> *rogab rígi i mBeind Étair;*
> *tallus lúag mo dúane de,*
> *ech d'echaib ána Aichle.*

> Amlaib of Ath Cliath the hundred-strong,
> who gained the kingship in Bend Etair;
> I bore off from him as price of my song
> a horse of the horses of Achall.[7]

Furthermore, John Carey has suggested that Amlaíb may have been the patron of Cináed's poems on Howth, *Étar étan ri dílind* ('Étar, forehead to the flood')[8] and possibly a poem on the death of the legendary king of Ulaid, Conchobar mac Nessa, *A chloch thall for elaid úair* ('O stone yonder upon the cold tomb'),[9]

---

4 Alex Woolf, 'Amlaíb Cuarán and the Gael, 941–81' in Seán Duffy (ed.), *Medieval Dublin III* (Dublin, 2002), pp 34–43 at p. 43. See also his comments on the gaelicization of the Vikings in Ireland: ibid., pp 34–5.   5 It is generally believed to be *cúarán* ('shoe/sandal'), a word derived from *cúar* ('crooked'). Andrew Breeze has suggested that the nickname should be understood as 'the Little Crooked One, the Little Hunchback': Andrew Breeze, 'The *Anglo-Saxon chronicle* for 949 and Olaf Cuaran', *Notes and Queries*, 44:2 (1997), 160–1 at 161.   6 An entry *s.a.* 949 states *Her com Anlaf Cwiran on Norðhymbra land* ('In this year Olaf Cwiran came into Northumbria'). Susan Irvine (ed.), *The Anglo-Saxon Chronicle: a collaborative edition, volume 7 MS. E* (Cambridge, 2004) (text) and Dorothy Whitelock et al. (trans.), *The Anglo-Saxon Chronicle: a revised translation* (London, 1961) (translation).   7 Edward Gwynn (ed. and trans.), *The Metrical Dindshenchas, part 1* (Dublin, 1903), pp 52–3, lines 81–4. Further Viking association with Howth may be seen in the derivation of its English place-name from Old Norse *höfthi* ('headland'): Anne-Christine Larsen, 'The exhibition: the Vikings in Ireland' in eadem (ed.), *The Vikings in Ireland* (Roskilde, 2001), pp 127–48 at p. 146.   8 Gwynn (ed. and trans.), *The Metrical Dindshenchas, part 3* (Dublin, 1913), pp 104–9.   9 Kuno Meyer (ed.

although the evidence for his patronage of these latter poems is circum-stantial.[10] Other fragments of verse, however, may actually refer to Amlaíb.[11]

Despite these Gaelic characteristics, important aspects of Dublin's kingship appear to have remained Scandinavian; for example, the items believed to have acted as regalia: the 'sword of Carlus' and 'ring of Tomar (Þorir)'.[12] Other aspects may outwardly appear (and have been read as) more Gaelic than they are.[13] Amlaíb's marriages to two Gaelic women, Dúnlaith (daughter of Muirchertach mac Néill, King of Ailech) and Gormlaith, daughter of Murchad mac Finn (king of Laigin),[14] should be understood in the contexts of political and military alliances, rather than as expressions of cultural identity. Undoubtedly the most visible indicators of ethnic and cultural identity occur at an elite level,[15] but Amlaíb's cultural outlook (whatever it was) need not have defined that of all (or even a majority) of his subjects. Powerful kings often moved between different cultural and political worlds, but it does not follow that their cosmopolitanism was mirrored at every level of society.

One figure farther down the social ladder (though by no means on the bottom rung) was an unnamed casualty of the Battle of Tara (AD980), who bore the Gaelic title *airlabraid* (variously translated as 'orator/spokesman').[16] His existence has implications for assessments of the Scandinavian/Gaelic character of Amlaíb's Dublin. Was there a Gaelic *airlabraid* in Dublin or is it possible that the Gaelic title *airlabraid* was applied to an institution of Scandinavian origin (which some scholars have equated with the Old Norse *þulr, stalleri* and *lǫgsǫgumaðr*)? In order to assess whether the Dublin institution was Gaelic, Scandinavian or a hybrid, an initial investigation of the records for the Battle of Tara will be followed by an assessment of the position of the *airlabraid* within Gaelic society. Only then can evidence for the

and trans.), *The death-tales of the Ulster heroes* (Dublin, 1906), pp 18–21. **10** John Carey, 'Cináed ua hArtacáin (Cineth O'Hartagain) (*d.* 975)' in H.C.G. Matthew and B. Harrison (eds), *Oxford dictionary of national biography* (Oxford, 2004), www.oxforddnb.com/view/article/20636, accessed 24 Mar. 2013. **11** Kuno Meyer (ed. and trans.), *Bruchstücke der älteren Lyrik Irlands*, i (Berlin, 1919), p. 13. **12** These were forcibly seized by Máel Sechnaill mac Domnaill: *AFM* 994; *CS* 995; *ATig.* 994; Denis Murphy (ed.), *The annals of Clonmacnoise: being annals of Ireland from the earliest period to AD1408* (Dublin, 1896; repr. Felinfach, 1993), 988. The sword of Carlus was later used to ransom the king of Dublin: *ATig.*; *CS*; *AFM*; *AU*, 1029. **13** For a nuanced discussion of Dublin identity, see Clare Downham, 'Living on the edge: Scandinavian Dublin in the twelfth century' in Beverley Ballin Smith et al. (eds), *West over sea: studies in Scandinavian sea-borne expansion and settlement before 1300; a Festschrift in honour of Dr Barbara E. Crawford* (Leiden, 2007), pp 33–52 at pp 34–8. **14** M.E. Dobbs (ed.), 'The ban-shenchus', *Revue Celtique*, 47 (1930), 283–339; 48 (1931), 163–234; 49 (1932), 437–89 at 48 (1931), 227. **15** Shannon Lewis-Simpson, 'Viking-Age queens and the formation of identity' in John Sheehan and Donnchadh Ó Corráin (eds), *The Viking Age: Ireland and the West; papers from the proceedings of the fifteenth Viking Congress, Cork, 18–27 August 2005* (Dublin, 2010), pp 217–26 at p. 224. **16** For a discussion of variations in the spelling of this term, see Roibeard Ó Maolalaigh, 'Varia III. Vocalic variation in *air-, aur-*', *Ériu*, 53 (2003), 163–9.

aforementioned institutions be examined, to ascertain whether any of these displayed similarities to the *airlabraid* of the Gaelic sources – similarities that might have prompted a tenth-century annalist to identify a hypothetical Dublin *þulr/stalleri/lǫgsǫgumaðr* (or even *lǫgmaðr* 'lawman') as an *airlabraid*. The results will highlight the difficulties of assigning a politico-cultural identity to the *airlabraid*, and more broadly to late-tenth-century Dublin.

ANNALISTIC RECORDS FOR THE BATTLE OF TARA (980)

Only three texts mention the existence of an *airlabraid* in Dublin. These are the Annals of Tigernach, *Chronicon Scotorum* and the Annals of the Four Masters, all of which record the death of the *airlabraid* at the Battle of Tara.[17] The relationships between these texts (and the close textual parallels in these three entries in particular), indicate that they represent the testimony of a single source, rather than multiple attestations of the title *airlabraid*.[18] The relevant portions of these three records are as follows:

Annals of Tigernach

Cath Temrach re MaelSechnaill Mór mac nDomnaill maic Donnchaidh maic Flaind, ria ríg Erenn, for Gallaib Atha cliath, for macaib Amlaim intíndrudh, dú a torcair ili im Ragnall mac Amlaim, rigdamna na nGall, 7 im Conmael mac Gilli Airi, 7 im Irlabraidh Atha clíath, et alíí muilti.[19]

The Battle of Tara gained by Maelseachnaill the Great son of Domhnall son of Donnchadh son of Flann, by the king of Ireland, over the Foreigners of Dublin, over the sons of Olaf specially, wherein many fell, including Raghnall son of Olaf, crown prince of the Foreigners, and Conmael, son of Giolla (Airi) and the Orator of Dublin, and many others.[20]

Chronicon Scottorum

Cath Temrach ria Maolseclainn mac Domnaill la rig hÉrenn for Gallaibh Atha Cliath & for macoib Amlaoib an t[sh]ainriudh dú a ttorchair ile um

17 Other annalistic sources record the battle, but not the presence of the *airlabraid*: G. Mac Niocaill (ed.), 'Annála gearra as proibhinse Ard Macha', *Seanchas Ardmhacha*, 3:2 (1959), 337–40, *s.a.* 980; A.M. Freeman (ed. and trans.), 'The annals in Cotton MS Titus A. XXV', *Revue Celtique*, 41 (1924), 301–30; 42 (1925), 283–305; 43 (1926), 358–84; 44 (1927), 336–61, *s.a.* 980; *AI* 980; *AU* 980; Murphy (ed.), *Annals of Clonmacnoise*, 974. 18 It has been suggested that the record of the Battle of Tara in the Annals of Ulster also derived from this lost source: Nicholas Evans, *The present and the past in medieval Irish chronicles* (Woodbridge, 2010), p. 245. 19 Stokes (ed. and trans.), 'Annals of Tigernach', *s.a.* 979. As Stokes noted, the form *irlabraigh* is found in the MS (Rawl. B488, fo. 15r); ibid., n. 1. 20 *ATig.* 980: available online at www.ucc.ie/celt/published/T100002A/index.html, where parenthesis in the translation by

Raghnall mac Amlaoibh rigdamna Gall & um Conamail mac Gille Airre uel i & arlabraid Atha Clíath & socaide.

The Battle of Temair [won] by Mael Sechnaill son of Domnall, king of Ireland, over the foreigners of Áth Cliath and the sons of Amlaíb in particular, in which many fell including Ragnall son of Amlaíb, heir designate of the foreigners, and Conamail son of Gille Aire and the spokesman of Áth Cliath and a large number [besides].[21]

Annals of the Four Masters

Cath Temhra ria Maoilseclaind, mac Domhnaill, for Ghallaibh Atha cliath, 7 na nindsedh, for macaibh amhlaoibh an tsainriudh, du i ttorcrattar ile im Raghnall mac Amhlaoibh, ríoghdhamhna Gall, 7 im Chonamhail, mic Gilliairri, 7 saerlabhraidh Atha cliath, 7 ro ladh dearg ár Gall imaille friú.

The Battle of Teamhair [was gained] by Maelseachlainn, son of Domhnall, over the foreigners of Ath-cliath and of the Islands, and over the sons of Amhlaeibh in particular, where many were slain, together with Raghnall, son of Amhlaeibh, heir to the sovereignty of the foreigners; Conamhail, son of Gilla-Arri; and the orator of Ath-cliath; and a dreadful slaughter of the foreigners along with them.[22]

As may be seen, Gearóid Mac Niocaill – the most recent translator of both the Annals of Tigernach and *Chronicon Scotorum* – offered two different translations of *airlabraid*: 'orator' and 'spokesman', in that order. The nineteenth-century translators of those two texts, Whitley Stokes and William Hennessy respectively, and John O'Donovan in his edition of the Annals of the Four Masters, all translated it as 'orator'.[23] These translations do not explain what functions the *airlabraid* may have performed, nor do they offer grounds upon which to speculate on the society in which he lived. Evidence for a hybrid society is suggested by the name of the *airlabraid*'s fallen comrade, Conmáel/Conamail; an ambiguous figure owing to scribal variations in his name/title.

Gearóid Mac Niocaill, enclosing *Airi*, may refer to ambiguity in the manuscript orthography, where the first 'i' is not unambiguously identifiable as such. **21** *CS* 980. Gearóid Mac Niocaill's editorial additions to the text and translation (available online at www.ucc.ie/celt/published/G100016/index.html) are enclosed in square parenthesis. *Uel i* was a scribal note to indicate that the final letter of *Airre* could be an 'i'; it does not refer to the *airlabraid*: Hennessy (ed. and trans.), *CS, s.a.* 978, n. 1. **22** *AFM* 978. O'Donovan's editorial addition in the translation is enclosed in square parenthesis. O'Donovan did not have access to two of the manuscripts of the Annals of the Four Masters when compiling his edition: RIA MS C iii 3 and UCD-OFM MS A 13. Both show deletion and reworking of the *sa-* of *saerlabhraidh* (RIA MS C iii 3, fo. 381v and UCD-OFM MS A 13, fo. 394r), www.isos.dias.ie, accessed 24 Mar. 2013. **23** In contrast, Diarmuid Ó Murchadha rendered it 'spokesman' in his index of the names in the Annals of Tigernach: idem, *The annals of Tigernach: index of names* (London,

His given name is clearly Gaelic, but 'son of Gille Aire' (an otherwise unattested name), may have been a corruption of *m. airri Gall* ('son of a tributary king of the foreigners'), as found in the Annals of Ulster.[24] Thus it is possible that Conmáel/Conamail was also the holder of a Gaelic title who fought for Amlaíb, or at least someone whose position was readily identifiable in Gaelic terms.

THE *AIRLABRAID* IN GAELIC SOCIETY

In Gaelic sources not concerned with Dublin, the noun *airlabraid* is also very poorly attested. *Airlabraid* is derived from the verb *ar-labrathar* ('to speak for/plead for') or its verbal noun *airlabrae* ('speaking on behalf of another'), while *saerlabhraidh* (in the Annals of the Four Masters) is the noun *airlabraid* with the prefix *so-* ('good/excellent'). Thus, an *airlabraid* is 'one who speaks on behalf of another' and consequently is defined in the *Dictionary of the Irish language* as 'spokesman, advocate, representative'.[25] It is important to draw a distinction between the official position of *airlabraid* and the function of speaking on behalf of another. Speaking on behalf of another does not imply that the speaker held a formal position as an *airlabraid*, even if similar vocabulary was used to describe the act. To illustrate the point: in 1 Timothy 2:12, St Paul stated 'I do not permit a woman to teach or to exercise authority over a man; rather, she is to remain quiet', to which an eighth-century Gaelic glossator of the Würzburg Pauline Epistles added *arislour infer diairlabri* ('for the man is enough to speak for her').[26] The Pauline man's speech on behalf of a woman does not, *ipso facto*, make him an *airlabraid*; otherwise a considerable portion of the male population would hold the title, owing to women's general lack of independent legal capacity.[27] Consequently, in the following discussion the focus will be confined to those individuals who are given the title *airlabraid*, rather than those who speak on behalf of others in general.

1997), *s.v. airlabraid*. **24** *AU* 980. The Annals of Clonmacnoise follows the other Clonmacnoise-group texts in calling him 'Conawill mcGillearrie': Murphy (ed.), *Annals of Clonmacnoise*, 974. F.J. Byrne argues that *air-rí* should be interpreted as 'viceroy' and that the *Dictionary of Irish language*'s primary definition 'tributary king, chieftain' is misleading: F.J. Byrne, 'Ireland and her neighbours, *c*.1014–*c*.1072' in Dáibhí Ó Cróinín (ed.), *A new history of Ireland, i: prehistoric and early Ireland* (Oxford, 2005), pp 862–98 at pp 877–8. It was probably this latter form that influenced *Conmael mac Gilli, ardri ele gall* ('Conmael, son of Gille, another high king of the foreigners') found in *Cogadh Gáedhel re Gallaibh*: J.H. Todd (ed. and trans.), *Cogadh Gaedhel re Gallaibh: the war of the Gaedhil with the Gaill, or the invasions of Ireland by the Danes and other Norsemen* (London, 1867), pp 46–7. **25** E.G. Quin et al. (eds), *Contributions to a dictionary of the Irish language based mainly on Old and Middle Irish materials* (Dublin, 1913–76), *s.v. airlabraid*. **26** Whitley Stokes and John Strachan (eds and trans.), *Thesaurus palaeohibernicus: a collection of Old-Irish glosses, scholia, prose and verse*, i (Cambridge, 1901), p. 681, n. 15. **27** Fergus Kelly, *A guide to early Irish law* (Dublin, 1988),

Legal evidence

The earliest attestation of the word *airlabraid* is that found in the pre-Viking-Age law text, *Críth Gablach* (*c.*AD700), which was particularly concerned with regulating the status of laymen in the highly stratified and inegalitarian society of early medieval Ireland. In its discussion of one of the highest grades of commoner (*aire coisring*), it states:

> *Aire coisring, cid ara n-eperr? Arindí consrenga túath 7 rí 7 senod tar cenn a chenéoil, ná[d] dlig a shlán doib, for curu bél, acht atndaimet do thoísiuch 7 aurlabraid remib. Is é aire fine insin tobeir gell tar cenn a fhine do ríg 7 senud 7 óes cherdd dia timorggain do réir.*[28]

Lord of obligation, why is he so called? Because kingdom and king and ecclesiastical authority bind him by contracts on behalf of his kin and he is not entitled to any indemnity from them, but they acknowledge him as leader and spokesman of them. That is the noble of a kin. He gives a pledge on behalf of his kin to king and ecclesiastical authority and poets, to constrain them to discipline.[29]

The *aire coisring*'s elevated status derived from his position as head of his *fine* (kin group).[30] The *fine* was a key legal and social unit in Gaelic society and possessed considerable powers over its members. In particular, the *aire coisring* was responsible for representing his kin in their dealings with the *nemed* ('privileged') members of society, namely kings, churchmen and poets.[31] He appears to have given a standing pledge on behalf of his *fine* and was entitled to heavy compensation should it be forfeited, presumably because it was pledged as a matter of obligation, rather than choice.[32] In some respects, he may be seen as a surety for their legal compliance.

Robin Chapman Stacey's excellent work on the performance of law in early medieval Ireland has demonstrated that speech and power were inextricably linked; the right to speak publicly was restricted within society and generally

pp 75–8.   **28** D.A. Binchy (ed.), *Críth Gablach* (Dublin, 1941), p. 11, lines 277–82. Binchy's editorial addition is enclosed in square parenthesis.   **29** My translation, based upon ibid., p. 32, n. 277. Robin Chapman Stacey suggests that *óes cherdd* should be read as 'tribal professionals', rather than 'poets': R.C. Stacey, *The road to judgement: from custom to court in medieval Ireland and Wales* (Philadelphia, 1994), pp 77–8. See, however, Kelly, *Guide to early Irish law*, p. 48, n. 84.   **30** For a discussion of the *aire coisring*, see Binchy (ed.), *Críth Gablach*, p. 70 and Kelly, *Guide to early Irish law*, pp 13–14, 48.   **31** For a brief discussion of the *fine*, see Kelly, *Guide to early Irish law*, pp 12–16. For a more detailed treatment, see T.M. Charles-Edwards, *Early Irish and Welsh kinship* (Oxford, 1993). Another legal text, *Míadshlechta*, suggests that actual lords, such as the *aire túise* ('lord of leadership'), were also kin representatives, who likewise spoke in public on behalf of their kin: Riitta Latvio, 'Status and exchange in early Irish laws', *Studia Celtica Fennica*, 2 (2005), 67–96 at 75.   **32** Binchy (ed.), *Críth Gablach*, pp 94–5. On the pledge lapsing, see R.C. Stacey, *Dark speech: the performance*

concomitant with social status.[33] This position is neatly summed up in the pseudo-historical prologue to the legal collection *Senchas Már*, where it is stated *tomus n-aí 7 innsce do chách iarna miad* ('lawsuit and speech to each man according to his rank').[34] In *Críth Gablach*, the two grades of the lowest rank of freemen (*fer midboth*) were distinguished by the extent to which they were granted the right to speak publicly, while the name of the highest of all noble grades, *aire forgill* ('lord of superior testimony'), incorporates the symbiosis of speech and power.[35]

Thus an *airlabraid*'s very ability to speak in public, and particularly to *nemed* figures, is an indicator of his importance. Although he was the possessor of a socially and legally elevated position, it is clear from the legal material that the *airlabraid* of *Críth Gablach* did not represent his kingdom; in contrast, the *airlabraid Átha Cliath*'s title suggests he probably had a kingdom-wide (rather than kin-orientated) function.[36]

Literary texts

The few literary texts in which the *airlabraid* features are generally several centuries younger than the legal material. One text, whose *airlabraid* appears to act in a quasi-legal capacity as a representative of subordinates before a higher power (like the *aire coisring*), is *Fís Adomnáin* ('Adomnán's [second] Vision'). That apocalyptic text probably dates from the 1090s, a little over a century after the death of the *airlabraid* of Dublin and almost four hundred years after *Críth Gablach* was written.[37] According to *Fís Adomnáin*, Adomnán of Iona (d. 704) is said to have received a vision of threatened divine punishment of the Irish, in consequence of which the long-dead St Patrick prayed to God to avert the disaster. Of Patrick it is stated: *is e bus brethem 7 bus erlabraid doib il-lou bratha* ('it is he who will be their judge and will be their spokesman on the Day of Judgment').[38] This appears to be a somewhat odd combination; the offices of judge and advocate are ostensibly incompatible and it seems unlikely that they are to be considered synonymous. It is possible that Patrick's function as an *airlabraid* was conceived as similar to that performed by an angel in the fragmentary Old Irish 'Vision of Laisrén', where the angel responds on behalf of a soul to accusations by a demon.[39]

In tales set in pre-Christian Ireland, particularly those concerning the Ulaid (the so-called Ulster Cycle of tales), the title *airlabraid* is associated with one

of law in early Ireland (Philadelphia, 2007), p. 44.   **33** Stacey, *Dark speech*, p. 98.   **34** Quoted and translated in ibid., p. 136.   **35** Ibid., pp 136–7.   **36** Indeed, Clare Downham has referred to him in passing as a 'civic official': eadem, *Viking kings of Britain and Ireland: the dynasty of Ívarr to AD1014* (Edinburgh, 2007), p. 238.   **37** Whitley Stokes (ed. and trans.), 'Adamnan's second vision', *Revue Celtique*, 12 (1891), 420–43.   **38** Stokes (ed. and trans.), 'Adamnan's second vision', 424 (my translation). Translated by Stokes as 'It is he who will be their judge and their advocate on Doomsday'; ibid., 425.   **39** *Frisgart aingel don arbar mór dar cheann na hanma don deman* ('an angel of the great host answered the demon on behalf of the soul'):

figure in particular, Senchae mac Ailella, who has been studied in detail by Kaarina Hollo.[40] Even Senchae, however, is rarely entitled *airlabraid*. In *Mesca Ulad* ('The drunkenness of the Ulaid'), Senchae is not actually called an *airlabraid*, although the character Cú Rúi does describe him as *sobérlaid fher in talman 7 fer sídaigthi slúaig Ulad* ('the skilful speaker of the men of the earth, and the peacemaker of the host of Ulster').[41] It is another character in this tale, Triscoth, who is entitled *airlabraid* by the Ulaid's enemies, although perhaps in a vein of mockery: *Driscoth sund oc erlabrai Ulad. Ní fuil aurlabraidi mathi leo chenae*[42] ('Triscoth is here speaking for the men of Ulster. They have no good spokesmen save him').[43] Similarly, Senchae is not given any title in the tale *Fled Bricrenn* ('Bricriu's Feast').[44] Rather, it is in the oldest recension of *Táin Bó Cúailnge* ('The cattle raid of Cooley') where he is called *erlabraid Ulad* ('the spokesman of Ulaid'), but he is not mentioned further in that recension.[45] In the second recension of *Táin Bó Cúailnge* (found in the twelfth-century Book of Leinster), Senchae is described as *so-irlabraid Ulad 7 fer sídaigthe slóig fer nHérend* ('the good spokesman of Ulaid, the man who pacifies the hosts of the men of Ireland').[46] An ambassadorial role is not implicit in this statement, as the closely related Stowe version of the *Táin* has *sluaig Ulad* ('hosts of Ulaid') for the Book of Leinster's *slóig fer nHérend* ('hosts of the men of Ireland'), and Senchae is generally depicted as a peacemaker among the Ulaid and never *fir Érend* ('men of Ireland').[47] In the second recension (Book of Leinster), Senchae is also described as a *láech* ('warrior')[48] and takes on a military role. Conchobar sends him to restrain the Ulaid until the battle omens are encouraging, before subsequently dispatching him to rouse the troops after the omens prove auspicious.[49] The role of *airlabraid* as battle inciter is also found at the beginning of the acephalous Middle Irish *History of Philip and Alexander of Macedonia*, in

Kuno Meyer (ed. and trans.), 'Stories and songs from Irish MSS', *Otia Merseiana*, 1 (1899), 113–28 at 115 (text) and 117 (trans.).   **40** Kaarina Hollo, 'Conchobar's "sceptre": the growth of a literary topos', *Cambrian Medieval Celtic Studies*, 29 (1995), 11–25 and eadem, 'The Ulster cycle, the law-tracts and the medieval court: the depiction of Senchae mac Ailella, *aurlabraid Ulad*', *Aiste*, 1 (2007), 170–80.   **41** J.C. Watson (ed.), *Mesca Ulad* (Dublin, 1941), p. 33, lines 757–8. J.C. Watson (trans.), 'Mesca Ulad', *Scottish Gaelic Studies*, 5 (1942), 1–34 at 24.   **42** Watson (ed.), *Mesca Ulad*, p. 43, lines 985–6. Watson noted of this passage, '*aurlabraidi*: the expansion is not quite certain, but gives distinctly better sense than *aurlabrai*, "speeches"'; ibid., p. 61, n. 986. The manuscript (*Lebor na hUidre*) has *aurlab* followed by a suspension stroke: RIA MS 23 E 25, p. 20 col. A.   **43** Watson (trans.), 'Mesca Ulad', 31.   **44** Hollo, 'The Ulster cycle', 172.   **45** Cecile O'Rahilly (ed. and trans.), *Táin Bó Cúailnge: recension I* (Dublin, 1976), p. 110, lines 3623–4 (my trans.). Trans. by O'Rahilly as 'the eloquent speaker of Ulster'; ibid., p. 222.   **46** Cecile O'Rahilly (ed. and trans.), *Táin Bó Cúalnge from the Book of Leinster* (Dublin, 1967), p. 120, l. 4356 (my trans.). Trans. by O'Rahilly as 'the eloquent speaker of Ulster, the man who appeases the armies of the men of Ireland'; ibid., p. 256.   **47** Hollo, 'Conchobar's "Sceptre"', 19, n. 33.   **48** O'Rahilly (ed. and trans.), *Táin Bó Cúalnge from the Book of Leinster*, p. 120, lines 4337, 4354.   **49** Ibid., pp 128–9, lines 4650–64. The poem Senchae recites bears verbal parallels with that uttered by Láeg, who was sent by Cú Chulainn to rouse the Ulaid to battle; ibid., p. 128, lines 4634–8. Senchae is not mentioned in a

which it states: *ro closa degurlabrada deigecnaide oc nertad 7 oc gressacht na slóg sin* ('there was heard very wise good spokesmen strengthening and inciting those hosts').[50] The death of the Dublin *airlabraid* at the Battle of Tara might suggest that he too performed a 'battle-rousing' function.

Another Middle Irish (possibly eleventh-century) translated text, *Togail Troí* ('The destruction of Troy', a translation of the popular *De Excidio Troiae Historia* ascribed to Dares Phrygius), features the character Antenor, *toisech sin 7 erlabraidh deirscaigthech do Tróíandaib* ('a leader and distinguished spokesman of the Trojans').[51] A second character, Panthus, was *primerlabraid na Tróiandai ule indegaid Antenoir* ('chief spokesman of all the Trojans after Antenor')[52] and elsewhere described as *fer airechdai do Throiánaib 7 degcomairlid ámra* ('a leading man of the Trojans and a wonderfully good counsellor').[53] Both Antenor and Panthus are portrayed as part of the Trojan king Priam's inner circle of advisors. Antenor was sent on a mission to the various Greek kings, to seek the return of Priam's captured sister and upon failing he advocated making war against the Greeks, while Panthus advised that war would result in Troy's destruction. Both Antenor and Panthus appear to speak at Priam's promptings and neither takes part in the battles, although Antenor did guide to Greece the Trojan fleet that captured Helen and subsequently betrayed Troy to the Greeks.

Overall, the Gaelic material does not provide a clear outline of the role of *airlabraid*. Senchae (who is only rarely entitled *airlabraid*) is a figure subject to varying portrayals although, as Kaarina Hollo has noted, he is usually depicted in association with Conchobar, king of Ulaid, and appears both to be the king's councillor and to have a formalized speaking role in his court.[54] In contrast to Senchae, however, neither Antenor nor Panthus appear to have formalized speaking roles within the king's court or act as pacifiers/arbiters among their own people or as battle rousers. Instead, Antenor functions mainly as an ambassador (a role Senchae does not perform) and councillor, and Panthus as a councillor.[55] As may be observed, there is little or no correlation between the *airlabraid* of the legal material and that of the secular narratives – even legal texts

restraining/rousing role in the first recension.   **50** Kuno Meyer (ed. and trans.), 'Die Geschichte von Philipp und Alexander von Macedonien aus dem Lebar Brecc, mit deutscher Uebersetzung und mit Excerpten aus dem Book of Ballymote' in Whitley Stokes and Ernst Windisch (eds), *Irische Texte mit Übersetzung und Wörterbuch*, 2:2 (Leipzig, 1887), pp 1–108 at p. 16, lines 2–3 (my trans.).   **51** Whitley Stokes (ed. and trans.), 'The destruction of Troy' in Stokes and Windisch (eds), *Irische Texte mit Übersetzung und Wörterbuch*, 2:1 (Leipzig, 1884), pp 1–142 at pp 9 and 71, lines 223–4.   **52** Ibid., p. 57, l. 1851 (my trans.). Trans. by Stokes as 'chief speaker of all the Trojans after Antenor'; ibid., p. 129.   **53** Ibid., pp 15 and 78, l. 414.   **54** Hollo, 'Conchobar's "Sceptre"', 18.   **55** It might be imagined that an *airlabraid* would act as a translator, but there is no evidence to support this. The *Dictionary of the Irish language* gives *tintathach* as 'translator', which is based on the verb *do-intaí* ('turns back, returns' with its verbal noun *tintúd*). See Quin et al. (eds), *Contributions to a dictionary of the Irish language*, *s.v. do-intaí, tintathach* and *tintúd*.

that mention Senchae never call him an *airlabraid*.[56] Naturally, this poses problems for assessing the source of inspiration for the tenth-century annalist.

SCANDINAVIAN INSTITUTIONS

In the search for Scandinavian institutions that may have laid behind the *airlabraid* of Dublin, the most obvious place to look is Northumbria, where Amlaíb had been king. Unfortunately, the few written sources that present a contemporary Viking perspective on Britain (mainly coin inscriptions and skaldic verse) are not particularly helpful, in this instance.[57] Even important Anglo-Saxon sources, such as Edgar's 'Wihtbordesstan' law-code (early 970s) or Æthelred's Wantage law-code for the Five Boroughs of the Danelaw (*c*.AD997) must be treated with caution; they were more concerned with spreading English practices than with enshrining Scandinavian customs. Instead, the net must be cast a little wider and three Scandinavian institutions that have been equated with the *airlabraid*, namely *þulr, stalleri* and *lǫgsǫgumaðr* (and another, which may have existed in Ireland – *lǫgmaðr* 'lawman'), will be examined.

Þulr

The *þulr* is the least likely of the three to have corresponded with an *airlabraid*. In a discussion of the *airlabraid* – as manifested in the form of Senchae in the Ulster Cycle – Michael Enright has argued for similarities between Senchae and Unferth the *þyle*, found in the Old English poem *Beowulf*, and by extension with the Old Norse *þulr*. Attempts to link descriptions of the Old English *þyle* with the Old Norse *þulr* have not proved fruitful, despite the cognate nature of the words.[58] Furthermore, the *þulr* is a very ill-defined figure; Margaret Clunies Ross and Russell Poole have noted that the *þulr* is associated with certain motifs (particularly occult, esoteric or Odinic practices and aspects of mediation between human beings and gods) and occasionally functions as a royal advisor.[59] Consequently, attempts to link the *airlabraid* of late tenth-century Dublin with the Old Norse *þulr*, via similarities between Senchae of the Ulster Cycle and Unferth of *Beowulf*, would be the antithesis of Ockham's razor – growing Ockham's beard.[60]

---

56 For a list of references to Senchae in legal texts, see Liam Breatnach, *A companion to the Corpus Iuris Hibernici* (Dublin, 2005), pp 363, 367.   **57** Downham, *Viking kings of Britain and Ireland*, p. 64.   **58** For some critical comments on such attempts, see Anatoly Liberman, 'Ten Scandinavian and north English etymologies', *alvíssmál*, 6 (1996), 63–98 at 71–7. **59** Margaret Clunies Ross, 'Poet into myth: Starkaðr and Bragi', *Viking and Medieval Scandinavia*, 2 (2006), 31–43 at 34. See also Russell Poole, 'Þulir as tradition-bearers and prototype saga-tellers: *þat er opt gott, er gamlir kveða*' in Judy Quinn and Emily Lethbridge (eds), *Creating the medieval saga: versions, variability and editorial interpretations of Old Norse saga literature* (Odense, 2010), pp 237–59.   **60** Enright appears to suggest that there are links:

Stalleri

Hollo has cautiously put forward the possibility that the *airlabraid* in the annals was a Norse *stalleri* ('marshal'), owing to similarities between Senchae of the Ulster Cycle and descriptions of the *stalleri*, citing Laurence Larson's account of the Norse *stalleri*:[61]

> This official was primarily a spokesman: he addressed the popular assemblies on the king's behalf and in turn advised the ruler as to the wishes and requests of the freemen. He was responsible for good order and proper discipline at court, and all disputes that might arise within the household were referred to him for settlement.[62]

Larson claims to have based his description upon the work of Rudolf Keyser, and it is essentially a summary of one passage in *Hirdskrå* ('The Book of the Hird').[63] Once again, chronological objections may be raised. *Hirdskrå* dates from the 1270s (though it may incorporate material up to one hundred years older), approximately three hundred years after the death of the *airlabraid Átha Cliath* at the Battle of Tara.[64] Steinar Imsen has argued that the *hird* (royal household) depicted in *Hirdskrå* is radically different from that of the eleventh century, and should be viewed as a developing 'national' aristocracy rather than an immediate household.[65]

In *Hirdskrå*, the *stalleri* is very much the king's servant, responsible for the king's horses on his travels and not offering council, but speaking only when bidden to act as the king's mouthpiece. His position as an arbiter is expressly at the recommendation of the king and even his representations on behalf of the *hird* occur in exceptional circumstances, rather than as a matter of course. *Hirdskrå* depicts a tiered elite in which the *stalleri* occupies a subordinate position in the *hird*, in the third tier and below figures like the *kanceler* ('chancellor').

M.J. Enright, 'The warband context of the Unferth episode', *Speculum*, 73:2 (1998), 297–337 at 336.   **61** Hollo, 'The Ulster Cycle', 176–7.   **62** L.M. Larson, 'The king's household in England before the Norman conquest', *Bulletin of the University of Wisconsin*, 100 (1904), 55–211 at 191.   **63** For this passage, see Rudolf Keyser and P.A. Munch (eds), *Norges gamle love indtil 1387*, ii (Christiania [Oslo], 1848), pp 387–450 at pp 410–11. L.G. Berge (trans.), 'Hirðskrá 1–37: a translation with notes' (MA, University of Wisconsin, 1968), pp 40–1; minds. wisconsin.edu/handle/1793/7575, accessed 24 Mar 2013. Larson also claims that *Konungs skuggsiá* (*Speculum Regale*, 'King's Mirror') – a text roughly contemporary with *Hirdskrå* – was an important source: Larson, 'The king's household', 190, n. 76. *Konungs skuggsiá* actually contains only one passing reference to a *stalleri*. Ludvig Holm-Olsen (ed.), *Konungs Skuggsiá* (2nd ed. Oslo, 1983), p. 46. L.M. Larson (trans.), *The king's mirror: speculum regale; konungs skuggsjá* (New York, 1917), p. 182.   **64** Steinar Imsen, 'King Magnus and his liegemen's "Hirdskrå": a portrait of the Norwegian nobility in the 1270s' in A.J. Duggan (ed.), *Nobles and nobility in medieval Europe: concepts, origins, transformations* (Woodbridge, 2000), pp 205–20 at pp 205–6.   **65** Ibid., pp 214–16.

Lǫgsǫgumaðr

Thirdly, it is possible that the *airlabraid* may have corresponded to the institution of *lǫgsǫgumaðr* ('lawspeaker', plural *lǫgsǫgumenn*);[66] a possibility given credence by the incorporation of 'speech' in both words, though objections may be raised on a number of grounds. Firstly, the office of *lǫgsǫgumaðr* is reliably attested only in Iceland.[67] According to *Grágás* (the corpus of Icelandic law), the *lǫgsǫgumaðr* was elected at the *Alþing* (Icelandic assembly) for a three-year term, where he was to preside over the *lǫgrétta* ('law council', which possessed legislative and judicial functions), and it was his duty publicly to recite one-third of the laws during each year of his office.[68] It is certainly possible that *þing* were held in Dublin and other parts of Ireland, as suggested by the presence of Thingmoot in Dublin and the place-name Ting, in the parish of Rathmacknee, in Co. Wexford.[69] Nonetheless, the manuscripts of *Grágás*, one of the two chief sources for the role of the *lǫgsǫgumaðr*, date from the thirteenth century and the information they contain probably dates from the twelfth century.[70] Even if *Grágás* is taken to contain an adequate representation of the function of the twelfth-century Icelandic *lǫgsǫgumaðr*, it does not follow that this testimony holds true for his late tenth-century counterpart, even in Iceland alone.

The second principal source for the *lǫgsǫgumaðr* is Ari inn fróði ('the knowledgeable') Þorgilsson's magnum opus, *Íslendingabók*, which he wrote and revised during the 1120s and 1130s. According to Ari's account, only the fourth Icelandic *lǫgsǫgumaðr* would have been in office when the *airlabraid* fell at the Battle of Tara and the office itself was only about ten years old when the Dubliners' king, Amlaíb Cúarán, first appears in the historical record – far away from Iceland. The first Norwegian settlement of Iceland is believed to have occurred in the decades around AD900 and Ari – the only source for the history of the early *lǫgsǫgumenn* – suggests that the first *lǫgsǫgumaðr* was Úlfljótr, who is said to have modelled the law on the law of the *Gulaþing* in Norway, and held office around AD930.[71] Evidence for Norway at that time is little better. The thirteenth-century *Heimskringla* (written by the *lǫgsǫgumaðr* Snorri Sturluson) appears to suggest that Úlfljótr's establishment of the *Alþing* in Iceland occurred

---

66 This possibility has been raised in passing in Doherty, 'The Vikings in Ireland', p. 302, Donnchadh Ó Corráin, 'The Vikings and Ireland', www.ucc.ie/celt/General%20Vikings%20in%20Ireland.pdf, accessed 24 Mar. 2013, p. 37 and more tentatively in Downham, *Viking kings of Britain and Ireland*, p. 238 ('spokesman (law-speaker?) of Dublin', though he is called 'orator' at ibid., p. 267).   **67** John Haywood, *Encyclopaedia of the Viking Age* (London, 2000), pp 118–19.   **68** Helgi Þorláksson, 'Historical background: Iceland, 870–1400' in Rory McTurk (ed.), *A companion to Old Norse–Icelandic literature and culture* (Malden, MA, 2005), pp 136–54 at p. 142.   **69** Doherty, 'The Vikings in Ireland', p. 302.   **70** Hans Fix, 'Grágás' in Phillip Pulsiano (ed.), *Medieval Scandinavia: an encyclopedia* (New York, 1993), pp 234–5. **71** Gunnar Karlsson, 'Social institutions' in McTurk (ed.), *A companion to Old Norse–Icelandic literature and culture*, pp 503–17 at p. 509.

not long after the establishment of the *Gulaþing*, namely both were innovations *c*.AD930.[72]

Both the *airlabraid* of Dublin and the Icelandic *lǫgsǫgumaðr* appear to have been public officials in their respective territories; beyond that, there seems to be little to connect the two, apart from the 'speech' element in both their titles. Since the performance of law was so intimately bound with speech in both cultures, this is hardly a strong connection. When comparing the Gaelic and Icelandic legal texts, there seems to be no link between the *airlabraid* of *Críth Gablach* (a representative of his kin) and the *lǫgsǫgumaðr* of *Grágás*. The most common role of the *airlabraid* in the Gaelic narrative material is that of royal councillor, while the Icelandic *lǫgsǫgumaðr* was certainly not a royal councillor, as Iceland was an oligarchic (rather than a monarchic) society.

Lǫgmaðr

Although the Old Norse *lǫgmaðr* ('lawman', plural *lǫgmenn*) has not been suggested as an inspiration for the *airlabraid*, the possibility ought to be explored, especially as it has been proposed that lawmen may have been present in the Insular region during the second half of the tenth century. In Norway, it was the duty of the *lǫgmaðr* to summon individuals to royal assemblies and deliver the decisions made in cases brought before the assembly. However, it has been argued that the *lǫgmaðr* did not come into existence until as late as the twelfth century,[73] while the *lagman* ('lawman') in Sweden is not reliably attested before the committal of the laws to writing in the thirteenth and fourteenth centuries.[74] Evidence from Anglo-Saxon England is hardly more promising: the lawmen of the *Libellus Æthelwoldi episcopi* ('The little book of Bishop Æthelwold') – relating to the 970s, though written in the twelfth century – amount to little more than a lexical borrowing.[75]

Clare Downham has suggested that it is unlikely that lawmen were absent from Viking territories in Ireland; unfortunately, there is no unambiguous evidence for their presence either.[76] It is possible, however, that the *lagmainn* mentioned in Gaelic sources were lawmen, but they are very poorly attested, appearing only twice in the annals.[77] Although they appear in sources referring to the two decades preceding the Battle of Tara, these sources (namely the Annals of the Four Masters and *Leabhar Muimhneach*) date from the seventeenth and eighteenth centuries respectively.[78] Furthermore, the Annals of the Four Masters

72 Gudmund Sandvik and J.V. Sigurðsson, 'Laws' in McTurk (ed.), *A companion to Old Norse–Icelandic literature and culture*, pp 223–44 at p. 231.   **73** Ibid., pp 234–5.   **74** Ibid., pp 240–1. His function seems quite similar to that of the Icelandic *lǫgsǫgumaðr*.   **75** Alan Kennedy, 'Law and litigation in the *Libellus Æthelwoldi episcopi*', *Anglo-Saxon England*, 24 (1995), 131–83 at 158–9.   **76** Downham, *Viking kings of Britain and Ireland*, p. 185.   **77** *AFM* 960, 972. Alex Woolf has suggested that they might have been leaders of 'farmer republics' in the Isles: idem, 'The wood beyond the world: Jämtland and the Norwegian kings' in Ballin Smith et al. (eds), *West over sea*, pp 153–66 at pp 164–5.   **78** Diarmuid Ó Murchadha, 'Lagmainn,

appear to suggest that the *lagmainn* originated in the Irish Sea region (possibly the Hebrides) and were inimical to the interests of Amlaíb Cúarán of Dublin.[79] Unfortunately, knowledge of the legal and administrative system of the Hebrides derives from much later sources and is largely relevant to later periods.[80] Donnchadh Ó Corráin has suggested that the *lagmainn* were not lawmen but an 'aristocratic kindred', whose name derived from treating the occupational title *lǫgmaðr* as a proper name.[81] Furthermore, Diarmuid Ó Murchadha has argued that the annalists may have treated *lagmainn* as a population name; the dative plural *lagmannaibh* suggests that *lagmainn* was treated as an o-stem noun, thus similar to population names like Bretain. He proposed an alternative etymology from *ladg* ('snow'); they were 'snow people', that is, people from the north. This etymology is supported by the alternative spelling in the annals, *ladgmainn*.[82]

An important obstacle to equating *airlabraid* with *lǫgmaðr* quickly becomes apparent. If the annalists were comfortable using the term *lagmainn* for *lǫgmaðr* at this very time, why did they abandon it for the equally obscure *airlabraid* in this instance? Whether or not the Annals of the Four Masters can be accepted as representative of contemporary accounts of lawmen in the Isles, they do not support the assumption that they existed in Dublin (and the title *airlabraid Átha Cliath* suggests that the *airlabraid* slain at Tara was not an ally from the Isles).

CONCLUSION

In a recent historiographic overview of Viking ethnicities, Downham suggested that one can speak of a multiplicity of regional Viking cultures throughout Europe (*c.*AD1000), which were simultaneously integrated into their local

Lǫgmenn', *Ainm: Bulletin of the Ulster Place-name Society*, 2 (1987), 136–40 at 136. For some remarks on the unreliability of AFM for tenth-century Viking history, see Woolf, 'Amlaíb Cuarán and the Gael', 39–40. The unverifiable reference in *Leabhar Muimhneach* simply states that Mathgamain, king of Dál Cais (d. 976), fought a battle against the *lagmainn*: Tadhg Ó Donnchadha (ed.), *An Leabhar Muimhneach maraon le suim aguisíní* (Dublin, 1941), p. 127. **79** They appear to have been in the service of the sons of Óláfr Guðrøðsson: Downham, *Viking kings of Britain and Ireland*, pp 49, 184. It should be noted, however, that both AU and AFM claim that Amlaíb had support from the Isles at the Battle of Tara, and he did die on Iona. Mary Valante has suggested that this support was motivated by economic concerns: M.A. Valante, *The Vikings in Ireland: settlement, trade and urbanization* (Dublin, 2008), p. 116. **80** Magnús Stefánsson, 'The Norse island communities of the western ocean' in Knut Helle (ed.), *The Cambridge history of Scandinavia 1: prehistory to 1520* (Cambridge, 2003), pp 202–20 at p. 207. Similarly, although the Orkneys had an assembly headed by a *lǫgmaðr*, knowledge of this also derives from later medieval sources, particularly *Orkneyinga saga*: ibid., p. 206. It is possible that some of the insular assemblies are comparably late, such as that in the Shetlands, which may have developed only after the direct imposition of Norwegian royal control in the last decade of the twelfth century: ibid., p. 208.   **81** Donnchadh Ó Corráin, 'The Vikings in Scotland and Ireland in the ninth century', *Peritia*, 12 (1998), 296–339 at 308–9.   **82** Ó Murchadha, 'Lagmainn, Lǫgmenn', 137.

setting and consciously maintained awareness of their Scandinavian heritage.[83] Furthermore, in discussing the evidence for lawmen in the Isles, she elsewhere suggested that 'a fusion of aspects of Scandinavian and Gaelic law may have occurred in areas of mixed Gaelic-Scandinavian culture'.[84] Indeed, an example of legal fusion may be seen in the conquered Danelaw, where the practice of recognizing distinctive legal traditions continued into the eleventh century (as witnessed in the law codes associated with Archbishop Wulfstan II of York).[85] The *airlabraid* of Dublin may have been a feature of one such hybrid legal system, but his role is almost impossible to discern. Whoever and whatever he was, he had features familiar enough to bear the semantic weight of the Gaelic term *airlabraid*, as understood by one annalist at least. Unfortunately, the picture remains unclear, owing to the poor attestation (and heterogeneous depiction) of the *airlabraid* in Gaelic sources.

In short; defining and translating *airlabraid* within the framework of current knowledge of tenth-century Dublin society may be an impossibility. Scholarly attempts to translate it as (or equate it with) 'orator', 'spokesman', *þulr*, *stalleri* and *lǫgsǫgumaðr* may have more to say about historiographic methodologies and underlying cultural perceptions concerning the intensity of Dublin's Scandinavian character (or lack thereof), than they do about the institution itself. Short of holding a séance and actually questioning the *airlabraid* of 980 himself, it is unlikely that his role within Dublin society, or how he viewed himself culturally, will ever be known. That is not to say that our ghostly interlocutor would have any clear-cut answers, for, as Edward T. Hall noted, 'culture hides much more than it reveals and, strangely enough, what it hides, it hides most effectively from its own participants'.[86]

83 Clare Downham, 'Viking ethnicities: a historiographic overview', *History Compass*, 10:1 (2012), 1–12 at 6–7.   84 Downham, *Viking kings of Britain and Ireland*, p. 185.   85 D.M. Hadley, *The Vikings in England: settlement, society and culture* (Manchester, 2006), p. 69. 86 E.T. Hall, 'The power of hidden differences' in M.J. Bennett (ed.), *Basic concepts of intercultural communication: selected readings* (Yarmouth, ME, 1998), pp 53–67 at p. 59.

The coinage and economy of Hiberno-Scandinavian Dublin

ANDREW WOODS

Hiberno-Scandinavian Dublin boasts an extensive number of coin finds, with over one hundred coins from archaeological excavations in addition to four hoards from within the walled area of the town. This volume of pre-Anglo-Norman finds places it among a relatively small number of northern European towns with large early medieval assemblages; the numbers of coins published from York, Winchester and Trondheim is smaller than those from Dublin, although the large-scale excavations within London unsurprisingly produced numbers in excess of any of these (Pirie 1986; Biddle 2012; Risvaag 2006; Stott 1991; Kelleher & Leins 2008). The number of finds from the town is a testament to the extent of excavation, and good survival, of material from early medieval Dublin. The excavated finds are included in a forthcoming publication of single finds from Ireland (Woods forthcoming (a)) while the hoards have been described previously (Blackburn 2008, 118–23; Dolley 1966, 78–9).

Most analysis of Hiberno-Scandinavian coinage has utilized the evidence of hoards, which has yielded important results including an interpretation of chronology (Dolley 1966) and insights into those using coinage (Kenny 1987). Analysis of hoards has tended to consider Ireland as a whole, with the role of Dublin inferred from the discussion of silver finds beyond its walls. This essay moves the focus away from Ireland's hoards and instead considers the finds of coins from within the town. This is not the first time early medieval coins from Dublin have been discussed, but on the whole the coinage has been an under-utilized resource for the interpretation of the town. When it has been discussed, it has been largely used for the purposes of dating, most spectac-ularly at Fishamble Street, where a series of coins allow for quite precise dating of the successive phases (Wallace 1992). It has also been included in discussion of the importance of commerce to the town, with Patrick Wallace including analysis of this material within a broader overview of the town's early medieval economy (Wallace 1987, 206–14). Wallace's analysis built upon his earlier publication of the coin finds that had been excavated by the mid-1980s, examined in the context of the English presence in Dublin (Wallace 1986). However, there has been little recent and detailed analysis of coinage. This is regrettable, as the volume of finds, coupled with the excellent and extensive excavations, allow for quite detailed analysis with good chronological and spatial resolution. Much of the discussion revolves around evidence from excavations within the town. These are referred to by name here, as summaries and associated bibliographies can be found in previous syntheses of the archaeological evidence from the town (Simpson 2001; Simpson 2011).

The purpose of pursuing an analysis of the coins from Hiberno-Scandinavian Dublin is to examine the economy of the town. It is clear that commerce played an important role within the early medieval town. There are indications of the presence of traders from Dublin in a number of English towns, and mention is made of Dublin's merchant ships in contemporary accounts (Wallace 1987, 224–5; Hudson 2005, 42; Valante 2008, 131). Finds of material culture within the town also point towards exchange relationships. Amber, jet, walrus ivory, silk and soapstone would all have needed to be imported (Wallace 1987, 211–19). Although unattested by the archaeological record, there is also good evidence from the eleventh and twelfth century for a flourishing trade in skins from Dublin (Valante 2008, 159; Hudson 2005, 43). It is clear that significant trade occurred in Dublin, but the precise mechanics of this – when, where and how – are still fairly obscure. The coin finds from early medieval Dublin combine strong chronological resolution with the possibility of quantification. They allow the patterns of exchange to be traced, particularly the manner in which these evolved through the history of the town. The following will pursue a biographical approach, focusing upon coinage in each of its three contexts; minting (primary), use (secondary) and deposition (tertiary) (Kemmers & Myrberg 2011, 90). This will begin by considering the Hiberno-Scandinavian mint of Dublin and move on to a discussion of the use of coinage within the urban environment before progressing to a consideration of deposition within a wider Irish and Irish Sea context.

BACKGROUND

There is little archaeological evidence to suggest that silver was widely utilized as a means of exchange in Ireland before the settlement of the Vikings in the ninth century. There are references to weighed silver ounces in seventh- and eighth-century law tracts, but these are only matched by archaeological evidence in the ninth century (Kelly 1988, 112–16). From 850 to 950, a period generally associated with extensive Viking activity in Ireland, a large number of hoards with mixed silver, indicative of a metal-weight mentality, are known across much of Ireland (Sheehan 2007). John Sheehan has published extensively on this material and it is apparent from his work on the hoards that coinage played only a minor role in Ireland at this early date (Sheehan 2000; Sheehan 2007). As the tenth century progressed, the silver economy of Ireland became increasingly orientated towards coinage, although it must be stressed that this was neither a simple nor an inevitable process. This is visible in silver hoards, which frequently include imported Anglo-Saxon coins, mostly unadulterated and particularly focused in areas around Dublin (Kenny 1987;

A   B   C   D

*c.*1000   *c.*1050   *c.*1080   *c.*1120

3.1 Examples of Hiberno-Scandinavian coinage.

Blackburn 2007; Bornholdt-Collins 2010). The relationship between metal weight and coin-using economies has been extensively discussed elsewhere, with variety of chronology and practice stressed (Blackburn 2007; Williams 2007; Bornholdt-Collins 2010). Broadly speaking, however, the tenth century saw the emergence of coin-use in Ireland and this was particularly focused in and around Dublin.

The silver economy of Ireland fundamentally altered *c.*995 when Sygtryggr *silkiskeggi* (Sitriuc Silkenbeard), the Hiberno-Scandinavian king of Dublin, had his own coinage struck within the town. This was the first coinage manufactured in Ireland and it was modelled upon the contemporary English coinage, as was the norm across a number of European coinages, featuring an image of the king on the obverse with a cross design on the reverse. These coins are usually referred to as 'Hiberno-Norse', but it has been suggested that the more neutral term 'Hiberno-Scandinavian' should be utilized in its stead and that convention will be followed here (Sheehan et al. 2001, 93–4; Bornholdt-Collins 2003). The Hiberno-Scandinavian coinage continued to be struck until the Anglo-Norman invasion, although the form of the coins underwent significant change during this period, as is visible in figure 3.1.

Michael Dolley classified the coinage into seven successive phases (Dolley 1966, 92–150). This classification is open to criticism over its absolute chronology, but the main scheme sketched by Dolley still broadly holds. The coinage began with imitations of English coins with successive English types imitated contemporaneously in Dublin. Coin A of figure 3.1 is an example of a

Dublin imitation of an English Long Cross design and was struck around the year 1000. The imitation of England's coinage was succeeded *c*.1020 by stylized versions of this Long Cross design, as can be seen on coin B. Mark Blackburn has termed these early eleventh-century changes as the evolution of a 'coinage of national identity', with production changing from imitation to innovation (Blackburn 2008). During the first half of the eleventh century, the coinage gradually became illiterate, with the legend represented by 'pseudo-epigraphy', often just a series of vertical strokes. This is unlikely to be indicative of deficiency in Dublin's mint and is much more likely to show the relatively limited scope of Latin literacy in the Hiberno-Scandinavian town. In the late eleventh century, there was a period of iconographic heterogeneity, with a range of complex images, as demonstrated on coin C, used alongside one another. This was replaced from the 1120s by the striking of 'bracteate' coins. The bracteates were extremely thin with only one design, visible on both faces, rather than the usual two. Coin D illustrates the fact that these were usually geometric designs, often featuring crosses. The end of the chronology also saw a reduction in the silver standard with bracteate coins struck in very debased silver in the 1150s and 1160s (Kenny 2012). This is a very brief outline of the coinage, but serves to emphasize that the evolution of the coinage was quite dramatic. It should also be stressed that while the earliest coins had imitated English exemplars, from *c*.1020 onwards Dublin had a novel and successful coinage of its own.

PRODUCING COINAGE IN EARLY MEDIEVAL DUBLIN

All of the coins struck in pre-Anglo-Norman Ireland appear to have been manufactured in Dublin. Where legends exist, they name Dublin as their place of issue, usually rendered as DYFLIN or similar, as can be seen on coin A in figure 3.1. Among the illiterate coins of the eleventh and twelfth centuries, stylistic continuity and the pattern of coin finds suggest that the coins continued to be struck in Dublin. However, beyond the evidence of the coins themselves, there is very little evidence for the practicalities, organization or authority for the mint. Much can be inferred from the coins, including the technical capability of the mint, which could maintain a very high and consistent silver alloy throughout the eleventh century (Heslip & Northover 1990). A number of technical features could be discussed in relation to production but, drawing upon the evidence of the finds, the following discussion will focus upon the site of the Hiberno-Scandinavian mint. It will be argued that the Hiberno-Scandinavian mint is most likely to have been in proximity to modern-day Christchurch Place, as is marked on figure 3.2.

Utilizing the term 'mint' is slightly problematic, as it gives an impression of organization that is probably unjustified for the early medieval world

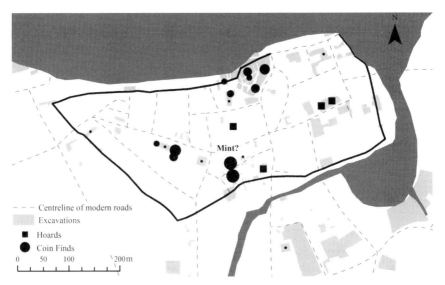

3.2 Map showing conjectural site of the mint and all coin finds from Dublin, 900–1170.

(Allen 2012, 1). In England, where there is both archaeological and historical evidence for coin production, 'mints' have been argued to be a series of work-shops run by individual moneyers. Indeed, there were specific prohibitions regarding multiple moneyers working in the same building (Allen 2012, 46). As a result, attempts to identify a specific 'mint' are problematic. However, evidence from both York and Winchester suggests that the physical production of coinage was clustered into one area. There is evidence for up to six forges being in close proximity in Winchester and at least two buildings associated with coin production at Coppergate in York (Barlow & Biddle 1976, 420; Pirie 1986, 18–20). While a 'mint', as either an institution or a building, may not have existed as we currently understand it, it seems likely that those responsible for the striking of coinage were in relatively close proximity to one another. The term 'mint' will be used as a means of convenience here and is best understood as the area in which moneyers/craftsmen worked, rather than a building or institution in which official minting activity occurred.

The positioning of Dublin's 'mint' cannot be determined through historical enquiry as, to the best of my knowledge, the pre-Anglo-Norman mint is not directly mentioned in any source. The moneyers of the town are noted in a passage in the twelfth-century *Lebor na Cert* ('The Book of Rights') contained in the Book of Uí Maine, where Armagh is due to receive, among a number of things, a 'scruple from every moneyer' of Dublin (Etchingham 2010, 28–9; Ó Corráin 1997, 107–8). That the moneyers are referred to specifically in the text suggests that there was more than one moneyer and that they were reasonably identifiable within the town. This would fit within broader European patterns in which moneyers represented a distinctive and fairly high-status group within towns (Lopez 1953, 1–16). While this does not mean that every moneyer was based in the same area of the town, comparison with contemporary English exemplars suggests that this is the most likely occurrence.

The consideration of minting requires comparison with other areas where evidence is stronger than in Dublin. A number of early medieval mints have been investigated across England and Scandinavia. York and Sigtuna have been investigated archaeologically, equipment associated with minting has been recovered from London, while Winchester is known from documentary sources (Barlow & Biddle 1976, 396–421; Pirie 1986, 15–25; Malmer et al. 1991; Stott 1991; Archibald et al. 1995; Archibald 1991). Comparison with these sites suggests that the fingerprint of a mint has three main elements: evidence of precious metalworking, specific topography and certain types of small find.

These comparative sites suggest that minting is likely to have occurred in proximity to the working of metals. This would be expected, as forges, benches, tools and the skills for working of metals would have been common across the two practices (Allen 2012, 103–14). At York, the excavations at Coppergate have shown an overlap between metalworking, visible in the form of crucibles and extensive hearths, and the striking of coins (Pirie 1986, 20–1). A similar situation is observable at Sigtuna, where a furnace and forge were found in the same building as a lead trial piece associated with Olof Skötkonung's mint (Malmer et al. 1991). In Dublin, the site of Christchurch Place has produced ample evidence for metalworking, with numerous moulds, trial pieces and crucibles (Ó Ríordáin 1971; Wallace 1987, 211). It was described as a 'metalworking quarter' by its excavator (Wallace 1987, 212).

At both Sigtuna and Winchester, the position of the mint was on the major route through the town, where it would be expected that travelling traders, those who might be expected to use the mint most frequently, would pass (Barlow & Biddle 1976, 420; Ros 2001, 83; Malmer et al. 1991). The site of the mint in both of these cases also lay just beyond an area of political authority. In the case of Winchester, this was just beyond the boundary of the church's lands, while in Sigtuna it was just outside of royal land. This was manifest physically at Sigtuna where a boundary ditch divided the royal lands from the mint building (Malmer et al. 1991). The proposed mint site in Dublin would fit with both of these topographic features, as Christchurch Place is situated on the intersection between the major east–west route and one of the two major north–south roads. It is also a short distance from modern Christ Church Cathedral. This was originally founded by Sitriuc Silkenbeard in the early eleventh century on land that may have been previously under royal authority (Kinsella 2000). Assuming the modern roads represent the medieval streets,

3.3 One of two lead tokens (E122:8700) found at Christchurch Place in 1973.
Image © National Museum of Ireland.

then this may have been the edge of the royally sponsored church's lands.
Christchurch Place could be interpreted in a similar way to Winchester or
Sigtuna; close to an area of authority but perhaps just beyond the boundary of it.

The other piece of evidence is in the form of two small finds (E122:6143
and E122:8700) recovered in the course of excavation at Christchurch Place.
They are two thick discs of lead that have been struck using coin dies and have
subsequently been drilled through their centre. One is illustrated as figure 3.3.
Assuming that it dates form the same period as the coin, it can be dated early
within the bracket of *c*.1040–60. It has not been possible to photograph the
other piece, but it can be dated to the early 1060s.

Taken in isolation, interpreting the purpose of these objects is difficult.
Fortunately, Marion Archibald has worked on a similar group of objects from
contemporary sites in England (Archibald 1991). While it might be tempting
to describe these objects as 'trial pieces', related to minting, Archibald has
preferred an explanation of them as customs receipts. Customs and tolls were
common in medieval towns and markets (Middleton 2005). They are known in
Ireland too, and a passage from *Lebor na Cert* lists the tax due to the 'folk of the
royal citadel' from merchants trading in Ireland (Valante 1998, 250). The lead
pieces may have existed to prove that these, or similar tolls, had been paid
(Archibald 1991, 333). Archibald argues that they must have been officially
sanctioned pieces, as they are struck from genuine coin dies. There is also
frequent damage, normally a deliberate nick in the edge, which is explained as
'cancellation' after they have been used. She also notes that the find-spot of the
tokens is normally at sites of 'mints, customs or royal tax activities, with
possibly more than one of these functions being carried out in the same place'
(Archibald 1991, 333). In many ways, there are similarities to the Dublin

pieces. The lead discs from Dublin were struck from coin dies, used for striking normal coins, meaning their purpose must have been official. They also appear to have been 'cancelled' with a hole drilled through the centre suggesting a completion of their function. There are quite rough edges around this drilling, with little sign of wear subsequent to this, suggesting that the hole may have been created towards the end of their period of usage. The association that has been noted in relation to royal activities is probably equally relevant in the context of Dublin. It seems likely that the pieces were officially sanctioned, connected to toll-payment and may have been lost in an administrative centre of some form. Their presence at Christchurch Place in a cancelled form suggests that this was where they were returned after use and would accord well with the possibility of this being a mint. At the very least, this must have been an area with some form of administrative function. It is possible that they were on their way to be 'recycled', at the mint, into new pieces in a similar way to the Coppergate or Clifford's Castle pieces in York (Archibald 1991, 333).

It is impossible to prove that the area around Christchurch Place was the site of the mint striking Dublin's coins but, at least for the mid-eleventh century, for which the lead pieces provide good corroborative evidence, it is a possibility. Further evidence in favour of such an interpretation can be found in the fact that this area was the location of a significant number of coin finds from the eleventh century, as is visible in figure 3.6. In the absence of finds of coin dies, and documentary evidence, it is difficult to be certain, but comparison with a range of other mints suggests that this area had an official, administrative purpose with circumstantial evidence that suggests that this may have been connected to minting.

USING COINAGE IN EARLY MEDIEVAL DUBLIN

Turning to the evidence for the use of coins in the town, as is discussed above, this is reliant upon a comparison of single finds, rather than hoards, from across a range of archaeological contexts. In analysing this assemblage it becomes apparent that coin-usage was far from static in early medieval Dublin. This is apparent in Table 3.1, which lists the number of finds across the various excavations in Dublin . The table provides a listing of all coins known to the author, but it is possible that there are omissions. The numbers from some of the major sites show substantial chronological variability and the monetary economy of early medieval Dublin will be considered in three phases: the tenth, eleventh and twelfth (to 1170) centuries. These chronological boundaries are chosen to enable comparison with previous research on the topographical development of the town (Halpin 2005).

Table 3.1 The number of coins from excavations in Dublin, by century (for references, see Woods forthcoming (a)). (* = lead trial piece)

	Square	C9th	C10th	Early C11th	Late C11th	C12th	Total
High Street	1962–3					1	1
	1		3				3
	2					1	1
	3					17	17
	4	1		3		3	7
Christchurch	1		4	9	6	2	21
Place	2			11	5	5	21
	uncertain			2*	2	1	3
Winetavern	1				1		1
Street	2				4		4
	5					3	3
Fishamble	FS I		1		4	2	7
Street	FS II		8	8			16
	FS III		5	1	1		7
Temple Bar West			1				1
Werburgh Street			2				2
Wood Quay			2			2	4
Bride Street					1		1
Winetavern Street						1	1
Back Lane						1	1
Patrick Street	B					2	2
	C					1	1
All sites		1	26	32	24	42	**125**

In general terms, during the course of the tenth century, coinage became an increasingly important element within the town. This is particularly notable if finds are plotted chronologically, as is summarized in figure 3.4. A general upward trend in the number of finds is visible. Coinage struck from the 920s onwards was lost quite consistently in Dublin. The finding of a very early coin of Alfred struck in the 880s might suggest that this occurred even earlier, but at a low, almost archaeologically invisible, level. The single-find evidence would suggest that some Dubliners embraced a mixed silver and, ultimately, coin-

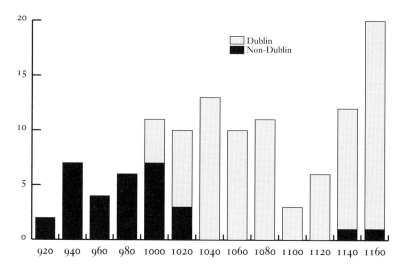

3.4 Single finds from Dublin, divided by origin.

using economy, probably from *c*.920 onwards. This may be connected to the close dynastic links between York and Dublin at this point, as has been suggested for the Isle of Man (Bornholdt-Collins 2003, 334–40; Downham 2007, 29). It is impossible to be certain about the relationship of coinage with other forms of silver, in advance of their full publication, but it seems likely that Dublin broadly paralleled the situation in other areas of Ireland, which continued to utilize mixed silver means of exchange into the latter half of the tenth century (Blackburn 2007, 129–30; Bornholdt-Collins 2010). This is suggested by finds of bullion weights from eleventh-century contexts at Fishamble Street (Wallace 2013, 305). The higher incidence suggests that Dublin was an environment increasingly comfortable with the use of coinage during the late tenth and early eleventh century. Further evidence in favour of such an interpretation is the decision to begin to strike coins *c*.995. The striking of coins can be argued to presuppose an audience willing to use them.

When considered spatially, the pattern of finds of tenth-century coin is centred on Fishamble Street, on the River Liffey, as is illustrated in figure 3.5. These finds are spread over a number of plots, with only one plot associated with more than one coin. There are also a number of coins to the south, on the slightly higher ground, at Christchurch Place. The smaller number of coins at Christchurch Place might be explained in chronological terms, as it appears the site was only occupied from the mid-tenth century. Coins of Æthelstan (924–39) from Fishamble Street suggest that the site was utilizing coinage from the early part of the tenth century onwards. Even allowing for the

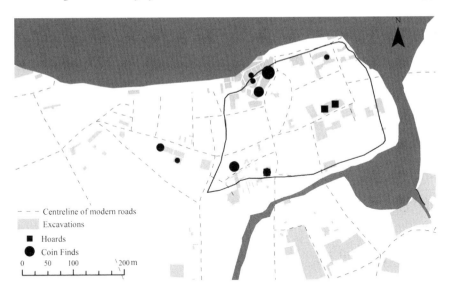

3.5 Distribution of tenth-century coin finds.

chronological difference between the two sites, it seems likely that Fishamble Street was of greater economic importance in the tenth century.

There are also a small number of coins further to the south and west, at High Street. These coins are of interest as one, a coin of Alfred struck in the period *c*.880–5, is the earliest known from Dublin. It should be stressed that this is a production date rather than a deposition date, so it may have been lost as late as the tenth century. It was found in square 4 of the High Street excavation, a significant distance to the west of the conjectured extent of the tenth-century town. It suggests that the western area of the town was settled earlier than is often assumed or, as is more probable, that coins were lost along the route-way to the west of the tenth-century town.

The presence of the three hoards within the town is of some interest, as much for their composition as for their location. The three hoards are all of broadly comparable date, in the range *c*.985–95, and are reasonably uniform in the types of coins they contain and the mints they represent (Blackburn 2008, 121). The consistency of the hoards suggests that there was something of a common pool of currency within the town (Blackburn 2008, 122). This suggestion is broadly supported by the analysis of hoards from outside of the town where, again, a consistency of currency is emphasized (Bornholdt-Collins 2003, 265–74). In the absence of later hoards from the town, it is difficult to be certain that this continued to be the case beyond the tenth century, but it seems likely, especially given the increasingly common usage of

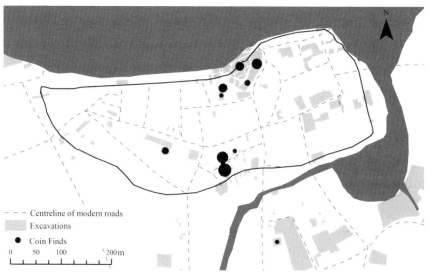

3.6 Distribution of eleventh-century coin finds.

coinage. It is significant, as it suggests that, from a relatively early date, coinage was circulating within, rather than merely passing through, Dublin.

The coin finds parallel the other archaeological evidence that suggests a formalization, and greater permanence, of the town in the tenth century. While the settlement appears to have been quite transitory in the ninth century, there is a far greater sense of stability in the tenth century, with encircling banks and more systematically laid out streets (Wallace 1992; Simpson 2011, 36–58). The period also saw the first traces of significant production within the town, with metal- and bone-working occurring (Wallace 1985, 212; Wallace 1987, 238). It is tempting to view coinage in this period as quite closely aligned with trade along the Liffey, especially given the slight shift in distribution in the following periods. However, linen and amber production was also occurring in riverside areas (Geraghty 1996, 8–10, 29; Wallace 1992, 133). Thus, while coinage and maritime trade can be linked, this should not be to the exclusion of other forms of economic activity.

The general upward trend of the number of coin finds from the tenth century continued into the eleventh. This is demonstrated in figure 3.4, where the middle of the century is represented by the top of fairly flat peak. Coins of Dolley Phase II, struck between *c*.1020 and *c*.1040, are the most common find in the town until the light bracteates of the mid-twelfth century, described below. They comfortably outnumber finds of any English type of the tenth century. This is a point worthy of emphasis, as a concentration of hoards in the tenth century may lead to the misconception that this represented a peak for

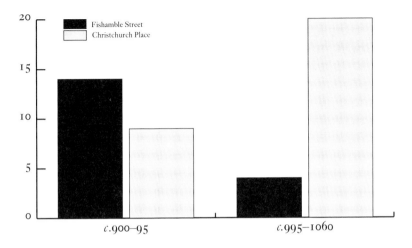

3.7 Comparison of finds from Fishamble Street and Christchurch Place.

coinage in Dublin and Ireland. In fact, the excavated evidence suggests that the peak occurred in the eleventh century and was during a period in which Dublin struck a distinct and successful coinage of its own. It is certainly possible to describe this period as something of an economic 'boom' for the town. This is visible in the evidence from the coins, but also in a number of other proxies. The century saw the defended area of the town double in size and the construction of a number of churches (Simpson 2011, 34–56). The emergence, or concentration, of productive craft activities is also highly visible, with metalworking at Christchurch Place, wood at Winetavern Street and combs in a number of areas (Ó Ríordáin 1984, 140–2).

In spatial terms, eleventh-century coin-usage saw elements of continuity from the tenth. As is visible in figure 3.6, the area from Fishamble Street in the north, including Winetavern Street, to Christchurch Place in the south boasts the greatest concentration of finds. The relative absence of finds to either the east or the west of this can be deemed significant, as both of these areas have been reasonably extensively excavated. The absence of coinage in the eastern area of the town, where there was evidence of coinage in the tenth century, and the west, where there is evidence from the twelfth, suggests that the pattern is a genuine one rather than merely a product of the positioning of areas of archaeological investigation.

Continuity should not be stressed too much, however, as within this central area, Christchurch Place emerges as the most significant site for coinage. This is quite clear when the finds from the tenth and first half of the eleventh

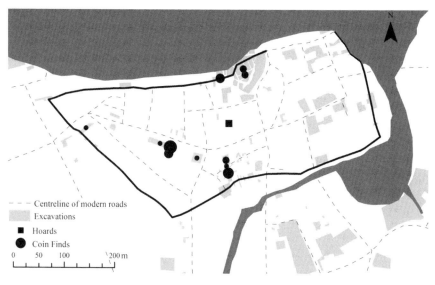

3.8 Distribution of twelfth-century coin finds.

century are compared, as in figure 3.7. Christchurch Place has twenty coins, which is more than double the nine from Fishamble Street. This period has been selected as it is before the significant truncation of Fishamble Street in which many of the late eleventh-century strata were lost. Rather than being a coincidence of recovery, the argument can be advanced that the most intensive use of coins had shifted somewhat further to the south in the first half of the eleventh century. This shift is also mirrored in the variation of coin types between sites. There is a slightly greater proportion of foreign silver at Fishamble Streets which suggests that it was more closely aligned with international trade than other areas of the town. Such an interpretation is endorsed by its tenth-century assemblage of Anglo-Saxon silver, which is the largest from the town (cf. Wallace 1986). The difference in assemblage may be explained by the topography of the sites. Fishamble Street is very close to the Liffey, while Christchurch Place is further from the river and uphill somewhat. Both topography and coin assemblages suggest that Fishamble Street was engaged more in international trade while Christchurch Place was a more general, or better regulated, area of exchange in the heart of the town.

Determining what drove the growth in coin-use and presumed success of the town in the eleventh century is difficult, but it is tempting to connect it with specialist production. There are overlaps between concentrations of finds and sites of production, as can be seen by comparing figure 3.2 and figure 3.9. The coin finds suggest that there was a slight shift from Fishamble Street to Christchurch Place, perhaps reflecting a greater emphasis on production rather than longer-distance trade in the eleventh century. However, it is unlikely that either was ever pre-eminent. Exchange in commodities must have occurred early in the life of Dublin, to enable it to feed itself. The peak in coinage also coincided with a peak in slavery and it has been suggested that the eleventh century may also represent the beginnings of significant trade in bulky commodities (Holm 1986; Barrett et al. 2004). While longer-distance trade out into the Irish Sea and beyond continued to play an important role within the economic life of the town, the coinage suggests that production and commodities became increasingly significant.

A slightly less ambiguous change in the political economy of the town is the increased administrative control that is visible in the eleventh century. This is very clearly demonstrated by the coinage. Figure 3.4 divides the coin finds from Dublin according to their place of manufacture. The figure highlights the fact that while foreign, overwhelmingly English, coins predominate in the tenth century, from the early eleventh century onwards the Hiberno-Scandinavian coins are the only finds. This change is not indicative of a reorientation of trade; instead, it demonstrates the ability to enforce the re-coinage, into Hiberno-Scandinavian coins, of foreign silver upon its entry into Dublin. The ability to exclude foreign silver from circulating within an early medieval polity has been demonstrated in a number of areas of contemporary Europe, including Norway and England, where it has been described as a 'demonstration of effective royal power' (Gullbekk 1992; Stewart 1990; Campbell 2000, 32). It is appropriate to extend such an argument to Dublin, where the Hiberno-Scandinavian ruler of the town appears to have had the political power and effective administration to insist upon his own coins being used. Similarly, a shift in coin finds, from the liminal space at the riverside Fishamble Street to the central space at Christchurch Place, suggests an increased regulation of trade. This is not surprising, as attempts at royal control over trade in towns are well known from contemporary England, and it is not difficult to envisage something similar in Dublin (Screen 2007, 157–60). The overlap between concentrations of coin finds and lead discs discussed above is suggestive of a link between economy and oversight in early medieval Dublin. The evidence of the coin finds suggests that an extensive and effective administration existed with an interest in the control, and likely taxation, of economic matters in eleventh-century Dublin.

The evidence suggests that the twelfth century saw an initial decline before a dramatic explosion in the number of coins in circulation. The fall in the number of coin finds dating to the early part of the century, visible in figure 3.4, is probably to be connected with a general scarcity of silver on a European scale (Woods forthcoming (b); cf. Spufford 1988, 96). The subsequent peak is quite pronounced and this is largely connected to finds of late bracteate coins, which are quite common. This is despite their fragility and the truncation of twelfth-century strata at many archaeological sites. It is likely that if similar amounts of twelfth-century material to the amounts of material from the preceding century had been excavated, a greater number of coins would have been found from this later period (Wallace 1981). The end of the Hiberno-Scandinavian coinage has been portrayed as something of a collapse, due to their light weight and debased alloy (cf. Dolley 1966, 87). But the evidence suggests that coins were being used, and lost, more regularly in twelfth-century Dublin than at any point before. Indeed, the fact that they may have had less silver and were of presumably lower value may have encouraged even wider usage in the town. The fact that a largely token currency, with little silver remaining in the coins, could function within the town suggests a fairly deep-rooted, coin-using mentality. This can be contrasted with other areas of Ireland that did not use the debased bracteate coins (Woods forthcoming (a)).

The distribution of coins shows one significant change between the eleventh and the twelfth century, with High Street emerging as the most significant site for the loss of coinage. However, that there are finds at all from the heavily truncated twelfth-century layers at Christchurch Place and Fishamble Street suggests that coinage remained important in these areas (Murray 1983, 204). Nonetheless, it seems likely that the area in which coins were used within the town expanded somewhat from a north/south axis in the eleventh century, from Fishamble Street to Christchurch Place and somewhat further to the west during the course of the twelfth century. This move would mirror the gradual expansion of the town from east to west.

The concentration of finds at High Street emphasizes the link between certain types of production and coinage. The number of bracteates from High Street, where shoemakers were based, is very notable (Ó Ríordáin 1984, 142–3). It seems inconceivable that those producing the leather in this area were not familiar with coinage, in much the same way as the metalworkers at Christchurch Place in the eleventh century.

COINS, MARKETS AND CRAFTS

Drawing these three chronological phases together, it can be noted that a significant majority of coins were used within a relatively defined space in the town. This area may have originally been that by the river at Fishamble Street, expanding south and uphill towards Christchurch Place in the eleventh century and westwards in the twelfth, as is summarized in figure 3.9. A concentration of single finds in these areas suggests either that they had a greater number of coins or, perhaps more plausibly, that these were the areas in which more transactions were carried out. Similar patterns of find distribution are visible in York and Trondheim. In each, a central area, with intensive coin

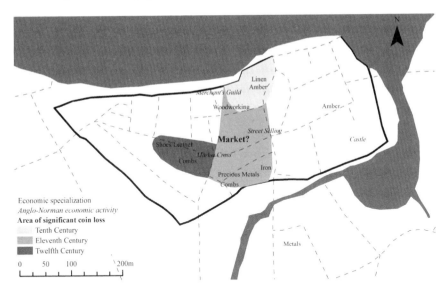

3.9 Summary of areas of coin usage.

loss, is detectable. At York, the area in and around Coppergate has produced a concentration of finds (Pirie 1986). A central, coin-using area was also present at Trondheim, centred on a street formally known as Kaupmannastratet, the 'Merchant Street' (Risvaag & Christophersen 2004, 76). The Trondheim parallel suggests that the coin finds in Dublin are likely to be related to commercial activity. This is difficult to prove beyond doubt in Dublin, but there is later Anglo-Norman evidence for the economic importance of the area around modern Christ Church Cathedral. The name Booth Street is seen as likely to be indicative of the selling of wares on the street (Clarke 2002, 8). This may also have been formalized as this area had a market cross, situated on the meeting point of modern High Street, Christchurch Place and Nicholas Street (Clarke 2002, cf. Crawford 1911). While all of this evidence is circumstantial, it does raise the possibility that this may have been the site of a regulated marketplace in the early medieval period. Even if this suggestion is not accepted, the volume of coin finds from within the walled town suggests that trade occurred readily and frequently at the heart of the town, not only at an occasional market beyond its walls.

While there is a concentration of coin finds in the centre of the town, small numbers are found across most of the occupied area of Dublin, as is visible in figure 3.2. The earliest coin found outside the walled town dates to the eleventh century – it is a single coin from Bride Street. This would support the increasing body of evidence for settlement in 'suburbs' to the north and south of the later walled town (Simpson 2011, 51). Similarly, during the twelfth century, bracteate coins were used quite some distance from the centre of the town. Coins at Winetavern Street and Patrick Street were found in residual layers behind Anglo-Norman river revetments. The Patrick Street coins were found some way to the south of the walled town. It is unknown where the revetting material was drawn from, but if it was taken from the immediate vicinity then it might suggest that there was a coin-using community living along the Poddle waterway to the south of the town. These finds coupled with isolated finds at Back Lane, Temple Bar West and Castle Street all suggest that coinage was present across most of the town. A distribution of this sort – generally widespread with a large central concentration – suggests that coinage was known to those in most areas of the town, but that its intense usage was largely confined to a commercial core. This is a point emphasized by the Castle Street hoards. These were deposited outside of this commercial core, implying that coinage was known and used by those who lived there. The Castle Street excavations produced no single finds, however, suggesting that coinage was not exchanged in significant volumes in this area. Similarly, in both York and Trondheim, small numbers of coins are found across the breadth of the settlement, but nothing to match the intensity of finds from the central area (Pirie 1986; Risvaag 2006, 65–8). In each case, it would appear that the town had a relatively clearly defined centre. In this area, exchange using coinage occurred on a much more significant scale than across the rest of the town. The evidence of the coinage suggests that commerce was, both literally and figuratively, at the heart of the town.

The changing pattern of coin finds also suggests a fairly strong connection between craft and coinage. The tenth-century production of flax and amber at Fishamble Street is matched by a concentration of coin finds in this area. Similarly, the 'metalworking quarter' suggested for the area around Christchurch Place in the eleventh century is matched by a large number of coin finds. It is most clearly demonstrated at High Street, an area of concentrated leatherworking in the twelfth century, from which large numbers of bracteates have emerged. Wherever evidence has been found for significant production within the town, coin finds have matched this. It is also notable that coinage was used in the exchange of relatively low-status materials including worked leather and wood. It is unlikely that these were particularly valuable, certainly in comparison to the products of crafts such as precious metal-working, but it appears that they were bought and sold nonetheless. This would suggest that there existed a market for almost all goods within the town. Dublin should not be envisaged as a high-status emporium of exotic goods, but a place in which the staples of everyday life were bought and sold. This also raises an important point about commodity exchange. The exchange of bulky commodities, including foodstuffs, has been seen as an important element within the early medieval economy (Barrett et al. 2004). Evidence from Dublin for exchange of this type is sparse, as it is archaeologically almost invisible. There is a textual reference to the international supply of foodstuffs from Dublin and it is known that there was a trade in skins (Harris 2003, 13–16; Hudson 2005, 43). The fact that Dublin had a market for fairly low-value objects such as shoes or wood suggests that slaves, skins and food could have been exchanged in a similar manner. This is, of course, impossible to prove. However, the animal-bone assemblage from Dublin suggests specific management of cattle resources and the economic exploitation of animals used elsewhere as pets (Wallace 1987, 203). Similarly, the eleventh-century boom in slave-raiding matches the chronology of the expansion of Dublin and coin-usage (cf. Holm 1986). The coin finds certainly suggest that specialized production played an important role in the economy of Dublin. They also suggest that if leather and wood can be taken as a proxy for other bulkier commodities, then these may also have been significant, if largely archaeologically-invisible, for the town's economy.

HIBERNO-SCANDINAVIAN COINAGE BEYOND DUBLIN

If the evidence from Dublin is broadly suggestive of an important role for coins within the economy, then the distribution beyond the town emphasizes the fact that this was quite unusual in early medieval contexts. The distribution of coin finds from across Ireland is mapped in figure 3.10 (reproduced from Woods forthcoming (a)). This map combines the evidence of single finds, usually taken to be indicative of the use of silver, with that of hoards, indicative of the removal of silver from circulation. The map emphasizes the pre-eminence of Dublin, with both hoards and single finds attesting to its central importance for the use of coinage in early medieval Ireland. There are more single finds of coins from the town than across the rest of Ireland combined. Furthermore, as has been noted by a number of authors, the hoards are arrayed in an arc around the town leading to the suggestion that Dublin acted as the conduit for silver into Ireland (Kenny 1987; Sheehan 2000; Blackburn 2007, 66). The combined evidence of the single finds and hoards suggests that Dublin was certainly the conduit for silver into Ireland, but that it also represented the most likely place for coins to be used. The number of finds from the town suggests that it had an economy that was far more monetized than any other part of Ireland. Dublin was the earliest consistently coin-using area, has evidence for monetary activity on a scale that dwarfs all other Irish sites and was the location of the only mint in Ireland. Its importance for coin-usage in early medieval Ireland cannot be overstated.

The evidence of the finds also suggests that, beyond Dublin, monetary activity was relatively confined, geographically. Hoards might suggest a semi-

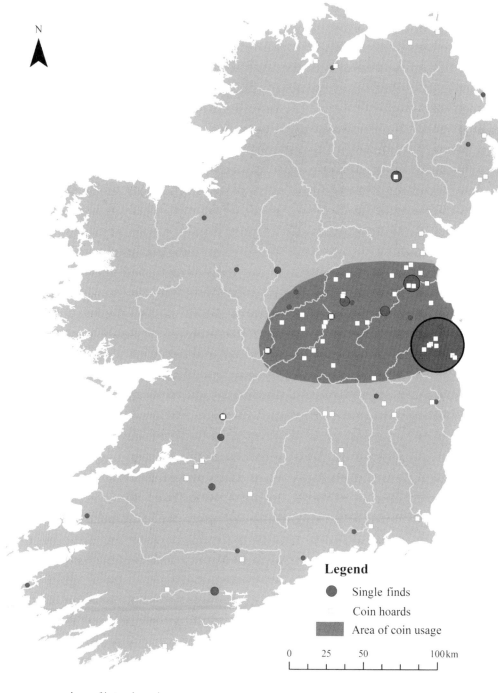

N

3.10 Area of intensive coin usage, 900–1170.

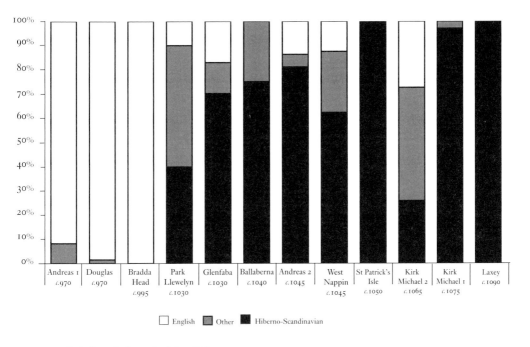

3.11 Coin hoards from the Isle of Man.

circular area around Dublin as a coin-using area, but the single finds seem to suggest that coin-use was confined even within this arc, largely to the north-west of Dublin. Coin-usage was most common in Mide and Brega, with the northern part of the medieval kingdom of Leinster (that is, the area to the south of Dublin) less engaged with monetary activity. Sixty per cent of hoards and 80 per cent of single finds can be placed within this area. The area from which there are significant numbers of hoards and single finds that appear to be indicative of relatively active coin-use is very constrained, representing only around 10 per cent of the total area of Ireland. This is not to say that other areas never used coinage, but more to make the point that it is likely that the majority of coinage in Ireland never made it more than around 120km from Dublin. Within this area, coin types fairly closely mirrored the finds from the towns, implying regular and peaceable contact.

This pattern can be contrasted, to a certain extent, to the situation in the Irish Sea region. Anglo-Saxon silver had dominated the silver currency of the Irish Sea during the tenth century (Blackburn 2007). This situation was dramatically reversed in the eleventh century, when the Hiberno-Scandinavian coinage came to dominate. This is most clearly demonstrated by the Manx hoards, which are plotted in figure 3.11, divided according to the origin of the coins they contain (Bornholdt-Collins 2003; Bornholdt-Collins et al. forthcoming). The dominance of English silver is visible in the tenth-century hoards, which are almost exclusively composed of Anglo-Saxon silver. This situation fundamentally altered by the middle of the eleventh century, when a majority of coins in hoards were struck in Dublin. To a certain extent, this may be due to the political links that existed between Dublin and Man during the eleventh century (Duffy 1992), but the existence of a currency on Man, the 'Hiberno-Manx' coinage, suggests that the dominance of Dublin's coinage was in spite of rather than because of political coercion. A more likely explanation for the dominance of Dublin coins among the Manx hoards is that the Hiberno-Scandinavian coinage had become the de facto currency of the Irish Sea region.

Expanding the focus to its widest, it is also worthy of note that Hiberno-Scandinavian coins have been found some distance from Ireland. Significant numbers have been recovered in Scandinavian hoards. Hundreds of coins struck in Dublin in the first half of the eleventh century have been found in a number of Scandinavian hoards. These are generally present in small numbers and mixed alongside Anglo-Saxon coins. The eleventh century was a period that saw the movement of significant volumes of silver to Scandinavia from the west, and the Irish coins must be seen as one element of this. It highlights the fact that the silver did not come exclusively from England but was also drawn from the Irish Sea region. The flow of silver highlights the interconnected trading networks that Dublin was involved with during the eleventh century, with coins from the town reaching as far as the eastern Baltic (Dolley 1979). It is difficult to assess the importance of Scandinavian trade in relation to other areas, as most other areas re-coined silver into the local type upon its entry into a port. Thus, there are only a handful of Hiberno-Scandinavian coins found in England. Blackburn was able to list seven coins from England, to which can be added a further two found in Nottinghamshire and another in Suffolk (Blackburn 2008, 134). I know of only a single coin, currently in the Fitzwilliam Museum in Cambridge, that has a northern French provenance. However, it is likely that there was extensive trade with England and quite probably northern Continental areas, but it is beyond the scope of the coinage to prove this. Moving even further afield, there are two hoards and at least one single find of Hiberno-Scandinavian coins from northern Italy (Dolley and Lane 1968; Orlandoni 1983, 112–14; Serafini 1951). The finds must be linked with pilgrimage routes, as is emphasized by the single find that derives from Rome itself. In this case, the silver coins are likely to be indicative of the movement of people, bringing with them local currency, rather than trade. The finds span the eleventh century and suggest regular pilgrimage from Ireland to Rome.

The distribution of finds of Hiberno-Scandinavian coins highlights the extensive networks with which Dublin was connected. Coinage struck in the town travelled east into the Baltic, south to Rome and west to reach remote areas of south-west Ireland. However, the areas in which the coinage was used on a regular basis are likely to have been relatively limited. The overlap of single finds and hoards outlined in figure 3.10 suggests that only a small area of Ireland was monetized. Furthermore, in an Irish Sea context, the Isle of Man is likely to have been party to significant exchange using Dublin's coins during the eleventh century. In both of these cases, Dublin is of central importance and regular economic links with the town are likely to have encouraged use of its coinage.

DUBLIN AND ITS COINAGE: CONCLUSIONS

The above discussion has followed the several phases in the biography of a Hiberno-Scandinavian coin; outlining where it was produced and used within Dublin and its ultimate deposition beyond the town. Several general points can be drawn from this analysis, the first of which concerns the evolution of the use of coinage. The earliest coin from Dublin dates to the late ninth century and there was a peak in coin-use in the middle of the eleventh century. It is likely that this represented both an expanding economy and an increasingly monetized environment. Other archaeological proxies suggest that the eleventh century was a boom time for the town. It roughly doubled in size between 1000 and 1100, several churches were founded and there is archaeological evidence for economic specialization (Simpson 2011, 34–58). Occurring alongside this economic growth was the emergence of a monetary mentality within the town. Consistently increasing numbers of finds, presumably reflective of coin-use and the decision to strike coinage at the end of the tenth century suggest an environment fairly comfortable with the use of coins. Furthermore, the ability to ensure that foreign coins were excluded, despite close similarity in terms of appearance, suggests a coin-literate audience within the town.

The use of coins is unlikely to have been highly restricted within the town, with an array of activities that involved their use. Leatherworkers at High Street are unlikely to have been of high status, but it does appear that they utilized coinage. Coins are found in conjunction with materials suggestive of external, long-distance trade, but also with evidence suggestive of specialized production. Determining which was of greater importance to the economy of the town at any point is a difficult matter, as it appears that both external exchange and specialized production were important aspects of Dublin's economy for the entirety of the archaeologically visible period. They were probably mutually reinforcing, with trading networks helping to distribute objects produced within the town. The occurrence of coinage in this range of material suggests that this was, at least within the town, carried out in a commercial manner. The variety and low value also suggest that there was a market, using coinage, for most goods rather than merely the most valuable objects. The unknowable element of this is the importance of commodities – such as slaves or provisions – to Dublin's economy. However, it is likely that these were significant, given the chronological correlation between a peak in eleventh-century coinage and evidence for exploitation of these commodities (cf. Holm 1986; Barrett et al. 2004).

It is unsurprising that political authority within the town took an active interest in controlling, and quite probably profiting from, the expanding early medieval economy. The role of royal authority within Dublin was not insubstantial. The exclusion of foreign coinage from the town is suggestive of effective administration, and it is not surprising that this occurred at a similar time to the provision of encircling banks and walls. These are likely to have been accompanied by taxes and tolls, as the finds of lead tokens would suggest. Indeed, the beginning of a mint in the late tenth century is suggestive of an attempt to control, and tax, the economic output of the town. This could also be suggested by the reorientation of trade from a riverside site to a more central site between the tenth and eleventh century. The end of the tenth and beginning of the eleventh century emerges as a time at which a controlling royal element became particularly visible in Dublin's economy.

Probably the most important element that analysis of the coins highlights is the importance of Dublin. In an Irish context, the town was comfortably the most likely place for coins to be used. It sat at the heart of a zone of monetary activity. Inland areas that became coin-using over the course of the tenth and eleventh centuries are likely to have become commercialized in this way through continued and peaceable contact with the town. Expanding the focus, Dublin's coins dominated the economy of the Irish Sea region. The town is likely to have been the most important economy within this context, with its coinage representing the de facto currency of the eleventh century in much the same way as Anglo-Saxon coins had in the tenth. If the distant find-spots of hoards are taken as representative of trade networks, then Dublin was connected to a trade network that extended south to the near Continent, east into the Baltic and north across much of Scandinavia. Whichever level of focus is preferred, the coinage highlights the vibrancy and impressive scale of the economy of Hiberno-Scandinavian Dublin.

BIBLIOGRAPHY

Allen, M.R. 2012 *Mints and money in medieval England*. Cambridge.
Archibald, M.M. 1991 'Anglo-Saxon and Norman lead objects with official coin types'. In A. Vince (ed.), *Aspects of Saxo-Norman London: 2. Finds and environmental evidence*, 326–46. London.
Archibald, M.M., J. Lang & G. Milne 1995 'Four early medieval coin dies from the London waterfront', *Numismatic Chronicle* 155, 165–200.

Barlow, F. & M. Biddle 1976 *Winchester in the early Middle Ages: an edition and discussion of the Winton Domesday*. Oxford.

Barrett, J.H., A.M. Locker & C.M. Roberts 2004 '"Dark Age economics" revisited: the English fish bone evidence, AD600–1600', *Antiquity* 78, 618–36.

Biddle, M. (ed.) 2012 *The Winchester mint*. Oxford.

Blackburn, M.A.S. 2007 'Currency under the Vikings, part 3: Ireland, Wales, Man and Scotland', *British Numismatic Journal* 77, 119–49.

Blackburn, M.A.S. 2008 'Currency under the Vikings, part 4: the Dublin coinage, *c*.995–1050', *British Numismatic Journal* 78, 111–37.

Bornholdt-Collins, K. 2003 'Viking-Age coin finds from the Isle of Man: a study of coin circulation, production and concepts of wealth'. PhD, Cambridge.

Bornholdt-Collins, K. 2010 The Dunmore Cave [2] hoard and the role of coins in the tenth-century Hiberno-Scandinavian economy. In J. Sheehan & D. Ó Corráin (eds), *The Viking Age: Ireland and the West. Proceedings of the Fifteenth Viking Congress, Cork, 2005*, 19–46. Dublin.

Bornholdt-Collins, K., A. Fox & J. Graham-Campbell forthcoming 'The 2003 Glenfaba Hoard (*c*.1030), Isle of Man'. In M.R. Allen, R. Naismith, & E. Screen (eds), *Early medieval monetary history: studies in memory of Mark Blackburn*.

Campbell, J. 2000 *The Anglo-Saxon state*. London.

Clarke, H.B. 2002 *Dublin. Part 1, to 1610: Irish historic town atlas no. 11*. Dublin.

Dolley, M. 1966 *Sylloge of coins of the British Isles, 8: Hiberno-Norse coins in the British Museum*. London.

Dolley, M. 1979 'The last(?) Hiberno-Norse penny to reach the USSR', *Irish Numismatics* 12:67, 22–5.

Dolley, M. & S.N. Lane 1968 'A parcel of late eleventh-century Hiberno-Norse coins found in Northern Italy', *British Numismatic Journal* 37, 25–8.

Downham, C. 2007 *Viking kings of Britain and Ireland: the dynasty of Ívarr to AD1014*. Edinburgh.

Duffy, S. 1992 'Irishmen and Islesmen in the kingdoms of Dublin and Man, 1052–1171', *Ériu* 43, 93–133.

Etchingham, C. 2010 *The Irish 'monastic town': is this a valid concept?* Cambridge.

Geraghty, S. 1996 *Viking Dublin: botanical evidence from Fishamble Street*. Dublin.

Gullbekk, S.H. 1992 'Renovatio Monetae i Norge i Middelalderen', *Nordisk Numismatisk Årsskrift*, 52–87.

Halpin, A. 2005 'Development phases in Hiberno-Norse Dublin: a tale of two cities'. In S. Duffy (ed.), *Medieval Dublin VI*, 94–113. Dublin.

Harris, C.P. 2003 *A history of the county of Chester: volume 5, part 1. The city of Chester: general history and topography*. Oxford.

Heslip, R. & J.P. Northover 1990 'The alloy of the Hiberno-Norse coinage'. In K. Jonsson & B. Malmer (eds), *Sigtuna Papers: proceedings of the Sigtuna symposium on Viking-Age coinage, 1–4 June 1989*, 103–11. London.

Holm, P. 1986 'The slave trade of Dublin, ninth to twelfth centuries', *Peritia* 5, 317–45.

Hudson, B.T. 2005 *Viking pirates and Christian princes*. Oxford.

Kelleher, R. & I. Leins 2008 'Roman, medieval and later coins from the Vintry, city of London', *Numismatic Chronicle* 168, 167–240.

Kelly, F. 1988 *A guide to early Irish Law*. Dublin.

Kemmers, F. & N. Myrberg 2011 'Rethinking numismatics: the archaeology of coins', *Archaeological Dialogues* 18:1, 87–108.

Kenny, M. 1987 'The geographical distribution of Irish Viking Age coin hoards', *Proceedings of the Royal Irish Academy* 87C, 507–25.

Kenny, M. 2012 'Coins, tokens and related numismatic material from Knowth'. In G. Eogan (ed.), *Excavations at Knowth 5: the archaeology of Knowth in the first and second millennia AD*. Dublin.

Kinsella, S. 2000 'From Hiberno-Norse to Anglo-Norman, *c.*1030–1300'. In K. Milne (ed.), *Christ Church Cathedral, Dublin: a history*, 25–52. Dublin.

Lopez, R.S. 1953 'An aristocracy of money in the early Middle Ages', *Speculum* 28:1, 1–43.

Malmer, B., J. Ros & S. Tesch 1991 *Kung Olofs Mynthus: i kvarteret Urmakaren, Sigtuna*. Stockholm.

Middleton, N. 2005 'Early medieval port customs, tolls and controls on foreign trade', *Early Medieval Europe* 13:4, 313–58.

Murray, H. 1983 *Viking and early medieval buildings in Dublin: a study of the buildings excavated under the direction of A.B. Ó Ríordáin in High Street, Winetavern Street and Christchurch Place, Dublin, 1962–3, 1967–76*. Oxford.

Ó Corráin, D. 1997 'Ireland, Wales, Man and the Hebrides'. In P.H. Sawyer (ed.), *The Oxford illustrated history of the Vikings*, 83–109. Oxford.

Ó Ríordáin, B. 1971 'Excavations at High Street and Winetavern Street, Dublin', *Medieval Archaeology* 15, 73–85.

Ó Ríordáin, B. 1984 'Excavations in Old Dublin'. In J. Bradley (ed.), *Viking Dublin exposed: the Wood Quay saga*, 134–43. Dublin.

Orlandoni, M. 1983 *Antiche Monete in Val d'Aosta*. Aosta.

Pirie, E.J.E. 1986 *Post-Roman coins from York Excavations, 1971–81*. London.

Risvaag, J.A. 2006 'Mynt og by. Myntens rolle i Trondheim by i perioden ca. 1000–1630, belyst gjennom myntfunn og utmynting'. PhD, Trondheim.

Risvaag, J.A. & Christophersen, A. 2004 Early medieval coinage and urban development: a Norwegian experience. In J. Hines, A. Lane & M. Redknap (eds), *Land, sea and home: proceedings of a conference on Viking-Period settlement*, 75–92. Leeds.

Ros, J. 2001 *Sigtuna: Staden, kyrkona och den kyrkliga organisationen*. Uppsala.

Screen, E. 2007 'Anglo-Saxon law and numismatics: a reassessment in the light of Patrick Wormald's *The making of English law, I*', *British Numismatic Journal* 77, 150–72.

Serafini, C. 1951 'Appendice numismatica'. In B. Mario & A. Ghetti (eds), *Esplorazioni sotto la Confessione di San Pietro al Vaticano eseguite negli anni 1940–1949* 225–44. Vatican City.

Sheehan, J. 2000 'Ireland's early Viking-Age silver hoards: components, structure and classification', *Acta Archaeologica* 71:1, 49–63.

Sheehan, J. 2007 'The form and structure of Viking Age hoards: the evidence from Ireland'. In J. Graham-Campbell & G. Williams (eds), *Silver economy in the Viking Age*, 149–61. Walnut Creek.

Sheehan, J., S.S. Hansen & D. Ó Corráin 2001 'A Viking maritime haven: a reassessment of the island settlement at Beginish, Co. Kerry', *Journal of Irish Archaeology* 10, 93–119.

Simpson, L. 2000 'Forty years a-digging: a preliminary synthesis of archaeological investigations in medieval Dublin'. In S. Duffy (ed.), *Medieval Dublin I*, 11–68. Dublin.

Simpson, L. 2011 'Fifty years-a-digging: a synthesis of medieval archaeological investigations in Dublin city and suburbs'. In S. Duffy (ed.), *Medieval Dublin XI*, 9–112. Dublin.

Spufford, P. 1988 *Money and it use in medieval Europe*. Cambridge.

Stewart, B.H.I.H. 1990 'Coinage and recoinage after Edgar's reform'. In K. Jonsson (ed.), *Studies in late Anglo-Saxon coinage*, 455–86. Stockholm.

Stott, P. 1991 'Saxon and Norman coins from London'. In A. Vince (ed.), *Aspects of Saxo-Norman London: 2. finds and environmental evidence*, 279–325. London.

Valante, M.A. 1998 'Tolls and tribute: the language of economics and trade in Viking-Age Ireland', *Proceedings of the Harvard Celtic Colloquium* 18–19, 242–58.

Valante, M.A. 2008 *The Vikings in Ireland: settlement, trade and urbanization*. Dublin.

Wallace, P.F. 1981 'Anglo-Norman Dublin: continuity and change'. In D. Ó Corráin (ed.), *Irish antiquity: essays and studies presented to Professor M.J. O'Kelly*, 247–68. Cork.

Wallace, P.F. 1986 'The English presence in Viking Dublin'. In M.A.S. Blackburn (ed.), *Anglo-Saxon monetary history: essays in memory of Michael Dolley*, 202–22. Trowbridge.

Wallace, P.F. 1987 'The economy and commerce of Viking Age Dublin'. In K. Düwel, H. Jankuhn, H. Siems & D. Timpe (eds), *Untersuchungen ziu Handel und Vekehr der vor- und frühgeshichtlichen Zeit in Mittel- und Nordeuropa*, 200–45. Göttingen.

Wallace, P.F. 1992 *The Viking Age buildings of Dublin*. Dublin.

Wallace, P.F. 2013 'Weights and weight systems in Viking Age Ireland'. In A. Reynolds & L. Webster (eds), *Early medieval art and archaeology in the northern world*, 301–16. Leiden.

Woods, A.R. forthcoming (a) 'Monetary activity in Viking-Age Ireland: the evidence of the single finds'. In M.R. Allen, R. Naismith & E. Screen (eds), *Early medieval monetary history: studies in memory of Mark Blackburn*.

Woods, A.R. forthcoming (b) *Economy and authority: a study of the coinage of Hiberno-Scandinavian Dublin and Ireland*. PhD, Cambridge.

How Dublin remembered the Battle of Clontarf

LENORE FISCHER

This essay is concerned not so much with historical events themselves as with the stories about a specific historical event. So let me start with a story:

> There was a merchant in Doubling called the White Merchant (he was the King of Denmark's son) and had a fair wife, and he, minding to travel in other realms for merchandise, came to Brene Borowe, then chief and principal King of Ireland, and desired the King to take the charge of his wife in his absence, for her beauty was such that he feared all men; which promised to do in his absence; and so the merchant departed. And while the merchant was in his merchandise, Morcke McBren Borow, the King's son, made suit to her, and wan her love, and lay with the merchant's wife. And by chance and fortune the merchant arrived after his long voyage in other realms with seven great ships upon the sudden at Pollbeyeg, by Doubling, in a great fog and mist, in the morning early, and so came to his house, and found … Morhewe McBrene in bed with his wife … the White Merchant went to Bren Boro the King, to complain and declared to him the trust he put him in, and how he was deceived by his son, and demanded judgement; who willed the White Merchant to give what sentence or judgement he would, seeing he was his son. The White Merchant said, this was his judgement, and none other, that he would be in the field of Clontarff by that day twelve-month, to fight there a field with Morhe and all his that would take his part, and there trusted to be revenged on that wrong, and so departed, and went to seek his friends to Denmark, from whence his generation came; and by the day appointed brought a great number of stalworth soldiers out of Denmark, and landed at Clontarff, and there proclaimed a field, and after fought a terrible battle for all the forenoon.

Such is the story of how the Battle of Clontarf came about, as recorded *c.*1572 by Christopher St Lawrence in his *Book of Howth*.[1]

* * *

Why should we talk about stories? What might they have to tell us? Stories are our way of encoding information, of taking discrete happenings or items of

---

1 St Lawrence's 'The Book of Howth' is published in *Calendar of the Carew manuscripts preserved in the archiepiscopal library at Lambeth*, 6, ed. S.J. Brewer (London, 1871), pp 24–7.

data and stringing them together in a manner that creates relationships, fashions images and imbues them all with meaning. Stories can range from 'what happens when two hydrogen atoms meet', which we classify as science, to 'what happened when Auntie Mary dropped her false teeth in the soup', which we classify as gossip, to 'what happened to Seamus Ennis when he spent the night in a fairy fort', which we classify as folklore. Groups of people tend to own stocks of stories in common. Georges Zimmermann, in his introduction to the *Irish Storyteller*, tells us that 'people with a common stock of stories ... form a community; conversely, different repertoires may divide audiences'. Stories do not necessarily remain static. As a group's interests and involvements change, stories become altered to fit the new circumstances. 'Aspects of the past', Zimmermann tells us, 'are selected, interpreted, if necessary invented ... traditions shift over time ... in form or in function'.[2]

We shall examine Howth's story, then, and compare it with the other main version of events that was current in Ireland at the time, using Zimmermann's guidelines as a framework: that stories characterize a community and mark their separation from other communities. Adding some scattered references made by other Dubliners at the time, and putting this together with what we know through other means of Dublin at the end of the Middle Ages, we can form a picture of the population, their allegiances and something of their relations with the native population of the hinterland around them.

* * *

First let us look at how the prelude to the Battle of Clontarf was interpreted in the rest of Ireland, as codified in the *Cogadh Gáedhel re Gallaibh*, a piece of literature composed within a century of the battle.[3] Here, Máelmórda, the king of Leinster, is taunted by his sister, Gormflaith, a wife of Brian's, for being subservient to Brian. He quarrels with Murchad, Brian's eldest son, and flies off to raise a revolt against Brian's overlordship. Dublin's only appearance in this version, at this point in the story, is as an ally called in to assist Leinster.[4]

It is immediately obvious that this differs wildly from Howth's version with which we started off. Dublin, scarcely even a player in the older Irish version, occupies centre stage in Howth's story. Dublin is represented there as an aristocratic Danish merchant, the hero of the story; he is called 'the White Merchant', white being the colour of all Good Guys. Elizabethan Dublin clearly felt comfortable with its Viking trading origins. We are even provided

2 George Denis Zimmermann, *The Irish storyteller* (Dublin, 2001), pp 9, 11.   3 Máire Ní Mhaonaigh, '*Cogad Gaedel re Gallaib*: some dating considerations', *Peritia*, 9 (1995), 354–77 at 377; cf. Denis Casey, 'A reconsideration of the authorship and transmission of *Cogadh Gáedhel re Gallaibh*', *Proceedings of the Royal Irish Academy*, 113C (2013), 1–23.   4 For the full version, see *Cogadh Gaedhel re Gallaibh: the war of the Gaedhil with the Gaill*, ed. and trans. J.H. Todd (London, 1867), chs lxxxi–lxxxv; it should be noted that these chapter

with a topographically precise image of the merchant arriving home 'with seven great ships upon the sudden at Poolbeg'.

The merchant, or in other words, Dublin, acknowledges Brian Bóraime as his overlord. The *Cogadh Gáedhel re Gallaibh* claimed that Brian ruled over all Ireland, maintained such peace and justice during his reign that a woman bedecked with gold could walk from one end of the country to the other unmolested.[5] Our Dublin storyteller's image, in which the merchant lodges his wife with Brian for her protection, fits in well, then, with what was being told of Brian in general elsewhere at the time. Brian appears again in his role as justice-giver when the merchant appeals to him after his betrayal. But what sort of justice does Brian dispense? In an Irish court of law, we might expect the correct value of an honour-price to be worked out for payment; but here we have nothing of the sort, instead Brian grants the merchant self-judgment, a ruling of a sort common in Icelandic saga (see, for example, *Vatnsdœla saga*, or Bolli Bollason's Tale), but as far as I know unknown in Irish contexts.[6]

The villain of Howth's story is Murchad, Brian's son, a marplot and reckless seducer of women. Murchad seems to have enjoyed a mixed reputation. In the *Cogadh*, too, he was rather hot-headed, quarrelling with his brother-in-law and rushing into battle before his troops were ready.[7] Yet Murchad became a popular hero among the people of Ireland, more popular even, for a time, than his father Brian, for Murchad became the centre of a group of wonder-tales much like those told of Finn Mac Cumaill. Fairytale aspects of Murchad surface even as early as the *Cogadh* itself, but complete stories remained current in oral lore into the nineteenth century.[8] Moreover there may be historical reasons why Dublin did not love Murchad: both the *Cogadh* and the annals maintain that in the months preceding the battle, Brian had sent Murchad out plundering the Leinster countryside from Glendalough to Kilmainham.[9] So, in portraying Murchad as the villain, the storyteller is picking on a character unbeloved by Dublin but prominent elsewhere and carrying intimations of youth and recklessness; one moreover, already associated in the *Cogadh* with the crucial dissension that led to the battle.

divisions are of Todd's own devising and are not present in any of the original manuscripts. **5** Todd (ed.), *Cogadh*, lxxx.   **6** See *The sagas of Icelanders*, ed. Örnólfur Thorsson et al. (New York, 2000), pp 236, 431. Denis Casey has been kind enough to point out to me that self-judgment does occur in Irish saints' tales, notably in 'the Migration of the Ciarraige'; I have nevertheless left my text as it was delivered in the lecture, even if in this point it is erroneous.   **7** Todd (ed.), *Cogadh*, lxxxii, xcvii.   **8** For Murchad's involvement with the Otherworld in the *Cogadh*, see Todd (ed.), *Cogadh*, xcviii; his role in wonder-tale cycles is described in Alan Bruford, 'The Dalcassian Cycle' in idem, *Gaelic folk-tales and mediaeval romance: a study of the early modern Irish 'romantic tales' and their oral derivatives* (Dublin, 1969), pp 134–46. See also Meidhbhín Ní Úrdail (ed.), *Cath Cluana Tarbh* (London, 2011), pp 51–9 for this and other aspects of Murchad's role in wonder-tales and in Howth. **9** Todd (ed.), *Cogadh*, lxxxvi; *AU* 1013.7, *CS* 1013.4.

Dublin has replaced Leinster as centre stage and is interpreted now as the hero rather than as the villain; Murchad's rash qualities have been redrawn to make him a dastard; a third ingredient yet remains: the woman in the plot. For a woman still remains central to the action, although the merchant's wife in Howth's story is but a pliant marionette compared to the fiery and ambitious Gormflaith of Irish tradition.

* * *

Moving on to the battle itself, our closest approach to an objective source consists of the annals of Ireland that were being recorded in monasteries around the country at the time of the events in question. The Annals of Inisfallen (*AI*), Chronicon Scotorum (*CS*) and Annals of Ulster (*AU*) tell us that the battle was fought near Dublin in 1014.[10] They do not give causes, merely recording that Leinster and the 'Foreigners of Áth Cliath' (that is, the Vikings of Dublin) were broken and wiped out, and they list the deaths on their side of the king of Leinster, the earl of Orkney, various Dublin notables and Bródar, chief of the fleet. On the other side, they record the deaths of Brian, his son Murchad and others of his family, along with Tadc Ua Cellaig and other kings of Munster and south Connacht. The battle must have taken place outside the town defences, but Dublin itself does not seem to have been sacked or plundered, which perhaps made it possible for the two diametrically opposed stories to develop as to the outcome of the battle.

Here is Howth's description of the battle:

> The Irish wan, and drove the strangers to seek aid to their ships, and found them borne to collis. When they saw that they returned again to the battle, and so wan the field by very force of fight, and killed both Bren and left his son Morhowe for dead, benorth the stinking stream, lying upon his shield; to whom came a priest called Segert Ne Fenemy, and asked for his son … The priest's son … did confess the treason done … And so he was taken, and brought to a hill twelve mile from Dubling, called the Weyn-gattys, and there put him in the earth [with stones], standing … and there doth it rest to this day, a great heap of stones. There was the end of the field of Clontarff, wherein was a soldier of Morhe called Douling of Hertackane, which that day fought best …
>
> The causes that the field was lost. First the haste that Bren the King made to the field, and did not tarry till his friends came to his aid, as his sons and others, which came three days after the field with 7,000 men. This great haste and worse speed may be an example to all men. Another cause was … [Bren] placed his men in this order. The horsemen was put

10 *AI* 1014.2, *CS* 1014.2; *AU* 1014.2.

on the right hand of his woward [vanguard] as nigh the sea as might be
… The left wing was kerne and men with slings, spears, stones, and
shields, all naked men … These horsemen was the force of the King's
army … and by reason of the slimy and deep ground towards the sea, the
horsemen did nothing, being there placed afore as their ill fortune was …
The King's horsemen stood him in no stead. By reason thereof the King
lost the field and his life and 11,000 men and his son.[11]

The *Cogadh* is a longish work, a good third of which is dedicated to the
retelling of the battle. And yet, the Battle of Clontarf there is functionally not
so much a battle as a stage setting for the tragic deaths of Brian and his heir,
Murchad. The hosts opposing Brian are turned and sent fleeing to their ships,
which they find borne away on the tide,[12] but who it was that set Brian's foes to
flight is not recorded. Murchad meets an old pal, Dúnlaing ua hArtacáin, who
has come back from the Otherworld to help him; Murchad admits that he, too,
had once been invited to take up life in the Fairy World,[13] but that he had
refused; on entering battle, he becomes filled with battle frenzy and is crowned
Cú Chulainn-style by a 'moon of valour'.[14] The action is divided up by
punctuating episodes deriding the Dublin Vikings and their king in particular,
who stand observing the events from the safety of the town walls.[15] Murchad's
great deeds, and his fatal wounding,[16] serve as a build-up to the devotions and
death of Brian Bóraime himself,[17] the central figure of the entire work. Brian,
compared with Lug Lámfhata and Finn mac Cumaill for greatness,[18] is
discovered at prayer by Earl Bródar of Caer Ebroc (York), and he and Bródar
kill each other.[19]

Now, in Howth's version the Vikings found their ships gone, just as the
Cogadh says, but instead of giving up, the Vikings turn and rally, breaking the
Irish opposition. Brian's death gets little mention, Murchad's slightly more,
but Murchad's death is tangled up with a strange tale about a priest's son. The
passage is very confused: what treason the priest's son committed is never
explained. Nevertheless, the garbled fragments play an important role because
they result in a topographical story about a mound at Windgate (Delgany
parish, Rathdown, Co. Wicklow), which lies just south of Bray Head, anchoring
the events of the fateful day in the visible landscape around victorious Dublin.
Another fractured story contained in this narrative is that of Douling of
Hertackane, a soldier of Murchad's who 'that day fought best'. For this can be
none other than Dúnlaing ua hArtacáin of the *Cogadh*, Murchad's fairy-world

---

11 Brewer (ed.), 'Book of Howth', pp 25–7.   12 Todd (ed.), *Cogadh*, cix.   13 Ibid., xcviii.
14 Actually a 'bird of valour' in Todd (ed.), *Cogadh*, cviii; Máire Ní Mhaonaigh also draws
the parallel: see *Brian Boru: Ireland's greatest king?* (Stroud, 2007), p. 72.   15 Todd (ed.),
Cogadh, cii, viii, cx.   16 Ibid., cvii, cviii, cxi, cxii.   17 Ibid., cxiii–cxvi.   18 Ibid., cxv.
19 Ibid., cxiv.

companion who fights what the *Cogadh* calls 'one of the three hardest combats that took place at Cluain Tarbh'.[20] Douling or Dúnlaing seems to have been a vibrant figure: he played an even bigger role when the *Cogadh*'s story was reworked in the seventeenth- and eighteenth-century Munster texts *Cath Chluana Tairbh* and *Leabhar Oiris*.[21]

Overall, though, Howth is most emphatic of all about Brian's defeat. His is by far the most tactical description of the battle that has survived, and seems largely of late manufacture: his main battle scene has a very Elizabethan ring to it, with its mired cavalry, its ill-placed vanguard and its naked kerne. He seems at pains to show Dublin's opponents in as bad a light as possible. Brian is dismissed as hasty and incompetent. The manner of Brian's death, so resounding in the *Cogadh*, is of no interest whatever, and the name of his killer is never even mentioned.

* * *

What led to the recording of these very different traditions? The *Cogadh* is believed to have been written as deliberate propaganda to promote the interests of Brian Bóraime's immediate descendants.[22] It is a composed piece of literature, drawing heavily on all the literary forms extant at the time: annals, poetry, oral folklore and mythology, welding them into a powerful unity. The name of its author is unfortunately not known.

The *Book of Howth* is a compilation formerly dismissed as random material. Its structure has recently been studied intensively by Valerie McGowan Doyle, however, who has shown how St Lawrence employed a series of scribes to collect background information, entered miscellaneously at the rear of the manuscript, while the front pages of the manuscript were used to build up a narrative history of Ireland based both on transcribed and on original material.[23] St Lawrence himself was the seventh baron of Howth, a member of the Old English stock who had settled in Ireland in the wake of the Anglo-Norman invasion. Howth participated in the parliament convened by Sidney in 1569, a parliament in which conflict became increasingly apparent between the New English settlers who were coming in under Queen Elizabeth and the Old English, as they began to call themselves at that time. The newcomers spoke of having to remedy the defects of their predecessors' so-called 'failed conquest'. Howth, increasingly embittered by the political process, sought to support the Old English cause by putting together a history of Ireland that would demonstrate how they had made Ireland their own.[24] His story of Clontarf

20 Ibid., civ.   **21** Eoin MacNeill (ed.), 'Cath Cluana Tairbh', *Gaelic Journal*, 7 (1896), 8–11, 41–4, 55–6. (1896); R.I. Best (ed.), 'The Leabhar Oiris', *Ériu*, 1 (1904), 74–112.   **22** Ní Mhaonaigh, 'Some dating considerations', p. 355; Casey, 'A reconsideration of the authorship and transmission'.   **23** Valerie McGowan-Doyle, *The Book of Howth: Elizabethan conquest and the Old English* (Cork, 2011), pp 40–2.   **24** MacGowan-Doyle, *The*

might be said to foreshadow the main narrative, showing how Viking Dublin succeeded in vanquishing the natives, just as Howth's own ancestors did in turn upon their arrival.

Howth's was not the only voice expressing such a point of view. Richard Stanihurst, in his *Description of Ireland* published in 1577, was likewise writing in defence of the Old English. He too speaks of the Battle of Clontarf, describing how the Danes of Ostmantown

> discomfitted at Clontarfe in a skirmish diverse of the Irishe. The names of the Irish Capitaynes slayne, were Bryanne Borrogh, Miagh mack Bryen, Tadg Okelly, Dolyne Ahertigan, Gylle Barramede. These were Irish potentates, and before their discomfiture they ruled the rest. They were interred at Kilmaynanne over against the great cross.[25]

While Stanihurst confirms Howth's main points, he is obviously not drawing directly on it, and indeed amplifies it, brief though his description is. Who Gylle Barramede might be, I have not been able to ascertain, but Dúnlaing ua hArtacáin significantly appears again. Tadc Ua Cellaig, like Dúnlaing, provides us with another Irish connection. Tadc was not a member of the Fairy World, he was the king of Uí Máine, and he was certainly at Clontarf, as attested from the annal accounts onwards.[26] But so were many others. Why should Tadc Ua Cellaig be singled out for mention? If we look at what was happening in native Irish traditions about Clontarf, we find that in the period between the writing of the *Cogadh* in the early twelfth century and Geoffrey Keating's seventeenth-century account in his *Foras feasa ar Éirinn*, there were a number of ways in which Brian material was being reworked. One of the most productive of these consisted of poetry produced in the Uí Máine court. There are some four poems relating to Brian in the Book of Uí Mháine, more than in any other medieval collection.[27] Most of these are attributed to Muirchertach mac Liacc, a contemporary of Brian's. They are conspicuously focused not so much on Brian as on the greatness of his cohort, Tadc Ua Cellaig. I have discussed these poems elsewhere, and argued there that the bulk of them are not mac Liacc works, but Uí Máine productions written *c.*1316, to encourage a younger Tadc Ua Cellaig, his descendant, who was facing political difficulties connected with the Bruce Invasion.[28] That Tadc Ua Cellaig should be singled out for mention

Book of Howth, p. 87.   **25** Richard Stanihurst, 'A description of Ireland' in Raphael Holinshed, *Chronicles*, 3 (London, 1577), p. 582.   **26** *AI* 1014.2; *AU* 1014.2; *CS* 1014.3; *The annals of Clonmacnoise*, ed. Denis Murphy (Dublin, 1896; repr. Llanerch, 1993), *s.a.* 996=1014. **27** These are: '*Da mac dec do chin ó Chas*', reproduced in *The Book of Uí Maine*, facs. ed., ed. R.A.S. Macalister (Dublin, 1941), p. 326; '*Leasg amleasg sind gu Áth Clíath*', printed by Kuno Meyer, '*Mittelungen aus irischen Handschriften*', *Zeitschrift für Celtische Philologie*, 8 (1911–12), 229–31; '*Scíath rígh Gaela, glantar hí*', printed in ibid., 227–9; and '*Beannacht, a Bruin, ar Brigit*' in ibid., 225–7.   **28** Fischer, Lenore, 'Two poets and the Legend of Brian Bóraimhe',

in Stanihurst's account suggests that Dublin was not unaware of the poetry and propaganda of the Uí Máine court in Connacht.

Stanihurst's description may be brief, but it has a pungency that bites deep. 'These were Irish potentates', he says, 'and before their discomfiture they ruled the rest'. Stanihurst wants us to be quite clear that Dublin threw off the might of all the rest of Ireland in the one battle. To drive the point home, he could even point to the place where they were buried, 'over against the great cross' at Kilmainham.

Meredith Hanmer, a Welsh minister who came to Ireland in the 1590s,[29] wrote *A chronicle of Ireland* (not published until 1633), in which he claims that the king of Dublin had gathered allies unto himself to withstand Brian, gaining aid from Máelmórda, king of Leinster, and hiring in

> Danes, Norwegians, Scots, Britaines, pirates and sea rovers. The fight was desperate, the field all blood, a horse … sometimes up to his belly in blood. There were slain that day of the one side, Brian the Monarch, and his sonne Murchard; of the other side, Mailmordha king of Leinster, Rodericke the arch-pirate and captain of the strangers, with others of both sides, innumerable. Sutrick was sore wounded, was brought to Dublin, and shortly after died of his wounds. I pray the gentle reader, who got best the bargain? As far as ever I could learn, a woman set them together by the ears.[30]

So far, this description seems drawn largely from the *Cogadh* tradition, although the horses bogged down in blood recall Howth's mired cavalry. But Hanmer goes on to paraphrase Howth's description extensively. His details are in many cases different, however, and he gives the full story of the priest's son and his treason. So Hanmer must have had other, probably oral, sources.

Such descriptions belong almost exclusively to this burst of Elizabethan writing in which the Old English sought to justify their position in Ireland. Brian Bóraime and Clontarf do not appear in an English context again until Sir James Ware's *De Hibernia et antiquitatibus eius* appeared in 1654. Ware was a second-generation man, the son of one of the New English, but he was passionately devoted to the study of Ireland's history, and his manuscript collections according to James Kenney's *Sources* form the core of the Irish collections in the Bodleian Library and British Museum today.[31] Ware is even more emphatic as to the causes of Clontarf than any writer previous:

North Munster Antiquarian Journal, 49 (2009), 91–109 at 105.   **29** I am following here the biographical essay by Robert Dunlop, in *Dictionary of national biography* (1885–1900), p. 297. For other versions of Hanmer's life, see his entry in Alfred Webb, *A compendium of Irish biography, comprising sketches of distinguished Irishmen and of eminent persons connected with Ireland by office or by their writings* (Dublin, 1878).   **30** Meredith Hanmer, *The chronicle of Ireland* (Dublin, 1663; repr. Amsterdam, 1971), p. 91.   **31** James Kenney, *The sources for the*

About the beginning of the year 1014, or a little before, Brian Boro
treated with most of the Kings of Ireland to joyne their forces with him,
and endeavor the expulsion of the Danes as publick enemies of the
kingdom. Sitricus on the other side understanding the design, neglected
nothing that might contribute to his defence; and therefore having made
his peace with Maelmorrius, son of Murchad king of Leinster, he
procured assistance both from him and from the Danes of the Isle of
Man and the Hebrides.[32]

Ware afterwards goes on to summarize both the *Cogadh*'s and Howth's
versions as alternate explanations of the battle's outcome. His story as to the
battle's causes, however, is simpler than either of theirs and turns very neatly
upon the *Cogadh* itself. For the *Cogadh*, in its biography of Brian, claimed that
Brian's rule over Ireland was a Golden Age of peace and justice, and that he

extirpated, dispersed, banished, caused to fly, stripped, maimed, ruined
and destroyed the Foreigners in every district and in every territory
throughout the breadth of all Erinn. He killed also their kings, and their
chieftains, their heroes and brave soldiers, their men of renown and
valour. He enslaved and reduced to bondage their stewards and their
collectors, and their swordsmen, their mercenaries and their comely,
large cleanly youths; and their smooth youthful girls.[33]

Such a pogrom is inconsistent, of course, with the presence later in the tale of
a very robust and flourishing Viking Dublin. Historians writing later in the
native tradition reconciled the problem by claiming that Brian had deliberately
left pockets of Vikings in order to benefit from their trading activities, but Ware
takes the *Cogadh*'s story to its most brutal and logical conclusion: that Brian
was bent on a racial cleansing that would sweep Viking Dublin off the map.
Ware's story allies Leinster with Dublin in, as it were, a nod to the *Cogadh*, but
for Ware it is Dublin that calls the shots, and Leinster just tags along. Ware's
story might in fact be considered Dublin's ultimate answer to the *Cogadh*,
saying in effect: 'You tried to exterminate us, but we fought back to protect
ourselves, and we won!'

Ware is the last writer to declare that Dublin won the battle, although he
prefaces this with 'others say', having given the alternative version first.[34]
Although later Dublin authors continue to insist on Dublin's central role in
the whole episode, they no longer try to portray Dublin as being the wronged

early history of Ireland: ecclesiastical (New York, 1929), pp 48, 88.   **32** James Ware,
Antiquities and history of Ireland, trans. Walter Harris (Dublin, 1705), p. 63. Although Harris
expanded the work in his translation, comparison with the Latin original shows no deviation
in this section of the work.   **33** Todd (ed.), *Cogadh*, lxxix.   **34** Ware, *Antiquities*, p. 63.

party, nor do they accord to Dublin the victory.[35] The *Cogadh*'s version had won out.

* * *

Howth's and Stanihurst's stories tell us first and foremost of a population that felt a strong identity with the town and with its pre-Anglo-Norman history. Dubliners were clearly very proud to think that they had vanquished the king of Ireland and all his forces, and could point to landmarks associated with the battle and to the place where he and his people were buried not far beyond the town gates. The Old English and the Ostmen, as the Vikings came to be called, felt themselves to be sufficiently unified that pride in the Ostmen's past could be shared by the Old English who had settled among them. A Scandinavian flavour continued to be preserved in Howth's tale, both in the style of law-giving described and in the account of the merchant as both aristocrat and trader, a combination more common to the Viking world than to the Anglo-Norman.

This tallies well with the vision of Dublin as it is being pieced out in the modern historiography. We know that the Ostmen enjoyed special legal status under Anglo-Norman law.[36] Far from having expelled the Vikings from Dublin into a new suburb of Oxmantown upon the Anglo-Norman capture of Dublin, Emer Purcell has shown that Oxmantown had been a thriving part of Dublin well before the Anglo-Norman conquest;[37] James Lydon stated categorically that there was 'essential continuity between Ostman Dublin and the Anglo-Norman city'.[38] Given this mixed population, it can be expected that some tales with a Scandinavian bent might survive in oral tradition. That a specifically Dublin version of Clontarf remained current shows us how Dublin felt its cultural identity to be separate from the rest of Ireland.

Though separate, Dublin's cultural identity was not utterly divorced from native Irish tradition. We have seen that significant aspects of the story are common to the two main accounts that we have looked at here. A woman, be it Gormflaith or the merchant's wife, remains at the hinge point of the story; Murchad also is present at that hinge point in both traditions. In both versions the battle veers at one stage in favour of the Irish, who drive the foreign Vikings back to the sea where their ships are found to be missing.

35 See Thomas Leland, *The history of Ireland from the invasion of Henry II with a preliminary discourse on the antient state of that kingdom*, 1 (Dublin, 1773), p. li; A.G. Richey, *Lectures on the history of Ireland, down to AD1534* (Dublin, 1869), p. 69; C.B. Gibson, *Historical portraits of Irish chieftains and Anglo-Norman knights* (London, 1871), pp 22, 25. 36 Edmund Curtis, 'The English and Ostmen in Ireland', *English Historical Review*, 90 (1908), 209–19 at 211. For some examples from the records, see Hodkinson 'Serious crime in early fourteenth century Co. Limerick', *North Munster Antiquarian Journal*, 34 (1992), 37–43 at 37. 37 Emer Purcell, 'Land-use in medieval Oxmantown' in Seán Duffy (ed.), *Medieval Dublin IV* (Dublin, 2003), pp 193–228. 38 James Lydon, 'Dublin in transition:

The woman, Murchad's role, and the initial Irish success in the battle all seem to be elements embedded deep in the tale, and point to a common core. We should remember that Viking Dublin was not an exclusively Scandinavian settlement, but should rather be regarded as a Hiberno-Viking settlement. How much Irish presence there was among the commoners of the population we cannot know, but certainly in the upper echelons there is extensive evidence for mixing. Intermarriage was frequent and, as political power shifted into the hands of the Irish lords, it became increasingly common for Irish kings to install their sons as kings of Dublin as a stepping stone to greater things. Brian's great-grandson Muirchertach Ua Briain, for whom or for one of whose relatives the *Cogadh* was written, had himself been king of Dublin from 1075 onwards, possibly until 1086, when he succeeded his father as king of Munster.[39]

One further element unites the two versions: Dúnlaing ua hArtacáin, the fairy warrior. Though he is but a peripheral character, his persistent presence, along with Tadc Ua Cellaig's appearance in Stanihurst's record, suggests a continued intercourse with the population of the rest of Ireland. Many of the Old English who had settled outwith the Pale had become heavily hibernicized over the course of time, but contemporary accounts suggest that Dubliners themselves were not wholly averse to Irish ways. Colm Lennon quotes a newcomer of the early Elizabethan period as saying that 'all the English and the most part with delight, yea, even in Dublin, speak Irish and are greatly spotted in manners, habit and condition with Irish stains'.[40]

But Dublin was not to remain culturally distinct from the rest of Ireland. In the end, it was the *Cogadh*'s version that won out. At the time of the Elizabethan re-conquest of Ireland, the Pale was still a separate entity with its own traditions. By the time Ware was writing his history a generation later, there were still memories of these traditions, which he duly records, but he is the last to do so. Keating, a hibernicized member of the Old English community outside the Pale, had succeeded in writing a narrative history of Ireland that became the foundation stone for later historians. In writing that history, Keating drew heavily on native Irish tradition, and it is the *Cogadh*'s version of Brian's life and of Clontarf that he narrates there. Dublin's own twist on that story drifted into oblivion as Dublin became but the administrative centre of a country that, though torn by wars and uprisings, nevertheless was increasingly unified under British rule.

from Ostman town to English borough' in Seán Duffy (ed.), *Medieval Dublin II* (Dublin, 2001), pp 128–41 at p. 134.   **39** *AI* 1075.4; *AI* 1086.4, 1086.5, 1086.7.   **40** Colm Lennon, *Sixteenth-century Ireland* (Dublin, 2005), p. 193.

The church lands of the diocese of Dublin: reconstruction and history[1]

PAUL MacCOTTER

INTRODUCTION

This essay comes in three sections. Firstly, the church lands or crosslands of the medieval diocese of Dublin are reconstructed as they must have existed at the time of the Anglo-Norman invasion (fig. 5.1). Secondly, the question of the origins of the diocese and how it acquired these lands is examined. Thirdly, the earlier history of these ecclesiastical lands is discussed. This essay does not seek to deal with the issues of parish origins or pastoral care within the diocese. These are partly addressed in my forthcoming publication, *Medieval Ireland: the lands of the Church*.

SOURCES AND ORIENTATION

The diocese of Dublin has left an unequalled – in an Irish context – wealth of documentation, both from the pre-Invasion period and especially the Anglo-Norman period, and is thus a unique diocese. It is important to note that the diocese under study here is that recognized or reconstructed at Kells-Mellifont in 1152, when some kind of division appears to have been made of the area that later became the modern archdiocese of Dublin, whose lands lay in Cos Dublin, Wicklow and Kildare. This division was between the sees of Dublin and of Glendalough, which were reunited as a single diocese in 1214, and the exact line of the border between both is uncertain. The church of Glendalough was much older than that of Dublin, and for long eclipsed Dublin in power and prestige. Hence it possessed more property and had a broader area of ecclesiastical dominance than Dublin. This must account for the possession by Glendalough of lands and churches near Dublin itself. Yet Dublin also possessed lands and churches in modern Wicklow not far from Glendalough itself. It is unclear whether these were simple estates or if, in addition to land, the eponymous churches of these estates, both later parochial,

1 This essay was researched as part of my Irish Research Council post-doctoral fellowship. I also wish to acknowledge the assistance of Prof. Donnchadh Ó Corráin and Mr Kenneth Nicholls in the preparation of this essay. I use acres rather than hectares in this essay for historical reasons. 2 See Paul MacCotter, *Medieval Ireland: the lands of the Church* (forthcoming).

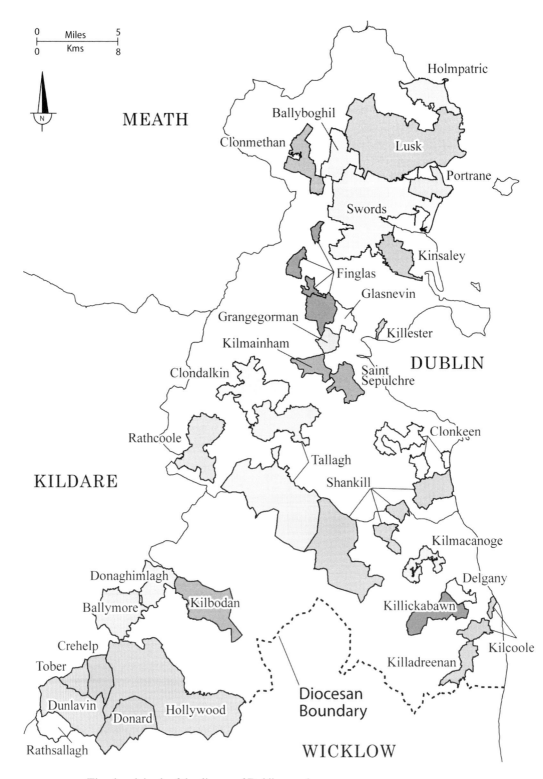

fulfilled some pastoral function in the pre-Invasion period. It may be that this pattern of churches whose lands belonged to both bishoprics in the area from Dublin itself south to Newcastle in Wicklow reflects the normal pattern of fragmented *paruchiae* seen in the pre-'Reform' Irish Church, where bishoprics did not occupy a single coherent territorial block of land but rather exercised pastoral care over various churches, some lying contiguously and others discretely. Equally, we sometimes find a situation in which diocesan sees possess lands in other dioceses but which do not have pastoral significance.[2]

We are fortunate in possessing several lists of lands for both Glendalough and Dublin dating to before their final union.[3] It is likely that the area of the diocese of Dublin corresponds with that of the original rural deaneries of Lusk, Swords, Taney, Dublin, Ballymore and Bray, which in turn are quite similar, if not identical, to the boundaries of the medieval county of Dublin.[4] Yet a note of caution must be sounded here. Among the parameters of the diocese of Glendalough as set down in a papal bull of 1179 is Dulgen, which must be Carrickgollogan Hill in Rathmichael parish, in southern Dublin near the Wicklow border. This occurs as Carrikdolgyn etc. in early records.[5] It may be that before the final union of both dioceses Dublin acquired the area of Bray deanery, most of which lay south of Carrickgollogan. As certainty is impossible here, I have chosen to follow the medieval county boundaries (of Dublin) for this reconstruction, within which one finds lands belonging to both Dublin and Glendalough. The aim here has been to attempt to establish the lands in diocesan possession at the time of the Invasion, while also noting other church estates of relevance.

The only example of medieval diocesan crosslands reconstruction attempted prior to my own efforts in Ardfert/Kerry was that undertaken by Otway-Ruthven in reconstructing those of Dublin.[6] Her work here is sound, apart from the unfortunate omission of those lands in the medieval county not in modern Dublin, for she limited her excellent work to the area of the modern county. In addition to reconstructing the medieval crosslands, Otway-Ruthven researched the date of acquisition of those lands acquired after the Invasion. Her work does not, however, distinguish between pre- and post-Invasion church lands, nor does it deal with the origins of the former. I have used the

3 Charles McNeill (ed.), *Calendar of Archbishop Alen's register* (Dublin, 1950), pp 2–8, 20–1. 4 Paul MacCotter, *Medieval Ireland: territorial, political and economic divisions* (Dublin, 2008), pp 162–6. 5 *Alen*, pp 5, 91, 196, 222. 6 A.J. Otway-Ruthven, 'The mediaeval church lands of County Dublin' in J.A. Watt, J.B. Morrall and F.X. Martin (eds), *Medieval studies presented to Aubrey Gwynn SJ* (Dublin, 1961) (hereafter Otway-Ruthven, 'Church lands'), pp 54–73; see also, Ailbhe MacShamhráin, 'The *Monasticon Hibernicum* project: the diocese of Dublin' in Seán Duffy (ed.), *Medieval Dublin VI* (Dublin, 2004), pp 115–43. The online version of the same source has also been used as a source of references both to documentary source-material and to archaeology and has been consulted in all cases. Hence it is not referenced (http://monasticon.celt.dias.ie).

same sources as Otway-Ruthven to attempt to reconstruct the diocesan lands she omitted to trace, but most of these lay within the area of the Gaelic resurgence in northern Wicklow, and a complete reconstruction may not have been achieved due to major changes in the toponymy of the area resulting from its loss to the colony. A broad outline of these lands does emerge, however, and with this we must be satisfied.

The principal sources for the crosslands of medieval Dublin are *Archbishop Alen's register*, a compilation of transcribed documents dating from the late twelfth to sixteenth century, and the diocesan register known as *Crede Mihi*, which dates from the late thirteenth century. Both of these sources contain abundant records of the crosslands of Dublin. In addition, two series of manorial extents survive for those lands within medieval Dublin: an incomplete one from *c.*1260 and a fuller one from 1326.[7] The following extent follows the order of manors of 1326.

I. THE CHURCH LANDS

The lands of the archbishops of Dublin

The manor of St Sepulchre This contained lands in the parishes of Crumlin, Donnybrook, St Catherine's, St Nicholas Without, St Peter's and Taney, all lying in a single block. The lands in Taney – half of its *baile* – were acquired by donation from an Ostman at some stage before the Invasion, though they were later re-granted by John de Clahull, perhaps in answer to church claims on these. The remainder of these lands also appear to date from the pre-Invasion period, apart from the ploughland of St Kevin's itself.[8] Otway-Ruthven's reconstruction appears to omit most of the lands of the parish of St Nicholas Without, including parts of the Coombe, but these were not substantial.[9] These pre-Invasion lands total 3,071 acres approx.

The manor of Finglas This contained most of the modern parish of Finglas, in four distinct parcels, acreage: 4,487.[10]

The manor of Swords (and the 'lost' lands of Rush in Lusk) This large manor contained several large parcels scattered throughout northern Co. Dublin. The lands of Swords itself included most of Swords parish, excluding the townlands of Ballymadrough, Brackenstown and Knocksedan, and three townlands outside of the parish, and was thus a single parcel (acreage: 9,273).

7 Otway-Ruthven, 'Church lands', pp 118–28, 170–98.   8 Otway-Ruthven, 'Church lands', 57–8; *Alen*, p. 28.   9 H.B. Clarke, '*Urbs et suburbium*: beyond the walls of medieval Dublin' in Conleth Manning (ed.), *Dublin and beyond the Pale: studies in honour of Patrick Healy* (Bray, 1998), pp 45–58 at pp 53–4.   10 Ibid., p. 57.

The lands of Portraine are that of the parish, which includes Lambay (2,186). The lands of Clonmethan, which lay in a single large parcel apart from one small outlier, comprised 2,676 acres.[11]

The crosslands of Lusk all lay within that parish, in two distinct parcels, divided by secular lands, while much of the east of the parish was not crossland either.[12] The explanation for this anomalous situation is of great interest for a number of reasons, and has its roots in a grant of the vill of Lusk to Hubert Walter, by the Lord John, apparently a few years after 1185.[13] Walter, brother of Theobald, ancestor of the Butler earls of Ormond, was one of John's leading bureaucrats at this time, and a very prominent man in the government of England. Now, Lusk, as one of the great churches of the pre-Invasion period, was clearly church property at the time it was granted to Walter, such contradictory grants of lands being a feature of John's behaviour in Ireland. Archbishop John Cumin of Dublin was a substantial figure, and clearly did not acquiesce quietly in this loss of a substantial manor. While we know nothing directly of subsequent events, we can reconstruct something of these by reference to the subsequent history of these lands. As we have seen above, the archbishop's lands in Lusk parish comprised only 6,977 acres, while the parish itself comprises over 16,000 acres (although the seventeenth-century parish was somewhat smaller). To this total must be added the lands of the nunnery of Gracedieu in Lusk, whose lands totalled 1,005 acres, and which had originally been given to the nunnery upon its foundation by Archbishop Cumin and thus had been church land.[14] Most of the lands in the parish not part of the episcopal manor of Lusk formed part of the large manor of Rush and the much smaller manor of Corduff. These belonged to the earls of Ormond, and their lands can be largely reconstructed from a number of extents.[15] (Corduff appears to have been the subject of litigation between Edmund le Butler and Richard, archbishop of Dublin, as late as 1305.)[16] The identifiable townlands in these give an acreage of 6,205, and it is probable that the total there was bigger

11 Ibid., pp 57, 72; *Alen*, pp 118–19, 175–6, 178; Otway-Ruthven, 'Church lands', p. 57. 12 See Otway-Ruthven's map at the end of her essay. 13 Edmund Curtis (ed.), *Calendar of Ormond deeds* (6 vols, Dublin, 1932–43), i, p. 366. See also C.R. Cheney, *Hubert Walter* (London, 1967), p. 21 and, for Walter's career, passim. 14 Otway-Ruthven, 'Church lands', p. 71. 15 *Cal. Ormond deeds*, iii, pp 221–2; iv, p. 168; v, pp 17–18; Margaret Griffith (ed.), *Calendar of inquisitions formerly in the Office of the Chief Remembrancer of the Exchequer* (Dublin, 1991), pp 21, 57, 60, 117, 272. The identified townlands in Rush manor are Rush, Rush Demesne (Kinure), Ratharton, Horestown, Baldrumman, portion of Corduff, Effelstown, Jordanstown, Tirrelstown, Oberstown, Loughshinny, Dromanagh, Thomastown, Ballykea, Deanstown, Ballystrane, Colecot and Hedgestown. It is clear from their positioning that Rush also certainly included Ballustree, Ballyhavil, Blackland, Carnhill, Drumlattery, Lane, Piercetown and Popeshall. Those in Corduff manor are Corduffhall, Coldwinters, Thomondstown, the detached portion of Deanstown adjoining, and both Ballealys (see Griffith, *Inquisitions*, pp 38, 136; Robert Simington (ed.), *The Civil Survey (AD1654–56)* (10 vols, Dublin, 1931–61), vii, p. 65). 16 *Alen*, p. 160.

and can be accounted for by those unidentified denominations in the extents. Therefore, it is likely that the manors of Rush and Corduff contained most of the lands of Lusk not part of its crosslands, giving an approximate acreage of 16,000 for the original area of the church lands of Lusk. The distribution of these lands is significant. While the bulk of them lie in the east of the parish, along the coast, a second group of five townlands divides the crosslands of the archbishop there into their two main sections,[17] while there are some other examples of small parcels of lands of one lying surrounded by those of the other.

Three conclusions emerge from this survey. It must be that the manor of Lusk was divided evenly at an early stage between Archbishop Cumin and Hubert Walter by means of a legal agreement. The intermixed pattern of the parcels, as distinct from an even east/west division, also suggests that both parties had been actively engaged in infeudating the lands of the manor before the agreement to divide was made. Finally, it is clear that, upon Walter's death without heirs in 1205 (as archbishop of Canterbury), his lands at Rush passed to his brother Theobald. One last point should be made. The lands of Rush were not considered part of the County of the Cross of Dublin, indicating that the shire system, with its separate administration for church lands, was established *after* Rush had been quitclaimed by the archbishop. The acreage there is thus approximately 30,000.

The manor of Tallaght   This manor comprised the greater portion (twenty-nine of fifty townlands) of the parish of Tallaght. Townlands in this parish but not in the manor are: Ballymaice, Ballymana, Ballyroan, Bohernabreena, Brittas Little, Corbally, Corrageen, Friarstown Lower and Upper, Gibbons, Killinardan, Killininny, Kilnamanagh, Kiltalowen, Knocklyon, Lugmore, Mountpellier, Newlands Demesne, Oldbawn, Oldcourt and Piperstown.[18] Acreage: 14,330.

The manor of Rathcoole   This manor contained the medieval parish of Rathcoole, which consisted of the modern parish excluding the lands of the obsolete parish of Calliaghstown (Calliaghstown Upper and Lower, Farmersvale, Slademore and Badgerhill). Calliaghstown parish (as its name suggests) comprised the lands of the nunnery of Hogges. While the latter appears to have been a pre-Invasion foundation, there is no evidence that its lands were already church land when granted, and I do not count them as crossland. Also excluded is Westmanstown, which belonged to the Hospitallers. Included are Newtown Upper and Lower, which were part of Rathcoole even though in Saggart parish.[19] Acreage: 4,045.

17 Colecot, Baldrumman, Jordanstown, Oberstown and Ballystrane.   **18** Otway-Ruthven, 'Church lands', pp 57, 73.   **19** Ibid., pp 57, 66, 69; *Alen*, pp 125, 183–4.

The manor of Clondalkin   This contained all of Clondalkin parish except Collinstown and Coldcut, as well as Aungierstown and Ballybane in Kilmactalway, and Rowlagh in Esker.[20] Acreage: 4,544.

The manor of Shankill   Otway-Ruthven identifies 2,059 acres in this manor within modern Co. Dublin (at Shankill itself and Rathmichael) but does not attempt to locate its lands in Wicklow.[21] The reconstruction of the crosslands within those parts of medieval Dublin in modern Wicklow is a difficult task. Two dioceses possessed lands there – Dublin and Glendalough – and made several exchanges of lands before they were eventually united. While several lists of these lands survive, many of the toponyms are obsolete and careful cognisance of the surrounding secular fees must also be taken in order to arrive at some certainty regarding their extent. This manor is first noted in 1228, when described as that of 'Senekil & Kilmacburn'.[22]

The church and lands of Stagonill in Powerscourt parish appear in the 1326 extent. This is now Churchtown, a sub-denomination in the south of Powerscourt Demesne. The 'grange' of Stagonill (Techugonnell) originally belonged to Glendalough but was given to St Patrick's by John Cumin before 1192.[23] The confirmation of Dublin's lands in 1179 includes 'Cell Critaich and the mountains from Digis to Sudi Cheli'. Digis is Djouce, a top on the ridge marking the original southern bounds of Powerscourt parish, while Suidhe [Uí?] Cheallaigh is identified by Liam Price with one of the tops on the ridge between northern Powerscourt parish and Castlekelly townland in Dublin, perhaps Killakee Mountain. Cell Critaich is probably the old graveyard in Tonygarrow.[24] Another church parcel there is Killegar, with another early church site, originally belonging to Glendalough and later occurring in the Shankill extent of 1326.[25] This list also includes lands at Stamelyn, 'Moling's House', now Kilmalin, a townland that originally extended into northern Powerscourt Demesne.[26] It is clear from the extent that these lands were substantial, significantly bigger than the mere townlands themselves, and we may get some idea of their borders by noting the secular fees there. The bulk of Powerscourt Demesne must be the earlier Balitened (Powerscourt itself), which was a royal manor in 1308 and so cannot have been crossland.[27] Other lands in this manor include Glencree, Balichathel and Donderk. Balicathel is the Ballycale of the late seventeenth-century 'Book of Survey and Distribution',

20 Otway-Ruthven, 'Church lands', pp 57, 61.   **21** Ibid., p. 58.   **22** *35th report of the deputy keeper of the public records in Ireland* (Dublin, 1903), p. 32.   **23** *Alen*, pp 5, 20; Liam Price, *Place-names of Co. Wicklow* (Dublin, 1945–67), pp 296–8.   **24** Price, *Place-names*, pp 302–3; MacShamhráin, 'The *Monasticon Hibernicum* project', p. 117.   **25** *Alen*, pp 2, 21, 24, 42, 195.   **26** Ibid., p. 196; Price, *Place-names*, pp 291, 295.   **27** James Mills et al. (eds), *Calendar of the justiciary rolls, Ireland* (3 vols, Dublin, 1905–56), iii, p. 112; H.S. Sweetman and G.F. Handcock (eds), *Calendar of documents relating to Ireland* (5 vols, London, 1875–86), iii, p. 309 (hereafter *CDI*).

now Annacrivey, while Donderk also lay in Glencree.[28] From other sources, we learn that Ballybrew, Curtlestown, Monastery ('Keliniebren') and Cookstown were part of the manor of Bray and thus were also secular fees.[29] Therefore, the crosslands there, at a minimum, must have included parts of Powerscourt Demesne, Kilmalin, Killegar, a couple of townlands lying just west of Powerscourt Demesne, and the mountainous upper reaches of the western part of the parish. Approximate acreage: 12,000 (much of which was mountain).

Kilmacanoge occurs among the Glendalough lands in 1176, and had passed to Dublin by 1216, with its lands.[30] Its church and lands are again noted in the early fourteenth-century papal taxation.[31] It does not occur in the Shankill extent, unless Warynston is the modern Ballyorney.[32] The parish of Kilmacanoge contained a large royal manor, Glencap, which appears to have had its own parish of the same name, whose church is that of Kilmurray alias Templeglencap, while another obsolete church in this parish was that of Kilcrony, a distinct chapel *c*.1280.[33] Later records note the distinct vills of Glencap and Kilmacanoge, whose members are listed, and it may be that these preserve the area of the original manors there.[34] Those of Kilmacanoge are: both Kilmacanoges, both Glencormicks, both Ballybawns, Ballinteskin, both Killoughs. Acreage: 1,340.

The parish of Delgany contained the Mac Gilla Mo-Cholmóc fee of Rathdown, but also held some crosslands. Delgany itself and Bali Udunetha occur as Glendalough lands in 1176, and both eventually passed to Dublin.[35] Delgany parish contained two rectories, those of Delgany and Karrec. The latter is now Templecarrig, and this may represent the rectory of the Mac Gilla Mo-Cholmóc fee here, just as that of Delgany the crosslands.[36] The lands of Delgany comprised at least one carucate, and the modern townland seems too small for this measure. Price is correct in his identification of Bali Udunetha with modern Ballydonagh, which occurs as Ballydonenagh in the 1326 extent.[37] Originally, this townland contained Bellevue Demesne as well, and the acreage of these three contiguous townlands is 956. The crosslands in this parish are likely to have been greater in extent than this, but we cannot uncover them. The crosslands there adjoin those in neighbouring Kilcoole parish.

28 J.T. Gilbert (ed.), *Chartularies of St Mary's Abbey, Dublin* (2 vols, Dublin, 1884), i, pp 118–19; *Dinnseanchas*, 4/2 (1970), p. 37, n. 15.   29 Colmán Etchingham, 'Evidence of Scandinavian settlement in Wicklow' in Ken Hannigan and William Nolan (eds), *Wicklow: history and society* (Dublin, 1994), pp 113–38 at pp 129–30; J.T. Gilbert (ed.), *Register of St Thomas' Abbey, Dublin* (Dublin, 1889), pp 145–8, 153; MacCotter, *Medieval Ireland*, p. 73; Price, *Place-names*, pp 286–7.   30 *Alen*, pp 2, 55–6; Price, *Place-names*, pp 313–14. 31 *CDI*, 5, pp 240–1.   32 *Alen*, p. 195.   33 *Crede Mihi: the most ancient register book of the archbishops of Dublin before the Reformation*, ed. J.T. Gilbert (Dublin, 1897), pp 142–3; Price, *Place-names*, pp 310–16.   34 Book of Survey and Distribution, Co. Wicklow (NLI MS 969).   35 *Alen*, pp 2, 21, 24, 67, 128.   36 *Crede Mihi*, pp 142–3; Price, *Place-names*, pp 320–1, 324–5.   37 Price, *Place-names*, p. 318.

The earliest list of Glendalough includes Killickabawn (Cellmacabuirinn), while that of Dublin contains Kilcoole (Cellcomgal).[38] By 1216, both places occur in a list of Dublin lands, while the lands of the former are again mentioned in a contemporary grant, and later in the 1326 extent, which indicates them to have been fairly extensive.[39] Kilcoole appears to be the Kilconwill of 1326, and a reference from 1395 mentions its five temporalities(?).[40] Therefore, the lands of Kilcoole may well have been extensive, and certainly contained Ballyronan 'beyond Powerscourt' of the 1326 extent, definitely bigger than its modern descendant (it contained that part of Mount Kennedy Demesne to its south, but was certainly larger),[41] and perhaps also the townlands linking both, Bullford and Kilquade. These all lay in the original parish of Kilcoole, as did the parcel of Kilfernoc (a church) in modern Ballynerrin, which belonged to St Patrick's Cathedral later in the thirteenth century.[42] Another such parcel there may have been Kilpedder, but this is uncertain.[43] In any case, it is clear that much of the original Kilcoole was crossland, and the acreage suggested (*c*.1,100), even including the linking townlands, is an underestimation.

We are on surer ground with the lands of Killickabawn, originally part of the Glendalough lands, which were granted to Dublin by an abbot of Glendalough *c*.1228. These are referred to in an early exchange as 'Kilmaccabirn, Toman, Balymacdouergilla and Ballyhuchaide'.[44] Killickabawn Church, listed *c*.1280, is the church of the Downs, in modern Woodlands (St Mary's), and so its lands must have included Killickabawn, Woodlands, Holywell, both Drummins, Downs and Tooman.[45] Tooman was in fact the old name for the entire Downs Hill, originally part of Delgany parish and even earlier certainly part of the lands of the church of Killickabawn. Adjoining Downshill townland to the south is Carrigagower, and Price is correct in identifying this place with that granted to St Thomas' Abbey by the abbot of Glendalough *c*.1200.[46] Acreage: 2,605.

Killadreenan did not lie in Shankill manor but in that of Castlekevin further south. This manor lay outside our study area but its member did not. As Cell Achaich Dreignig, this place occurs in the first confirmation of Dublin's lands in 1179. Archbishop Alen noted its lands, and Killadreenan was originally a distinct parish, later absorbed by Newcastle.[47] These references suggest that its lands were extensive, but these cannot be uncovered. They certainly included Killadreenan itself, and probably Kilmullin to its north, which seems to be an alias for Killadreenan. The place-name Le Kelote, of the 1326 extent, occurs among fees in the Kilcoole/Killickabawn area, and is probably to be identified

38 *Alen*, pp 2–3.   **39** Ibid., pp 38–9, 76, 194.   **40** Ibid., pp 195, 229.   **41** Ibid., p. 195; Price, *Place-names*, p. 389.   **42** *Alen*, pp 128, 298; Price, *Place-names*, p. 384.   **43** Price, *Place-names*, p. 386.   **44** *Alen*, pp 2, 20, 24, 39; Ailbhe MacShamhráin, *Church and polity in pre-Norman Ireland: the case of Glendalough* (Maynooth, 1996), pp 164–5.   **45** *Crede Mihi*, p. 142.   **46** Price, *Place-names*, pp 390–1.   **47** *Alen*, pp 3, 123, 229; *Crede Mihi*, pp 142–3.

with the townlands of Keeloge in Upper Newcastle parish, near Killadreenan.[48] If we include all of these townlands, as well as those linking Keeloge with Killadreenan, we get an estimate of between 1,500 and 2,000 acres, but this is an underestimate.

Finally, we might note the lands of Glennmuneri, usually identified with Ballyman (Old Connacht parish). This occurs in the early confirmations to Glendalough but its subsequent history is unclear, and there is no record of it passing to Dublin. It later occurs among the lands of the Hospitallers.[49] It is likely to have included Ballyman, Prompstown and Fassaghroe, and the original church location there, in Ballyman, appears to have been later abandoned in favour of a site at Old Connaught.[50]

The manor of Ballymore   Reconstructing the original church lands of this manor is difficult, as the evidence is somewhat contradictory. At the core of this manor lay the pre-Invasion lands of Glendalough 'west of the mountains', which were granted to Archbishop Comyn by John during the 1180s, when described as 'the half-cantred of Glendalough nearest to Ballymore'.[51] Unfortunately, around the same time John had granted Comyn 'the land of Coillaght' in barony.[52] This lay in approximately the same area as the church lands of Glendalough there, and crucially, its status is unclear. A grant 'in barony' suggests that these lands were earlier secular lands and not ecclesiastical, even though it is stated in a grant of deforestation of 1229 that Coillaght (along with Ballymore and Fertir) was formerly demesne of Glendalough and the property of its last abbot.[53] While Edmund Curtis accepted the ecclesiastical status of Coillaght, two more recent authorities, Liam Price and Kenneth Nicholls, consider it to have originated as secular land.[54] Therefore, it is best to proceed by identifying the original half-cantred of Glendalough 'west of the mountains'. These lands are listed in confirmations of 1172×6, 1179 and 1198, which mostly mention the same places.[55] The first list contains twenty-four place-names, of which eight have proved entirely beyond identification. Two more appear to have lain in medieval Kildare and so lie outside the parameters of the present study.[56] The later lists add a number of other names while omitting some of the originals, and it would seem from this that these new names must represent some of the unidentified names of the first list. The identified lands from these sources follow.

> *Crehelp*: Crehelp and Baliloman (now Lemonstown) occur, so clearly the entire parish of Crehelp is included.

---

48 Price, *Place-names*, pp 394, 402; *Alen*, p. 195.   **49** *Alen*, p. 2; Otway-Ruthven, 'Church lands', p. 66.   **50** John Dalton, *The memoirs of the archbishops of Dublin* (Dublin, 1838), p. 325.   **51** *Alen*, p. 18.   **52** Ibid., p. 25.   **53** Ibid., p. 62.   **54** Edmund Curtis, 'The family of Marisco', *JRSAI*, 61 (1931), 22–38, 89–112; 62 (1932), 50–74 at 51–2; Price, *Place-names*, pp 245–6.   **55** *Alen*, pp 2, 5, 23.   **56** Ardmeicbrein alias Armacrenan is Colbinstown while

Donard: again, the entire parish is included; Donard, Kilbaylet, Kilcoagh and Ballymooney all occur in the early lists, while Irishtown and possibly Ballylion occur in later extents of Ballymore.[57]

Rathsallagh: this parish formed a complementary manor and all of this is included.[58]

Dunlavin: while only Dunlavin occurs in the early lists, probably the whole parish is included; Tornant, Merginstown and Milltown occur in later extents of Ballymore.[59]

Tober: the vill of this grant equates with the entire parish.

Burgage: the Balivdalig of the early lists is modern Glashina in Burgage parish; Burgage itself is the older Domnach Imlech. While this is not recognizable in the first list, it does occur in that of 1179. The whole parish appears to have belonged to the vill. Thus, we should also include Glebe East and Kilmalum in modern Tipperkevin, but which lay in seventeenth-century Burgage. These lands also have ecclesiastical associations with Domnach Imlech.[60]

Kilbodan: this is the Cellbodan of the lists and a later parish subsequently absorbed by that of Boystown. The church site is in Lackan. The Cellugarcon of the lists is now Kilbeg within Kilbodan, and it would seem that all of this old parish – the northern third of Boystown – was Glendalough land there, containing Lackan, Kilbeg, Ballynultagh, Carrig and Sroughan townlands.[61] Another possible identification here is that of Ballivlaccuane of the first list, which later occurs as Ballilaghnan, when associated with a place called Adkyp. Adkyp is described as lying between the Liffey and the mountains, and this and other references suggest that this place lies in the area of Carrig and or Sroughan townlands.[62]

Ballymore (Eustace): while the reference to 'the half-cantred of Glendalough nearest to Ballymore' might suggest that Ballymore was not part of these lands, and it cannot be recognized in the first list, it does occur in the list of 1198 and so must occur earlier as one of the unidentified vill names. The onomastic pattern in the parish suggests that all of Ballymore was meant here. While now in Kildare, Ballymore lay in medieval Co. Dublin.

Hollywood and Dunboyke: Dunboyke appears to have been an early parish and its estate must correspond to this. It was one of three original parishes in the present Hollywood, and its area must have included that part of Hollywood lying to south of Dunboyke itself.[63] While

---

Cellfraim seems to be Freynstown (*Alen*, p. 124; Price, *Place-names*, pp 156, 202).   **57** *Alen*, pp 121, 123, 192.   **58** Price, *Place-names*, pp 154–5.   **59** *Alen*, pp 121, 123; Price, *Place-names*, p. 200.   **60** Price, *Place-names*, pp 250–2, 254.   **61** Ibid., pp 237–43.   **62** *Alen*, pp 34, 73, 91, 125, 191–2.   **63** Price, *Place-names*, pp 207–8, 212–13.

Hollywood itself does not appear on the early lists, it is almost certainly
to be identified with the Kilnee (*Coillidh Naomh*) exchanged by the last
bishop of Glendalough before 1192, while another church name
relating to a place adjacent to Hollywood, Killenkeyvin, occurs on the
list of 1179.[64] The final parish there was Killerk in the very north of
Hollywood, and there is no evidence to include this in the lands of the
cross.

The picture thus given is of an area comprising intermixed fees, those of
'the half-cantred of Glendalough' on the one hand, bearing a single if sinuous
shape, and those of Coillaght on the other, in two sections. Coillaght seems to
have comprised two principal areas: in the north, the area of the Wicklow
parishes of Kilbride and Blessington, and, further south, the bulk of the parish of
Boystown and a portion, at least, of that of Hollywood, at Killerk. Therefore, the
church lands of Ballymore contained approximately 47,200 acres.

The lands of Christ Church Cathedral
These were organized into five manors, but two of these (Balscadden and
Kilmashogue) were composed entirely of lands acquired after the Invasion,
and so are ignored here, as is the isolated townland of Astagob.[65]

The manor of Glasnevin This consisted of the lands of Glasnevin,
Kinsaley, Drumcondra and Killester.[66] Acreage: 2,625.

The manor of Grangegorman Acreage: 878.[67]

The manor of Clonkeen Consisting of lands in the parishes of Kill and
Tully, as well as a detached portion, Killiney.[68] Acreage: 2,834.

The lands of St Patrick's Cathedral
These were either acquired after the Invasion or are already included in the
archbishop's lands listed above.[69]

The lands of St Mary's Abbey (Ballyboghil)
While this abbey acquired extensive lands in the pre-Invasion period, their
nomenclature is strongly indicative of lands of secular origin, with many
secular terms (*ráith, baile, lios* etc.) and almost no ecclesiastical toponyms
occurring.[70] Accordingly, these are ignored. One post-Invasion grant to the

64 *Alen*, p. 20; Price, *Place-names*, pp 208, 215–17. **65** Otway-Ruthven, 'Church lands', p.
59; James Mills (ed.), *Account roll of the priory of the Holy Trinity, Dublin* (Dublin, 1891;
repr. Dublin, 1996), pp 194–8. **66** Otway-Ruthven, 'Church lands', pp 59–60. **67** Ibid.,
p. 59. **68** Ibid. **69** Ibid., pp 61–2. **70** Ibid., pp 63–4.

abbey was of a significant ecclesiastical pre-Invasion estate; that of Ballyboghil, a Patrician house donated by the archbishop of Armagh *c*.1175.[71] These lands contained 2,789 acres.

Holmpatrick Priory

This Augustinian priory was a pre-Invasion foundation deriving directly from an older and significant Patrician church there.[72] The original lands of this parish are likely to represent the area of the earlier indigenous church. Acreage: 2,088.

All Hallows Priory

As with St Mary's, its pre-Invasion lands appear to have been secular before being granted.[73]

Kilmainham

Kilmainham was granted to the Hospitallers by Strongbow, but its earlier history suggests that it was probably church land previously, and probably usurped by Strongbow. Its original lands appear to be represented by that part of the medieval parish of Kilmainham south of the Liffey. Acreage: 1,040.[74]

II. THE DIOCESE OF DUBLIN AND ITS LANDS: ACQUISITION

Uniquely in Ireland, the foundation of the diocese of Dublin can be approximately dated. Howard Clarke dates it, and the building of its cathedral, to *c*.1030, events that follow on closely from the conversion of the leaders of Ostman Dublin.[75] The subsequent difficulties and rivalries between the dioceses of Dublin and Glendalough are well documented, with the unsuccessful efforts begun at Ráith Bressail to subsume Dublin by Glendalough leading to the complete reversal of the situation at Kells-Mellifont thirty-four years later, where Dublin gained archiepiscopal status and Glendalough became a mere suffragan, eventually to be absorbed by Dublin in 1214.[76] By the time the Anglo-Normans arrived, it seems clear that the area of the diocese of Dublin corresponded, as noted above, and at least approximately, to that of the four reserved cantreds that later became the first county of Dublin.

We know something of the grantors of the early estates of Dublin, and can

71 Ibid., p. 64.   **72** Ibid., p. 68; Aubrey Gwynn and Neville Hadcock, *Medieval religious houses: Ireland* (London, 1970), p. 178.   **73** Otway-Ruthven, 'Church lands', pp 68–9. **74** Ibid., pp 65–6.   **75** H.B. Clarke, 'Conversion, church and cathedral: the diocese of Dublin to 1152' in James Kelly and Daire Keogh (eds), *History of the Catholic diocese of Dublin* (Dublin, 2000), pp 19–50 at pp 33–5.   **76** MacShamhráin, *Glendalough*, pp 160–7; idem, 'The emergence of the metropolitan see: Dublin, 1111–1216' in Kelly and Keogh (eds), *History of the Catholic diocese of Dublin*, pp 51–71; Clarke, 'Conversion, church and

be certain that the lands so granted lay within the diocese. The earliest grants –
those datable securely to before Kells-Mellifont – concerned the lands of
Grangegorman, Lambay and Portraine, and Clonkeen. Other grants follow but
are not securely datable, yet probably date to the first half of the twelfth
century.[77] These include lands at Tully and Kill o' the Grange. All of these
lands lay within the Ostman kingdom of Dublin, whose extent again is
approximately preserved in that of the area of the medieval county. The one
significant exception is that of the cantred of Fyngal 'north of Goure', which
was part of the medieval county but also claimed by the Anglo-Norman lords
of Meath. Significantly, this same area lay outside of the diocese of Glendalough
(and thus Dublin) as perambulated in 1111, when it lay in Mide. It is
represented by the kingdom of Saithne, corresponding approximately to the
modern baronies of Balrothery.[78] Significantly, the monastery of Lusk in
Saithne had been absorbed by the diocese of Dublin by 1148, just as Saithne
itself came to lie within the kingdom of Dublin. Therefore, the territories of
kingdom and diocese were similar: as the kingdom grew, so did the diocese. It
is likely that the pre-1148 extent of the kingdom is represented by the area of
the medieval county, less Saithne. Certainly, this area agrees with that of
Ostman settlement within the Hiberno-Scandinavian 'shire' of Dublin
(*Dyflinarskiri*), which stretched from Lambay in the north to Delgany in the
south-east, and Rathturtle (Deerpark near Blessington) in the south-west.[79]
That these bounds were of some antiquity is suggested by the evidence that
locates the church of Swords within the kingdom of Dublin in the 990s.[80]

Within the area of this pre-1148 Ostman kingdom, there had existed a
number of churches that had bishops: Swords (1023), Finglas (791, 796, 812,
817, 838, 867), Rechru or Lambay (739?), Clondalkin (789, 879), Tallaght (792,
874, 962, 966).[81] Even allowing for *lacunae* in the annalistic record, is it not
remarkable that no bishop of these sees is recorded after 1023, just a few years
before the foundation of the see of Dublin? Rather than suggest that these
churches maintained their independence from Dublin until Kells-Mellifont, as

cathedral', pp 44–50.   **77** *Alen*, pp 28–9; Otway-Ruthven, 'Church lands', p. 60; Clarke, 'Conversion, church and cathedral', pp 35–6; Edel Bhreathnach, 'Columban churches in Brega and Leinster: relations with the Norse and the Anglo-Normans', *JRSAI*, 129 (1999), 5–18 at 13–14.   **78** MacCotter, *Medieval Ireland*, pp 165–6; M.T. Flanagan, *Irish royal charters: texts and contexts* (repr., Oxford, 2008), p. 72; James McErlean, 'Synod of Raith Breasail, boundaries of the dioceses of Ireland', *Archivium Hibernicum*, 3 (1914), 1–33 at 25. The northern boundary of Glendalough/Dublin as established at Ráith Bressail lay at Greenoge, on the Dublin–Meath boundary. Greenoge is south of the Broadmeadow Water, and hence lay on the southern border of Saithne, which thus cannot have lain in Dublin. **79** John Bradley, 'The interpretation of Scandinavian settlement in Ireland' in idem (ed.), *Settlement and society in medieval Ireland: studies presented to F.X. Martin* (Kilkenny, 1988), pp 49–78 at pp 55–8; Price, *Place-names*, pp 263, 319.   **80** *AU* 994.3, 995.2 (where Swords is clearly within Dublin).   **81** These obituaries are taken from *AU* and *AFM*.

has been implied,[82] is it not more likely that, with the foundation of the see of Dublin *c.*1030, any surviving episcopal seats within the Ostman kingdom were extinguished and their churches placed under the governance of Christ Church? I suggest elsewhere, however, that this may not have been the case with the temporalities of these churches, which perhaps did not follow into Christ Church's hands until Kells-Mellifont.[83]

Some of these churches maintained a status as mother-churches into the early colonial period – before that of colonial parish formation – with extensive territories under their lordship that may represent earlier territorial dioceses, and certainly in some cases represent earlier *túatha*. Indeed, Dublin in general, and Fingal in particular, provides near unique evidence for the nature of pastoral care and pre-Invasion layered 'proto'-parish structures in Ireland. While this subject lies outside the remit of the present essay, we should note in passing that at least six such pastoral mother-churches existed in the county: Swords, Finglas, Lusk, Clonmethan, Hollywood and Clondalkin, and there were doubtless others.[84] Lusk was also an episcopal see, with bishops recorded in 616, 791, 836, 875, 883, 891, 904, 907, 929 and 965.[85] In this context, we might finally note the church of Tully or Tulach na nEpscop, which, as we shall see, may have been the seat of a territorial bishopric serving Uí Briúin Cualann.

III. THE EARLIER HISTORY OF THESE LANDS

Duiblinn / liberty of St Sepulchre
This estate lay immediately south of the city, and the bulk of its lands appear to have belonged to the see from the pre-Invasion period. As the senior manor of the archbishopric, it was the site of both the archbishop's palace and St Patrick's Cathedral.[86] The manor bore two names in the early period: St Sepulchre's, after the chapel of the archbishop's palace, a post-Invasion foundation; and Colonia, a Latinization of Cullen, a rural estate whose general location is indicated by the townland of Cullenswood. While this name may have originated as an Irish toponym, from *Cuileann* or some such, equally it may have derived from a settlement of ecclesiastics from Cologne in Germany, with whose ecclesiastical establishment the early diocese of Dublin had major links.[87]

82 Clarke, 'Conversion, church and cathedral', p. 49.   83 See my forthcoming *Medieval Ireland: the lands of the Church*; Charles Doherty, 'Cluain Dolcáin: a brief note' in A.P. Smyth (ed.), *Seanchas: studies … in honour of Francis J. Byrne* (Dublin, 2000), pp 182–8 at pp 186–8.   84 See my forthcoming *Medieval Ireland: the lands of the Church*.   85 Taken from *AU* and *AFM*.   86 For much of what follows, see Clarke, '*Urbs et suburbium*', pp 45–58 at pp 52–4; idem, 'Conversion, church and cathedral', pp 25–33.   87 Raghnall Ó Floinn, 'The founder relics of Christ Church Cathedral' in Seán Duffy (ed.), *Medieval*

Several churches lay within the pre-Invasion lands. The first St Patrick's existed as early as *c*.1121, while a possible church site has been identified at Clonskeagh, where there is a well dedicated to St Brigit.[88] It is St Peter's Church that is of most interest, however. This lies within what is possibly an early ecclesiastical enclosure, whose shape may still be preserved by the street pattern surrounding Aungier Street. Its size indicates this to have been a significant site, and Clarke's identification of this enclosure and its church of St Peter with the early medieval monastery of Duiblinn is very probable. This church bore the name of the eponymous pool of Dublin, possibly on the Poddle, beside which it sat, and obituaries are recorded of its abbots in 656 (Beraid) and 790 (Siadal).[89] All of this points to the early importance of this site, and this is confirmed by the remains of a cross-shaft found in excavations.[90] The most remarkable feature here is, however, the way the parish boundary of St Peter's follows exactly the curving line of the enclosure. While doubt has been expressed about the ability of this monastery to survive the initial Viking onslaught in Dublin, the fact that the site remained crossland into the colonial period, and that the border of these lands agrees with the line of the putative early enclosure there, is quite remarkable. I suggest that this essentially indicates that a portion, at least, of the pre-Invasion church lands of this estate descend directly from the lands of the monastery or church of Duiblinn, a tenure that must have survived, in some form, the early Viking period in Dublin, and that the church of St Peter is built directly upon the site of this early church, whose existence throughout the period 800–1170 in some form or shape, if even intermittently, is thus certain. While the objection may be raised that the annals fall silent about Duiblinn after 790, a counter-argument can be made that the same silence affected the churches of Finglas and Glasnevin, also quite near to Viking Dublin, yet these churches also formed part of the pre- and post-Invasion estate of the see of Dublin, and their continued existence throughout the Viking period is not disputed. Given the obvious importance of Duiblinn, it is likely that the bulk of the lands of the St Sepulchre estate derive from its temporalities, and probably date to the pre-Viking period.

The final church here is St Kevin's, but this was a post-Invasion grant, along with its carucate of land, in 1185. This church clearly belonged to Glendalough, and was certainly a pre-Invasion foundation, perhaps even dating to the early tenth century, if we allow the possibility of a missionary effort being made from Glendalough to the still-pagan Ostmen.[91]

Dublin VII (Dublin, 2006), pp 89–102 at pp 97–102.   **88** Clarke, 'Conversion, church and cathedral', p. 45; MacShamhráin, 'The *Monasticon Hibernicum* project', p. 136.   **89** *AFM* 650.6=656; *AU* 790.2.   **90** MacShamhráin, 'The *Monasticon Hibernicum* project', p. 136. **91** As suggested to me by Donnchadh Ó Corráin.

Finglas

Annalistic references to this church span the period 763 to 867, and refer to several bishops and abbots. Among these was Abbot Duibliter, who died in 796, and who is commemorated in all three main martyrologies, when of 'Finglas Cainnig beside Dublin', a reference that indicates that the church was then dedicated to Cainnech of Aghaboe, an early saint with dedications throughout Ireland. This name-form occurs in several sources.[92] The Martyrology of Tallaght includes a number of other memorials of Finglas saints, including two of its abbots, and all of this suggests an early foundation there.[93] Of the three other churches on the estate of Finglas, two – Kilshane and Kilreesk – each occupy one of the two northern outliers of the parish, while both are *cell* toponyms, suggesting that these were pre-Invasion chapels of ease. That parish and ecclesiastical estate correspond in Finglas indicates that the parish was erected upon the estate, and Finglas is described as a mother-church early in the thirteenth century, when Artane was a member.[94] Interestingly, Artane was considered a detached part of Finglas parish in the seventeenth century, and yet does not appear to have been crossland. The ecclesiastical family there, Uí Dímai Lecerda, were of Uí Failgi, whose lands had, in the sixth century, extended much further northwards than later, and this suggests that this church may have been in existence in the sixth century.[95]

Swords

First mentioned in the annals as Sord 'of Colum Cille' in 994, regular references to this church continue until 1166. Most of these references are to *airchinnig*; there is just one to a bishop.[96] The twelfth-century Irish Life of Colum Cille makes him founder of Swords, but this is highly unlikely, while the church is mentioned in the ninth-century *Bethú Brigte* in a context that suggests it was then a Brigidine church.[97] The contemporary Martyrology of Tallaght makes no mention of this connection: it makes Finán the Leper the patron of Swords, and both sources attest to the importance of this church in the early ninth century, which is confirmed by annal material in *Cogadh Gáedhel re Gallaibh* recording Viking raids on Swords in the 830s and 840s.[98] Finán is given a Ciannachta pedigree, and this suggests that Swords may date back to the period when much of north Co. Dublin was part of the overkingdom of Ciannachta Breg, a situation that ceased during the seventh

92 *AU* 796.1; R.I. Best and H.J. Lawlor (eds), *The martyrology of Tallaght* (London, 1931); Whitley Stokes (ed.), *Félire Óengusso céli Dé; the martyrology of Oengus the culdee* (London, 1905), and idem (ed. and trans.), *Félire hÚi Gormáin: the Martyrology of Gorman* (London, 1895), all under 15 May; J.H. Todd (ed. and trans.), *Cogadh Gaedhil re Gallaibh: the war of the Gaeidhil with the Gaill* (London, 1867), p. 19; *AFM* 786.2. **93** Mart.T, 21 and 27 Jan., 24 Sept. **94** *Alen*, p. 33. **95** MacShamhráin, *Glendalough*, pp 48, 56. **96** *AFM* 1023.1. **97** Máire Herbert, *Iona, Kells and Derry: the history and hagiography of the monastic familia of Columba* (Oxford, 1988), pp 234, 281, n. 357, 282, nn 371–6. **98** Mart.T, 16 Mar.; Todd

century. The local rulers there, Uí Chormaic of Túath Tuirbhi, were also of Ciannachta stock.[99] In the later period, Swords lay securely within the Norse kingdom of Dublin, while its personnel show both local and Columban associations. This triple-stage history, in addition to its large estate, suggests that this church was both significant and ancient. The Brigidine associations in particular may date to the sixth-century period of Brigidine influence north of the Liffey.[1] At least two minor churches existed on the estate. The exact location of Tech Ingen Baíti, a female house, is unknown, while Glas Mór (Mooretown) is associated with Crónán mac Melláin in the early martyrologies.[2] Once again, the parish there seems to be based on the ecclesiastical estate.

Lusk

This church is recorded regularly in the annals between 616 and 1133, with retrospective obits of its founder, Mac-Cuilin, being given in the 490s.[3] An early tradition gives his real name as Cunnid, which, like the name of Bishop Petrán (d. 616), is British.[4] This suggests that this church may be early indeed, and be associated with British missionaries of the sixth century, if not even earlier. The Martyrology of Tallaght describes Mac-Cuilin as a bishop, again emphasizing his possible missionary status, while he is given a Ciannachta pedigree in line with the kinship of the locals in Lusk.[5] These comprised the *túath* of Uí Cholgáin, and they feature regularly among the ecclesiastical personnel of Lusk from the late seventh century until the mid-eleventh. Indeed, it would appear that the area of this *túath* was coterminous with that of the church estate of Lusk.[6] Among these was Odar Ua Muiredaig, *airchinnech* of Lusk and *taísech* of Uí Cholgáin (d. 1055).[7] The eponym here appears to be Abbot Colgú mac Maenach (d. 702), who occurs as a witness to Cáin Adamnáin *c*.697.[8] The last *airchinnech* of this family recorded there was Odar's son, Aneslis mac Uidhir (d. 1059), who was probably eponym of the later McWether tenants of Ballymaguire in Lusk, who can be found there into the 1320s.[9] The townland of Regles besides Lusk itself derives from *reiclés*, a word

(ed.), *Cogadh*, p. 19.   **99** Donnchadh Ó Corráin, 'The early Irish churches: some aspects of organisation' in idem (ed.), *Irish antiquity: essays and studies presented to Professor M.J. O'Kelly* (Cork, 1981), pp 327–41 at p. 328; *The Book of Leinster*, ed. R.I. Best et al. (6 vols, Dublin, 1954–83), 350c 56; Paul Walsh, 'Meath in the Book of Rights' in John Ryan (ed.) *Féilsgríbhinn Eoin Mhic Néill* (Dublin, 1940), pp 508–21 at p. 520.   **1** For Swords *within* Dublin, see *AU* 993.3, 995.2. For the cult of Brigit, see MacShamhráin, *Glendalough*, pp 68–9.   **2** Idem, 'The *Monasticon Hibernicum* project', p. 141.   **3** For earliest and latest, see *AU* 616.1 and *ATig.* 1133.8. For Mac-Cuilin see *AU* 496.2, 498.4; *CS* 493; *ATig.* 496.1.   **4** MacShamhráin, 'The *Monasticon Hibernicum* project', p. 131.   **5** Mart.T., 6 Sept.; *Book of Leinster*, 352g.   **6** See my forthcoming *Medieval Ireland: the lands of the Church*.   **7** For a pedigree table of Uí Cholgáin, see Kathleen Hughes, *The church in early Irish society* (New York, 1966), p. 162, and for additions to this table, see *AU* 702.4, 1055.2, 1059.7; *AFM* 1055.7.   **8** Máirín Ní Dhonnchadha, 'The guarantor list of Cáin Adamnáin, 697', *Peritia*, 1 (1982), 178–215 at 180.   **9** *Alen*, pp 104, 177.

that can denote a subsidiary ecclesiastical enclosure within a larger one and is a term that also bears eremitical associations.[10] This may be the female *reiclés* mentioned at Lusk *c.*1150.[11] Lusk appears to have had another female house attached, Cell Lusca.[12]

Rush (Ros Éo)

This church was in existence as early as 721, when the Annals of Tigernach record the death of its patron, Cuanna. He is the virgin, Cuanna, 'in Mag Locha in Brega or in Ros Éo' of the Martyrology of Tallaght, given a Cenél nÉnda pedigree in the Martyrology of Óengus. This church must early have come under the rulership of Lusk.[13]

Portraine (Rechra)

The church of Port Rechrann is named from the harbour of Rechru island, alias Lambay, and the island and mainland estate formed an ecclesiastical unit. Here we have a rare accurate foundation date, for this Columban church was founded in 635 by Ségéne, abbot of Iona.[14] This data comes in an annal, unlike the alleged foundation of the island monastery by Colum Cille according to his twelfth-century Life.[15] The church is noted in the annals a number of times between 635 and 1038, but seems to have suffered from much plundering towards the end of this period, which may have resulted in the church going into decline, and may also account for the Norse name for the island, Lambay.[16] It was donated to the see of Dublin – apparently before Kells-Mellifont – by one of the Meic Duib family, elsewhere associated with Swords, and these were probably a clerical family.[17]

Ireland's Eye (Inis mac Nessáin)

The Martyrology of Óengus records the dedication of this church to the three sons of Nessán, although by the time of the Martyrology of Gorman this memory had become corrupt.[18] This island was part of the archbishop's estate.

Clonmethan

Glen Medóin does not occur in the annals but may be found in the martyrologies, where its patron is given as Lassar, a virgin. She is probably the Cenél Lóegaire saint of that name who is genealogically placed in the sixth century.[19] There is no other secure church identification on these lands, and this modest church has a surprisingly large estate. This probably reflects its

---

10 Colmán Etchingham, *Church organisation in Ireland, AD650 to 1000* (Maynooth 1999), p. 344 and n.   11 Flanagan, *Irish royal charters*, pp 383–4.   12 MacShamhráin, 'The *Monasticon Hibernicum* project', p. 130.   13 *ATig.* 721.4.   14 *AU* 635.3.   15 Herbert, *Iona, Kells and Derry*, p. 234 (and cf. pp 42, 74).   16 *AU* 975.3; *ATig.* 1038.1.   17 Bhreathnach, 'Colomban churches', 12–14. I do not understand Clarke here ('Conversion, church and cathedral', p. 35).   18 Mart.O; Mart.G, 15 Mar.   19 Mart.T;

erstwhile status as the mother-church of the Uí Chathasaig kingdom of Saithne.[20]

Tallaght

This church was founded in 769 by the Céle Dé ecclesiastic, Máelruain.[21] There is no reason to doubt the genealogical record that names Cellach mac Dúnchada, king of Uí Dúnchada (d. 776), as the donor of Tallaght to Máelruain.[22] The site was possibly a greenfield one: *tamlacht* is a term for plague burial sites. The Tallaght estate was large, and was possibly further enlarged by a grant made by a later king of Uí Dúnchada during the middle of the twelfth century, Muirchertach (Óc) Mac Gilla Mo-Cholmóc.[23] The monastery of Tallaght became the centre of the Celi Dé 'movement' and was a very important house as such. Its scriptorium produced the famous Martyrology of Tallaght, and this volume contains entries concerning a number of early clerics of Tallaght.[24] Annalistic references continue to occur until 1125, and Tallaght shared personnel with a number of other churches, such as Ferns, Glendalough and Bec Éire.[25] In this case, the crosslands do not contain the entire parish but are located in two main discrete parcels around Tallaght itself and in the southern, upland portion of the parish. This southern portion contains Kill Saint-Ann (townland Glassamucky), that is, Cell Epscoip Sanctáin, a church that occurs in the martyrologies as that of Bishop Sanctán, who is also associated with Templeusk near Arklow, and is thus at least as old as the eighth century. The genealogies make Sanctán a Welsh saint, suggesting an early date for this foundation.[26] This southern portion must originally have been the estate of this church, later absorbed by Tallaght.

The church of Templeogue (Tech Mo-Lóce) originally belonged to Glendalough, coming to Dublin after the union of dioceses.[27] The Leinster saints' genealogies note 'Mo-Lóce of Tig Mo-Lóca' in Uí Chellaig Cualann, and this is perhaps the Cloyne saint, Mo-Lóca of Templemolaga, Co. Cork (see also under Killiney, below).

Two further early churches are found in this parish but they are not associated with later crossland. Kilnamanagh appears to be the Cell Manach Escrach associated with Lochán and Énna in the Leinster saints' genealogies, while Kilininny is the Cell na nIngen of the Martyrology of Óengus, dedicated to 'Iar's four [named] daughters'.[28] These churches do not occur in Gorman,

Mart.G, 18 Feb.; Pádraig Ó Riain, *A dictionary of Irish saints* (Dublin, 2011), p. 70. **20** See my forthcoming *Medieval Ireland: the lands of the Church*. **21** *AFM* 769.13. **22** J.T. Gilbert, *A history of the city of Dublin*, i (repr. Dublin, 1978), pp 404–5. **23** Gilbert, *History of Dublin*, p. 407; Kenneth Nicholls, 'The land of the Leinstermen', *Peritia*, 3 (1984), 535–8 at 537. **24** Mart.T, 5, 21 Jan., 25 Feb., 7 July, 10 Aug. **25** *AU* 868.3, 937.5, 964.4. **26** Mart.O; Mart.T, 9 May; MacShamhráin, 'The *Monasticon Hibernicum* project', p. 131. **27** *Alen*, p. 2. **28** Edel Bhreathnach, 'The genealogies of Leinster as a source for local cults' in John Carey et al. (eds), *Studies in Irish hagiography: saints and scholars*

and may have been churches 'in decay' that had become secularized by the twelfth century. In this context, it is interesting to note the references to Kilnamanagh in the Life of Eógan of Ardstraw (Co. Tyrone) suggesting it to have been part of the *paruchia* of Ardstraw. The genealogies give Eógan an Uí Bairrche and thus Laigin filiation, suggesting that this Ardstraw–Kilnamanagh connection pre-dates the rise of Uí Dúnlainge there. Kim McCone dates this Life to the eighth century.[29]

Rathcoole

The church of Rathcoole and its estate must be of pre-Invasion date, given its dedication to Brigit.[30] There are no pre-Invasion references, when it may have been subject to Clondalkin.

Clondalkin

Once again, there is close correlation between parish and crosslands, though it is not exact in this case. The church of Cluain Dolcáin occurs in the annals between 781 and 1086, and survived the erection of a Norse raiding fortress adjacent to it in 867.[31] The martyrologies name the patron as Crónán mac Lugadach alias Mo-Chua, who is given an Uí Chétig pedigree and thus was a local saint.[32] His relics, alone with those of Coémgen (Kevin) of Glendalough, were taken on tour in 790, when the saint's name is given as Mochua moccu Lugedon.[33] This reference suggests that Clondalkin was already then allied with Glendalough, if not even part of its *paruchia*, while the usage of the obsolete 'moccu' suggests that this saint may be of sixth-century provenance. The Martyrology of Gorman's reference to 'populous Cluain Dolcáin' suggests that the church was fully operational in the late 1160s.[34] Hereditary descent of the abbacy is shown. The first abbot, Ailbran mac Lugaid (d. 781), was father or uncle to Abbot Fedelmid Ua Lugaid (d. 801), and these men may perhaps have been of the founder's stock.[35] Abbot Cathal mac Cormaic (d. 879) was father to abbot Rónán (d. 885), in turn probably ancestor to the *airchinnech* Fiachna Ua Rónáin (d. 1086). The Uí Rónáin were also associated with Glendalough, and possibly with Saggart, though this may be erroneous. They seem to have remained as tenants in Clondalkin and Tallaght into the thirteenth century, and also at Ballyronan on the crosslands of Kilcoole in Wicklow.[36]

(Dublin, 2001), pp 250–67 at p. 258.   **29** Kim McCone, 'Clones and her neighbours in the early period: hints from some Airgiallian saints' Lives', *Clogher Record*, 11 (1984), 305–25 at 319–20.   **30** MacShamhráin, 'The *Monasticon Hibernicum* project', p. 139.   **31** *AU* and *AFM*.   **32** Mart.T; Mart.O, 6 Aug.; *Book of Leinster*, 351d 21, 373b 44.   **33** *AU* 790.5. **34** Mart.G, 6 Aug.   **35** *AU* 781.3, 801.1.   **36** *AU* 879.4, 885.4, 1086.2; MacShamhráin, *Glendalough*, pp 152, 166n; Doherty, 'Clondalkin', pp 185–7; I think the reference to Tech Mo-Shacru in the Uí Bairrche genealogies refers to Tomhaggard, Co. Wexford, and not to Saggart, Co. Dublin (where the adjacent Banba is modern Bannow, Co. Wexford): see my *Medieval Ireland*, p. 251.

Clondalkin was a mother-church in the early thirteenth century: Rathcoole was among its dependant chapels.[37]

Shankill and Dalkey

Senchill ('the old church') is associated with Berchán, a local Dál Messin Corb saint with Glendalough associations.[38] Its name may derive from its abandonment and the building of a new church at Rathmichael nearby, where there are some significant cross-slabs and a round-tower base (yet Rathmichael is a pre-Romanesque ruin).[39] The existence of a church at Dalkey (Deilg-inis) is implied in an annal of 940.[40] The name itself relates to Dalkey Island, while a second church, the later parish church, and bearing the same name, lies on the mainland. Both sites have significant early archaeology, that on the island dating from perhaps as early as the eighth century. There are two dedications, to the Dál Messin Corb saint Beccnat ingen Colmáin and to Senán mac Midrán.[41] Another church there is the Kiltuck of the post-Invasion records (in Shanganagh).[42] Its cemetery had a pre-Invasion cross.

Glenn Muniri (Ballyman)

The martyrologies record this church and its patron, Sillán, both church and saint having Glendalough associations.[43]

Glasnevin

The church of Glas Noíden features in the martyrologies with its patron Mobí alias Berchán, a saint of the Corcu Fir Trí of Luigne Connacht, whose obituary is given under the year 541.[44] It was purchased by Christ Church in the pre-Invasion period, and its continued importance is indicated by its mention in the late twelfth-century Latin Life of Coémgen of Glendalough.[45] The dedication here suggests that this was an early foundation. Another possible dedication to the same saint occurs in Donnybrook, where there are vague traditions of a holy well dedicated to Mobí.[46]

Grangegorman (Cell Dúilich) and St Doolagh's

This church and estate was granted to Christ Church upon the latter's foundation by King Sitriuc of Dublin c.1030.[47] Nothing is known of its earlier

---

37 N.B. White (ed.), 'The *Reportorium Viride* of John Alen, archbishop of Dublin', *Analecta Hibernica*, 10 (1941), 171–222 at 188.   38 MacShamhráin, 'The *Monasticon Hibernicum* project', p. 122; Bhreathnach, 'genealogies of Leinster', 258; Ó Riain, *Dictionary*, p. 99. 39 Ó Riain, *Dictionary*, pp 122–3; Tomás Ó Carragáin, *Churches in early medieval Ireland* (New Haven, CT, 2010), p. 241.   40 *CS* 940.   41 MacShamhráin, 'The *Monasticon Hibernicum* project', pp 130, 136; Mart.G, 5 Dec.; Ó Riain, *Dictionary*, p. 94.   42 MacShamhráin, 'The *Monasticon Hibernicum* project', pp 122, 137.   43 Mart.T; Mart.G, 21 July.   44 See my forthcoming *Medieval Ireland: the lands of the Church*.   45 *Alen*, p. 28; MacShamhráin, 'The *Monasticon Hibernicum* project', p. 120.   46 See 'Donnybrook' at http://monasticon.celt.dias.ie.   47 *Alen*, p. 28.

history. A second church associated with Dúilech is Clochar Dúilich (St Doolagh's, Balgriffin parish), whose church ruin has Romanesque features. This church was listed among the cathedral lands in 1179 but was subsequently lost. Church and saint occur in the Martyrology of Óengus, and the cult is mentioned in *Cáin Adamnáin*, and hence is at least of seventh-century date. The genealogical filiation of the saint, with the distant Conmaicne of Connacht, may indicate significant antiquity for this cult.[48]

Clonkeen, Tully and Killiney

These three lie in proximity and formed part of a single manor under the colony. The church of Cluain Caín (the modern Kill o' the Grange) with its lands was donated to Christ Church by Donnchad mac Domnaill Remair *c.*1088. Its earlier history is obscure; it bears a medieval dedication to a native saint, Fintan. Its importance is indicated, however, by its mention in twelfth-century hagiography.[49]

The church of Tully (in modern Laughanstown) was earlier the important church of Tulach na nEpscop, with its 'seven holy bishops' of the Litany, who are also mentioned in a twelfth-century(?) Irish Life of Brigit (when the seven holy bishops of T. 'came out of Uí Briúin Cualann to Kildare', perhaps indicating that Tully was the seat of the bishopric of Uí Briúin Cualann).[50] The Brigidine connection is again mentioned in a gloss in 'Óengus', and this suggests an early association, perhaps dating from the eighth century, when the power of Kildare and the *paruchia* of Brigit were benefitting from support from the expanding Uí Dúnchada in northern Laigin.[51] Tully was donated to Christ Church by one of the Mac Turcaill Ostman family of Dublin, perhaps before the end of the eleventh century.[52]

Killiney (Cell Ingen Léinín) commemorates the daughters of Léinín and thus sisters of Colmán, patron of the diocese of Cloyne, who flourished during the second half of the sixth century.[53] This cult was well-established there when the Martyrology of Tallaght was composed, and may be part of a pattern of churches in the south Dublin area bearing dedications to Munster saints, reflecting a pattern of population linkage between Munster and this area that appears to be of sixth-century provenance.[54]

A number of grants to Christ Church were made of places now difficult of identification, mostly by Ostmen and apparently in the decades before the Invasion. Among these are places such as Drommin and Tirodran, which

48 Ibid., p. 3; Mart.O, 17 Nov.; Ó Riain, *Dictionary*, p. 276. **49** *Alen*, p. 28; MacShamhráin, 'The *Monasticon Hibernicum* project', pp 120, 136. **50** Whitley Stokes, *Lives of saints from the Book of Lismore* (2 vols, Oxford, 1890), i, p. 50; C. Plummer (ed. and trans.), *Irish Litanies* (London, 1925), p. 66. **51** Mart.O, p. 65; MacShamhráin, *Glendalough*, pp 72, 133–4. **52** *Alen*, p. 28. **53** Paul MacCotter, *Colmán of Cloyne: a study* (Dublin, 2004), pp 18, 29–30, 32, 63, 65. **54** MacShamhráin, *Glendalough*, p. 121; MacCotter, *Colmán*, pp 29–30.

clearly lay in or around Clonkeen and its hinterland. Another was of lands in Ballyogan, which now probably lie in Murphystown in Clonkeen.[55]

Kinsaley, Killester and Drumcondra
Although granted to the cathedral by Strongbow, the church of Cenn Sáile occurs in the Martyrology of Tallaght with its patron, Garbán, and is mentioned in the twelfth-century Latin Life of Coémgen, all of which suggests that this was church land before the Invasion and the re-grant may merely have been part of a dispute settlement.[56] Details of this saint's cult are confused; he may have been of the local Uí Chéthig.[57] Nothing certain is known of Killester, while Drumcondra appears to have been an estate without a church.

Inis Pátraic (Holmpatrick)
Tírechán, writing *c.*670, states that this island was the original arrival point of Patrick in Ireland, from which we may take its existence as a Patrician church when he was writing. In 798 it was burned by the Vikings and the shrine of St Do-Chonna was carried off. Do-Chonna may have been a British saint, which might indicate an early date for this foundation, but may also be identified with an historical abbot of Glendalough who died in the late seventh century (see under 'Kilmacanoge', below). A major synod was held on the island in 1148 under St Malachy, and it may already have been an Augustinian foundation at that time.[58] The inclusion of a detached portion of Lusk parish in the centre of the lands of Holmpatrick may indicate an earlier relationship with the church of Lusk. We may see both Inis Pátraic and Ballyboghil (below) as discrete parts of the *paruchia* of Armagh in Dublin down to the twelfth century.

Ballyboghil
This place derives from Baile Bachaill, the estate of the staff (of St Patrick, the *Bachall Ísu*), a relic venerated there in the twelfth century.[59] The pre-Invasion history of this Patrician church is obscure. It was certainly in the possession of Archbishop Cellach of Armagh (d. 1129). In 1113 Cellach brokered a peace at Greenoge on the Dublin–Meath border with the staff, and it has been suggested that the Ballyboghil estate was gifted to him by Bishop Samuel of Dublin (d. 1121).[60] Such a donation is rather unlikely, however, as bishops at

---

55 *Alen*, pp 7, 13, 28; Otway-Ruthven, 'Church lands', p. 60; Clarke, 'Conversion, church and cathedral', p. 36.   **56** Otway-Ruthven, 'Church lands', p. 60; Mart.T; Mart.G, 9 July; MacShamhráin, 'The *Monasticon Hibernicum* project', p. 120.   **57** Ó Riain, *Dictionary*, pp 362–3.   **58** Whitley Stokes (ed. and trans.), *The tripartite Life of Patrick* (2 vols, London, 1887), vol. 2, p. 34; *AFM* 793.7; *CS* 1148; MacShamhráin, 'The *Monasticon Hibernicum* project', pp 119–21, 131; Gwynn and Hadcock, *Medieval religious houses*, p. 193.   **59** White, '*Reportorium Viride*', 195; Otway-Ruthven, 'Church lands', p. 64; MacCotter, *Medieval Ireland*, pp 74, 85.   **60** *AU* 1113.8; Colmcille Ó Conbhuí, 'The lands of Saint Mary's

this time were not noted for giving away chunks of their estates. In any case, as we have seen, Ballyboghil appears to have lain outside of the kingdom of Dublin until the late 1140s at the earliest. It is quite likely that this estate belonged to Armagh before 1113. We should note the obituary of Tuathal mac Óenacáin, scribe and bishop of Lusk and Duleek, and '*maor* of Patrick's *muinntir* south of the mountain', in 929 (AU). Ballyboghil adjoins the parish of Lusk to the west, and this Patrician linkage between Armagh and Lusk may well explain the origins of Ballyboghil, which may originally have been part of Lusk. Indeed, Ballyboghil may have been in Armagh custody as early as 789, when the staff was 'dishonoured' by the Clann Cholmáin king, Donnchad mac Domnaill, at an *óenach* at Ráith Airthir in Mide, to which it must have been brought (from Ballyboghil?) to give protection to those attending.[61] Was Ballyboghil one of the unidentified Patrician foundations located in Brega mentioned in the seventh-century Patrician literature? The original church site there may have lain in modern Brownstown, earlier Techkelsi, apparently from **Tech Cellaigh*, perhaps from Cellach above.

Kilmainham

Cell Maighnenn was in existence by 787 and its eponym occurs in all three martyrologies, incidentally indicating its continued existence as a church as late as the 1160s. It was 'plundered' in 1013.[62] The saints' genealogies make Maigniu the son of a historic king of a branch of the Airgialla who died in 610, and this association, along with the existence of another Kilmainham in Meath and the location on Brega's original border of the Dublin Kilmainham, suggest that these were actual seventh-century foundations.[63]

Modern Wicklow 'east of the mountains'

Stagonnil derives from Tech Ua Conaill, whose saint is recorded in Óengus as Beccán, glossed as he of Kilpeacon in Munster. This Munster saint was a historical personage, a witness to *Cáin Adomnáin c.*697.[64] The name suggests that this was a kinship or *túath* church. Three other churches occur as crossland in this area. Cell Chrithaich in Tonygarrow has an early enclosure but no corresponding documentary evidence.[65] Cell Adgair (Killegar), while not mentioned in the martyrologies, bears a genealogical dedication to Finbarr, a local (Dál Messin Corb) saint, and the site has significant archaeology,

Abbey, Dublin', *PRIA*, 62C (1962), 21–86 at 36–7; Gilbert, *Reg. St Mary's*, ii, pp 141–2. For the incorrect claim that Ballyboghil belonged originally to Dublin, see M.V. Ronan, 'Saint Patrick's staff and Christ Church' in H.B. Clarke (ed.), *Medieval Dublin: the living city* (Dublin, 1990), pp 123–34. **61** *AU* 789.18. **62** *AU* 787.1, 1013.7; Mart.T., 9 Oct., 18 Dec. 18; Mart.O., and Mart.G, 18 Dec. **63** Ó Riain, *Dictionary*, pp 424–5. **64** Mart.O, May 26; Kenneth Nicholls, 'A charter of John, lord of Ireland', *Peritia*, 2 (1983), 267–76 at 271–2. **65** Price, *Place-names*, pp 302–3; Archaeological Survey of Ireland, SMR no. WI007-002.

including some eleventh-century slabs, and is enclosed.[66] Finally, Stamolin (now Kilmalin) bears a dedication to Moling of St Mullins in Carlow, so must also have been an early site.[67]

Kilmacanoge (Cell Mo-Channóc) has left little beyond its dedication, Mo-Channóc (or Mo-Chonnóc) being a local saint, of Dál Messin Corb filiation. Another source makes him a brother to Mo-Gorróc of Delgany and claims both to have been British saints. Yet Mo-Channóc appears to have been an historical figure, an abbot of Glendalough who died in 687. Reference to 'Deircne of Mo-Gorróc' occurs in the Martyrology of Tallaght.[68]

Kilcoole is Cell Comgaill, apparently dedicated to Comgall of Bangor, but there are no early references.[69] Among its lands was Ballyronan, suggesting a link with the powerful Uí Rónáin clerical family of Glendalough, Clondalkin etc. In the early thirteenth century, it was a mother-church with the dependant chapels of Kilfernoc, Kilpedder and others.[70]

Killickabawn derives from Cell Moccu Birn, who were a *forsloine* of Osraige origin, as their name indicates. Both the genealogical context and the usage of *moccu* indicate a pre-600 origin for this church, and this is echoed in the Martyrology of Tallaght's treatment of its saint, Ném moccu Birn, said to have visited Énda in Aran and to have been a brother to Ciarán of Seir.[71]

Killadreenan is the Cell Achaid Draignige of the Book of Leinster, when associated with Fedelm and Bishop Daurthech, who have Brigidine associations.[72]

Modern Wicklow 'west of the mountains'
The bulk of the places mentioned in the early Glendalough charters and confirmations there appear to be landed property or estates without a church on site rather than *termon*-lands surrounding a particular church foundation. The bulk of the places mentioned bear the prefixes *baile*, *ráith* etc. Furthermore, there is a regrettable tendency among scholars to suggest possible identifications that then, in the course of time, take on the mantle of certitude. In this context, we may note several churches. Dunboyke is tentatively identified with the Cluain Duach of the Latin Life of Coémgen by Price, yet the *Monasticon Hibernicum* website treats this identification as a certainty.[73] Again, Ailbhe MacShamhráin makes a tentative identification of Church Mountain in Ballymoony (Donard parish) with the church of Inis Ulad mentioned in the annals in 951 and the *Borúma* saga, and associated with one Mo-Chritóc in the hagiographical material.[74] Yet again this identification is

66 Ibid., WI003-028004; MacShamhráin, *Glendalough*, pp 182, 195; Bhreathnach, 'Genealogies of Leinster', 258.   67 Price, *Place-names*, p. 291.   68 MacShamhráin, *Glendalough*, pp 113, 124; Mart.T, 23 Dec.   69 *Alen*, p. 3.   70 White, '*Reportorium Viride*', 203.   71 Mart.T, 14 June; MacShamhráin, *Glendalough*, p. 57.   72 *Book of Leinster*, 353c 61; Price, *Place-names*, p. 394.   73 Price, *Place-names*, p. 208; see http://monasticon. celt.dias.ie.   74 MacShamhráin, *Glendalough*, pp 87, 109, 188, 193, 195, 213.

treated as a certainty by the *Monasticon*. Both identifications are, at best, rather speculative.

A number of early churches can be identified on these lands. The only significant church in this entire area of whose identification we can be certain is Domnach Imlech (Burgage), associated with Mo-Lumma in the *Notulae* of the Book of Armagh and in the Martyrologies of Tallaght and Gorman.[75] This is the saint, Lomán of Trim, said in the early Patrician material to be of British origin, and hence illustrating significant antiquity of cult. This association must also account for the dedication of Kilmalum, near Burgage. This church thus has Patrician associations, as well as significant archaeological remains.[76] May we speculate that it was a major foundation and probably possessed the various church lands adjoining Burgage, such as those of Ballymore and in northern Boystown parish?

Cell Bélat (Kilbaylet) occurs in the *Borúma* saga and so may have been in existence by *c*.1100 or earlier.[77] The other churches in Cell/Cill there must again be of pre-Invasion origins, but little is known of them. The etymology of Kilcoagh is uncertain. Kilbodan clearly derives from Cell Báetáin, the saint having a possible identification with one of Coémgen's kindred, and lies within an early ecclesiastical enclosure.[78] The 'Cellugarcon' of the early lists (Kilbeg in Boystown) is tentatively derived by MacShamhráin from Cell Ua nGarrchon and thus associated with St Áedán Ua nGarrchon of the lists of saints.[79] This again has become fully accepted on the *Monasticon* website. I would rather suggest an etymology Cell Uí Garrchon and suggest that this was a *túath* church of a branch of Uí Garrchon who remained west of the mountains when their fellows migrated eastwards. It has early archaeology.[80]

Ballymore Eustace, while appearing to be a late foundation when scrutinized by several diagnostic measures, has a high-cross that, at the least, shows it to have been a significant pre-Invasion church.

Finally, we should note the church of Hollywood, which bears an alias showing that Coémgen was its patron, while the name itself, deriving from 'holy wood' (*Sanctum Nemus*), may derive from a passage in the Irish Lives of the saint.[81] These references suggest that this was originally a church of some importance here: can we again speculate that this was therefore a senior church possessing many of the estates surrounding it, such as Donard, Dunlavin etc.? None of these others appear to bear dedications to St Coémgen.

75 Price, *Place-names*, pp 250–2 and the sources there quoted.   **76** Ó Riain, *Dictionary*, p. 401; Eoin Grogan and Annaba Kilfeather (comp.), *Archaeological inventory of County Wicklow* (Dublin, 1997), p. 154.   **77** Ibid., pp 191–2.   **78** MacShamhráin, *Glendalough*, pp 118, 196.   **79** MacShamhráin, *Glendalough*, p. 196; *Book of Leinster*, 366e33.   **80** MacCotter, *Medieval Ireland*, p. 172.   **81** Price, *Place-names*, pp 207, 215–16.

Mormaors, mayors and merchants: the early development of municipal government in Dublin[1]

NIALL Ó SÚILLEABHÁIN

In certain respects, high-medieval Dublin is a city that is surprisingly well covered by the surviving sources, relative to some other medieval cities in Britain and on the Continent. What is more surprising is how little these sources have been utilized by historians of the city in order to reconstruct the day-to-day structures of the early municipal government of the city and their development from the eleventh century onwards. This essay will provide a basic outline of the early development and characteristics of the medieval municipal government in the hope of laying the foundations for further research into this important aspect of Ireland's medieval urban history.

In order to understand properly the development of municipal government in Dublin, it is necessary to devote some attention to the governance of the city in the period prior to the English invasion and conquest. The older view that the arrival of the English meant the city starting with a clean slate 'as the old inhabitants were compelled to settle outside the walls in what became known as Oxmantown' is no longer credible, as there is ample evidence that, although outside the walls, there was no jurisdictional or legal separation between Oxmantown and Dublin proper.[2] Irishmen and Ostmen were not excluded from the city or its citizen body: James Lydon has made a convincing argument that a municipal administration had developed before the arrival of the English,[3] based on the city's ability to organize the construction of defences, the ability to raise taxes on property and the existence of burgage plots (albeit probably in the general rather than technical sense of the word 'burgage').[4]

This raises questions about the actual structures of this municipal organization in pre-conquest Dublin. Most scholars see it as centred on the

1 This essay is a revised version of an essay submitted for Seán Duffy's Sophister special subject 'Medieval Dublin' at Trinity College Dublin in Hilary Term 2012. The analysis of the sources presented is neither systematic nor exhaustive, and should not be interpreted as such. It claims only to be a preliminary overview of the subject, in the hope of inspiring further research in the area. I would like to thank Prof. Duffy for allowing me the opportunity to publish this piece.   2 R. Dudley Edwards, 'The beginnings of municipal government in Dublin' in Howard Clarke (ed.), *Medieval Dublin: the living city* (Dublin, 1990), p. 145. The city's boundaries as defined in John's charter of 1192 include Oxmantown: *Calendar of ancient records of Dublin, in the possession of the municipal corporation of that city*, 1, ed. J.T. Gilbert (Dublin, 1889), pp 2–3 (hereafter *CARD*). 3 James Lydon, 'Dublin in transition: from Ostman town to English borough' in Seán Duffy (ed.), *Medieval Dublin II* (Dublin, 2001), pp 128–41.   4 Ibid., pp 137–41.

Þing, or assembly, which is mentioned by Giraldus Cambrensis.[5] The assembly place for the Dublin *Þing*, the 'Thingmoot' was to the east of the city walls, in what is now the Dame Street/College Green area.[6] It was such a major focus of power and authority in the city that it even affected Henry II's choice of residence in Dublin during the winter of 1171–2.[7] There is little doubt that pre-conquest Dublin possessed a *Þing*, but its function and workings remain a mystery. The idea of an assembly of free men, where each had a voice and a vote to administer justice or legislate, in a primitive precursor to democracy, as presented in some texts, has little support in the evidence and is unlikely to be realistic.[8] The most detailed descriptions of a Scandinavian *Þing* are found in the thirteenth-century Icelandic sagas, and these show assemblies dominated by kings, jarls, judges and lawmen, all clearly powerful community leaders. The leaders pronounce their verdict or edict to the assembly, who give consent by raising or clashing their weapons. The presence of the king or jarl's armed retainers (*hirð*) at the *Þing* makes one wonder how much choice the assembly truly had in giving their consent.[9]

Although some scholars are inclined to dismiss out of hand any information drawn from the often colourful stories of the *Þing* from the Icelandic sagas, if specific instances are not used to try to reconstruct political history but rather broad trends used to construct social and institutional history, many of the pitfalls associated with backwards extrapolation can be avoided.[10] It should be borne in mind that most of the sagas were committed to writing at a time when living memory would have existed of the last days of the Dublin *Þing*, so that a model of such a phenomenon as an assembly for the confirmation and dissemination of decisions, rather than a decision-making assembly in and of itself, based on saga sources, is an acceptable hypothesis. Lending support to this model is the known existence of similar assemblies held by contemporary rulers, in particular the kings of England, in order to legitimize and communicate decisions.[11]

It is apparent that Dublin's government changed quite dramatically as the city declined from a political power in its own right to a political prize and asset fought over by Irish provincial kings.[12] The near-constant domination of

5 Ibid., p. 137.   **6** Seán Duffy, 'A reconsideration of the site of Dublin's Viking *Thing-mót*' in Tom Condit and Christiaan Corlett (eds), *Above and beyond: essays in memory of Leo Swan* (Bray, 2005), pp 351–60.   **7** Seán Duffy, 'Ireland's Hastings: the Anglo-Norman conquest of Dublin' in Christopher Harper-Bill (ed.), *Anglo-Norman Studies XX* (Woodbridge, 1998), pp 69–85.   **8** For example, James Graham-Campbell, *The Viking world* (London, 3rd ed., 2001), p. 196.   **9** Stefan Brink, 'Law and society: politics and legal customs in Viking Scandinavia' in Stefan Brink with Neil Price (eds), *The Viking world* (London, 2008), pp 25–6.   **10** Eric Christiansen, *The Norsemen in the Viking Age* (Oxford, 2002), pp 165–6.   **11** Robert Bartlett, *England under the Norman and Angevin kings, 1075–1225* (Oxford, 2000), pp 143–6.   **12** See Séan Duffy, 'Irishmen and Islesmen in the kingdoms of Dublin and Man, 1052–1171', *Ériu*, 43 (1992), 93–133, for a detailed account

Irish provincial kings in the twelfth century led to new titles such as *tigerna* ('lord') and *mórmaor* ('great steward' or *mormaor*, 'sea-steward') being adopted in place of the older term *rí gall* (king of the Foreigners).[13] These new titles are quite ambiguous, *mórmaor* in particular, which has been subject to various suggestions as to its meaning, ranging from a *primus inter pares* nobleman to a royal official to a hereditary descendant of a former king. *Mórmaor* is usually translated as 'earl' or *comes* (and indeed, there are many references in post-conquest documents to the earls of Dublin), but it remains unclear whether it is a functional or a social equivalence being drawn.[14] Whatever their exact meaning, these titles seem to imply a diminished authority on the part of the city's ruler. It is reasonable to assume that he would be more involved with the municipal affairs of the city, given that the wider political decision-making was now in the hands of Dublin's Irish overlords. Dublin's ruler, whichever title he chose to apply to himself, would be restricted to local affairs and administration in most circumstances, most likely working in close conjunction with the Þing.

Many of the issues that would have faced this municipal administration concerned trade, as it is clear that this was a major activity in the city.[15] Because of this, it is very likely that the city possessed a guild or at the very least an association of merchants. Dubliners would have been aware of the concept, and were possibly also members, of guilds from English cities, in particular Bristol, where guilds had existed since 'the time of Robert and William his son, earls of Gloucester' (*c.*1121–47 and 1147–83, respectively).[16] The organization provided by the guild (if it existed) and the city authorities is evidenced in Henry II's confirmation of *c.*1175 to the men of Chester of their rights and privileges as merchants in Dublin, as they had existed in the time of Henry I (1100–35).[17] It is certainly justifiable on the present evidence to conclude that Dublin had an organized municipal administration by the time of the English conquest, even if its exact structures and activities can only be guessed at.

The constitutional evolution of the city from the time of the English conquest of the city, on the other hand, is well understood due to the preservation of successive royal charters granting the citizens of Dublin various liberties and privileges.[18] Henry's own charter issued at Dublin in 1171–2 is recognition

of Dublin's political history in the period after the Battle of Clontarf.   **13** *AFM* 1167; Lydon, 'Dublin in transition' in Duffy (ed.), *Medieval Dublin II*, p. 138.   **14** Alex Woolf, *From Pictland to Alba, 789–1070* (Edinburgh, 2007), pp 342–50; Richard Oram, *Domination and lordship: Scotland, 1070–1230* (Edinburgh, 2011), pp 216–22. The application of *mórmaor*, a term otherwise found only in relation to Scottish rulers, to Dublin by the Irish annalists emphasizes the continued alien nature of the Dubliners in Irish eyes.   **15** David Griffiths, *Vikings of the Irish Sea: conflict and assimilation, AD790–1050* (Stroud, 2010), pp 126–9.   **16** N. Dermott Harding (ed.), *Bristol charters, 1155–1373* (Bristol, 1930), p. 13.   **17** Lydon, 'Dublin in transition', p. 140.   **18** Seán Duffy, 'Town and crown: the kings of England and their city of Dublin' in Michael Prestwich, Richard Britnell and Robin Frame

of the city's status as distinct and separate from the lordships surrounding it.[19] The city's boundaries are delineated in detail by the Lord John's charter of 1192, and the liberties and customs of Bristol alluded to by his father twenty years earlier are spelled out.[20] John's charter of 1215, this time as king, granted the citizens of Dublin the fee-farm of the city, along with the right to appoint a prevost/provost in order to administer it.[21] The effect of this was to give the citizens control over the raising of taxes in the city in return for a fixed payment of two hundred marks per annum to the king's exchequer. Any taxes surplus to this amount could be kept by the city for its own use. The movement towards self government was complete with the right to elect a mayor, granted in 1229 by Henry III.[22]

Despite this seemingly direct and simple progression of the citizens' rights, culminating in the mayoralty in 1229, there remain many aspects of both the progression to civic autonomy and the day-to-day running of the city that are not fully understood. By examining the main groups of sources that survive, an insight can be gained towards answering these vital questions of Dublin's history.

The first and most obvious place to search for clues about the development of the city is in the charters themselves. Aside from the main constitutional privileges sought in the charters (for the charters would have been sought, bargained and paid for rather than spontaneously granted) are a series of rights and privileges related to trade, both within and without the city. One of the best examples of this is also one of the earliest, granted by Henry II at St Lô in Normandy and conjecturally dated to 1174. It grants the 'burgesses of Dublin freedom from toll, passage, pontage, lestage, pavage, murage, quayage, carriage and all custom … throughout [the] land of England, Normandy, Wales and Ireland'.[23] What is notable here is that a group representing the burgesses of Dublin made the journey to Normandy to seek a charter benefiting only traders from Dublin active overseas, not those operating in the city.

Internal trade measures relating to the city do not appear until John's charter of 1192, which places severe limits on non-Dublin merchants trading there.[24] The charter also confirms the existence of guilds in the city, an example of the common phenomenon of charters merely confirming retro-spectively a development that had already occurred in a town.[25] The mention of guilds raises the possibility that the guild merchant of Dublin, which we know was in existence from at least this time, was the body responsible for organizing the community to collectively seek these privileges. The fact that the charter is modelled on a Bristol charter of four years earlier would support

(eds), *Thirteenth Century England X* (Woodbridge, 2005), pp 95–117. **19** *CARD*, p. 1. **20** Ibid., pp 2–6. **21** Ibid., p. 6. **22** Ibid., p. 8. **23** Ibid., pp 1–2. **24** Ibid., p. 4. **25** Susan Reynolds, *An introduction to the history of English medieval towns* (Oxford, 1977), pp 107–8, 111.

this view, given Dublin's close trading relationship with the city.[26] This practice of modelling a town's privileges on those already granted to a neighbour was common in towns throughout England.[27]

When representatives of the city were sent to Marlborough in 1215 to gain confirmation of the fee-farm and prevostship (another example of confirmation after the fact in Dublin charters, as the citizens are recorded as paying the farm to John in 1212), they also sought and were granted permission to hold a two-week fair.[28] Once again, a strong emphasis on trade emerges from an early Dublin charter.

The focus on the issues of trade in the charters should not be over-emphasized. Many other important rights and privileges, including legal and tenurial liberties, were obtained and these would benefit the entire population of the city.[29] The establishment of such things as monopolies and fairs would have benefited craftworkers and artisans in the city as well as merchants. The fact that many craftworkers and tradespeople were part of the guild merchant, however, as indicated by the names on the Dublin guild merchant roll, increases the likelihood of the guild playing an important role in obtaining the city's charters.[30] The sense of mercantile concerns being at the forefront of the minds of those who drafted the city's charters is hard to escape, despite the lack of direct evidence linking the merchant guild or any other specific group to the process.

The next documents that can shed light on early municipal administration in Dublin are the White Book (*Liber Albus*) and the Chain Book of the city. Both are cartularies begun in the fourteenth century, possibly with the transfer of the city's administration from the guildhall on Winetavern Street to the Tholsel on Bothe Street (Skinner's Row).[31] As sources, they are rich, but must be used with extreme caution. Many of the entries are undated, few are in chronological order and neither of the books has been properly studied or published in full.

The ordinances of the city written into the Chain Book describe how it gained its fee-farm. They credit four individuals – Gilbert Lyuet, Ralph de la More, Thomas de la Cornere and Robert Pollard – with obtaining the city's franchise from the king and establishing the offices of mayor and bailiffs (a later name for the office of prevost), as well as three councils of twenty-four *jurats*, forty-eight 'younger men' and ninety-six other men, 'to secure the city

---

26 Harding (ed.), *Bristol charters*, pp 8–13; cf. *CARD*, pp 2–6.   27 Reynolds, *English medieval towns*, pp 82–3.   28 *CARD*, p. 7; See Lydon, 'Dublin in transition', p. 139, for the 1212 fee-farm.   29 *CARD*, pp 3, 5.   30 See *The Dublin guild merchant roll, c.1190–1265*, ed. Philomena Connolly and Geoffrey Martin (Dublin, 1992), pp 157–9, for an index of occupations. Some of the most numerous enrolled in the guild were bakers, tailors, tanners, smiths and millers.   31 Mary Clark, 'People, places and parchment: the medieval archives of Dublin city' in Seán Duffy (ed.), *Medieval Dublin III* (Dublin, 2002), p. 148.

from ill or damage'.[32] It has long been recognized that this document was written no earlier than the fourteenth century and that it reflects the organization of the municipal institutions from that point onwards.[33] Robin Dudley Edwards suspected that only the council of twenty-four jurats existed in the earliest days of the prevostship and mayoralty and he credits the introduction of the other two groups to an unspecified 'general uprising of the guildsmen of Dublin' in the fourteenth century.[34] As no specific instance of a workers' uprising can be identified, it must be acknowledged that the development of these councils is unknowable unless new evidence comes to light. Although a narrowing of the numbers admitted to the councils seems unlikely, it is not impossible that these three levels of twenty-four, forty-eight and ninety-six existed from the early thirteenth century.

The most important piece of information regarding the city's government found in this passage, however, is that election to office was almost always from the top down rather than from the bottom up. Thus, although the jurats chose the mayor (from among themselves, it is likely), the mayor elected the prevosts, the jurats elected the forty-eight and these in turn elected the ninety-six.[35] This system would surely have resulted in a self-perpetuating oligarchic council running the city and it almost certainly dates back to the purchase of the city's fee-farm. A contemporary example of the purchase of Ipswich's fee-farm in 1200 led to two bailiffs being appointed, who hand-picked an electoral college to elect a council of twelve 'chief portmen'.[36] Something similar to this mode of election is likely to have happened in Dublin in 1215.

One feature that can be detected in the Dublin oligarchy, and is present in almost every oligarchy, is the use of political power for its members' own ends. The White Book in particular is full of deeds granting lands in the city to influential members of a small ruling group. Ralph le Hore (prevost in 1233–4, 1237–8), for example, was granted by 'the commonalty of the city' a meadow outside the walls, a tower by Ostman's bridge and a parcel of land by the church of St Saviour.[37] Richard Olof and William Flamstede, both mayors, held a rabbit warren and pasture in succession from the city.[38] John la Warre, who was mayor four times, received a tower from the city, while Reymond the Poitevin (prevost 1258–9), received an entire gate.[39] Roger de Assebourne, mayor three times, received the towers above one of the city gates along with

---

32 *CARD*, pp 230–1.   33 Edwards, 'The beginnings of municipal government', p. 150. 34 Ibid.   35 Jacqueline Hill, 'Mayors and lord mayors of Dublin from 1229' in T.W. Moody, F.X. Martin and F.J. Byrne (eds), *A new history of Ireland, IX: maps, genealogies and lists* (Oxford, 1984), p. 548.   36 Bartlett, *England under the Norman and Angevin kings*, pp 340–1.   37 *CARD*, pp 81–2, 85. All prevostal dates in this essay are from the list given in Connolly and Martin (eds), *Dublin guild merchant roll*, pp 111–12. All mayoral dates are from the list given in Hill, 'Mayors and lord mayors', pp 548–9.   38 Connolly and Martin (eds), *Dublin guild merchant roll*, pp 89–90.   39 Ibid., p. 90.

adjoining lands, with rent remitted for four years. Some years later, these towers were re-granted rent free.[40]

It is clear from these grants that those at the top of Dublin's political ladder did well for themselves, but this should not necessarily be seen as a symptom of corruption. In all but one case, rent was due to the city from the office-holders who were granted lands, and there are many other similar deeds in the White Book recording grants to people unconnected to the mayoralty or the prevostship (although they could have been *jurats* or other council members). Influence with the civic authorities was likely a factor in the award of grants to office-holders and ex-office-holders, however, and it almost certainly was the reason that these deeds were chosen for preservation in the White Book.

One final document from the cartularies that is of interest is the 'Ordinances of the Common Council of the City of Dublin' preserved in the Chain Book.[41] Although still fourteenth-century in date, this document may have originated at a slightly earlier date than those ordinances containing the account of the city council's structure, due to the fact that they are written in Latin as opposed to French and mention no rank between *jurat* and citizen when it comes to paying fines for insulting persons of standing.[42] These ordinances are interesting because they focus for a large part on market regulations (for example, where certain products may be sold), quality of produce (particularly bread and ale), maximum prices and maximum wage rates. This focus on retail activities recalls the similar focus in the charters of the late twelfth and early thirteenth centuries and once again raises the question of the level of the guild merchant's involvement in the politics of the city.

There are two documents that have the potential to shed light on the relationship between the guild and the city administration. These are the guild merchant roll and the free citizens roll, published together in 1992.[43] Both consist of lists of the names of those admitted to the guild merchant and the freedom of the city, respectively. Both begin with a long list of undated names followed by the names of those admitted on a yearly basis, from 1222 to 1265 for the guild merchant roll and from 1234 to 1249 for the free citizens roll. As sources, they present a huge range of challenges to the historian. The guild merchant roll is almost certainly incomplete, missing its earliest entries, although the amount that has been lost is impossible to tell. Identifying relationships or even individuals on the rolls can be nearly impossible; for example, in attempting to identify the mayor William de Bristol (1271–2, 1288–92) on the roll, eight William de Bristols were found to be enrolled in the guild in the decade 1236–46 alone![44] With these caveats and the limitations of this essay in mind, a preliminary effort was made to identify Dublin's thirteenth-century mayors on the rolls.

---

40 Ibid., pp 100–1, 107–8.   41 Ibid., pp 219–22.   42 Ibid., p. 219.   43 Ibid.   44 Ibid., pp 70–84.

The results do little to clarify the relationship between the municipality and the guild. While some of the mayors were clearly enrolled in the guild merchant, others were not. Several mayors had relatives enrolled in the guild but were not enrolled themselves. Of the four men credited with obtaining the franchise for the city, although three subsequently became mayors, only one, Robert Pollard, is enrolled on the guild merchant roll.[45] Thomas de la Cornere did, however, have a relative (son?) enrolled in 1236–7.[46] A future mayor, William de Flamstede, was enrolled in the year he first became prevost (1223–4), while the latest mayor to be found on the guild merchant roll, Henry de Mareschal (mayor 1279–80) was enrolled in the guild in 1262–3.[47] Several mayors appear on the free citizens roll also, such as Roger Oen (guild roll 1224–5, free citizens roll pre-1234 and mayor 1234–5, 1245–6, 1249–50), Richard Olof (guild roll and free citizens roll 1236–7 and mayor 1256–7) and Thomas de Winchester (free citizens roll 1247–8 and mayor 1263–4, 1265–7, 1270–1).[48] Mayors who had several possible relatives in the guild include Richard Mutun (Dublin's first mayor), Elias Burel, John le Warre and Walter Unred.[49]

The relationship between the city authorities and the guild as presented in these sources seems very complex. While there appears to be a mercantile focus in Dublin's early charters and, by the fourteenth century, the city council was passing ordinances impacting directly on the day-to-day work of guild members, there are surprisingly few links visible between the guild and the occupants of the mayoralty. This is the opposite of what one would expect to find, given the very blurred lines between town and guild in medieval cities in general.[50] There are several possibilities for why this might be so, foremost among them the unreliability or incompleteness of the guild merchant roll. Very little is known specifically about the activities of the guild and it could well be that it played more of a social or religious role within the mercantile community. Not every merchant in Dublin may have been a member. It could even be that there existed a non-mercantile urban elite in Dublin, supported perhaps by landholding outside the city and controlling the government of the city through the councils and municipal offices. There is no evidence for any of these speculations, and further research is needed if the municipal government of Dublin is to be properly understood.

Overall, however, a reasonably coherent picture has emerged from an examination of the sources for the history of Dublin's early municipal government. From clear pre-conquest foundations, the municipal government developed into an oligarchic system centred on a mayor, prevost and twenty-four *jurats*. There was clearly a complex and important relationship between the municipal government and the Dublin guild merchant, although, for now, the details remain a mystery.

---

45 Ibid., p. 18. **46** Ibid., p. 70. **47** Ibid., pp 49, 106. **48** Ibid., pp 51, 70, 114, 115, 119. **49** Ibid., pp 12, 15, 20, 21, 25, 27, 38, 42, 44, 49, 54. **50** Reynolds, *English medieval towns*, pp 82–4, 100–2.

The merchant conquistadors: medieval Bristolians in Dublin

GRACE O'KEEFFE

A glance through any list of names from medieval Dublin (such as mayors and provosts, guild merchants' rolls, franchise rolls, or any number of witness lists) testifies to the representation in Dublin of settlers and visitors primarily from throughout England and Wales. One English town in particular, Bristol, has long been recognized as holding a particular significance in the history of transmarine relations and trade between England and Ireland.[1] Trade between the two cities had in earlier centuries included slaves, causing one visitor to Bristol in the early twelfth century to be apparently cautioned 'about the way in which Irish traders would suddenly raise anchor and sail away with unwary visitors'.[2] Indeed, according to Giraldus Cambrensis, and him alone, in 1171, two years after the first English settlers arrived in Ireland, an ecclesiastical council was held in Armagh at which the presence of these new conquistadors in Ireland was discussed, where it was held that 'because it had formerly been their habit [that is, the Irish habit] to purchase Englishmen indiscriminately from merchants as well as from robbers and pirates', the Irish had, 'by the stern judgment of divine vengeance', brought their new misfortune upon themselves.[3] For the remainder of the Middle Ages, ships crossed the Irish Sea carrying goods for consumption. Large quantities of cloth were exported from

---

1 Aubrey Gwynn, 'Medieval Bristol and Dublin', *Irish Historical Studies*, 5:20 (1947), 275–86 may be over sixty years old, but it provides a good explanation of how the collation of Bristol's medieval records was completed. Chester was also an important port trading with Ireland, but Bristol featured much more prominently. This was no doubt due to King Henry II's 1171–2 charter (discussed later in the main text of this essay) granting Bristolians the same trading customs in Dublin as they enjoyed in Bristol. The merchants of Chester may have attempted to counteract the loss of privileged trading rights by securing from Henry II a confirmation of their trading rights with Dublin as they had been granted under Henry I: J.H. Round, 'Early Irish trade with Chester and Rouen' in idem, *Feudal England* (4th ed., London, 1964), pp 353–4. For an exposition of earlier trading practices in Ireland, up to this period, see Charles Doherty, 'Exchange and trade in early medieval Ireland', *Journal of the Royal Society of Antiquaries of Ireland*, 110 (1980), 67–80; Michael Richter, 'The European dimension of Irish history in the eleventh and twelfth centuries', *Peritia*, 4 (1985), 328–45. 2 David A.E. Pelteret, *Slavery in early mediaeval England: from the reign of Alfred to the twelfth century* (Woodbridge, 1995) p. 78. See Poul Holm, 'The slave trade of Dublin, ninth to twelfth centuries', *Peritia*, 5 (1986), 317–45, for an examination of the practice. 3 Giraldus Cambrensis, *Expugnatio Hibernica: The conquest of Ireland*, ed. A.B. Scott and F.X. Martin (Dublin, 1978), pp 69–71.

Bristol to Dublin and other Irish ports, while in return Bristol received foodstuffs (corn, fish and cattle) in addition to linen and timber and animal skins (deer, otter, squirrel, lamb etc.).[4] Even before the 1169 invasion and certainly following it, pottery made its way from Bristol and the wider Gloucestershire region to Dublin. One particular type, called Ham Green Ware, takes its name from the kilns that operated in that area near Bristol, examples of which have been found from archaeological excavations through-out Dublin.[5] Indeed, it was the (probably overstated) opinion of Giraldus that Ireland could not 'survive without the goods and trade which come to it from Britain'.[6]

In 1166 an Irish king, Diarmait Mac Murchada, crossed the Irish Sea to Bristol in the hope of gaining assistance against his enemies in Ireland. Diarmait may initially have planned only to request aid from Bristol, whose inhabitants would have been familiar with Dublin and the east coast. Perhaps it was his host in Bristol, Robert Fitz Harding, then one of its leading citizens, who persuaded him to expand his operation, seeing in it further opportunities for the economic advancement of his city.[7] From Bristol, Diarmait then travelled to King Henry II, who gave the Irish king his permission to recruit support among his subjects. Diarmait returned to Bristol and to Fitz Harding, who, one source tells us, Henry had ordered to give Diarmait all the assistance he needed.[8] King Henry II was himself long familiar with Bristol; during the reign of his predecessor, King Stephen, Henry had spent some time in Bristol and had apparently received some religious education from the canons in St Augustine's Abbey, founded by Robert Fitz Harding.[9]

If Fitz Harding had perhaps hoped to benefit himself from advancement in the relationship between Kings Diarmait and Henry, and, by extension, trade between Bristol and Dublin, his death in 1171 meant that he did not live long enough to benefit from Henry's generous charter granted during his 1171–2 visit to Dublin, by which he granted the city of Dublin to his men of Bristol. The charter has been discussed at length elsewhere; in the context of this discussion, its importance is perhaps more as an explanation for why certain individuals came to be found in Dublin.[10] If, as Seán Duffy has suggested, the

---

4 E.M. Carus-Wilson, *The merchant adventurer of Bristol in the fifteenth century* (Bristol, 1962), pp 2–3; Wendy Childs, 'Irish merchants and seamen in late medieval England', *Irish Historical Studies*, 32:125 (2000), 22–43.   **5** Patrick Wallace, 'North European pottery imported into Dublin, 1200–1500' in Peter Davey and Richard Hodges (eds), *Ceramics and trade: the production and distribution of later medieval pottery in north-west Europe* (Sheffield, 1983), p. 226; Clare McCutcheon, *Medieval pottery from Wood Quay, Dublin* (Dublin, 2006), pp 42–53.   **6** Giraldus Cambrensis, *Expugnatio Hibernica*, p. 253.   **7** John Cottrell, 'Leinster, South Wales, Bristol and Angevin politics, 1135–72: some influences on the earliest English in Ireland' (PhD, Bristol, 2000), p. 33.   **8** *The deeds of the Normans in Ireland, La Geste des Engleis en Yrlande*, ed. Evelyn Mullally (Dublin, 2002), lines 304–6, pp 60–1.   **9** Robert B. Patterson, 'Bristol, an Angevin baronial capital under royal siege', *Haskins Society Journal*, 3 (1991), 174.   **10** H.B. Clarke, 'The 1192 charter of liberties and

charter has survived because it was believed by the men of Dublin to be of 'fundamental importance', for 'constitutional and commercial' purposes, might Bristolians like Haim of Bristol and his siblings, along with Thomas le Martre and the brothers William and Roger Cordwainer, all discussed below, have been directly influenced by Henry's charter of settlement?

As well as being part of a group of citizens in Dublin who were immigrants and settlers, many of these men and their extended families now found themselves living in close proximity in Dublin. Large numbers of charters surviving among the institutional sources for medieval Dublin record the names of these individuals and of those who held properties neighbouring the land in question, names that in many instances are not recorded in any other fashion. The area outside the western gate of medieval Dublin, in the neighbourhood of the hospital of St John the Baptist and St Thomas' Abbey, was one of high-density settlement. Undeveloped prior to the English conquest of Dublin, it would appear to have been an area inhabited primarily by the new arrivals into the city. While these men and women might not have shared a common background prior to arriving in Ireland, their decision to relocate to Dublin and the proximity of their domestic environment meant that they would quickly have become acquainted with each other outside the Newgate.

In addition to being neighbours in Dublin, these Bristolians may also have socialized with each other. In 1209, in an event known as 'Black Monday', later tradition has it that several hundred men, women and children, reportedly from Bristol, were killed in Cullenswood (today part of the Dublin suburb of Ranelagh) while taking a break on Easter Monday from the city air. These Bristolians, Sir James Ware reports, had flocked from their home city to inhabit Dublin as it had been left waste and desolate. On the day, the story goes that the Irish O'Byrnes and O'Tooles came down from the Dublin Mountains and attacked the group as they relaxed and socialized, killing three hundred men, other than women and children, who were 'led into their hands', perhaps meaning that they were taken as hostages. Apparently undeterred by the fate meted out to their fellow-citizens, more Bristolians arrived in Dublin following the massacre to repopulate the city.[11]

the beginnings of Dublin's municipal life', *Dublin Historical Record*, 46:1 (1993), 5–14; Mary Clark, 'People, places and parchment; the medieval archives of Dublin city' in Seán Duffy (ed.), *Medieval Dublin III* (2002), pp 140–50; Seán Duffy, 'Town and crown: the kings of England and their city of Dublin' in Michael Prestwich, Richard Britnell and Robin Frame (eds), *Thirteenth century England X* (Woodbridge, 2005), pp 100–2; *Bristol charters, 1378–1499*, ed. H.A. Cronne, *Bristol Record Society*, 11 (1946), 28–30.   11 James Ware, 'The annals of Ireland during the reigns of King John' in *Inquiries concerning Ireland, and its antiquities* (Dublin, 1705), pp 41–2. An earlier source, with the same details, Meredith Hanmer, *The chronicle of Ireland, collected by Meredith Hanmer in the year 1571* (repr. Dublin, 1809), pp 370–1. The O'Byrnes and O'Tooles of east Leinster had a changing and often difficult relationship with English settlers in the area: see Emmett O'Byrne, *War, politics and the Irish of Leinster, 1156–1606* (Dublin, 2003), esp. pp 30–2; idem, 'Cultures in

In his introduction to the *Dublin guild merchant roll*, Geoffrey Martin commented on the value of the topographical information provided from the surnames of those listed in the roll, though noting that 'Bristol is quite modestly represented'.[12] Many years prior to this, H.A. Cronne remarked that evidence 'of the extent of early Bristol colonization in Dublin is disappointing' due, he noted, to the 'small minority' of those named in records with the topographical designation 'of Bristol'.[13] For all the advantages that topographical or occupational names provide, especially to the prosopographer, Martin's statement is indicative of the danger of relying on toponymic surnames alone to trace an individual's origins. The group of settlers from Bristol discussed here were rarely, and in some cases never, identified by their English origins, and that only becomes clear when a study of contemporary English records demonstrates that their experiences as testators, benefactors and holders of civic offices were not confined to one side of the Irish Sea. The consequences of this approach suggest that although the presence of these early settlers has long been acknowledged, the numbers of settlers or stakeholders in the city may be much higher than previously thought. Patrick Wallace suggested that for 'about thirty years or so after the initial invasion, no major concerted effort was made to develop, improve and enlarge the city, though this impression could be due to the absence of historical data'.[14] The construction of two new religious houses outside the western gate of the city, the Victorine house of St Thomas in the 1170s and the hospital of St John the Baptist in the 1180s seems to negate this view: closer analysis of the surviving historical data may help to demonstrate that in Dublin the process of change began much earlier than Wallace concluded.

The research into those who are discussed below was conducted primarily from the register of the hospital of St John the Baptist, supplemented by the surviving registers and cartularies of Dublin's other medieval religious houses. The hospital of St John the Baptist was the first known foundation in Ireland of the Fratres Cruciferi, regular canons under the rule of St Augustine. Located outside the Newgate, in the western suburb of medieval Dublin, it was in existence by *c*.1188 and was suppressed in 1539 as part of Henry VIII's dissolution of the monasteries. An edition of the register was published in

contact in the Leinster and Dublin marches, 1170–1400' in Seán Duffy (ed.), *Medieval Dublin V* (Dublin, 2004), pp 111–48, esp. pp 119–20; for an archaeological study of the area, see Linzi Simpson, 'Anglo-Norman settlement in Uí Briúin Cualann, 1169–1350' in Ken Hannigan and William Nolan (eds), *Wicklow: history and society* (Dublin, 1994), pp 191–235. Black Monday and its parades are given a full treatment in this volume (see Declan Johnson, 'Black Monday: the power of myth in medieval Dublin', below).   **12** *The Dublin guild merchant roll, c.1190–1265*, ed. Philonema Connolly and Geoffrey Martin (Dublin, 1992), p. xix (hereafter *DGMR*).   **13** *Bristol charters, 1378–1499*, p. 30.   **14** Patrick Wallace, 'Anglo-Norman Dublin: continuity and change' in Donnchadh Ó Corráin (ed.), *Irish antiquity: essays and studies presented to Professor M.J. O'Kelly* (Dublin, 1994), p. 249.

1936. Transcribed and edited from the original Latin manuscript by Eric St John Brooks, it provides an excellent means by which to study the patrons of the hospital and their associates.[15] Aside from the register, two other documents frame the history of the hospital of St John the Baptist. Neither is to be found in the register of the hospital, although in their own way they respectively mark the beginning and end of that institution. Both are official pronouncements on the status of the hospital; one papal and one royal, but both are concerned to varying degrees with the possessions of the hospital. A 1320 papal bull contains the 1188 bull of Pope Clement III in which he confirmed the hospital in its possessions. This is as close to a foundation charter as is now extant.[16] In 1539, King Henry VIII granted a surgeon, Edmund Redman, the site of the hospital, by then defunct by reason of Henry's dissolution of the monasteries.[17] Apart from stating that the hospital had been founded by *Alredo Magistro domus hospitalis sancti Iohannis de Dubellinia*, or Ailred Palmer, and that he and Henry II had given donations to the hospital by 1188, Pope Clement III's confirmation provides the names of six other donors, four other incidental names and two unnamed wives. By tracking the path of this small number of men through contemporary sources, it is possible to provide evidence for connections with many more, mostly men, who were merchants and adventurers in Ireland from the earliest days of the conquest. Some cannot be identified beyond their appearance in the papal confirmation: Augustine of Bristol could be any number of Augustines but, despite the fact that we cannot identify him with any one particular individual, he is still significant for supplying one of many links between the patrons of St John's and Bristol.

Where it is possible to ascribe a definite origin, the earliest benefactors were overwhelmingly from western England, Gloucestershire and in particular Bristol. When their associates in Dublin, those not named in Clement's bull,

15 *Register of the hospital of St John the Baptist, without the New Gate, Dublin*, ed. Eric St John Brooks (Dublin, 1936) (hereafter *HSJB*). The fourteenth-century manuscript, MS Rawl. B498, is housed in the Bodleian Library, Oxford. The Bodleian Library have digitized most of the manuscript and it is available for view at http://image.ox.ac.uk/show?collection=bodleian&manuscript=msrawlb498. The hospital was the subject of my doctoral thesis, 'The hospital of St John the Baptist, Dublin, *c.*1188–1539: a historical and prosopographical analysis' (PhD, TCD, 2012). In the course of examining the patrons of the hospital, it became clear that among the large Bristolian community in medieval Dublin, some were operating on both sides of the Irish Sea and continued to be found in documentation together in Bristol. The families here are only those who were connected to St John's, and in the first few decades of its existence; many more Bristolians in medieval Dublin await examination.   16 *Vetera monumenta Hibernorum et Scotorum historiam illustantia quae ex Vaticani, Neapolis ac Florentiae tabularis depromsit et ordine chronologico diposuit, 1216–1547*, ed. Augustinus Theiner (Rome, 1864), pp 214–15 (hereafter *VMH*). For a brief discussion of its contents, especially the grants, see *HSJB*, pp v–vii.   17 *The Irish fiants of the Tudor sovereigns during the reigns of Henry VIII, Edward VI, Philip & Mary, and Elizabeth I* (4 vols, Dublin, 1994), i, no. 85, p. 15.

are investigated, does this same geographic principle apply? Along with those named in Clement's confirmation were those who, through family or social standing, appear to have been associated with each other. These individuals and their wider social circle are those others who were either grantors or witnesses to charters in the hospital's register in the first two decades of its existence. Twenty names are all that comprise the grantors in those documents dated by St John Brooks to the 1190s. There are many more regular attestors in the witness lists of the register and, from the list of all those who attested these charters, another small group emerges. The use of the witness lists of private deeds (as opposed to royal ones) as evidence for social groupings within a particular society has not been universally accepted as a sound methodology. The difficulty has centred on the reliability of the assumption that all named witnesses to a particular deed were present when the transaction recorded in the deed was carried out. As part of Keith Stringer's study of the diplomatic of the late twelfth- and early thirteenth-century deeds of David, earl of Huntingdon, he examined the witness lists to the earl's *acta*.[18] He maintained that the terminology used by the scribes gave no particular indication that the witnesses were necessarily present when the 'substantive transaction' took place, but that they may have attended the 'issue of the written acta'.[19] In addition, he noted that the physical presence of the witnesses was not legally required.

A comprehensive study of the legalities of witness-list attendance has been undertaken by Dauvit Broun, who noted that while it is generally accepted that those charters produced in Anglo-Norman Britain recorded witnesses who were physically present when their names were noted, there is some lingering doubt about the security or reliability of assumptions based on witness lists.[20] Broun conducted analysis of the historiography of those who doubted the veracity of witness lists, coupled with a palaeographic analysis of charters where the witness list appears to have been added after the main body of the text. While there are some examples of witnesses being added to charters when they were not actually present at the time of the transaction of the gift, or the drawing up of the written deed, Broun concluded that the evidence, on the whole, for witnesses being present, and in fact actively desiring the recording of their name for posterity, outweighed the contrary.[21]

The approach taken here has been to take the witnesses as being present, and therefore where many of the same names appear on the witness lists of each other's charters to take this as evidence of a particular social grouping. Of

---

18 Keith Stringer, 'The charters of David, earl of Huntingdon and lord of Garioch: a study in Anglo-Scottish diplomatic' in idem (ed.), *Essays on the nobility of medieval Scotland* (Edinburgh, 1985), pp 72–101, esp. pp 92–4 for the section on witness lists.   **19** Ibid., p. 93. **20** Dauvit Broun, 'The presence of witnesses and the writing of charters' in idem (ed.), *The reality behind charter diplomatic in Anglo-Norman Britain: studies by Dauvit Broun, John Reuben Davis, Richard Sharpe and Alice Taylor* [www.poms.ac.uk/ebook/index/html], p. 236.   **21** Ibid., pp 238, 280.

all those whose names are recorded in this period, only those who were frequent attestors and who were regularly in each other's company have been chosen for more in-depth investigation here. There was surely a practical purpose to neighbouring landowners witnessing each other's charters – though they may have been on friendly terms, a dispute concerning boundary properties was one definite way to provoke hostilities. By being aware of how land in one's locality was being managed, such disputes could be kept at bay.

I. ROGER, HAIM AND ADHELM (fig. 7.1)

In Clement's list, Roger's donation appears as follows:

> … from a donation of Roger brother of Haim in his house which is next to St John, three marks, thus nevertheless that if the same Roger should die in the aforesaid hospital, or if he dies elsewhere, from the house of the same hospital to 20s. in the same house let it be gratefully withdrawn.[22]

From this then, it is known that Roger had a residence in the western suburb by St John's. A couple of years later, Roger, this time with his wife Margaret, donated rent of 12s. to be paid in two instalments at Michaelmas and Easter from land that was in the same street as the hospital.[23] In this witness list, another brother of Haim's, Adhelm, is listed.[24] Haim, his brothers and their own extended families appear to have been part of Dublin city life from its earliest days as an English royal possession. Adhelm is the earliest English settler in Dublin recorded in an official capacity. During Henry II's sojourn in Dublin in 1171–2 and in a charter witnessed by Hugh de Lacy among others, the king granted Adhelm (noted as brother of *Hamundi de Bristowe*, which supplies the link to Bristol) land outside the eastern gate of Dublin.[25] As Duffy

---

22 *VMH*, p. 215: *ex dono Rogerii fratris Haimi in domo eius, que est propinquior sancto Iohanni tres marchas, ita tamen quod si predictus Rogerius moriatur in predicto hospitali, si autem alibi morietur, et gratus recedat de domo dicti hospitalis viginti solidos in eadem domo.* 23 *HSJB*, no. 38. 24 These names were, like Ailred's, probably Anglo-Saxon. William George Searle, *Onomasticon Anglo-Saxonicum: a list of Anglo-Saxon proper names from the time of Beda to that of King John* (Cambridge, 1897), p. 279 for Haim and p. 41 for Adhelm (Æthelhelm). In his article on the connections between the Hereford Jewry and marcher lords in the twelfth and thirteenth centuries, Joe Hillaby suggested that Hamo of Hereford, a prominent Jewish financier, 'may have come from the Continent in the recent wave of immigration. The name would suggest northern France, unless it is a corrupt form of the Hebrew, *Haim* or *Hayyim*, meaning 'life', but this was normally rendered Hagin in England': Joe Hillaby, 'Hereford gold: Irish, Welsh and English land, parts 1 & 2. The clients of the Jewish community at Hereford, 1179–1253: four case studies', *Transactions of the Woolhope Naturalists' Field Club*, 45:1 (1985), 212. 25 *Chartularies of St Mary's Abbey Dublin*, ed. J.T. Gilbert (2 vols, London, 1884), i, no. 118g, pp 140–2 (hereafter *CSMA*).

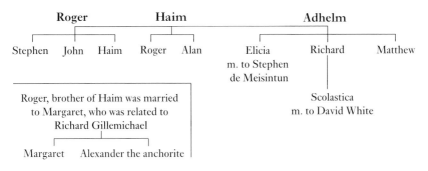

7.1 Genealogical table of the Haim family.

has previously noted, the site of this grant held its own significance. These lands were those on which Dublin's Thingmoot had stood, prior to the establishment of Henry's temporary court there in 1171. By granting it to one of the city's new men, the transference of power from the old to the new order was easily displayed.[26] This same land was later granted by Adhelm's daughter, Elicia, with the consent of her husband, Stephen de Meisintun, to the Cistercians of St Mary's in Oxmantown.[27] In the early thirteenth century, Elicia granted Germanus Dubeldai her lands outside the gate of St Mary del Dam, between the city wall and a mill, land that had been held of her father by William Dubeldai, Germanus' uncle.[28] The mill, in addition to its water, situated between the gate of St Mary del Dam and St Andrew's Church, had been granted to William Dubeldai by John (noted as the son of the king, hence it was probably when he was lord of Ireland and before becoming count of Mortain in 1189).[29] William later granted half of this mill, and his body, presumably for burial, with half his house beside St Olaf's, to the monks of St Mary's Abbey.[30] In the early 1230s, Adhelm's granddaughter, Scolastica, along with her husband David Albus, further gave to St Mary's all rights and claims that had been Adhelm's outside the eastern gate.[31]

In addition to being perhaps one of the earliest landowners in the eastern suburb, Adhelm also appears to have held land and a house in Donore, in the western suburb.[32] Adhelm was also occasionally referred to as *divitis*,[33] and he and his two brothers, Haim and Roger, appear to have been prominent landowners along Dublin's riverine walls.[34] Given the early date of Henry II's

26 Duffy, 'Town and crown', p. 102. **27** *CSMA*, i, no. 273, pp 325–6. Stephen de Mesintun (also spelled as Meisintun) makes several appearances in the register as a witness in the early thirteenth century; a Roger de Mesintun similarly so several decades later. **28** Ibid., no. 202, pp 224–5. **29** Ibid., no. 200, p. 223. **30** Ibid., no. 198, p. 222. **31** Ibid., no. 203, pp 225–6. Made in the presence of Gilbert de Livet, as mayor. Gilbert is examined below. **32** *HSJB*, nos 136, 137; *Calendar of Archbishop Alen's register, c.1172–1534*, ed. Charles McNeill (Dublin, 1950), p. 32 (hereafter *Alen*). **33** Ibid., nos 136, 137; *CSMA*, i, no. 203, pp 225–6. **34** *CSMA*, i, no. 178, p. 208; no. 240, p. 250.

charter, it seems safe enough to assume that this family were from Bristol, and may even have been members of a party of Bristolians who encouraged or petitioned for Henry's other more famous charter issued in Dublin, that of course being the granting of the city to Bristol, for the settlement of the former with merchants from the latter. This would certainly provide a link with another of the original donors, Augustine of Bristol. In one of Strongbow's charters, dated to 1174, Ailred (the hospital's founder), Roger brother of Haim, and Augustine are listed, while an Augustine the clerk can be found on several occasions sharing witness lists with Haim's family.[35] Roger and Adhelm are usually referred to by their fraternal link to Haim, but the latter is more difficult to identify. In the guild merchant roll, a Robert brother of Heim (presumably a variant of Haim) is listed, most likely then from this same family. From his place in the roll, his membership of the guild probably dated to the late twelfth century; this, however, is the only reference to him that has been unearthed.[36]

Based on only the extant evidence of religious cartularies, Roger and his family were actively involved in the life of medieval Dublin. The abbey of St Mary was, more than any other institution, their chosen destination for benefaction. This continued into the next generation, with donations and confirmations of their parents' donations by Stephen, Roger's son and Elicia, Adhelm's daughter.[37] In a charter of Stephen's to St Mary's, his brother John is listed as a monk, which may explain the link between the family and the abbey.[38] He was also among the benefactors to Holy Trinity as his grant of land in Crockers' Street to that institution was confirmed by King John.[39]

Other extended family can be traced through Roger's wife Margaret. In a charter of Margaret's in which she gave a part of her land opposite the church of St Nicholas in Dublin to Adam Palmer, the witnesses are listed as Richard Gillemichael, *genere meo*, and Simon, also *genere meo*.[40] A 1234 inspeximus of earlier charters of another Margaret, daughter of Richard Gillemichelle, contains details of several rents and plots held by her in Dublin but also a messuage held of her in Bristol and half a mark due from the same fee by a Richard Cordwainer.[41] The inspeximus gives an insight into the impressive number of land holdings claimed by Richard's daughter: land in Cornmarket by St Audoen's, in Bertram's Court, more by St Patrick's and in Oxmantown, in addition to her stone messuage in Bristol. Among those mentioned as owing

35 *Christ Church deeds*, ed. M.J. McEnery and Raymond Refaussé (Dublin, 2001), no. 468f., p. 124; no. 471, p. 124; no. 472, p. 124 (hereafter *CCD*).   36 *DGMR*, p. 1 (2nd col.). 37 See *CSMA*, i, no. 287, pp 350–2, for a confirmation of St Mary's lands, which lists several donations from the Haim family.   38 Ibid., i, no. 177, pp 207–8. This witness list also includes a relative of his mother, Richard Gillemicheal, discussed in the next paragraph.   39 *Alen*, pp 28–9.   40 *The register of the abbey of St Thomas, Dublin*, ed. J.T. Gilbert (London, 1889), no. 432, pp 380–1 (hereafter *RAST*).   41 *Calendar of documents relating to Ireland*, ed. H.S. Sweetman (5 vols, London, 1875–86), i, no. 2210, pp 327–8

her rent was Elena de Plumton, who may be the same Helena, wife of Elias Burel, four-time mayor of Dublin (of whom more below), and daughter of Richard de Plumton. Margaret's grant was made to the nuns of St Mary's de Hogges, for her soul and that of Alexander, the anchorite of St Clement's. In the late 1230s, this same Alexander made a grant to All Hallows Priory for the salvation of many souls, including those of his sister Margaret.[42] Although connected through marriage to a Bristolian family, Richard Gillemichael is perhaps a man of mixed ethnic background. A man bearing that name is listed in the Dublin guild merchant roll, as is another by the name Willekin Gillemichel.[43] Gille Mhichíl is a Gaelic name and he presumably originated from a Gaelic-speaking milieu in Ostman Dublin, Man, Gaelic Scotland or even Cumbria.

Roger brother of Haim did not restrict his social circle to fellow Bristolians. He appeared as witness to a charter of Milo le Bret,[44] and was noted in a charter of Milo's to the white monks as formerly holding the land that was the subject of the donation.[45] Others who regularly occur on the same witness lists as Roger, his siblings and offspring include William Brun (whose son Audoen was at one time a clerk to Archbishop John Comyn and later a chamberlain of the exchequer),[46] Walter Goldsmith and, to a lesser extent, the de Feypo family. In one charter to St Mary's by which Roger gave the monks a garden over the bank of the Liffey, also on the list of witnesses were Walter Goldsmith, William Brun, Roger's brother Adhelm, his sons John and Hamo, another Hamo (or Haim, as the form of the name seems to have been interchangeable) who may have been Adhelm's brother, and an Augustine who may be the elusive Augustine of Bristol who gave the hospital of St John the Baptist some land neighbouring its own property.[47]

Brun and Goldsmith were certainly resident in Dublin by the late 1170s, as Archbishop Lorcán Ua Tuathail (Laurence O'Toole, who died in 1180) confirmed to Brun land in Killester that the canons of Holy Trinity had given him in return for a rent of half an ounce of gold, a pair of boots and all tithes due from the land.[48] Unless the grant was made in Laurence's absence, it must have been given prior to 1178 when the archbishop left Ireland to attend the Third Lateran Council.[49] The witnesses include Walter Goldsmith and

(hereafter *CDI*).   **42** *Registrum Prioratus Omnium Sanctorum juxta Dublin*, ed. Richard Butler (Dublin, 1845), no. 47, p. 49.   **43** *DGMR*, p. 17 (2nd col.) for Richard and p. 23 (1st col.) for Willekin.   **44** *RAST*, no. 19, pp 25–6.   **45** *CSMA*, i, no. 108, p. 125.   **46** *Alen*, pp 13–14; H.G. Richardson and G.O. Sayles, *The administration of Ireland, 1172–1377* (Dublin, 1963), p. 118; *CDI*, i, no. 357, p. 54; *Rotuli litterarum clausarum*, ed. Thomas Duffus Hardy (2 vols, London, 1833), i, p. 576 (a); 'The Irish pipe roll of 14 John, 1211–12', ed. Oliver Davies and David B. Quinn, *Ulster Journal of Archaeology*, 4 (1941), supplement, pp 25, 43, 45.   **47** *CSMA*, i, no. 178, p. 208.   **48** *CCD*, no. 468a, p. 123; Liam Howlett, 'The Killester Charter', *Dublin Historical Record*, 32:2 (1979), 69–71.   **49** Archbishop Laurence's involvement with the new settlers in Dublin has been well documented and examined. A

Aelamus (Adhelm?) brother of Hamo. Included also is the only other direct reference to another person on Pope Clement's list, Gilbert Gude. William Goldsmith acted as benefactor to St John's on only one occasion, in a charter witnessed by Richard Gillemichael.[50]

The charter given to Adhelm by Henry II (mentioned above) does suggest that he, and perhaps his two brothers, were trusted Bristolians. Given their high status in Dublin, one could expect that the Haim siblings would be prominent landowners and burgesses of Bristol, but surprisingly they do not appear to have left the same impact on Bristol's records as they have on Dublin's. Despite their relative importance in the early stages of the English settlement of Dublin, and the trust that Henry II must have had in Adhelm to grant him land beside one of the entrances to the city, the records for medieval Bristol are overwhelmingly silent regarding Adhelm, Haim and Roger.

II. WILLIAM ABBOTSTONE

As Roger, brother of Haim, held land and a garden over the bank of the Liffey, it is possible that both Thomas le Martre and William Abbotstone were not only his neighbours in Dublin, but were also known to him in Bristol. In the records of St Augustine's Abbey in Bristol, Roger son of William the Cordwainer, rector of St Mary-le-Port, confirmed to Dionisia, daughter of William Abbotstone, all his land in Worship Street. For this, Dionisia was to pay the landgable due and 5*s.* to St James' in Bristol. In exchange for these payments, Roger was to receive from Dionisia land in Dublin, land that was beside the Newgate and held by William de Abbotstone from Robert la Warre. In addition, Roger, son of William the Cordwainer, was to receive a rental payment from her father's land by the bridge to Oxmantown.[51] These were not the only plots held by William de Abbotstone in Dublin; in memory of his father Walter and his mother Dionisia, William gave to the monks of St Mary's rent from his land between St Audoen's Church and the house of William Blundel, who also attested the charter.[52] William also held part of a tenement in Rochelle Street, across from St Audoen's, a tenement that was noted as being Roger Cordwainer's (discussed in detail below). A William de Abbedestuna was an early member of Dublin's merchants' guild, and, in what may be only a coincidence, is only one place removed from a Roger le

selection includes: M.T. Flanagan, 'Laurence (*c.*1128–1180)', *Oxford dictionary of national biography* (Oxford, 2004): www.oxforddnb.com/view/article/20934, accessed Feb. 2013]; John Ryan, 'The ancestry of St Laurence O'Toole', *Reportorium Novum*, 1 (1955), 64–75; J.F. O'Doherty, 'St Laurence O'Toole and the Anglo-Norman Invasion', *Irish Ecclesiastical Record*, 50 (1937), 449–77, 600–25; 51(1938), 131–46.   **50** *HSJB*, no. 157.   **51** *Cartulary of St Augustine's Abbey, Bristol*, ed. David Walker, *The Bristol and Gloucestershire Archaeological Society*, 10 (1998), no. 547, p. 349.   **52** *CSMA*, i, no. 230, p. 243.

Cordwainer of (*de*) Hereford on the same list.[53] William de Abbedestuna also made payments in 1194 in the same honour in Gloucestershire as Roger and William Cordwainer.[54] As witness, William was less visible than as a landowner. He appears in the company of Adhelm and Roger, brothers of Haim and Roger's sons Haim and John in a charter of Thomas le Martre to St Mary's.[55]

In the charter of Roger, son of William the Cordwainer, the land held by de Abbotstone from Robert la Warre by the New Gate is described as *totam terram suam in Dublinia versus novam portam*, but it is unclear if this is the same land referred to as *apud Duuelinam* in an indenture between Walter, son of Herbert la Werra, and Thomas, his brother, witnessed in Bristol in March 1199.[56] In this, Walter was to have 20*s.* from William de Abbotstone's land *apud Duuelinam*, among other transactions. If this was not the land William held of Robert la Warre, it is probable that he is the Robert listed as one of the attestors, the first four being John la Werra, David la Werra, Robert la Werra *clericus*, and Roger Werra brother of John.[57] The wording suggests that while all were of the la Warre/Were family, they were perhaps of different branches, though if this is true, both branches were represented in Dublin, and from the earliest days of the English colony there. In 1172, a William le Puhier and Hugh *pincerna* had been granted £4 to hire a ship to carry equipment and provisions (*ad portandum harnesium et guarnisonem*) of Robert Power (*Puherii*)

---

53 *DGMR*, p. 3 (2nd col.). In 1232–3, another William de Abbedestrune is listed: ibid., p. 64 (2nd col.).   54 *The great roll of the pipe for the sixth year of the reign of King Richard the first, Michaelmas 1194*, ed. Doris M. Stenton (London, 1928), p. 240.   55 *CSMA*, i, no. 182, p. 211. In what may be only a coincidental reference, a Hamo son of Roger appears in Essex in 1165–6: *The great roll of the pipe for the twelfth year of the reign of King Henry the second, 1165–6* (London, 1888), p. 127.   56 *Descriptive catalogue of the charters and muniments in the possession of Lord FitzHarding at Berkeley Castle*, ed. I.B.T. Jeayes (Bristol, 1892), no. 52, p. 24. Abbreviated version listed also in *Catalogue of the medieval muniments at Berkeley Castle*, ed. Bridget Wells-Furby (2 vols, *The Bristol and Gloucestershire Archaeological Society*, vols 17 & 18, 2004), 445.   57 *CSMA*, i, no. 153, p. 181 refers to John le Warre of (*de*) Bristol. Dating from the time of the archbishopric of Henry of London (1213–28), this might be the John la Werre (or a son of same) who was involved in wine provision for the king in Bristol *c.*1205: *Rotuli Litterarum Clausarum*, i, p. 38 (b). A John la Were can be found as witness to a charter of John as count of Mortain, in the company of the future chief governor of Ireland, Hamo de Valognes and also the recipient of a manor from the future king: see *Earldom of Gloucester charters: the charters and scribes of the earls and countesses of Gloucester to AD1217*, ed. R.B. Patterson (Oxford, 1973), no. 72, p. 79 and no. 108, p. 106. A John le Warre was also mayor of Dublin on ten occasions, and provost once throughout the 1240s and 1250s: H.F. Berry, 'Catalogue of the mayors, provosts and bailiffs of Dublin city, AD1229 to 1447' in Howard Clarke (ed.) *Medieval Dublin: the living city* (Dublin, 1990), pp 156–7. He may be the John de la Werre granted citizenship of Dublin in 1227–8: *DGMR*, p. 58 (2nd col.). A John de la Warre is credited with founding St Bartholomew's hospital in Bristol, *c.*1230. For this and more on the de la Warre family, see Roger Price and Michael Ponsford, *St Bartholomew's hospital, Bristol: the excavation of a medieval hospital: 1976–8* (York, 1998), pp 20–24. Even as late as 1306, the prior of Holy Trinity, Henry la Warre, was referred to as *de Bristol*: *CCD*, no. 178, p. 68.

in Ireland. Among those vouched were Jordan Were and his brother David.[58] This may be the same David listed as witness above. It certainly proves that this Bristol family would have been familiar with Dublin from at least the time of Henry II's visit to Dublin, his grant of the city to Bristol, and his grant of land there to that other Bristol native, Adhelm, brother of Haim.

III. THOMAS LE MARTRE

Thomas le Martre (at times also called la Martre) was another Bristolian who held land by Ostmen's Bridge. One part of this land was granted to Richard Carpenter, while another one between the land he gave to his wife Margaret and the one he gave to the Hospitallers in Kilmainham, was granted to the canons of St Thomas'.[59] Like his fellow Bristolian, Adhelm brother of Haim, Thomas was a landowner in the Donore/Bertram's Court area.[60] There is evidence of land also being held by him in St Werburgh's parish,[61] and his ownership of a stall/shop (*selda*) that he gave to his son Jordan.[62] From extant records, it seems that Thomas provided a single grant only to St John's, of land between the land of St Stephen and the street (*viam*).[63] In a grant of rent to the Cistercians in St Mary's Abbey, le Martre specifies that it was from land inside the walls, land *ex conquestu meo*, and witnessed by William Brun, Adhelm and Roger, brothers of Haim, Roger's two sons and William de Abbotstone.[64] This is a phrase that appears sporadically in Dublin charters from the late twelfth century, the use of which to describe their properties could mean that they were 'simply providing the technical clarification that they held them by acquisition rather than inheritance', while still allowing for the likelihood that they had been part of the initial conquest of the city.[65] Thomas was not the last Bristolian with this name to donate to the hospital; in 1259, a Peter le Martre (also known as le Mere) gave 8*d*. from land opposite the church of the Franciscans.[66]

---

58 *The great roll of the pipe for the eighteenth year of the reign of King Henry the second, 1171–2* (London, 1894), p. 32. For brief discussion of this, see *The great roll of the pipe for the thirty-second year of the reign of King Henry the second, 1185–6* (London, 1914), pp xxvi–xxvii. It has been suggested that a Jordan La Were was a possible relative of Robert Fitz Harding: Robert B. Patterson, 'Robert Fitz Harding of Bristol: profile of an early Angevin burgess-baron patrician and his family's urban involvement', *Haskins Society Journal*, 1 (1989), 115.   **59** *RAST*, no. 483, p. 414; ibid., no. 489, p. 418. Thomas also gave the Hospitallers land in Bertram's Court: *RAST*, no. 430, p. 379.   **60** *HSJB*, no. 127 references it as in Donore, while *HSJB*, no. 119 and *RAST*, no. 430, p. 379 mentions Bertram's Court.   **61** *CCD*, no. 18, p. 39.   **62** *CSMA*, i, no. 184, p. 212.   **63** *HSJB*, no. 158.   **64** *CSMA*, i, no. 182, p. 211.   **65** Duffy, 'Town and crown', p. 104.   **66** *HSJB*, no. 122. Peter is referred to as a burgess of Bristol. This may mean that he was related to Thomas and maintained the family's Bristol–Dublin connections: see also *CSMA*, i, no. 163, pp 425–6.

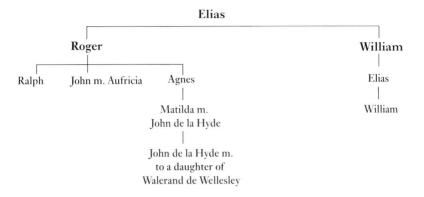

7.2 Genealogical table of the Cordwainer family.

Thomas' connections with Dublin's Bristolian population were not confined to his neighbours, the Haim siblings. In a grant from the Lord John to John Levesche of tenements in Dublin, Thomas le Martre was one of the attestors, in conjunction with William Cordwainer and Roger his brother.[67] In 1199, Roger Cordwainer and Jordan le Eveske (Levesche) were also part of the group that witnessed the indenture between Walter, son of Herbert la Werra, and Thomas, his brother. In a final concord dated November 1192 made in the Hundred Court of the city of Bristol, Thomas le Martre and William Cordwainer were noted as being provosts.[68]

IV. THE CORDWAINER FAMILY (fig. 7.2)

In 1194, the two brothers, William and Roger, are noted in the pipe roll for the honor of Gloucester regarding several payments.[69] In the same decade, they were attestors to a grant by Nicholas de Castello to the hospital,[70] while Roger, without William, attested a charter of William Brun and his wife Susanna.[71] It is from a grant made by this Nicholas to the monks of St Mary's Abbey that we learn of Roger Cordwainer's donation to the hospital. Nicholas described his donation as 'land which is between the land I gave to the hospital of St John and the land which Roger Cordwainer gave the same hospital, namely, opposite the church of St James to the south'.[72] William and Roger together made a grant to St Mary's in Dublin of half the land that Gille, son of Beorn, son of

67 *CCD*, no. 470, p. 124.   **68** *Historia et cartularium Monasterii Sancti Petri Gloucestriæ*, ed. William Henry Hart (3 vols, London, 1863–7), i, no. 45, p. 172 (Thomas here named as Thomas *la Matire*).   **69** *The great roll of the pipe for the sixth year of the reign of King Richard the first*, p. 240.   **70** *HSJB*, no. 1.   **71** Ibid., no. 30.   **72** *CSMA*, i, no. 213, p. 232. There is no record of Roger's grant in the register of St John's.

Haward, held in St Michael's Street.[73] In early 1200, letters of protection were issued for the brothers,[74] while in 1206 Roger was acquitted for three hundred marks paid to King John on behalf of the justiciar.[75] This entry also refers to him as Roger Cordwainer of Bristol.

William and Roger owned land in St Michael's parish in Dublin, which was held by Walter of Castleknock.[76] Roger again was one of a lengthy list of witnesses to a grant of a garden to the hospital by Baldwin, son of Gille, and his son-in-law Elias of Chester.[77] In this same list are Adhelm and Roger, brothers of Haim. Roger, brother of Haim, and Baldwin appear to have had links that pre-dated their patronage of St John's in Dublin, as in 1179–80 a Roger, brother of Haim, Daniel and Baldwin, son of Gille, are noted in the pipe roll for Gloucester as owing two marks for the chattels of a Gillemichel (no indication if this is the Richard Gillemichael mentioned above) for the work of his wife and his heirs.[78] The same entry appears annually until 1183–4 and again in 1186–7. In a charter of Robert de Berkeley (1218–20) in which he granted to St Augustine's Abbey in Bristol all his lands within that city's walls, Robert la Warre and William Cordwainer are among those listed as being the holders of the tenements in question, while William's brother Roger was one of the witnesses.[79]

Perhaps the most compelling evidence for the continued importance of the Cordwainers, and Roger in particular, to life in Bristol into the thirteenth century is Roger's position as mayor of Bristol, as he was termed in Walter de Escotot's grant to St Thomas'.[80] This is supported by a reference in the close rolls of 1216 to Roger Cordwainer, again named as mayor of Bristol.[81] In the same year, several other references in the same source mention a mayor of Bristol, but without specifically naming Roger.[82] That these all occur before Michaelmas of 1216 could mean that Roger had been appointed in Michaelmas 1215 and was mayor for the following year.[83] The entries further demonstrate that an important function of Bristol's medieval mayor was the care of the royal wine stores.[84]

73 Ibid., no. 189, p. 216.   74 *CDI*, i, no. 119, p. 18.   75 Ibid., no. 304, p. 45.   76 'Calendar of the *Liber Niger* and *Liber Albus* of Christ Church, Dublin', ed. H.J. Lawlor, *Proceedings of the Royal Irish Academy*, 27C (1908–9), 39.   77 *HSJB*, no. 41.   78 *The great roll of the pipe for the twenty-sixth year of the reign of King Henry the second, 1179–80* (London, 1908), p. 115.   79 *Cartulary of St Augustine's Abbey, Bristol*, no. 123, pp 71–2. An abbreviated version can be found in *Catalogue of the medieval muniments at Berkeley Castle*, p. 442. 80 *RAST*, no. 10, pp 17–18. For a short exploration of the beginnings of the mayoralty of Bristol and Roger's place in it, see *Bristol charters, 1378–1499*, pp 74–6.   81 *Rotuli Litterarum Clausarum*, i, p. 283 (a).   82 Ibid., pp 281 (b), 283 (a), 285 (a). In 1236, both Cordwainers, Roger and William, were noted as having held office as mayor of Bristol and provost of Bristol during John's reign: *Bristol charters, 1378–1499*, p. 75.   83 There is an entry in the close rolls for June 1216 in which Roger is named, but not as mayor, and again in early Sept.: *Rotuli litterarum clausarum*, i, pp 275 (a), 286 (b).   84 This might explain his interaction with King John, who was apparently a 'discerning' purchaser of wine: M.D.

While Roger was clearly referred to as the mayor, it is unclear if this meant that he was endowed with full mayoral privileges, or how he was elected. There is no extant record of Bristol receiving the right to a mayor, such as that given to Dublin by King Henry III in 1229, nor is there evidence of the citizens of Bristol being granted the right to select their mayor, as had been granted to Londoners by King John in 1215.[85] Given John's difficulties in the latter years of his reign, it could simply be that he instituted into an informal mayoralty a man who had proven himself to be a loyal servant over many years. Bristol had shown itself loyal to John's family and John, through his marriage to Isabella of Gloucester, had even more reason to secure the continued loyalty of the important port of Bristol.[86]

While both Cordwainer brothers, Roger and William, were clearly very much a continuing presence in the politics of Bristol, what of their wider family?[87] Roger's descendants are well represented as a result of their possession of land in Ballymadun (also referred to as Ballymacdon, in the barony of Balrothery, north Co. Dublin). Despite Roger's position as mayor of Bristol, and as an obvious trusted servant of the crown in England, it seems that his children were more prominent as Dubliners than Bristolians. From a 1270 inspeximus of the future Edward I in which the grant of Ballymadon by his grandfather John, as lord of Ireland, to Robert Ruffus in 1185, and Robert's subsequent grant of a moiety to both Roger and William Cordwainer is the subject, we derive much of what can be learned about both Roger and William's descendents.[88] While the details of the prolonged investigation into

Lobel and E.M. Carus-Wilson (eds), *Historic towns, 2: Bristol* (London, 1975), p. 6. See *Rotuli litterarum clausarum*, i, p. 283 (a), where Roger, as mayor of Bristol, was to deliver fifteen dolia (earthenware jar or vessel) of wine to the earl of Chester, two to John of Monmouth and three to Colin de Ruetot. **85** *Historic and municipal documents of Ireland, AD1172–1320, from the archives of the city of Dublin, etc.*, ed. J.T. Gilbert (London, 1870), no. 24, pp 91–2; for King John's agreement to allow Londoners formally elect their mayor, see *Rotuli chartarum in Turri Londinensi asservati*, ed. T.D. Hardy (London, 1837), i, p. 207. **86** John Gillingham, 'John (1167–1216)', *Oxford dictionary of national biography* (Oxford, 2004); online ed., Sept. 2010: www.oxforddnb.com/view/ article/14841, accessed Feb. 2013. **87** A Reginald Cordwainer also appears in the service of King John in Ireland, in the company of David, bishop of Waterford and Geoffrey Luttrell: *Rotuli litterarum patentium in Turri Londinensi*, ed. T.D. Hardy (2 vols, London, 1835), i, p. 48 (a). The shared surname may simply be coincidence. **88** *Calendar of the Gormanston register, c.1175–1397, from the original in the possession of the Right Honourable the Viscount of Gormanston*, ed. James Mills and M.J. McEnery (Dublin, 1916), p. 129 (hereafter *CGR*). The issue of who held right of seisin in Ballymadon involved many members of the extended Cordwainer family, the Trublevilles family and, by extension, the many tenants further enfeoffed by all claimants. References can be found across many sources, examples including: *CDI*, i, no. 1899, pp 282–3; *CDI*, ii, no. 67, p. 10, nos 564–5, pp 92–3, no. 696, p. 112; *Calendar of the close rolls … 1272–1509* (47 vols, London, 1892–1963), 1231–4, pp 111, 221, 344; in a 1252 inquisition calendared in *Inquisitions and extents of medieval Ireland*, ed. Paul Dryburgh and Brendan Smith (Kew, 2007), no. 7, p. 5, it is noted that the current tenants had all been enfeoffed by Roger Cordwainer.

which descendant rightfully held seisin is not of particular relevance here, the names of those involved are of significant interest.

In return for the sum of thirty-five marks, Robert Ruffus granted Roger Cordwainer a moiety of his land of Ballymadon, *c.*1204. It is likely that Robert Ruffus and Roger Cordwainer had become acquainted with each other through their involvement in serving the crown; in 1185, Ruffus, noted as being one of Lord John's serjeants, was responsible for the transport of one thousand marks from London to Bristol, part of the preparations being made there for John's visit to Ireland.[89] It is possible then that the original grant of Ballymadon by John to Robert had been in recognition of his role in the 1185 visit. One of the witnesses to Ruffus' grant was a representative of the la Warre family, in this instance John, while another was Nicholas, son of Nicholas, with both of whom Roger can be found a year later engaged on the king's business.[90] In the same year, Ruffus also granted to William Cordwainer the other moiety of his land of Ballymadon, with the same conditions given to his brother Roger. Two years later, in turn, William, noted as being the son of Elias the Cordwainer, released to John the Cordwainer all rights and claims in a moiety of Ballymadon.[91] This John Cordwainer appears to have been William's nephew, son of Roger. In the late 1230s, William son of Alan, with the consent of his wife Agnes, sister and heir of John Cordwainer, and daughter of Roger Cordwainer, granted another prominent Dubliner, Gilbert de Livet, half a stone house with cellar.[92] It appears that on John's death, his sister Agnes had retained the right of seisin, which on her death passed to her daughter Matilda, and subsequently to John de la Hyde, for whom the 1270 inspeximus was intended.[93]

The dispute as to the rightful holder of both moieties in Ballymadon seems to have begun with the grandchildren of those originally enfeoffed by Ruffus. Again, the actual details are outside the concerns of this study, but the affair allows us to trace the Cordwainer descendents into the late thirteenth century, over a hundred years after they originally arrived in Ireland. In the 1240s, William, grandson of William Cordwainer claimed that he was rightfully enfeoffed with his grandfather's moiety.[94] From his grandfather, the moiety had passed to Elias, his father and then to him, but five years later Robert Ruffus, the original enfeoffer, had died. As Robert's legitimacy was in question, his lands had been taken into the king's hands as an escheat. One of

---

89 *The great roll of the pipe for the thirty-first year of the reign of King Henry the second, 1184–5* (London, 1913), pp 217–18.   **90** *Rotuli litterarum patentium*, i, p. 54 (a). A decade later, Roger Cordwainer and Nicholas son of Nicholas were still engaged in John's work in Bristol: ibid, p. 136 (b) and 137 (a).   **91** *CGR*, p. 129. See also *Rotuli litterarum clausarum*, i, p. 416 (a) for a 1220 mandate to the Irish justiciar regarding Robert Ruffus' land in Ballymadon, which had been Elias Cordwainer's.   **92** *HSJB*, no. 83. In 1225–6, a John le Cordwainer was admitted to the merchant's guild of Dublin: *DGMR*, p. 54 (2nd col.) (John Palmer Cordwainer, p. 65, 2nd col.).   **93** A John de la Hyde granted land in the parish of St Michael in Dublin to William de Stafford, *c.*1253–4 (TCD MS 1207/33).   **94** *CGR*, p. 130.

the difficulties for the jurors in attempting to establish Robert's legitimacy was that, because he had not been born in Ireland,

> they have not deposed with certainty concerning his bastardy or legitimacy, which can be more fully declared in England; but as many coming from England say he was a bastard, the jurors believe he was bastard rather than legitimate.[95]

If Robert's legitimacy was confirmed, William's claim stood; if not, it was the king's right to enfeoff, as he had done to Ralph de Trubleville.[96]

William was not the only claimant to part of the Cordwainer lands in Ballymadon. John Cordwainer's wife, Aufricia, held approximately two hundred acres in what the inquisition calls Cordwainer's town in the manor of Ballymadon. These she held as her dower.[97] Following the death of John Cordwainer, Aufricia married a Roger Oweyn; however, John's grandnephew, John de la Hyde, was his heir, suggesting that John and Aufricia's marriage had not produced heirs.[98]

John Cordwainer's sister Agnes had at least one daughter, Matilda, who appears to have married Roger de la Hyde. This marriage brought new connections and brought Roger Cordwainer's descendants into a new sphere of politics. Of this other Roger, St John Brooks stated plainly that he was 'an important man'.[99] The earliest reference to his presence in Ireland appears to date to 1223,[1] and he was certainly in the employ of Earl William Marshal the Younger, receiving letters of protection in 1228 for having gone to Ireland on Marshal's service,[2] possibly in his capacity as seneschal of Leinster.[3] In the 1230s, he held a mill in Marshal land in Wexford,[4] and despite siding with

---

95 Ibid.   96 The Trubleville family were also landholders in various English counties and provided household knights to several English kings: see S.D. Church, *The household knights of King John* (Cambridge, 1999); Beth Hartland, 'English landholding in Ireland' in Michael Prestwich, Richard Britnell and Robin Frame (eds), *Thirteenth century England X* (Woodbridge, 2005), p. 121.   97 There is an earlier reference (1228) following the king's grant of Ballymadon to Ralph de Trubleville. In this, Roger Cordwainer's son, Ralph, and his unnamed wife were both to receive a payment, while Roger's wife, who held the manor as her dower, was to have her chattels and corn. This is the only reference to Ralph and his mother's concerns in Ballymadon that has been uncovered: *CDI*, i, no. 1611, p. 241. 98 Unless de la Hyde inherited following the death of any children; there is a reference to a John, son of John Cordwainer de Bristol in 1254–5: *DGMR*, p. 95 (1st col.). This Roger Oweyn may be the same Roger Owen/Audoen who was mayor *c.*1234–5, provost 1236–7 and mayor again twice in the 1240s. For mayoral dates, see Jacqueline Hill, 'Mayors and lord mayors of Dublin from 1229' in T.W. Moody, F.X. Martin and F.J. Byrne (eds), *A new history of Ireland, ix: maps, genealogies, lists* (Oxford, 1984), p. 548; for dates for the provosts, see *DGMR*, Table I, p. 111.   99 *Knights' fees in Counties Wexford, Carlow and Kilkenny (13th–15th centuries)*, ed. Eric St John Brooks (Dublin, 1950), p. 24.   1 Ibid.   2 *CDI*, i, no. 1597, p. 239.   3 *Calendar of Ormond deeds*, ed. Edmund Curtis (5 vols, Dublin, 1932–41), i, no. 75; *RAST*, no. 384, p. 339.   4 G.H. Orpen, 'Charters of Earl Richard Marshal of the

Richard Marshal against King Henry III he was restored to his lands and chattels in 1234.[5] This Roger was then father to John de la Hyde, whose marriage did produce at least one heir, and four generations removed from Roger Cordwainer another Roger appears in the family.

As descendant of a man who had at one time been mayor of Bristol and a trusted servant of the crown, it was perhaps fitting that John de la Hyde had married a daughter of Walerand de Wellesley.[6] His patronymic refers to Wellesley in Somerset and he first appeared in Ireland on the king's service in 1226.[7] Until his death, sometime before September 1276,[8] de Wellesley acted variously as justice itinerant and justice of the bench.[9] Not only would Roger de la Hyde and Walerand most likely have been familiar with each other as administrators and officials, they both had an interest in land in Dunoneghan (near Arklow?).[10] Walerand was also on one occasion a patron of the hospital of St John the Baptist, in 1260–1 granting 5s., four of which were owed to him from a tenement in St Patrick's Street in Dublin and another from a tenement Robert de Wayvill held of Elena de Bristol.[11] He too appears to have become embroiled in the Ballymadon affair; in 1260, William de Trubleville complained he had not received justice against John de la Hyde regarding land and rent in Ballymadon, 'owing to Walerand's influence'. It was ordered that 'two discreet and prudent men' should investigate.[12] Several years later, Walerand acted in his capacity as justice itinerant between his son-in-law and Archbishop Fulk in a case that resulted in Amicia, prioress of Grace Dieu, and her successors receiving from John de la Hyde the advowson of the church of Ballymadon.[13]

Outside of the immediate family circle, there are other Cordwainers whose exact relations with Roger, William and their descendants are unclear; one in particular, a Thomas Cordwainer, was called a burgess of Bristol in the 1230s.[14] That there was a connection between Thomas and Roger's family is probable; this deed describes the subject of the grant, a moiety of a stone house with cellar, having being held first by Roger Cordwainer, then his son John and then by Agnes, John's sister and heir, by right of her husband and grantor, William

---

forests of Ross and Taghmon', *Journal of the Royal Society of Antiquaries of Ireland*, 64 (1934), 56.   **5** *CDI*, i, no. 2129, p. 315; no. 2136, p. 317.   **6** *CGR*, p. 134 and Appendix to *36th report of the deputy keeper of the public records in Ireland*, p. 63 name Roger as John's son: *CDI*, ii, no. 696, p. 112 notes that John had married de Wellesley's daughter, unnamed. **7** Francis Elrington Ball, *The judges in Ireland* (2 vols, London, 1926), i, p. 46. In his entry on de Wellesley, Ball notes that Walerand 'was mentioned as father of John Delahyde 1260' but does not note the source. He was in fact his father-in-law.   **8** *Calendar of the patent rolls preserved in the Public Record Office, 1232–1509* (52 vols, London, 1891–1916), 1271–82, p. 161.   **9** Ball, *The judges in Ireland*, i, pp 46–7; Richardson and Sayles, *The administration of Ireland*, p. 32.   **10** *Calendar of Ormond deeds*, i, no. 77, p. 36.   **11** *HSJB*, no. 141.   **12** *CDI*, ii, no. 696, p. 112. William had been granted seisin of the manor of Ballymadon in 1249–50, while still allowing John Cordwainer's widow, Aufricia, her dower: *CDI*, i, no. 3035, pp 452–3. **13** *Alen*, p. 100.   **14** *HSJB*, no. 83.

son of Alan, against Thomas Cordwainer (*quam quidem medietatem tenui jure dicte Angnetis ... contra Thomam Cordewanerium, burgensem Bristollie*). The recipient was Gilbert de Livet, himself a prominent and important citizen of Dublin. This house may originally have been Thomas', as *c.*1220 he granted de Livet two stone cellars in the same location.[15] If they were his, there is no record of how they came to be in the possession of Roger and his children over a decade later, but it does provide a possible link to a Thomas Cordwainer who makes several appearances around the same dates in Bristol.[16] This Thomas, son of a Roger Cordwainer, who himself had a son Roger, may be a cousin of Roger and William. By the 1240s, Roger son of Thomas was in possession of at least a messuage, three shops and a cellar in Bristol.[17]

CONCLUSION

When writing about the Ireland–England–Normandy world of men such as William Marshal and Hugh de Lacy and his family, Robin Frame noted that in their involvement in events in each region, 'not only does the scene switch back and forth across the sea, alliances and enmities span it, and the leading actors are in some cases identical'.[18] Though the men considered here are lower on the social scale than the de Lacys and Marshals, and consequently in neither England nor Ireland had the same impact on politics or society, the actions of many of them mirrored the great magnates in keeping business options alive on both sides of the Irish Sea.

There is also the presence of an area in Bristol called 'Irish Mead' awaiting proper examination. Located north of Bristol Castle, and immediately north of the Dominican priory, Irishmead Street was in the area where Rosemary Street, Old King Street and Merchant Street meet in modern Bristol. The earliest reference appears to be in a deed dated *c.*1167x*c.*1200,[19] but it is still

15 Ibid., no. 84. The Cistercians were the recipients of the rent: *CSMA*, i, no. 176, p. 434.
16 A Thomas Cordwainer can be found as witness in Bristol: see 'Original documents of the thirteenth century relating to Bristol', ed. F.W. Potto Hicks, *Transactions of the Bristol and Gloucestershire Archaeological Society*, 58 (1936), no. 12, pp 233–4.   17 *Abstracts of feet of fines relating to Gloucestershire, 1199–1299*, ed. C.R. Elrington, *Bristol and Gloucestershire Archaeological Society*, 16 (2003), no. 415, p. 82; the same in more detail, in *The Great Red Book of Bristol*, ed. E.W.W. Veale (5 vols, Bristol, 1931–53), intro, pt I, no. 11, p. 183; *Cartulary of St Augustine's Abbey, Bristol*, nos 525 (pp 334–5), 542 (p. 345), 558 (pp 355–6) all mention other sons of Thomas Cordwainer.   18 Robin Frame, 'Aristocracies and the political configuration of the British Isles' in R.R. Davies (ed.), *The British Isles, 1100–1500* (Edinburgh, 1988), p. 147. Another study that examines the level of continued movement across the Irish Sea is Paul Brand, 'English royal justices in the lordship of Ireland, *c.*1300' in H.B. Clarke and J.R.S. Phillips (eds), *Ireland, England and the Continent in the Middle Ages and beyond* (Dublin, 2006), pp 128–43.   19 For the *c.*1200 date, see Potto Hicks, 'Original documents', no. 2, p. 221. The editor also refers to the presence of the phrase *corrigia hibernica* in an earlier deed, but provides no reference details. The same deed has

named as such in 1279,[20] and as late as 1480, when William Worcester conducted his topographical measurement of Bristol.[21] If this is an indication of Irish settlers in Bristol in the twelfth century, it raises the question as to their own ethnic background – Gaelic Irish, Hiberno-Norse or repatriated locals from Bristol and Gloucestershire? William Worcester commented that 'cooks and sellers of provisions formerly lived in the said street in the old days', which might suggest mercantile pursuits.[22] It is only by a full prosopographical examination of such sources as the roll of the Dublin merchants' guild and deeds of ecclesiastical institutions that the full extent of this settlement can be determined. Wendy Childs conducted an examination of the settlement of Irish (predominantly Anglo-Irish) merchants in the Bristol and Chester regions in the fourteenth and fifteenth centuries, with interesting results,[23] although, despite the much heralded trade between Dublin and Bristol, by the late fourteenth century, 'of 171 Irish ship movements recorded' in Bristol, there were only eleven that were from the Dublin–Drogheda area.[24]

The presence of the Anglo-Irish in Bristol was perhaps not only accounted for by passing merchants, but may also have been due to it being regarded as a place of refuge from Ireland in times of difficult economic circumstances, particularly in the fourteenth century.[25] If extensive numbers of settlers in Bristol were from Ireland, this might explain the distrust with which they were regarded and why attempts were made to exclude them.[26] In 1439, an ordinance was made in Bristol forbidding the election of an Irishman to the Common Council; specifically,

> it is ordained that no Irishman begotten and born within the country of Ireland of an Irish mother and father (*nullus homo Hibernicus infra terram Hibernie de partre et matre Hibernicis procreatus et natus decetero*) be in future admitted to the Common Council either by entreaty of reward.[27]

been dated *c.*1167 by the Bristol Record Office: Peter Fleming, 'Identity and belonging: Irish and Welsh in fifteenth-century Bristol' in Linda Clarke (ed.), *The fifteenth century vii: conflicts, consequences and the crown in the late Middle Ages* (Woodbridge, 2007), p. 176 and for the same [http://archives.bristol.gov.uk/dserve, accessed Feb. 2013].   **20** Potto Hicks, 'Original documents', no. 14, p. 235.   **21** *William Worcestre: the topography of medieval Bristol*, ed. Frances Neale, *Bristol Record Society*, 51 (2000), no. 61, pp 39–41; no. 167, p. 99.   **22** Ibid., p. 41.   **23** Wendy Childs, 'Irish merchants and seamen in late medieval England', *Irish Historical Studies*, 32:125 (2000), 22–43.   **24** Ibid., p. 24.   **25** Fleming, 'Identity and belonging: Irish and Welsh in fifteenth-century Bristol', p. 178.   **26** Childs, 'Irish merchants and seamen', p. 36.   **27** *The Little Red Book of Bristol*, ed. F.B. Bickley (2 vols, Bristol, 1900), i, p. 86. For any mayor who allowed such an election, a 'penalty of twenty pounds of good, lawful and usual money of England be levied and paid from the goods and chattels of the mayor'. By 'Irish', these Bristolian ordinances probably meant both the Gaelic and English of Ireland, although it is likely that the English of Ireland were present in Bristol in far greater numbers than their Gaelic counterparts. Fifteenth-century English sources are inexact in their terminology, and tend to use the term 'Irish' for both groups,

In an ordinance of 1479, the bowyers and fletchers of Bristol were ordered that 'no rebelle of Irelonde no alyen' was to be taken on as an apprentice, while the hoopers ordered the dismissal of Irish servants and aliens.[28] As a craft, cordwaining continued in Bristol, and its practioners too were concerned about the origins of their apprentices; in 1443, it was ordered that they should not 'receive any man born outside the power and allegiance of our lord the king to serve and occupy in the aforesaid craft'.[29] Fifteenth-century ordinances regarding the Irish were not restricted to occupational guilds; in 1489, in Dunster, Somerset, it was ordered that 'nobody shall henceforth keep in his service any Irish servants, save one, under pain of 10s'.[30]

The significance of the grant made by Henry II to Adhelm, Haim's brother, has been discussed above. It may be worth noting a further aspect of this, that is, the area of settlement by his siblings and their fellow émigrés from Bristol, although again a full investigation is needed. If Henry II was anxious to demonstrate the change in city rule by granting one of his Bristol subjects land in the old Viking Thingmoot, thus ensuring the security of the eastern access route into the city, might the same deliberate settlement have been planned for the newly reclaimed area on the riverfront by the north-western section of the 1100 wall?[31] By the time Dublin received its third royal charter, from John as lord of Ireland in 1192, reference was already being made to 'buildings over the water', while more significantly, the citizens were given the right to build on the riverbank, once the city or citizens were not adversely affected.[32] The area from the King's Gate on Winetavern Street, west to Gormond's Gate, became settled by several of the most prominent settlers from Bristol. Perhaps 'the building of revetments at Wood Quay was an attempt to provide better facilities for the merchants'.[33] One citizen who either did build, or at least

while sources from Ireland for the same period take care to distinguish between the two. The English of Ireland objected strenuously to being called 'Irish' and demanded that they be treated as English subjects of the crown. Their lobbying resulted in getting an exemption for the English of Ireland from alien's subsidies after 1443, but the prejudice against them persisted. Bans against all those born in Ireland – English or Irish – were put in place in various English port towns and at institutions like Oxford University and the Inns of Court in London in the second half of the fifteenth century: see J.L. Bolton, 'Irish migration to England in the late Middle Ages', *Irish Historical Studies*, 32:125 (2000), 1–21; Paul Brand, 'Irish law students and lawyers in late medieval England', *Irish Historical Studies*, 32:126 (2000), 161–73. **28** *The Great Red Book of Bristol*, text (pt 1), p. 151 and n. 1. **29** *The Little Red Book of Bristol*, i, p. 176. **30** H.C. Maxwell Lyte, *A history of Dunster and of the families of Mohun and Luttrell* (2 vols, London, 1909), i, p. 308. **31** This area has not undergone the same level of excavation as other waterfront sections of the city: Linzi Simpson, 'Forty years a-digging: a preliminary synthesis of archaeological investigations in medieval Dublin' in Seán Duffy (ed.), *Medieval Dublin I* (Dublin, 2000), pp 51–2. **32** *Calendar of ancient records of Dublin*, ed. J.T. and Lady Gilbert (18 vols, Dublin, 1889–1944), i, nos 24, 25, p. 5. **33** Clare McCutcheon, *Medieval pottery from Wood Quay, Dublin: the 1974–6 waterfront excavations* (Dublin, 2006), p. 17. For a description of the revetments excavated on this site in the same publication, see P.F. Wallace, 'Context and

acquired land in the region, was Roger, brother of Haim. He donated this to St Mary's, in a charter witnessed by the one-time provost of Bristol, Thomas le Martre.[34] Not only was le Martre a witness perhaps due to their common place of origin, he was probably a neighbour by the river, granting to Richard Carpenter his land towards Ostmen's Bridge.[35] Roger's son, Stephen, also made a grant to the Cistercians from land next to the wall, which may have been his father's, but given that he makes no reference to his father's donation in his own charter, it may be a separate property.[36] William de Abbotstone's land between the church of St Audoen and the house of William Blundel may have been on the city side of the wall, rather than riverine.[37] This is not to forget Roger Cordwainer, who had a stone house outside the old wall around Winetavern Street.[38]

Although Roger Cordwainer is the only one of these early settlers for whom written evidence of profession survives, and at that only long after he acquired a base in Ireland, the presence of these men on the merchants' guild roll and their relocation to Dublin from one of the city's main trading counterparts in England make it highly likely that they were themselves merchants. Living beside and owning property beside the newly expanding port would allow them ready access to inspection of a ship carrying their merchandise into the city.

location: Dublin's medieval waterfront at Wood Quay', pp 1–12.   **34** *CSMA*, i, no. 178, p. 208. Given the apparent lack of evidence in this area for the type of structures that denote habitation, the phrase 'over the bank (*super ripam*)', at this early stage might mean the area immediately outside the current Cook Street wall. Alternatively, as Roger also had land in Crockers' Street, this might refer to a riverine area in the western suburb.   **35** *RAST*, no. 483, p. 414.   **36** *CSMA*, i, no. 177, pp 207–8.   **37** Ibid., i, no. 230, p. 243. Attempts to locate a more precise description of Blundel's house were unsuccessful. While he did have land in that part of the city, it was described as stretching from the *magnus vicus* to Crockers' Street. In this instance, the former probably refers to Thomas Street, rather than High Street, otherwise the land would have had to straddle the division of the city wall: *RAST*, no. 469, p. 404.   **38** *CSMA*, i, no. 176, p. 434.

Black Monday: the power of myth in medieval Dublin

DECLAN JOHNSTON

Fateful days in Easter seem to be at the heart of Dublin city's historical mythology. Dublin's most hotly contested historiographical debates are fixated on the contemporary and current understandings of the events of 1014 and 1916. Yet for centuries it was another event that occurred on a fateful day at Easter, in this case Easter Monday 1209, that held a special significance for Dubliners. It was marked dutifully by them annually and while its weighty symbolism would evolve over the course of time, the story of Black Monday would remain one of the defining aspects of Dublin identity.

Unfortunately, it is practically impossible to ascertain what exactly happened on Easter Monday 1209. Most modern scholarship has accepted unquestioningly the narrative of the historians of Ireland in the sixteenth, seventeenth and eighteenth centuries, despite the fact that their sources remain obscure and undefined. In fact, it is highly doubtful that a contemporary account was ever recorded. Neither the traditional Irish annals nor the various Anglo-Irish annals record the occurrence (such as the chronicle sometimes associated with Philip Flattisbury or the ecclesiastical annals of the houses of Dublin's religious orders, such as St Mary's Abbey). The earliest surviving written account appears to be that of Richard Stanihurst, the chief composer of Raphael Holinshed's *The historie of Irelande from the first inhabitation thereof, unto the yeare 1509 within his Chronicles of England, Scotland and Ireland* [hereafter Chronicles] published in 1577:

> even to this daye, the Irish feare a ragged and jagged blacke standard that the citizens have, almost through tract of time worne to the hard stumps … The sight of which danteth the Irish above measure. Soone after Ireland was conquered by the Britons, and the greater part of Leinster pacified, diuerse townsmen of Bristow flitted from thense to Dublin, and in short space the ciuitie was by them so well inhabited, as it grew to bee verie populous. Whereupon the citizens having over great affiance in the multitude of the people, and so consequentlie being somewhat retchlesse [reckless] in heeding the mounteine enimie that lurked under their noses, were woont to rome and roile in clusters, sometime three or foure miles from the towne. The Irish enimies pieng that the citizens were accustomed to fetch such od vagaries, especiallie on the holiedaies, & having an inkling withall by some false clatterfert [traitor] or other, that a companie of them would have ranged abrode, on mondaie in the Easter

weeke towards the wood of Cullen, which is distant two miles from Dublin … and laid in sundrie places for their comming. The citizens … flockt unarmed out of the ciuitie to the wood, where being intercepted … they were to the number of five hundred miserablie slaine. Whereupon the remnant of the citizens deeming that unluckie time to be a crosse or a dismall daie, gaue it the appellation of Black mondaie. The citiesoone after being peopled by a fresh supplie of Bristollians, to dare the Irish enimie, agreed to banket yearelie in that place, which to this daie is observed. For the maior and the shiriffs with the citizens repaire to the wood of Cullen, in which place the maior bestoweth a costlie dinner within a mote or a rundell, and both the shiriffs within another: where they are so well garded with the youth of the ciuitie, as the mounteine enimie dareth not attempt to snatch as much as a pastie crust thense.[1]

Stanihurst admits in his preface that he was indebted to his close friend Edmund Campion (who was his tutor at Oxford)[2] for most of the material in his book, which he had decided 'to enrich with further addition'.[3] However, Campion's *A historie of Ireland* in two books contains no mention of Black Monday.[4] The fact that Black Monday therefore is an addition that can be attributed to Stanihurst would suggest that he was narrating an established tale for Dubliners, which Campion did not come across in his research of written records. It is also notable that in the *Chronicles* the original sources for events recorded were usually acknowledged in the margin,[5] which is not the case with the account of Black Monday. A study of Holinshed's listed additional authorities from the beginning of his *Chronicles* reveals no earlier source either.[6]

Stanihurst himself was much taken by 'urban legends' associated with the founding of the city and also talks in the *Chronicles* of how Little John had come to Dublin following the death of Robin Hood to partake in an archery contest.[7] If it is the case that Stanihurst was merely transcribing a popular legend of the city at the time, his particular version of it was no doubt shaped by his own biography. He was part of a family that had been active in municipal life in Dublin since the 1400s,[8] and was very much part of a settled

1 *Raphaell Holinshed (comp.), Holinshed's Irish chronicles: the history of Ireland from the first habitation thereof, unto the yeares 1509 & continued till the yeare 1547*, ed. Liam Miller and Eileen Power (Dublin, 1979), pp 42–3. 2 Colm Lennon, 'Richard Stanihurst and old English Identity', *Irish Historical Studies*, 21:82 (Sept. 1978), 121–43 at 124. 3 Ibid., 125. 4 Edmund Campion, *Two bokes of the histories of Ireland*, ed. A.F. Vossen (Assen, 1963). 5 *Holinshed's Irish chronicles*, p. x. 6 Jesus College Oxford launched an exhaustive examination of all of the sources listed in the *Chronicles*, in what was named *The Holinshed Project*. An examination of all the sources listed by Stanihurst, including the afore-mentioned Philip Flattisbury manuscript of Anglo-Irish Annals, which resides in Trinity College Dublin and forms the spine of the work, reveals no sources for Stanihurst's information. 7 *Holinshed's Irish chronicles*, pp 50–1. 8 Lennon, 'Richard Stanihurst and

community favouring an Anglo-Irish identity, attempting to prove to Elizabeth I that they were better equipped than a native English administration to rule Ireland.[9] Similarly, he was perpetually at loggerheads with the Gaelic Irish septs on the city's borders. His grandfather had been speaker of the Irish parliament and his father was a vocal advocate of Dublin's expansion, expressing a wish to 'reclaim our unbroken borders and unquiet neighbours'.[10] While it is clear why the story of Black Monday must have appealed to Stanihurst then, it was nevertheless a commonly accepted story at the time, as it was also being recorded by others.

Meredith Hanmer, a doctor of divinity, composed much of his *Chronicle of Ireland* in the 1590s and it was unfinished at the time of his death in 1604. Edited and completed by the Ulster King of Arms Daniel Molyneux,[11] it gives a damning account of both the Irish attack and the Black Monday parades, which Hanmer viewed as nothing but a blasphemous exercise:

> the occasion of blacke Munday, and the originall remembrance thereof, rose at Dublin. The citie of Dublin by reason of some great mortality, being wasted and desolate, the inhabitants of Bristoll flocked thither to inhabit, who after their country manner, upon holy dayes, some for love of the fresh ayre, some to avoyd idlenesse, some other for pastime, pleasure and gamings sake, flocked out of the towne towards Cullen wood upon Munday in Easter weeke. The Birnnes and Tooles (the mountaine enemies) like wolves lay in ambush for them, and upon espial [catching sight of] finding them unarmed, fell upon them, & slue some 300 persons, besides women & children, which they led in their hands, although shortly after, the towne was upon the report thereof, eftsoones [once more] peopled againe by Bristolians; yet that dismall day is yeerely remembred, and solemnly observed by the maior, sheriffes and citizens, with feast and banquet, and pitching up of tents in that place in most brave sort, daring the enemy upon his perill, not to bee so hardy, as once to approach neere their feasting campe; … now they have Munday in memory, making difference of dayes, not fitting the minde of the Apostle, which forbade the superstitions or vaine observations of daies &c. Gal. 4.[12]

This was written just twenty years after Stanihurst's version and contains many of the same basic points of information, and yet their sources are clearly

old English Identity', 122.   **9** Colm Lennon, *Richard Stanihurst, the Dubliner, 1547–1618: a biography, with a Stanihurst text on Ireland's past* (Dublin, 1981), p. 125.   **10** Campion, *Two bokes of the histories of Ireland*, ed. Vossen, p. 183.   **11** William Nicolson, *The English, Scotch and Irish historical libraries: giving a short view and character of most of our historians, either in print or manuscript* (London, 1776), p. 20.   **12** The biblical reference cited is a letter of Paul to the Galatians (Gal 4:10–11), criticizing the practice of marking days of the calendar: 'You observe days, and months, and seasons, and years! I am afraid I have laboured over you in

different. Most of Hanmer's work was also based on an original source – a set of Anglo-Irish annals – yet the Black Monday entry for 1209 is Hanmer's own addition, enhancing the idea of a traditional oral tale. The death toll given by Hanmer is three hundred, not five hundred, and he makes no mention of the black standard that Stanihurst claimed struck such fear into the Irish. There is also the indication that 'some great mortality' before 1209 had caused the town to be flooded by a fresh supply of Bristolians. It is known that a plague had ravaged Dublin and the surrounding areas specifically in 1204,[13] and this perhaps is what he is referring to. If Stanihurst and Hanmer, within years of each other, produced accounts so similar and yet tellingly different in key details, it suggests that at this stage of Dublin's history the legend of Black Monday was well known and considered important, even if it had no singular recognizable contemporary written source.

Hanmer's work was eventually completed and passed on to James Ware, who published it in 1633 in a collection of histories of Ireland. Ware went on to publish his own *Antiquities and history of Ireland* in 1654, which included Hanmer's account, repeated nearly verbatim, excluding only the biblical reference.[14] Ware had one of the greatest collections of historical manuscripts relating to Ireland ever assembled.[15] It would appear that nothing he owned would add to the account written by Hanmer. Walter Harris, married to Ware's granddaughter, produced his own work, *The history and antiquities of the city of Dublin*, in 1736. While borrowing much from Ware in his book, the account given of Black Monday is actually more faithful to Stanihurst's in style and structure and includes the figure of five hundred killed along with the first mention in any of the accounts of two parties of citizens playing 'hurling of balls', a sport he claims was introduced by Bristolians. Incidentally, this has often been mistakenly taken as proof of the Dubliners playing the Irish game of hurling.

All subsequent narratives of Black Monday are based on these original four accounts of Stanihurst, Hanmer, Ware and Harris. In the sixteenth century, the original Black Monday was considered a very real event. Mainstream historians all verified its occurrence and broadly agreed on its basic narrative. As with all historical events that are associated with such an emotive founding mythology, however – in this case of the Bristolians who established the city of Dublin – the exact truth has become lost somewhere across three centuries of retelling before it was recorded for the first time in writing. Similarly though,

vain'. Quotation is from Meredith Hanmer, 'The Chronicle of Ireland' in Sir James Ware (ed.), *Ancient Irish histories: the works of Spencer, Campion, Hanmer and Marleburrough* (2 vols, Dublin, 1809), ii, p. 370.   **13** *The annals of Tigernach*, ed. Whitley Stokes (repr., 2 vols, Felinfach, 1993), *s.a.* 1204.   **14** Sir James Ware, *The antiquities and history of Ireland* (Dublin, 1705), pp 235–6.   **15** William O'Sullivan, 'A finding list of Sir James Ware's manuscripts', *PRIA, 97C* (1997), 69–99 at 69–72.

mythologies are not created from nothing. For the story with such universally accepted dates and events to have survived, it suggests that some conflict did take place on Easter Monday 1209, but there is simply no evidence from which to ascertain the facts of the event. What we can track, however, is the evolution of the myth and its celebration. And it is perfectly understandable that this myth lasted through the ages.

By 1209, Dublin had been under Bristolian control for nearly forty years and the city's new elite had enjoyed a very robust and prosperous beginning to life in Dublin. A cartel of traders who had long dealt with the city now found themselves in its ownership. If we believe Hanmer's statement that the city had been restocked by Bristolians after the 1204 epidemic, this ruling class had been regenerated and its traditions perpetuated by a new generation of members. They showed a fierce loyalty to consecutive monarchs (having earlier offered support to Henry II in his struggle with Stephen and then to John in his attempt to seize the crown in the 1190s, and been rewarded with favourable charters in 1172, 1174, 1185, 1192, 1200) and by 1209 were governing the city as they had Bristol, with their own unique customs. The Dublin charters are nearly exact replications of the Bristol charters of 1164, 1170, 1171 and 1188. The Ostmen had no doubt been expropriated (some perhaps being expelled north of the Liffey to Oxmantown), the city had a set of defined boundaries within which they developed the town, and Dublin Castle had been constructed, as a symbol of dominance and rule and a measure of the level of taxes the city was taking in,[16] along with extensive city defences (which incidentally were viewed by the crown as the duty of the citizens, an indication of the level of responsibility they were expected to assume).[17] A merchant guild, a system presumably new to Dublin, had been established in order to monopolize the city's profits. Merchant guilds tended to be the most powerful element in any city,[18] and the elders within the guild no doubt ruled the roost, but in Dublin there were no older generations for these men of Bristol to vie with. These pioneers had imposed their own separate identity on Dublin.

Easter Monday sport is a medieval tradition and an important civic activity that, in some respects, persists to the present day. In the case of Dubliners on Easter Monday 1209, Harris even suggests that the very sport they were playing was of Bristolian origin. However, on that day, when they went to Cullenswood, they were taking their symbols of civic ownership beyond the city walls to an area that for centuries was the land of Irish septs, an encroachment that was sure to have engendered resentment. And it is easy to imagine how an Easter Monday hosting, targeting the revelries of the new settlers, would have appealed to the O'Byrnes and O'Tooles from their vantage point in the Wicklow Mountains.

16 James Lydon, 'Dublin Castle in the Middle Ages' in Seán Duffy (ed.), *Medieval Dublin III* (Dublin, 2002), p. 115.   17 Ibid., p. 116.   18 J.J. Webb, *The guilds of Dublin* (repr.

Robert Ware, son of Sir James, in his *Antiquities and history of Dublin*, tells the presumably apocryphal tale of how Richard Muton, the first mayor of Dublin, a man who had been raised in poverty, was married off to the daughter of a city provost, John Heath, and proceeded up through the ranks to initiate the building of the tholsel.[19] While this story is wholly problematic,[20] it is an example of the mythology surrounding the wealthy founders of the city in the thirteenth century that survived long into the seventeenth century. After 1209, the men who had established control over Dublin city sought to confirm an ever-growing sense of self-governance. Hence, the story of Black Monday would have become an important 'founding mythology' that legitimized their ownership of the city. It was one that perpetuated the idea of a constant threat to their survival, at the hands of barbaric enemies, and a common Bristolian heritage. Henry of London was appointed archbishop of Dublin in 1213 and immediately reserved one of the lucrative prebends of Dublin for himself – 1,150 acres of Cullenswood.[21] Perhaps, in the wake of Black Monday, this was a claim to ownership of the area for the city. He even established his own home manor there.[22] It was later destroyed in the Bruce Invasion, and the description of the destruction hints at the size of the establishment involved:

> a hall with stone walls now prostrate, a chamber for the archbishop with a chapel annexed, the chamber roofed with shingles … a kitchen formed of wood, a grange, a stable and granary … all now totally prostrate.[23]

The strengthening of the merchant guild continued to be a vital instrument of this Bristolian element's growing dominance and it is notable that the guilds led the Black Monday processions. The Dublin guild merchant roll lists 224 new members in 1226 alone (forty-two of whom were connected to some craft),[24] and more than fifty professions are suggested by the members' surnames, indicating a very robust and flourishing organization.[25] The existence of the guild merchant roll is an oddity in itself, the only other contemporary one being that of Leicester (which is also much smaller than Dublin's), which enhances the idea of a Dublin class of merchants legitimizing their own identity through procedure and process. Since 1169, Dublin trade had shifted from its concentration – a legacy of its Viking origins – on York, Scotland and

London, 1970), pp 1–8.   **19** Raymond Gillespie, 'Robert Ware's telling tale: a medieval Dublin story and its significance' in Seán Duffy (ed.), *Medieval Dublin V* (Dublin, 2003), pp 293–4.   **20** Ibid., pp 294–5.   **21** Deirdre Kelly, *Four roads to Dublin: the history of Rathmines, Ranelagh and Leeson Street* (Dublin, 2001), p. 18.   **22** Margaret Murphy and Michael Potterton, *The Dublin region in the Middle Ages: settlement, land-use and economy* (Dublin, 2010), p. 76.   **23** Kelly, *Four roads to Dublin*, pp 17–18.   **24** *The Dublin guild merchant roll, c.1190–1265*, ed. Philonema Connolly and Geoffrey Martin (Dublin, 1992); E.W. Eggerer, 'The guild merchant of Dublin' in Seán Duffy (ed.), *Medieval Dublin VI* (Dublin, 2004), p. 150.   **25** Webb, *The guilds of Dublin*, pp 8–10.

Iceland, and definitively moved south towards the Bristol Channel and France. While there are 150 names on the guild merchant roll that are specifically 'de Bristollo' and eighty-nine that are 'de Glovernia',[26] the overwhelming majority originate in southern Britain, specifically places in the West Country or Wales,[27] who presumably, as traders, were members of the Bristol merchant guild previously. The 1192 charter even specifies that Dublin would have the same guilds as were in Bristol.[28] Remarkably at this time, more than half of Dublin's new citizens were people migrating to the city.[29] As Dublin's independence gathered pace though, it formed an identity that became divorced from Bristol. While the charters of Dublin seemed to match the wording of the charters granted to Bristol in preceding years, the first major charter after Black Monday, in 1215, made a decisive break and Dublin was granted a provost and the fee-farm of the city, which took the responsibility of tax collection away from the king's sheriff and placed it in the hands of the city's own elected official, a significant act of self-governance.[30] In 1229, Dublin followed in the footsteps of London in securing the right to an elected mayor. While this may have been in return for the cancellation of a debt,[31] it is interesting that this is what the citizens of Dublin wanted in exchange – the right to elect their own leader, presumably one of their own elite, to further the prestige and independence of their frontier city. In a very short period, by 1230, Dublin had acquired everything needed for a self-governing polity under the English monarch – a mayor, a town clerk and a common seal.[32] Already the incoming settlers had tried to create a world of their own, which used all the basic civic guidelines of England, though with their own Dublin customs, which were gradually separating from those of Bristol. Black Monday and the structures of power built by the Dubliners in its wake were about forming a distinct separate municipality. Their new identity drew on Bristolian heritage, but was establishing itself as something new and independent: a Dublin identity.

On the other hand, Black Monday was no *Kristallnacht* for Dublin's large Irish population. Certainly there was a glass ceiling for Irish Dubliners. Irish members have been documented in the guild rolls of the fifteenth and sixteenth centuries,[33] but they were not listed in great numbers in the early city. The qualification attached to the charter of the smiths' guild of Dublin of 1474[34] that

---

26 Patricia Becker, 'An analysis of the Dublin guild merchant roll, *c*.1190–1265' (MPhil, TCD, 1996), pp 53–9.   **27** Eggerer, 'The guild merchant of Dublin', pp 150–1.   **28** *Calendar of ancient records of Dublin, in the possession of the municipal corporation of that city*, 1, ed. J.T. Gilbert (Dublin, 1889), pp 2–63 (hereafter *CARD*).   **29** Eggerer, 'The guild merchant of Dublin', p. 151.   **30** Mary Clark, 'People, places and parchment: the medieval archives of Dublin City' in Seán Duffy (ed.), *Medieval Dublin III* (Dublin, 2001), p. 145.   **31** Ibid.   **32** Ibid., p. 146.   **33** A great number of Irish members of Dublin guilds are listed by Sparky Booker, 'Gaelicization and cultural exchange in late medieval Dublin' in Seán Duffy (ed.), *Medieval Dublin X* (Dublin, 2010), pp 291–3, but none are before 1418.   **34** Booker, 'Gaelicization and cultural exchange', p. 291.

membership was reserved for those that 'be of English name and blood, of honest conversion and also a free citizen of the city',[35] has often been cited as proof of a widespread anti-Irish bias within the city. The truth is probably a great deal more complex than that. Irish people were intermarrying and participating in the business of the town,[36] but the new merchants who had grasped power were unwilling to relinquish it. Irish Dubliners and Irish traditions continued to creep into the city, but Dublin now identified itself as separate from the towns of England and separate from the Gaelic septs of Ireland. Within that, Irish people generally struggled to reach great heights within the city's echelons of power, despite being able to live relatively freely and participate in urban life. Black Monday parades, hence, were not about threatening the Irish who lived within the city, but about making a stand against those who lived beyond the city walls who would do damage to the colony and prosperity the new Dubliners had built.

The need for the show of defiance to the mountain enemy on Black Monday was perpetuated by the Dublin colony's ongoing struggle with the people of Wicklow. It seems that the Bruce Invasion reopened feelings of paranoia among the Dubliners against perceived local treachery. Certainly, the number of incursions into Wicklow, in pursuit of the O'Byrnes and O'Tooles, increased sharply and these were characterized by a certain brutality and a fear of Irish deceitfulness, features of English–Irish conflict that would persist for centuries. David O'Toole is said to have attempted to recreate the ambush of 1209 on the Black Monday commemorations in 1316, the year after the initial Bruce Invasion.[37] It is impossible to identify the aggressor, but in any case the Dubliners, led by Sir William Comyn and having their black standard running ahead of them, 'fought and chased the O'Tooles for six leagues, slaying 17 and wounding many desperately'.[38] It is plausible that this event was some sort of show of frustrated defiance on a day of theatre and feasting, while the Dubliners were still surrounded by the trauma of war with the invaders. The O'Tooles and O'Byrnes were lending considerable assistance to the Bruce Invasion.[39] On the other hand, the Wicklow men may have seen a vulnerability among the Dubliners. In either case, the Dubliners reacted fiercely. In the same year, just over £35, a not inconsiderable sum, was paid in wages to five crossbowmen to guard against 'the Irish felons and enemies of the king in the parts of Leinster who were threatening to burn the house of the exchequer'.[40] Again, whether that was the Irish intention is irrelevant: rumour, conjecture and fear of the 'mountain enemy', two words that seemed to be married

35 Kelly, *Four roads to Dublin*, p. 19.   **36** Booker, 'Gaelicization and cultural exchange', p. 298.   **37** Walter Harris, *The history and antiquities of the city of Dublin, from the earliest accounts: compiled from authentick memoirs, offices of record, manuscript collections and other unexceptionable vouchers* (Dublin 1766), p. 261.   **38** Ibid.   **39** Seán Duffy, *Robert the Bruce's Irish wars: the invasions of Ireland, 1306–1329* (Stroud, 2002), pp 31–2.   **40** *Irish exchequer payments, 1270–1446*, ed. Philomena Connolly (Dublin, 1998), p. 240.

together in the Dublin imagination at the time, spread on the streets. Treachery worked both ways too. In 1326, the Dublin exchequer paid out £6. 13s. 4d. for the capture of two of the O'Byrne brothers, for they were 'against the king's peace in Leinster'.[41] One of the brothers, 'Gerald Doulyngsone Obrynne, was later paid £2 6s. 8d. for 'his good service to the king in his war against those of the name of the Obyrnnes and Ototothels'.[42] The mountains remained a constant symbol of fear and the threat of invasion. In 1402, the mayor himself, John Drake, led a campaign into the mountains in which alternative Dublin chronicles by Henry of Marlborough and James de Redenesse give a grim exact total of victims slaughtered among the O'Byrnes: 493 and 487 respectively.[43] The 'short Dublin chronicle' recorded a string of hostings against the O'Tooles and O'Byrnes in the early sixteenth century: in 1513, 1516, 1517, 1519, 1521, 1523, 1530 and 1533.[44] Shane O'Toole's head was also sent as a grisly present to the mayor after the 1516 incursion.[45] By the early seventeenth century, nearly all the O'Toole lands had been parcelled out in grants and with them went a notion of insecurity and perpetual threat that lay behind Black Monday parades.

The Black Monday parades themselves must have been a quite considerable spectacle. The parades were awash with symbolism, celebrating prosperity, success, military order and a defiant challenge to the Irish. The city had four musters within the year: May Day, Midsummer Eve, St Peter's Eve and Black Monday.[46] Black Monday was one of the two musters associated with the mayor and his aldermen, indicating its priority as a civic function.[47] There was a military component to these celebrations. The tailors' guild (the oldest craft guild,[48] and one presumably particularly tied to tradition) paid out 32s. in 1622 for gunpowder for the occasion.[49] They must also have featured considerable feasting. Dublin's sixteenth- and seventeenth-century historians were always quick to point out the hospitality of the city – Robert Ware and Stanihurst both made reference to it – specifically relating it to the mayor, Black Monday's patron. David Duke, the schoolmaster, was paid 26s. 8d. by warrant of the mayor and his aldermen for playing an interlude on Black Monday in 1583. This is the earliest surviving record of an interlude in Ireland. Unfortunately, no additional information is added; we do not know whether Duke played it himself or if he used the children of the school to do so. The

41 Connolly (ed.), *Irish exchequer payments*, p. 320.   42 Ibid., p. 370.   43 A.J. Fletcher, 'The annals and chronicles of medieval Dublin: an overview' in Seán Duffy (ed.), *Medieval Dublin VIII* (Dublin, 2008), pp 206–7.   44 A.J. Fletcher, 'Earliest extant recension of the Dublin chronicle: an edition with commentary' in John Bradley, A.J. Fletcher and Anngret Simms (eds), *Dublin in the medieval world: studies in honour of Howard B. Clarke* (Dublin, 2009), p. 395.   45 Ibid.   46 A.J. Fletcher, *Drama, performance and polity in pre-Cromwellian Ireland* (Toronto, 2000), p. 130.   47 *Holinshed's Irish chronicles*, p. 42. 48 Mary Clark and Raymond Refaussé (eds), *Directory of historic Dublin guilds* (Dublin, 1993), p. 15.   49 H.F. Berry, 'The merchant tailors' gild: that of St John the Baptist,

considerable sum of money would suggest that he was paid for some production costs too, suggesting the use of children.[50] At the time, Dublin was
very consciously imitating London, where children had already been trained
for stage performances.[51]

The 'short Dublin chronicle' was a document dedicated to recording
everything that affected civic life in Dublin between 1504 and 1535.[52] This
document is very similar to its London counterpart,[53] which invoked a strong
sense of loyalty to the idea of London as a community.[54] Within it is the
announcement that in 1523 the rain was so heavy on Black Monday that the
mayor and his company had to head to Christ Church instead.[55] This was not
unheard of, as it also happened in 1578.[56] The inference of this being recorded
in the chronicle is that Black Monday parades were a landmark event on the
civic calendar. It even began to travel as a concept. By the late Middle Ages,
trade between Bristolian Dublin and Chester had become well established: the
English written in Dublin was significantly affected by a Cheshire and South
Lancashire dialect,[57] there are ninety-two names of Chester origin on the
Dublin guild merchant roll alone,[58] and Richard Stanihurst talks of an
established Chester enclave within the city,[59] and Black Monday parades duly
began to appear in Chester. In 1511, an archery contest, followed by a large
breakfast of calves' heads and bacon, noted as 'blakemondaye', took place in
Chester on Easter Monday.[60] By 1608, it was continuing in the same format,
but the reasons for it had long been forgotten by everyone,[61] and it was
continued right up until 1640.[62]

In Dublin too, the significance of Black Monday began to fade as the city
underwent a break with its medieval past in the early seventeenth century. The
assembly rolls of that period are filled with the words 'ruinous' and 'decayed'
as the city assembly justified the destruction of medieval buildings and
structures and went about creating a city for a new age.[63] The tradition must
have lapsed altogether at some point, because Mayor Mark Quine in 1655

Dublin, 1418–1841', *JRSAI*, 8:1 (1918), 19–64 at 27. **50** Fletcher, *Drama, performance and
polity*, p. 156. **51** E.K. Chambers, *The Elizabethan stage* (2 vols, Oxford, 2009), ii, pp 24–7.
52 Fletcher, 'Earliest extant recension of the Dublin chronicle', pp 390–1. **53** Ibid.
54 Fletcher, *Drama, performance and polity in pre-Cromwellian Ireland*, pp 155–6.
55 Fletcher, 'Earliest extant recension of the Dublin chronicle', p. 402. **56** Harris, *The
history and antiquities of the city of Dublin*, pp 318–19. **57** Angus McIntosh and M.L.
Samuels, 'Prolegomena to a study of medieval Anglo-Irish', *Medium Aevum*, 37 (1968),
1–11. **58** Becker, 'Dublin guild merchant roll', pp 43–5. **59** J.T. Gilbert, *A history of the
city of Dublin*, 1 (repr. Shannon, 1972), pp 27–30. **60** Elizabeth Baldwin, L.M. Clopper
and David Mills (eds), *Records of early English drama: Cheshire including Chester* (Toronto,
2007), p. 66. **61** Ibid., p. 346. **62** Ibid., p. 594. **63** Colm Lennon, 'The medieval town in
the early modern city: attitudes to Dublin's immediate past in the seventeenth and
eighteenth centuries' in Bradley et al. (eds), *Dublin in the medieval world*, pp 440–1.

revived the ancient custom of marching from Tholsel to Cullenswood on
Easter Monday ... The brethren and their servants from 16 to 60 years of
age were summoned to muster at 7 in the morning, fully armed and
equipped,[64]

and these revamped parades must have been extensive: the 1656 versioncost
£55 7s.;[65] the 1665 edition £40.[66] In 1671, though, presumably after an
unenthusiastic showing in previous years, the mayor thought it fit to order the
masters of the Trinity Guild to ensure that on Black Monday 'no disturbance,
disorders, debauchery or other profanation be committed, to the dishonour of
God or scandal of the government, but that all should demean themselves as
becometh sober citizens and good Christians'.[67] With time, however, even the
rekindled Black Monday commemorations disappeared. As long as they
survived, though, the macabre carnival of swirling black banners and the
armed muster of citizens must have made a deep impression on the city's
population. The meaning of the event changed significantly over the years, but
it was always bound to a municipal duty and a sense of shared tradition.

While the events of the Easters of 1014 and 1916 have become historical
facts, the exact events of Black Monday 1209 may never become known to
modern historians. We are at the mercy of the Dublin legend that lived on into
the era of Stanihurst and Hanmer, more than three hundred years after the
event. Yet, is it really important that we know what exactly happened? Black
Monday's importance lies in its story. We know it as it was known to the
Dubliners who paraded under black banners for centuries. It was an
importance that had been first recognized by the city's elite in the early
thirteenth century, and Black Monday served many purposes: it provided the
city with noble founding fathers who faced adversity, and it reaffirmed their
ideas of legitimacy in ruling the city and protecting themselves and their newly
found wealth from an enemy that they saw as fundamentally treacherous and
bloodthirsty. It was continued by a frontier capital that lived under the
constant threat of invasion, ambush and war, obsessed by the 'mountain
enemy'. And it provided the Dublin citizens with the opportunity to stage a
unique civic procession, which was bound to their identity as a city, eventually
even being exported, such was its popularity. Within the emotions, images and
mythology of Black Monday over the centuries, there are many ideas that are
central to Irish history as a whole – identity, defiance and heritage. As the dates
of 1014 and 1916 invoke thoughts and perspectives on those notions in modern
Dubliners, the year 1209 did likewise for centuries. Myth has always been a
powerful concept in Ireland.

---

64 Kelly, *Four roads to Dublin*, p. 24.   **65** Ibid.   **66** Webb, *The guilds of Dublin*, p. 164.
67 Ibid., pp 162–3.

The arrival of the Dominicans in Ireland in 1224 and the question of Dublin and Drogheda: the sources re-examined[1]

BERNADETTE WILLIAMS

This essay seeks to re-examine sources that have been, for the most part, uncritically accepted by historians with regard to the arrival of the Order of Preachers (the Dominicans) in Ireland. Contemporary medieval evidence places the arrival in 1224, and a seventeenth-century source, Sir James Ware (1594–1666), claims that both Dublin and Drogheda were founded in 1224. With regard to the arrival of the Dominicans in Ireland, statements have been made by historians that have been restated and become generally accepted as fact. In 1916, when discussing the reason for his research into medieval Dominican bishops in Ireland, M.H. MacInerny, a Dominican, said that he hoped that his work 'would correct many current errors … and save us repeating, for the thousandth time, the meagre details, often marred by mistakes and misrepresentations, which are to be found in Harris and Ware'.[2] Another Dominican historian, Hugh Fenning, stated: 'So meagre, indeed, are the sources for Irish Dominican history, above all for the Middle Ages, that one cannot afford the luxury of ignoring any detail, however insignificant'.[3] A re-examination of the sources is indeed a valid exercise.

Before examining the 1224 arrival of the Dominicans in Ireland and particularly in Dublin, it is essential to be very aware of the ethos and raison d'être of the Dominican order.[4]

FOUNDATION OF DOMINICANS AND FRANCISCANS, AND THEIR DIFFERENCES

The foundations of the first mendicant orders, the Dominican and Franciscan orders, took place at a time of great crisis in the church, and the momentous Fourth Lateran Council was called to address these problems in November

---

1 I am grateful to Colmán Ó Clabaigh for commenting on an earlier draft of this essay.
2 M.H. MacInerny, *A history of the Irish Dominicans from original sources and unpublished records: Irish Dominican bishops, 1224–1307* (Dublin, 1916), p. vi.   3 Hugh Fenning, 'Irish material in the registers of the Dominican masters general (1390–1649)', *Archivum Fratrum Praedicatorum*, 39 (1969), 249, 251.   4 The Dominican motto is 'To contemplate and to give to others the fruits of contemplation': W.A. Hinnebusch, *The early English Friars*

1215.[5] One major problem was that the church had largely neglected the spiritual needs of the laity of the growing cities, and this opened the way for heresy.[6] As notice of this proposed Lateran Council had been given by Pope Innocent III as early as April 1215, an extraordinarily large number of prominent and renowned ecclesiastics attended and the lay leaders were also represented. The Irish church was represented at the council by the four archbishops, fourteen bishops, two bishops–elect and some members of monastic houses and cathedral chapters.[7] In Rome also were both the Italian Francis of Assisi and the Spaniard Dominic de Guzman and these two idealistic and charismatic men were seeking ratification of their proposed new mendicant orders.[8] Despite the fact that both the proposed orders were similarly dedicated to improving the faith of urban society and combating heresy and that both espoused a mendicant ethos, they had many differences – differences dictated by their very dissimilar backgrounds and experiences. What is most important is that the different characters of Francis and Dominic influenced the nature of their respective orders, especially in the early centuries.

Dominic began his religious life as an Augustinian canon regular and a priest and, because of his background and his early experiences, was intent on founding a learned order to combat heresy. On the other hand, Francis was initially a layman,[9] who, after a dramatic conversion, founded an order based on the *vita apostolica*; his followers were to be 'simple evangelists preaching their Gospel more by the quality of their lives than by the eloquence of their words'.[10] According to Francis, the friars should only have their clothes and, if necessary, shoes, and carry nothing with them on their preaching journeys (*nihil tuleritis in via*).[11] Books were considered property and, as such,

Preachers (Rome, 1951), p. 228.　**5** Walter Ullman, *A short history of the papacy in the Middle Ages* (London, 1972), pp 221–3. One of the topics discussed at the council was the problem of new orders that had come into existence in recent years; Canon 13 stated that new religious orders must accept a rule already approved. The Dominican order based its lifestyle on the rule of St Augustine and enacted specific constitutions to deal with other areas of their ministry. For the Franciscan Rule, see William Short, 'The Rule and life of the Friars Minor' in Michael J.P. Robson (ed.), *The Cambridge companion to St Francis* (Cambridge, 2012), pp 50–67.　**6** R.F. Bennett, *The early Dominicans: studies in thirteenth-century Dominican history* (Cambridge, 1937; repr. New York, 1971), pp 3–17.　**7** P.J. Dunning, 'Irish representatives and Irish ecclesiastical affairs at the Fourth Lateran Council' in J.A. Watt, J.B. Morrall and F.X. Martin (eds), *Medieval studies presented to Aubrey Gwynn SJ* (Dublin, 1961), pp 90–2.　**8** There is a legend that they met: W.A. Hinnebusch, *History of the Dominican order, origins and growth to 1550* (2 vols, New York, 1965), i, p. 154. For a general history of the Franciscan order, see J.R.H. Moorman, *A history of the Franciscan order from its origins to the year 1517* (Oxford, 1968); Robson (ed.), *Cambridge companion to St Francis*.　**9** Francis became a deacon; I thank Colman Ó Clabaigh for this information.　**10** For a brief synopsis, see Michael Cusato, 'Francis and the Franciscan movement (1181/2–1226)' in Robson (ed.), *Cambridge companion to St Francis*, pp 17–33.　**11** R.M. Huber, *Documented history of the Franciscan order, 1182–1517*

contravened the ideal of the *vita apostolica* and, of course, if there was no need for books there was no need for a building to house books and 'St Francis did not institute his order as a teaching community'.[12] Because of this tenet, there was a marked anti-academic strain in the early days of the Franciscan order, but only in the early days. This attitude changed radically in later years when the Franciscan order became renowned for its intellectual excellence.[13]

Dominic, highly influenced by his close personal contact with the heretical Cathar (Albigensian) preachers, took the diametrically opposite viewpoint from Francis from the outset and vigorously pursued the idea of attracting the greatest number of able academics to the order who would therefore be capable of counteracting the influence of the Cathar preachers. Study was the core of the Dominican ethos and Dominic, we are told, carried his books with him everywhere he went.[14] Dominic's first contact with heresy had been in 1203, when he was among the entourage of the Spanish bishop of Osma (en route for Denmark on a diplomatic mission).[15] Later, in 1206, returning from Rome through southern France, Dominic encountered the abbot of Cîteaux and two of his monks who had been sent by Pope Innocent III to check the dangerously rapid growth of the Cathar heresy that was then taking control of the region.[16] The pope, very alert to the dangers of this rapidly growing heresy, had asked the Cistercians to address the problem, but, as the Cistercians were a monastic order and not in the general habit of preaching to the laity, they were not successful. Dominic quickly realized that many of the influential Cathar preachers were well-educated men, versed in the Scriptures, who preached convincingly to a laity who sought religious and spiritual enlightenment.[17] Dominic came to the conclusion that heresy could only be counteracted by the orthodox preaching of similarly well-educated preachers whose lifestyle gave

(Milwaukee,WI, 1944), pp 44, 615.   **12** Huber, *Documented history*, pp 788–95.   **13** Bert Roest, 'Francis and the pursuit of learning' in Robson (ed.), *Cambridge companion to St Francis*, pp 161–77. Assisi only began to assemble its famous library *c.*1230: Moorman, *History*, p. 184; for early Franciscan scholars, see ibid., pp 240–55. For a full discussion on the libraries of the mendicant friars, see K.W. Humphreys, *The book provisions of the medieval friars* (Amsterdam, 1964), pp 46–66. See also A.G. Little, 'The Franciscan school at Oxford in the thirteenth century', *Archivum Fratrum Praedicatorum*, 19 (1926), 803–74. For friars at Paris, see P.R. Szittya, *The anti-fraternal tradition of medieval literature* (Princeton, NJ, 1968), pp 11–17; Neslihan Senocak, 'Books acquisitions in the medieval Franciscan order', *Journal of Religious History*, 27:1 (2003), 14–28; idem, 'Circulation of books in the medieval Franciscan order: attitude, methods and critics', *Journal of Religious History*, 28:2 (2004), 146–61.   **14** Hinnebusch, *Dominican order*, p. 28: 'He had a consuming zeal for study': Ernest Barker, *The Dominican order and convocation: a study of the growth of representation in the church in the thirteenth century* (Oxford, 1913), p. 10. See also Michèle Mulchahey, *'First the bow is bent in study …': Dominican education before 1350* (Toronto, 1998).   **15** The journey was in connection with a proposed marriage alliance between Castile and Denmark: Hinnebusch, *Dominican order*, pp 20–1.   **16** It is important for the history of the Dominicans in Dublin to note Dominic's early connection with the Cistercian order.   **17** Hinnebusch, *Dominican order*, p. 120.

credence to their words. With the approval of the local Cistercian bishop, Dominic remained in southern France and became one of a small band of preachers in the Languedoc who had been entrusted with the task of counteracting the Cathar heresy.[18]

Between late 1216 and early 1217, Dominic gained full permission to found a new order called the *Ordo Praedicatorum*. The very name is vital for understanding the Dominican order, the Order of Preachers. In order that his followers could preach successfully, Dominic, from the very beginning, placed a great emphasis on education and urged his followers to study in order that they should be learned and able to combat the heretical ideas and beliefs circulating at that time. Dominic even 'led his companions to lectures ... in the cathedral school of Toulouse'.[19] He also sought out learned men such as Jordan of Saxony, Roland of Cremona, Reginald of Orleans, Hugh of St Cher and John of St Giles, among many others, and persuaded them to join him; indeed, most of the early members of the order were men of university background and training.[20] This emphasis on learning was reflected in Dominic's preference for founding houses in university cities such as Bologna, Paris, Montpellier and Oxford. As the famous verse states,

> Bernard liked the valleys, Benedict the hills,
> Francis the towns, Dominic the cities of renown.[21]

The first general chapter of the new Order of Preachers was held in Bologna at Pentecost 1220. Constitutions were quickly promulgated and included strict mendicancy.[22] Among the extensive legislation, it was decreed that the order comprised the master general (initially called abbot)[23] together with the general chapter and the priories.[24] Also decreed was that a Dominican priory 'must be established with no less than twelve friars (priests), a prior and a professor' and that each priory was also to be a school of theology. This number twelve had to be maintained or the priory would lose the right to send representatives to the provincial chapters. Indeed, if the provincial took some friars from any priory he was obliged to replace them so that the number

18 Ibid., pp 21–5. The mission was not a success and in 1209 Innocent III launched the Albigensian crusade under the leadership of Simon de Montfort, earl of Leicester: Michael Costen, *The Cathars and the Albigensian Crusade* (Manchester, 1997).   **19** Hinnebusch, *Dominican order*, p. 40.   **20** Ibid., p. 61; R.F. Bennett, *The early Dominicans*, pp 25–6; Mulchahey, *Dominican education*.   **21** *Bernardusvalles, montes Benedictus amabat, Oppida Franciscus, celebres Dominicus urbes*; Hinnebusch, *Dominican order*, p. 260.   **22** For the early constitutions of the Dominicans, see Barker, *Dominican order and convocation*, pp 13–18; Hinnebusch, *Dominican order*, pp 39–57, 145–63, 195–250.   **23** Simon Tugwell, 'The evolution of Dominican structures of government, I: The first and last abbot', *Archivum Fratrum Praedicatorum*, 69 (1999), 5–60.   **24** For first general chapter, see Hinnebusch, *Dominican order*, pp 80–7.

twelve could be maintained. There was to be a lector in each priory in order to continue the education of the brethren throughout their lives.[25] This 1220 general chapter also expanded the order by sending out friars to new areas. Then, in 1221, in the presence of Dominic, the second general chapter of the order was held, again in Bologna, and now the order was divided into eight provinces, and one of the new provinces was England.[26]

ARRIVAL OF THE DOMINICANS IN ENGLAND

The Dominicans arrived in England in 1221 under the authority of Friar Gilbert de Fresney. He remained their leader and, most importantly, also became the leader of the Dominicans in Ireland until *c*.1235. Gilbert and his friars came to Canterbury and, apart from preaching there, they moved onwards through London and then without any deviation proceeded to the university city of Oxford, which was their objective: 'London was not ... the final destination but only a station on their way to Oxford, where, in accordance with the principles of their order, novices were to be attracted from among the students and teachers'.[27] Furthermore, they all stayed together as a full priory complement in accordance with the general chapter of 1220. Founding a new priory was a complicated and sometimes lengthy process.[28] A 'quick job' was not in accord with the Dominican philosophy. The Dominican historian, William Hinnebusch, stated that the Dominican friars

> moved ahead with measured speed, especially when a new province was being formed. With their penchant for large priories, they aimed to consolidate and establish fully organized communities ... and thoroughly train their postulants before moving on to a new phase of development.[29]

25 As early as 1220, the order was in principal committed to making every house a school with its own *doctor*: Simon Tugwell, 'The evolution of Dominican structures of government, III: The early development of the second distinction of the Constitutions', *Archivum Fratrum Praedicatorum*, 71 (2001), 30; Hinnebusch, *Dominican order*, p. 86; idem, *Early English Friars Preachers*, p. 9. For founding of Dominican priories, see Hinnebusch, *Dominican order*, pp 251–78. The friar normally reached priesthood at the age of 25 and achieved a degree at 33–7: A.B. Emden, *A survey of Dominicans in England based on the ordination lists in episcopal registers (1268 to 1538)* (Rome, 1967), p. 22. Mulchahey, *Dominican education*, p. 39. 26 Simon Tugwell argues that the provinces emerged as a result of decisions to send friars to a new part of the world: idem, 'The evolution of Dominican structures of government, II', 67–8. For the second general chapter, see Hinnebusch, *Dominican Order*, pp 91–6. 27 Jens Röhrkasten, *The mendicant houses of medieval London* (Münster, 2004), p. 22. The principal authority is Nicholas Trivet, *Annales*, ed. Thomas Hog (London, 1845), p. 209; for translation of relevant passage, see Hinnebusch, *Early English Friars Preachers*, pp 3–4. 28 Barker, *The Dominican order and convocation*, p. 14. Hinnebusch, *Early English Friars Preachers*, p. 62. For the legal process of the founding of priories, see Hinnebusch, *Dominican Order*, ch. ix. 29 Hinnebusch,

This need for a properly constituted priory was partly because the friars were either already priests or were training to become priests and 'the law of the Church frowned on a clergy that was unsupported'.[30] A Dominican priory was always intended, from the very foundation of the order, to be a centre of learning with a good library and a library needs a building.[31] While, as with all institutions, hard and fast rules might not always have been followed in early years, the Dominican foundations in Ireland post-date the 1220 general chapter stating that a full complement was required.[32] It is quite clear that this is certainly how Gilbert de Fresney operated in England and he was also the head of the Dominicans in Ireland.

Hinnebusch states that

> it is enlightening to contrast the methods of making foundations followed by the first Dominicans and Franciscans. For example, the first Franciscans to arrive in England, a band of nine, separated at each important city, and by the end of October 1224 ... the same month as they arrived ... had already made three settlements.[33]

Of the nine original Franciscan friars, five remained at Canterbury and four set out for London and then, out of those four, two continued to Oxford.[34] Therefore 'planning friaries' is most unlikely in the case of the Franciscans but was a strong consideration for the Dominicans.[35] The Franciscans taught by example and to teach by example one just needed to live the *vita apostolica*; the Dominicans taught by theology and to teach by theology one needed an infrastructure of buildings, books, teachers and a library.[36] The Franciscans could and did split their group at each new place, leaving a few friars, often as few as two or three, to set up and establish a friary when new vocations joined. The first band of thirteen Dominicans stayed together and pushed on to Oxford to found a full legal priory.[37] Hinnebusch considers that the first Dominican friars desired to consolidate their position and establish fully organized priories, as required by the constitutions of the second general chapter of 1220.[38] It is instructive to note that, in the first ten years, the Franciscans in England founded twenty-three friaries, while, in the first ten

Dominican Order, pp 261, 279.   **30** Ibid., p. 147.   **31** Hinnebusch, *Early English Friars Preachers*, p. 109.   **32** Ibid., pp 56–62; smaller foundations were made prior to 1221: Hinnebusch, ibid., p. 9, n. 28. Hinnebusch, *Dominican Order*, p. 86.   **33** Hinnebusch, *Early English Friars Preachers*, p. 61.   **34** Ibid., pp 9–10, n. 28.   **35** Ibid., pp 67–8; Röhrkasten, *Mendicant houses of medieval London*, pp 67–8.   **36** Röhrkasten, *Mendicant houses of medieval London*, p. 482.   **37** For full description of Oxford Priory, see Hinnebusch, *Early English Friars Preachers*, pp 3–19.   **38** Hinnebusch, *Dominican Order*, p. 86. The Dominicans owned their priories; the Franciscans did not: Hinnebusch, *Early English Friars Preachers*, pp 62, 232–3; Röhrkasten, *Mendicant houses of medieval London*, pp 239–40. There was 'never any doubt that at all times the order owned the land upon which its houses

years, the Dominicans founded only five priories.[39] This pattern was the same in Germany, Scandinavia and other countries.[40]

For, both the Franciscans and the Dominicans, we are fortunate in having contemporary records of their early arrival in England. Friar Thomas of Eccleston wrote an account of the early years of the Franciscans in England.[41] Included in Nicholas Trevet's *Annales* of 1320 is some information about the Dominicans in England.[42] Apart from that, as in most areas of medieval research, we are hampered by the scarcity of primary sources. It is evident that before the Dissolution each convent had records of its own, but the survival rate is virtually nil.[43] In Ireland, the only exception is the register of Athenry.[44] In regard to England, two modern Cambridge Dominican historians bemoan the fact that 'the dispersal and destruction of the archives of religious houses at the Dissolution were particularly severe in the case of mendicant orders. Since (apart from the site of their houses) they were unlikely to hold landed endowments, they lacked successors in title … who might take over and preserve deeds and other records'.[45] A.B. Emden states that the history of the Friars Preachers of the English province 'has suffered irreparably from the loss of records of its constituent priories and of their provincial chapters'.[46]

ARRIVAL OF THE DOMINICANS IN IRELAND

In Ireland, we have no such information about the early years and early foundations of either of these two mendicant orders. Later sources preserve various versions of the foundation legends of both the Franciscans and

were built': Bennett, *Early Dominicans*, p. 176.   **39** There were forty Franciscan but only twenty Dominican houses in England and Wales before 1250: Jens Röhrkasten, 'Mendicants in the metropolis: the Londoners and the development of the London friaries' in Michael Prestwich, Richard Hugh Britnell and Robin Frame (eds), *Thirteenth century England VI* (Woodbridge, 1997), p. 61.   **40** J.B. Freed, *The friars and German society in the thirteenth century* (Cambridge MA, 1977), p. 52; during the first fifteen years they founded only seven houses in Scandinavia: Hinnebusch, *Dominican Order*, p. 262.   **41** *Fratris Thomae vulgo dicti de Eccleston tractatus de adventu fratrum minorum in Angliam*, ed. A.G. Little (Manchester, 1951). For an English translation, see E.G. Salter, *The coming of the Friars Minor to England and Germany* (London, 1926).   **42** Trivet is a modern spelling: Antonia Gransden, *Historical writing in England I, c.550 to c.1307* (London, 1974), p. 487, n. 4.   **43** The *obituaria* was compiled to serve as calendars for the commemoration of the obits of its former members and friends. Only one has survived: A.B. Emden, *A survey of Dominicans in England based on the ordination lists in episcopal registers (1268–1538)* (Rome, 1967), p. 15. **44** Ambrose Coleman, '*Regestum monasterii fratrum praedicatorum de Athenry*', *Archivium Hibernicum*, 1 (1912), 201–21.   **45** These historians further declared that they have never been able to trace a single original document from the archives of the Dominican convent of Cambridge: P. Zutshi and R. Ombres, 'The Dominicans in Cambridge, 1238–1538', *Archivum Fratrum Praedicatorum*, 60 (1990), 319; Emden, *Dominicans in England*, pp 15–16. **46** Emden, *Survey of Dominican in England*, p. 15.

Dominicans in Ireland, in each case attributing the initiative to the respective founders. The Franciscan legend is that they came to Ireland via Compostela in 1214, that is, before the death of Francis.[47] The Dominican legend is that Dominic himself sent two friars to Tyrconnel.[48] These attractive legends are totally without evidence and both have been thoroughly discussed and convincingly discarded by Colmán Ó Clabaigh.[49] What these early claims indicate, however, is the desire for primacy of foundation, very important to religious orders.[50] Without a written record, what we must do, therefore, is take some cognisance of the method of the very early foundations by both the Franciscans and Dominicans in England and – only for those very early years – extrapolate from that pattern; it is now fully accepted that both those mendicant orders first arrived in Ireland from England. It is important for the early history of Dominican Ireland to keep the characteristics of the early Dominican foundations in England to the forefront.

Rather surprisingly, we cannot be certain of the date of the arrival of the Franciscans in Ireland.[51] We are very fortunate, however, in having clear and unequivocal contemporary evidence of the date that the Domincans entered the country. That is 1224. The thirteenth-century Franciscan annals of Multyfarnham record 1224 as the date of the arrival of the Dominicans, and the Franciscan Kilkenny Chronicle corroborates this information.[52] By a very fortunate chance, there are two seventeenth-century transcripts containing

47 Luke Wadding, *AnnalesMinorum, Tomus 1, 1208–1220* (2nd ed., Rome, 1731–41), p. 225; E.B. Fitzmaurice and A.G. Little (eds), *Materials for the Franciscan Province of Ireland, 1230–1450* (Manchester, 1920), pp xi–xiv; G. Cleary, 'St Francis and Ireland', *Studies*, 15 (1926), 543–4.   **48** MacInerny, *History of the Irish Dominicans*, pp 78–81. There was even a suggestion that St Dominic himself came to Ireland: John Stevens, *Monasticon Hibernicum*, trans. with additions and alterations by John Stevens from Louis Alemand, *Histoire monastique d'Irlande* (London, 1722), p. 205.   **49** Of interest here is that the Scottish Dominicans and Franciscans made similar claims. The Scottish historian Hector Boece, writing in 1527, claimed that St Dominic had personally sent friars to establish the Dominicans in Scotland in 1219: Colmán Ó Clabaigh, *The friars in Ireland, 1224–1540* (Dublin, 2012), pp 4–6. In fact, the Dominicans ('Jacobin friars') first arrived in Scotland in 1230: *The Chronicle of Melrose: church historians of England*, trans. Joseph Stephenson (London, 1856; repr. Llanerch, 1988), p. 59; all five Welsh priories were founded between 1245 and 1269, R.C. Easterling, 'The friars in Wales', *ArchaeologiaCambrensis*, 14 (1914), 330, 333–40.   **50** The Carmelites in London also claimed an earlier date of foundation, now disproved: Jens Röhrkasten, 'The origin and early development of the London mendicant houses' in T.R. Slater and Gervase Rosser (eds), *The church in the medieval town* (Aldershot, 1998), p. 77.   **51** Richard of Ingworth is the first documented minister provincial of Ireland, a position he held from 1230 to 1239. The earliest reference in papal documents to the existence of the Franciscans in Ireland is a letter of 14 June 1233 from Pope Gregory IX to the minister provincial of the Franciscans in Ireland: Maurice Sheehy (ed.), *Pontificia Hibernia: medieval papal chancery documents, 640–1231*, 2 (Dublin, 1965), p 46–7, n. 1.   **52** Bernadette Williams (ed.), *The 'Annals of Multyfarnham': Connacht and Roscommon provenance* (Dublin, 2012), p. 150; Robin Flower, 'Manuscripts of Irish interest in the British Museum', *Analecta Hibernica*, 2 (1931), 331.

notes from two non-extant medieval Anglo-Irish Dominican annals of Ross and of Trim. The brief notes from the Dominican annals of Ross (not to be confused with the Franciscan annals of Ross) state that the Dominicans entered Ireland in 1224, and the brief notes from Trim corroborate this.[53] Ware had access to the medieval Cistercian annals of St Mary's, Dublin, and under 1224 he recorded the entry of the Dominicans into Ireland.[54] The fifteenth-century Dublin chronicler, Thomas Case, gives us the date of the arrival of the Dominicans in England (1221), but unfortunately his annals have a lacuna from 1221 to 1308.[55] John de Pembridge, the Dublin Dominican chronicler, offers no information, but equally the Franciscan Annals of Multyfarnham are silent on the arrival of the Franciscans in Ireland. Both the Franciscan Stephen de Exonia and the Dominican Pembridge probably would not have felt it necessary to enter this information in their annals. The information about their own orders would be readily available elsewhere in their friaries and priories. To the independent medieval evidence from Franciscan, Dominican and Cistercian sources can be added a further medieval source, the Gaelic Annals of Ulster, and this once again corroborates the date of the Friars Preachers entering Ireland as 1224. This is most significant, as it is the only medieval set of Gaelic annals to record the news.[56] A newly discovered seventeenth-century copy of annals, sourced from much earlier material, emanating from Dominican Roscommon does have the entry relating to the arrival of the Dominicans in Ireland in 1224.[57] It would be very difficult indeed to dispute such independent medieval evidence from Franciscan, Dominican, Gaelic and Cistercian sources stating that the Order of Preachers arrived in Ireland in 1224. What must be noted, however, is that, as is clearly evident, nowhere in these medieval sources is there any mention of where the Friars Preachers first settled.

---

53 The transcripts are only very brief extracts: *Chronicle of Ross*, Bodl. MS Rawl. B479, fos 68r–69r; this transcript has as its title *Annales*, but Ware appended the following note: *Anonymi Hibernici forte ord fratrum Praedicatorum Ross*. The reason for assigning the annal to Ross is clearly the entry in 1267 that states that the Dominicans entered Ross and gives the date 13 Kal Nov. (68v). This identification is strengthened by an entry in 1293 concerning Thomastown in Ossory (68v). From the beginning of the annal in the year 184 to 1259, entries, in the great majority of the cases, are virtually identical with the entries in the Annals of Multyfarnham; this might account for the entry concerning the arrival of the Dominicans in Ireland: Williams (ed.), 'Annals of Multyfarnham', p. 150. 'Chronicle of Trim', BL MS Add. 4789, fos 206v–207v; this transcript has as its title *q. Annal Coenob Dominic Trim* and *Chroncui usdam fratris ord Praedicatorum*. The chronicle is preceded by the list of thirteenth-century Dominican foundation-dates, ending with Killmallock in 1291, and a list of Dominican provincial chapters ending in 1347 (fo. 206r).
54 *Chartularies of St Mary's Abbey, Dublin: with the register of its house at Dunbrody, and annals of Ireland*, ed. J.T. Gilbert (2 vols, London, 1884), ii, p. 288 (hereafter *CSMA*).
55 *CSMA*, ii (Thomas Case annals), p. 281.   **56** The Annals of Ulster also record the arrival of the Friars Preachers in England in 1221.   **57** *Annales Dominicani de Roscoman*, ed. Benjamin Hazard and K.W. Nicholls (2012): at www.ucc.ie/celt.

The Dominicans who arrived in Ireland in 1224 can only have been sent from England under the auspices of Friar Gilbert de Fresney, the man who was sent by Dominic himself to found the English province. If they had not been sent from England they would not have been included in the English province, as they were. In Ireland the Dominican order (unlike the Franciscans) was not independent and formed part of the English province. Even when they became grouped under a vicar-provincial for Ireland in 1256, they were still subject to the English provincial.[58] Therefore, we cannot ignore the foundation process in England, especially when considering this early date of 1224, because the Dominicans who came to Ireland were part of the English province and they were English. There is no reason that they would act any differently in the first few years of their arrival in Ireland than they did in England. They were part of a very disciplined order and, furthermore, as previously noted, the first English prior was the leader in Ireland until *c.*1235.[59] Without a written record of these early years, it is vital to take some cognisance of the method of very early foundations of the Dominicans in England and extrapolate from that pattern.[60]

The Dominicans who were sent to Ireland by Friar Gilbert, under his authority, came either from their Oxford priory or from the newly constituted priory in London, because these were the only two houses established in England by 1224. We know that Oxford was established in 1221. Historians agree that the precise date of the London foundation is not known, although it is known that the benefactor was Hubert de Burgh, who donated a plot of land in London.[61] Also known is that when the first Franciscans arrived in London in September 1224, they were welcomed and entertained by the Dominicans. It appears that the Dominicans might only have been established there earlier in the same year.[62] If it took up to three years for the Oxford community to establish a house in London, it seems unlikely that London would establish Dublin and Drogheda in the same year. It is worth considering that the decision could have been made at Oxford to establish two new houses in the king's two capital cities of London and Dublin. The logic of progress from Oxford to London is evident; first the intellectual centre then the political capital.[63]

58 For a brief synopsis, see Aubrey Gwynn and R.N. Hadcock, *Medieval religious houses: Ireland* (Dublin, 1988), pp 218–19; Hinnebusch, *Early English Friars Preachers*, pp 209–10, 340. 59 The Dominicans, unlike the Franciscans, had a preference for big priories: Hinnebusch, *Dominican order*, p. 279. 60 Recently, our knowledge and understanding of the early Dominicans in England has been greatly enhanced by Jens Röhrkasten's research on the London mendicant houses: idem, *Mendicant houses of medieval London.* 61 Röhrkasten, *Mendicant houses of medieval London*, pp 30–1; Hinnebusch, *Early English Friars Preachers*, pp 20–55. 62 Simon Tugwell, 'The evolution of Dominican structures of government, III: the early development of the second distinction of the Constitutions', *Archivum Fratrum Praedicatorum*, 71 (2001), 40; Röhrkasten, *Mendicant houses of medieval London*, p. 30; Röhrkasten, 'Mendicants in the metropolis', p. 63, n. 8. Hinnebusch, *Early English Friars Preachers*, pp 20–1, 30. 63 Hinnebusch, *Dominican order*, p. 261.

After the medieval evidence for the arrival date of 1224, the next information about the dates of the early Dominican foundations in Ireland comes only in the seventeenth century and, as is so often the case, the information comes from one of our best known and esteemed antiquarians of that era, Sir James Ware, and every Dominican historian thereafter used Ware as a primary source. Another source was Walter Harris (1686–1761), who married Elizabeth, great-grandchild of Ware. Harris published an English edition of Ware's Latin works concerning Ireland (with some of his own additions). Ware claimed that there was a medieval list of Irish Dominican foundations, which is as follows:[64]

Dublin 1224	Sligo 1252[67]
Drogheda 1224	Athelathan [Strade] 1252[68]
Kilkenny 1225	Athy 1253
Waterford 1226	Roscommon 1253[69]
Limerick 1227	Trim 1263
Cork 1229	Arklow 1264
Mullingar 1237	Rosbercon [New Ross] 1267
Athenry 1241[65]	Youghal 1268
Cashel 1243	Lorrha 1269
Tralee 1243[66]	Rathfran 1274
Newtownards 1244	Derry 1274
Coleraine 1244	Kilmallock 1291[70]

This list claims that not one but two priories were founded from England under the authority of Gilbert de Fresney in 1224.[71]

---

64 BL MS 4789, fo. 206r; Sir James Ware, *The antiquities and history of Ireland* (Dublin, 1705), p. 22; Walter Harris, *The history and antiquities of Ireland … with the history of the writers of Ireland by Sir James Ware* (Dublin, 1764), p. 77. In Ware's catalogue, he does not mention this list after the annals of Multyfarnham, although he does correctly mention that the codex contains the prophecy of the prophet Wynne: William O'Sullivan, 'A finding list of Sir James Ware's manuscripts', *PRIA*, 97C (1997), 92–103. For brief notes on foundation, see relevant priories in Gwynn and Hadcock, *Medieval religious houses*, pp 221–320. **65** The register of Athenry does not actually give a foundation date: see Coleman, '*Regestum monasterii fratrum praedicatorum de Athenry*', p. 204. It was certainly built by Meiler de Bermingham, who died after 1264 (not 1252 as stated in the register: G.H. Orpen, *Ireland under the Normans* (4 vols, Oxford, 1911–20), iii, p. 212 (new ed., Seán Duffy (Dublin, 2005), p. 387). **66** Founded by at least 1253, Gwynn and Hadcock, *Medieval religious houses*, p. 230. **67** 'A monastery was erected, and a cemetery consecrated, for the Friars Preachers at Sligech': *Annals of Loch Cé*, *s.a.* 1253; *Annals of Connacht*, *s.a.* 1253; the foundation could have been at least a year earlier. **68** 'The Preaching-friars marked out the site of another monastery at Ath Lethan in Leyney': *Annals of Connacht*, *s.a.* 1253. **69** 'The monastery of Mary, in Roscomain, was consecrated by Tomaltach O Conchobhair for the Friars Preachers': *Annals Loch Cé*, *s.a.* 1257; *Annals of Connacht*, *s.a.* 1257. **70** *Calendar of documents relating to Ireland, 1285–1292*, ed. H.S. Sweetman (London, 1879), no. 967, p. 439. **71** This list claims that between 1224 and 1291

Whatever Ware wrote (unless of course contradicted by an extant medieval source) has been used and reused down the centuries; every Dominican historian copied Ware, who, most importantly and most significantly, had access to documents no longer extant. However, although the debt is indeed great, it cannot be assumed that Ware was never in error, and his statements do need to be re-examined and re-evaluated.

The earliest statement by Ware on the Dominicans comes in 1639 in his *De scriptoribus Hiberniae* and claims that Dominican annals to 1274 by an anonymous Dominican had attached to it a list of all the convents according to the date of foundation. Ware goes on to relate that he believes that those annals 'commonly called the annals of Multyfarnham' were written by the Franciscan whom he calls Stephen de Exeter.[72] This statement was repeated in the 1705 English translation of Ware's *Antiquities and history of Ireland*.[73]

Ware's list does not follow the annals of Multyfarnham, however, which are present in a Trinity College Dublin manuscript (TCD MS 347). Moreover, it is difficult to believe that the list could ever have followed the annals.[74] The manuscript that contains the annals is an entirely Franciscan codex and all the quires but one were together as a preaching manual in the late thirteenth century. The last quire contains the annals that end in 1274 and the last entry on Ware's list is 1291. After the last entry of the annals, there was at least two thirds of a folio unused. It is difficult to imagine that the young Franciscan friar, Stephen de Exonia, would record a list of Dominican foundations in a book wholly concerned with Franciscan matters.[75] The safest conclusion is that, unless that medieval document comes to light, the list must be treated with extreme caution. Nonetheless, the claim deserves study.

The main problem with this list is that Ware claims that both Dublin and Drogheda were founded in 1224. It can be argued that it is extremely unlikely that both Dublin and Drogheda could have been established as priories in 1224 as that would have required around twenty-four friars being taken from Oxford or, even more doubtful, from the new foundation in London.[76] Given that at the first general chapter of 1220, a mere four years earlier, it was

twenty-four priories were established. By 1228, in theory at least, the authority to allow a new foundation rested in the hands of the general chapter: Röhrkasten, 'Mendicants in the metropolis: the Londoners and the development of the London friaries', p. 62.   **72** Sir James Ware, *De scriptoribus Hiberniae. Libridvo. Prior continet scriptores, in Hiberniâ natos. Posterior, scriptoresalios, qui in Hiberniâ munera aliqua obierunt./ Authore Iacobo VVaraeo eq. aur* (Dublin, 1639), pp 61–2.   **73** Ware, *The antiquities and history of Ireland*, p. 22.   **74** The annals, known since the early seventeenth century as the Annals of Multyfarnham, survive in a late thirteenth-century manuscript volume in the library of Trinity College Dublin, TCD MS 347: Williams (ed.), 'Annals of Multyfarnham', pp 19–27.   **75** Colmán Ó Clabaigh has pointed out that the codex also contained the Rule of St Augustine and a commentary thereon, which is of no legislative significance for a friar minor but hugely important for a Dominican.   **76** Even the earliest constitutions of the order prescribed that no priory should be constituted without a lecturer in theology: Hinnebusch, *Early English*

decreed that a 'Dominican priory must be established with no less than twelve friars, a prior and a professor', and that each priory was also to be a school of theology with a lector to continue the education of the brethren throughout their lives, it is extremely unlikely that Dublin and Drogheda could both have been established as priories in 1224.[77] In three years in England there were only two foundations, and it is difficult to credit that two would be established concurrently in a new country at the same time.

Equally, it is difficult to believe the other early foundations on the list as it records the Dominicans in Ireland founding six new priories in five years, while England they had founded only five in ten years: Oxford (1221), London (1224), Norwich (1226), York (1227) and Bristol (1230). The question that must be posed is: why would Gilbert de Fresney, provincial prior of Ireland as well as England, approve of this speed in Ireland by his own English friars?[78] As the English contingent arrived as a full priory complement, it seems only logical to assume that they would do the same when they, in their turn, sent friars to Ireland just a few years later in 1224. It appears unlikely that those same friars would have any different agenda, a mere three years later, when they sent a contingent to Ireland.[79] The initiative for founding new convents came usually from inside a province, but, theoretically, approval was necessary from the general assembly of the order. However, often new approvals were given before the new convent was thought of and approvals were sometimes 'kept in reserve' for future needs.[80] Therefore, in the initial years, it was the decision of the provincial minister, de Fresney, as to what priories could be established and where. Arriving in a new country, they 'had to establish contact with ecclesiastical and secular authorities, present themselves to the people, find shelter and finally organize construction of a convent'.[81]

Given the intentions of Dominic, and the fact that when the Dominicans arrived in England in 1221 they came as a full complement of twelve friars plus Friar Gilbert de Fresney, enough to found only one priory in a new country, it seems only logical to assume that Fresney would do the same when he sent friars to Ireland just three years later in 1224. But how strictly were the

Friars Preachers, p. 9.   **77** Hinnebusch, *Dominican order*, p. 86; Hinnebusch, *Early English Friars Preachers*, p. 9. For founding of Dominican priories, see Hinnebusch, *Dominican order*, pp 251–5.   **78** There is always the possibility that there was a surge of applicants to join the order in Ireland. However, the Dominican order wanted the friars to be priests and demanded a high educational standard, including a good standard of literacy, so the process in any case could not have been swift: Mulchahey, *Dominican education*, pp 79–80, 83. Also, 'new convents had to be licensed in a lengthy procedure by the general as well as the provincial chapters, even though the formalities were not strictly adhered to': Röhrkasten, 'The origin and early development of the London mendicant houses', p. 83.   **79** Hinnebusch states that the first friars 'came to England with an express commission from St Dominic and the second general chapter of the order to set up a legal priory, requiring twelve friars at Oxford': Hinnebusch, *Early English Friars Preachers*, p. 20.   **80** The first approval was in 1249: Hinnebusch, *Early English Friars Preachers*, pp 56–62.   **81** Röhrkasten, 'Mendicants in the metropolis', p. 62.

formalities adhered to in these early years?[82] We cannot be sure, of course, but, would those same friars have any different agenda a mere three years later when they sent a contingent to Ireland (bearing in mind that they had only two houses in the whole of England at this date, Oxford and the very newly established London)?

It is difficult to test the veracity or otherwise of all of the dates on Ware's list, but, from independent medieval evidence supplied by a medieval Franciscan chronicler (Friar John Clyn, writing *c.*1333), we know that the date of Rosbercon is correct but the date of Youghal should be 1271 not 1268.[83] The date of Kilmallock is correct, as we know from administrative sources, but comes years after the cessation of the annals.[84] Foundations of mendicant houses are notoriously difficult to date accurately, as they usually had no large land grant, and therefore no deeds from a single benefactor. Furthermore, first mention of the house can be decades after the foundation.[85] An example is Waterford, where the first certain information dates to 1235, nine years after the date in Ware's list; the king, writing to the citizens of Waterford, 'approves of their proposal to construct an edifice for the use of the Dominicans in a vacant space under the walls of their city in which anciently existed a small field'.[86]

The main problem is that Ware's list claims that both Dublin and Drogheda were founded in 1224. It must be stressed again that nowhere in the extant medieval sources is there any statement to the effect that the Dominicans first arrived in Dublin or in Drogheda. To repeat, given that at the first general chapter of 1220, a mere four years earlier, it was decreed that a 'Dominican priory must be established with no less than twelve friars, a prior and a professor', and that each priory was also to be a school of theology with a lector to continue the education of the brethren throughout their lives, it is extremely unlikely that Dublin and Drogheda could both be established as priories in 1224.[87]

EVIDENCE FOR DROGHEDA

The Order of Preachers founded priories in cities important for ecclesiastical, academic, commercial or political reasons.[88] Drogheda was an important

---

82 Hinnebusch states that the first friars came to England with an express commission from St Dominic and the second general chapter of the order to set up a legal priory, requiring twelve friars at Oxford: Hinnebusch, *Early English Friars Preachers*, p. 9, n. 26, p. 20.   83 Bernadette Williams (ed.), *The annals of Ireland by Friar John Clyn* (Dublin, 2007), p. 148. See also Hugh Shields, 'The walling of New Ross: a thirteenth-century poem in French', *Long Room*, 12–13 (1975– 6), 24–33; T.S. Flynn, *The Dominicans of Rosbercon (1267–c.1800)* (Dublin, 1981). 84 *CDI, 1285–92*, no. 967, p. 439; see also Arlene Hogan, *Kilmallock Dominican priory: an architectural perspective, 1291–1991* (Limerick, 1991).   85 Röhrkasten, 'The origin and early development of the London mendicant houses', p. 76.   86 *CDI, 1171–1251*, no. 2249, p. 334. 87 Hinnebusch, *Dominican order*, p. 86; Hinnebusch, *Early English Friars Preachers*, p. 9. For founding of Dominican priories, see Hinnebusch, *Dominican order*, pp 251–5. 88 Hinnebusch, *Dominican Order*, pp 260–1.

commercial town and a leading international port and had some measure of ecclesiastical importance, as the then archbishop of Armagh, Luke de Netterville (1219–27), spent some time in Termonfeckin a few miles from Drogheda, and the de Netterville family came from that area.[89] However, although an important place, Drogheda could not compete with Dublin. Drogheda was neither a city, an academic centre, a political centre, an episcopal see, nor a centre of administration and the population was smaller.[90] A large population was important, as mendicant orders existed because of the charity of the local inhabitants. There is always the possibility that, perhaps, the Dominican friars first landed in Drogheda (as had been the case with Canterbury) and then had moved on to Dublin, their intended destination.[91]

The claim for the foundation of Drogheda in 1224 comes only from Ware's unsubstantiated list and has been followed by all Dominican historians. Ware also makes the statement that Luke de Netterville introduced the Dominicans to Drogheda in 1224 and that Patrick O'Scanlon was buried there in 1270.[92] The question is whether this was an historical fact known to Ware from a medieval source or was merely, to him, a logical deduction based on the list. There is no doubt that an archbishop of Armagh would indeed be an ideal person to invite the Order of Preachers to Ireland, and we know that the archbishop was present at the Fourth Lateran Council. However, this was not Luke de Netterville, as he did not become archbishop until September 1219.[93] If Netterville did indeed found Drogheda, then it must have been before 1227, as he died in that year. Interestingly, the Dominican historian, Hinnebusch, examined the claims of episcopal foundations for Dominicans in England and lists only seven possibilities, some of which he dismisses as mere conjecture. He considers that the bishops 'sought the help of the friars rather than helped them'.[94] It has to be remembered that, because the friars owed their primary

---

89 The Netterville family had connections with Drogheda area: Brendan Smith, *Colonisation and conquest in medieval Ireland: the English in Louth, 1170–1330* (Cambridge, 1999), pp 69, 65, 81, 84, 125. See also Arlene Hogan, *The priory of Llanthony Prima and Secunda in Ireland, 1172–1541: lands, patronage and politics* (Dublin, 2008), pp 108–24; for Netterville, see ibid., pp 88, 160.   90 H.B. Clarke, 'Decolonisation and the dynamics of urban decline in Ireland, 1300–1550' in T.R. Slater (ed.), *Towns in decline, AD100–1600* (Aldershot, 2000), p. 163. St Peter's Church in Drogheda did function as a pro-cathedral.   91 It is possible that they could have established a *locus* in Drogheda in or soon after 1224. A *locus* had a smaller community, enjoyed no constitutional rights and could not live up to all the obligations of a priory: Hinnebusch, *Dominican order*, p. 252.   92 Ware, *The antiquities and history of Ireland*, p. 90; Walter Harris (ed.), *The whole works of Sir James Ware concerning Ireland, revised and improved* (Dublin, 1739–64), pp 64–5.   93 Luke de Netterville (d. 1227) was chosen as archbishop of Armagh in 1216, but, as the king's assent was not sought, he did not become archbishop until Sept. 1219. He could not therefore have been present as archbishop of Armagh at the Fourth Lateran Council. But, was he perhaps present as archdeacon of Armagh? There are some indications that representatives of Irish monastic houses and cathedrals did attend: Dunning, 'Irish representatives and Irish ecclesiastical affairs at the Fourth Lateran Council', p. 91.   94 Hinnebusch, *Dominican Order*, pp 102–8.

allegiance to the papacy, they were largely exempt from episcopal jurisdiction.[95] The Dominican historian Hugh Fenning recently discovered in Rome a manuscript that is a 1647 list of founders of Irish Dominican friaries, written by an Irish Dominican. This lists Drogheda as being founded by the citizens and nobles of the neighbourhood (*a civibus fundatus et partim a vicinis nobilibus*).[96] Here we have the usual problem; no surviving medieval evidence, but evidence from seventeenth-century Ware and now contradictory Dominican evidence also from seventeenth-century Ireland. The author of this founders list was a Dominican, but he was from Munster and, therefore, while there must be a caveat over the reliability of his knowledge of eastern Ireland, he must have been trusted as a reliable historian by his own order.

It is interesting to note that, in the seventeenth century, the Dominican general chapter was well aware of the problem regarding Ware's list. In John Stevens' 1722 translation of Alemand's *Monasticon Hibernicum* (1690), we find the statement:

> I find likewise in the registers of the general chapter held at Rome, these following words: 'Whereas nothing is certainly known concerning the antiquity of the monasteries of this province, or of their boundaries or districts, we will, and decree, that for the future the priors among themselves take place according to the antiquity of their monasteries collected from an ancient manuscript by James Ware, knight, as it was ordained at the congregation held pro interim at Cork, in, the year l640; And the said ordination we do in particular confirm and revive ...' By which, it appears that it was not in the power of that general chapter to fix, with any certainty, the time of the foundation of the Dominican convents in Ireland; so that there will be no cause to find fault, if we fall short sometimes of evidences to ascertain the time of the foundation of some of those monasteries.[97]

So, in 1640 the decision was made in Cork to accept Ware's list of 1639 and the general chapter followed suit.

Thereafter, all historians of the Irish Dominican order followed the Ware list. In 1690, Louis-Augustin Alemand produced his *Histoire monastique d'Irlande*, in which he declared Dublin to be '*des plus anciens*' and established in 1223 and Drogheda established in 1224 by Luke de Netterville.[98] In 1706, the Dominican, John O'Heyne, in his *Epilogus chronologicus*, relied heavily on

95 Röhrkasten, *Mendicant houses of medieval London*, pp 291–2, 301–2, 337–8. **96** Hugh Fenning, 'Founders of Irish Dominican friaries: an unpublished list of *c.*1647', *Collectanea Hibernica*, 44/5 (2002–3), 62. **97** *Monasticon Hibernicum; or, The monastical history of Ireland*, trans. John Stevens (London, 1722), pp 210–11. **98** Louis-Augustin Alemand, *Histoire monastique d'Irlande* (Paris, 1690), pp 209, 210; for the section on the Dominicans

Ware.[99] In 1722, John Stevens translated Alemand's *Histoire monastique* with additions and alterations, and he discussed the early foundations and the problems of provenance surrounding them.[1] In 1762, the great Dominican historian Thomas de Burgo (Thomas Burke), bishop of Ossory, wrote his *Hibernia Dominicana* and, not surprisingly, used both Ware and O'Heyne.[2] In 1786, Mervyn Archdall produced his *Monasticon Hibernicum*, and relied very heavily on Ware, Harris and Alemand.[3] In the twentieth century, the Dominicans Ambrose Coleman (1902) and M.H. MacInerny (1916) both relied on Ware, though MacInerny did voice his strong reservations. Ambrose Coleman introduced a new claim, which is that Luke de Netterville was buried with the Order of Preachers in Drogheda in 1227.[4] Coleman claimed that this statement came from a source that he calls 'Ware. The *Liber Niger (ad annum 1227)*'. Coleman records *Anno 1224, aædificare cæpit in Pontanæ oppido abbatiam pro fratribus prædicatoribus, in quo sepultus fuit, die 27 Aprilis, anno 1227, defuntus.*[5] This statement, concerning Netterville's burial with the Dominicans of Drogheda, is not in Ware's account of the monasteries of Ireland under Drogheda, nor in Ware's annals under 1227, nor in Ware's account of Netterville as archbishop of Armagh. In fact, on the contrary, Ware claims that Netterville, 'according to his request', was buried in the abbey of Mellifont.[6] Ware, who recorded that Netterville was the founder of the Dominicans in Drogheda, would most certainly have stated so if he had believed that Netterville was buried in Drogheda. Finally, the manuscript known to Irish medievalists as the *Liber Niger* is the Christ Church Cathedral, Dublin, manuscript of that name, and those annals end in 1168 and nowhere in that manuscript is this information.[7] Coleman could have had access to a Ware manuscript – in a black book.[8] But, even if he did, it is unlikely, though not

(Jacobins), see ibid., pp 199–220.   **99** John O'Heyne, *Epilogus chronologicus exponens succinte conventus et fundationes sacriordinis praedicatorum in regno Hyberniae* (Louvain, 1760); ed. and trans. Ambrose Coleman as *The Irish Dominicans of the seventeenth century*, together with Ambrose Coleman, *Ancient Dominican foundations in Ireland* (Dundalk, 1902) (hereafter O'Heyne, *Irish Dominicans*).   **1** *Monasticon Hibernicum*, pp 212–13.   **2** For Ware's list, see Thomas Burke, *Hibernia Dominicana; sive, historia provinciae Hiberniae Ordinis Praedicatorum* (Farnborough, 1970), p. 38.   **3** Thomas Flynn, *The Irish Dominicans, 1536–1641* (Dublin, 1993), p. xix.   **4** In 1227, the Dominicans of Oxford were given permission for a cemetery, but only for the burial of themselves and members of their household who had served them for at least a year. In 1230, a founder was buried in Bristol: Hinnebusch, *Early English Friars Preachers*, pp 7, 88. Henry III had a clear preference for the Dominicans: Röhrkasten, *The mendicant houses of medieval London*, pp 344–8.   **5** Coleman, *Ancient Dominican foundations in Ireland*, p. 19.   **6** Ware, *The antiquities and history of Ireland*, p. 12; Harris, *The whole works of Sir James Ware*, pp 64–5.   **7** H.J. Lawlor, 'Calendar of the *Liber Niger* and *Liber Albus* of Christ Church, Dublin', *PRIA*, 27C (1908–9), 1–93; Colmán Ó Clabaigh, 'The *Liber Niger* of Christ Church Cathedral, Dublin' in Raymond Gillespie and Raymond Refaussé (eds), *The medieval manuscripts of Christ Church Cathedral, Dublin* (Dublin, 2006), pp 60–80.   **8** *Fragmentum per exiguum Annalium coenobij*

impossible, that in that manuscript Ware, who stated that Netterville was buried in Mellifont, could have had different information. Of course, there is no problem with the attribution of the Dominican priory of Drogheda as a burial place of the Dominican Archbishop O'Scanlan in 1271.[9] Incidentally, O'Heyne also tells us that, 'according to Ware, Patrick O'Scanlan, primate of Armagh ... was buried in the Dominican church, in the year 1270'.[10] But there must be a question mark over the burial of Netterville, especially as, according to Ware, his will stated Mellifont as his place of burial.[11] So there is no medieval evidence for the foundation of Dominican Drogheda in 1224. There is, however, no doubt that Drogheda was a very early foundation, because in 1246 the Dominicans of Drogheda were appointed as papal commissioners.[12]

All logic points to Dublin being founded in 1224. For another priory to be founded at the same time as Dublin, permission would have to be given by de Fresney. To reiterate, Hinnebusch states that the first friars desired to consolidate their position, establish fully organized priories and thoroughly train their new recruits 'before they moved on'.[13] All medieval evidence states that the Dominicans arrived in Ireland in 1224, but logic dictates that it was to Dublin that the Dominicans first came. Of course, without further evidence, no definite conclusion can be reached.

EVIDENCE FOR DUBLIN

In England, the Dominicans bypassed Canterbury, and even London, and went straight to the university town of Oxford. In Ireland, because there was no university, a different logic had to prevail. The ethos of the Dominicans was to teach, so the question then must be which town or city had the best intellectual centre. This was a necessary requirement in order to borrow and

Praedicatorum Pontanae. Ex quo constat loci fundatorem fuisse Lucan de Netterville, Armachanum Archiepiscopum qui decessit Aprilis 17 1227: O'Sullivan, 'A finding list of Sir James Ware's manuscripts', p. 93. I am grateful to Mark Empey for this reference.   **9** Ware, *The antiquities and history of Ireland*, p. 13. Harris, *The whole works of Sir James Ware*, pp 67–8. MacInerny (using Octavian's register as his source) gives the date as 1270 and his burial with the Dominicans of Drogheda: MacInerny, *History of the Irish Dominicans*, pp 269–70. Of interest here is that this Dominican archbishop introduced the Franciscans to Armagh. The Dominicans obtained the right to bury laity in 1229 but in 1250 the general chapter forbade burying inside the church: Hinnebusch, *Early English Friars Preachers*, pp 127–8, 322, 327. For excavation of Drogheda Priory and cemetery, see Andrew Halpin and Laureen Buckley, 'Archaeological excavations at the Dominican priory, Drogheda, Co. Louth', *PRIA*, 95C (1995), 175–253.   **10** Of interest is that this Dominican archbishop introduced the Franciscans to Armagh: O'Heyne, *Irish Dominicans*, p. 21; MacInerny, *History of the Irish Dominicans*, p. 269.   **11** Hinnebusch, *Early English Friars Preachers*, pp 127–8, 322.   **12** Fitzmaurice and Little, *Franciscan province of Ireland*, pp 13, 18.   **13** Drogheda could have been a *locus* initially: Hinnebusch, *Dominican order*, p. 252.

copy the manuscripts necessary for their primary function of preaching and teaching.

Dublin was arguably the most important ecclesiastical centre in Ireland. It was the seat of an archbishop. There were two cathedrals. The cathedral of the Holy Trinity (Christ Church) with its chapter of Augustinian canons was one of the wealthiest corporate bodies in the country.[14] It had a significant collection of manuscripts, which were needed to fulfil the liturgical and educational needs of that establishment.[15] We are told that, from the 1170s, 'this cathedral priory in Dublin commissioned, collected and used manuscript materials in its everyday life'.[16] The other Dublin cathedral, St Patrick's, was a collegiate church, founded by Archbishop John Comyn as the cathedral for the Anglo-Irish archbishops of Dublin. Given the well-known and well-documented rivalry between the two cathedrals, there would be no lack of funds to bring St Patrick's manuscript collection up to a similar standard to that of Christ Church.[17]

Furthermore, Dublin had the most important and wealthiest Cistercian monastery in Ireland: St Mary's, founded in 1139.[18] It was a daughter house to Buildwas in Shropshire and there were close contacts between the two houses, with at least two monks of Buildwas being abbots of St Mary's. As we have no record of the library of St Mary's, an examination of the library of Buildwas is

---

14 'It has been estimated that in modern County Dublin alone, the land of Christ Church Cathedral, Dublin, came to a total of 10,538 acres, most of which had been granted before the arrival of the English': J.F. Lydon, 'Christ Church in the later medieval Irish world, 1300–1500' in Kenneth Milne (ed.), *Christ Church Cathedral, Dublin: a history* (Dublin, 2000), pp 81–2.   15 Volumes included 'gospels, psalters, graduals, antiphonies and missals, cartularies and legal texts books of scripture writings of the fathers and devotional works to be read at meals': Raymond Refaussé, 'Introduction' in Milne (ed.), *Christ Church Cathedral*, pp 17–18.   16 Raymond Refaussé, 'The Christ church manuscripts in context' in Gillespie and Refaussé (eds), *Medieval manuscripts of Christ Church Cathedral*, pp 13–32. 'It is reasonable to assume that the collection of medieval manuscripts in Christ Church must once have been much larger': ibid., pp 30–1. See also Ó Clabaigh, 'The *Liber Niger* of Christ Church Cathedral', pp 75–80. 'The scriptoria of medieval Dublin were certainly capable of producing high-quality ecclesiastical codices': Alan Fletcher, 'The de Darby Psalter of Christ Church Cathedral' in Gillespie and Refaussé (eds), *Medieval manuscripts of Christ Church Cathedral*, p. 90. Sadly only a small, albeit significant, selection has survived: Refaussé, 'The Christ Church manuscripts in context', p. 31.   17 A high priority was given in the new Salisbury Cathedral to copying texts – even damaged ones. 'The acquisition of texts was one of the foremost concerns of the men associated with the new cathedral at Salisbury': Teresa Webber, *Scribes and scholars at Salisbury Cathedral, c.1075–c.1125* (Oxford, 1992), pp 29, 31. See also Fletcher, 'The de Darby Psalter', p. 90.   18 Founded in 1139 (Savigniac), it became Cistercian in 1147–8. It was one of the largest and richest in Ireland at that time and, unusually for Cistercians, it was close to Dublin: Aubrey Gwynn, 'The origins of St Mary's Abbey, Dublin', *JRSAI*, 79 (1949), 116–18. See also Colmcille Conway, 'The lands of St Mary's Abbey, Dublin, at the dissolution of the abbey: the demesne lands and the grange of Clonliffe', *Reportorium Novum*, 3:1 (1961), 94–107.

helpful and does indeed indicate the high quality of intellectual life there.[19] So St Mary's, both as a daughter house of Buildwas and as the wealthiest Cistercian house in Ireland, would have had a substantial library.

Dublin also had the largest population in Ireland, which was a very helpful prerequisite for alms and donations.[20] In England, the Dominicans had clearly recognized the importance of London and, with the assistance of Hubert de Burgh, had made it their second foundation: 'London's importance for the English church, symbolized by its cathedral, the numerous churches and religious houses, will not have been lost to them'.[21] Dublin was similar to London in these respects. It was the king's city, wealthy, important, the seat of the Anglo-Irish administration, the site of two cathedrals and had a large collection of manuscripts available to the Dominicans.[22] All logic suggests that Dublin was the obvious place for the first Dominican foundation.

POSSIBLE FOUNDERS

Using the word 'founder' in relation to the mendicants is, in the great majority of cases, misleading; the better term is 'patron'. The foundation of a Dominican mendicant convent needed support for the purchase (or gift) of land, and money for maintenance.[23] It is quite clear that the 'chief support of the mendicants came from the donations and alms of the ordinary people'.[24] As usual, we rarely have solid medieval information about the first years of the mendicant houses and we hear about most of them many years after they were founded; Kilmallock is one of the rare foundations with documentary evidence from the justiciary rolls. Therefore, the usual deductive reasoning has to be a substitute for medieval evidence. Our only Dominican medieval source is Pembridge's Dublin annals and, although Pembridge has only incidental

19 'More books survive from Buildwas than from any other English Cistercian library'. One surviving manuscript notes a dispute with St Mary's, Dublin, and was possibly made by the monk William of Ashbourne, who was interested in history. Later, as abbot of St Mary's, Dublin, he compiled a list of the early abbots of that house. Sheppard considers that Buildwas had a fairly large library, especially considering it was situated in the wilds of the Welsh borderlands (near Ironbridge). The Franciscans considered it of such importance that they visited there to examine manuscripts: J.M. Sheppard, 'The twelfth-century library and scriptorium at Buildwas: assessing the evidence' in D. Williams (ed.), *England in the twelfth century* (Bury St Edmunds, 1990), pp 193–204; J.M. Sheppard, *Buildwas books: book production, acquisition and use at an English Cistercian monastery, 1165–c.1400* (Oxford, 1997). See also Gwynn, 'The origins of St Mary's Abbey, Dublin', p. 118.   20 Röhrkasten, *The mendicant houses of medieval London*, p. 257.   21 Ibid., pp 22–3. London's mendicant houses were the largest in the British Isles, reflecting the importance of the principal city: ibid., p. 132.   22 For the Dominican library, see Hinnebusch, *Early English Friars Preachers*, pp 180–6, 297–307.   23 Röhrkasten, *Mendicant houses of medieval London*, pp 339–478.   24 Hinnebusch, *Early English Friars Preachers*, p. 249; Hinnebusch, *Dominican*

comments about the Dublin priory, his annals still need to be consulted for corroborating evidence.

The questions now to be addressed are: who initiated the move to Ireland and who gave support and in what form? The Dominicans had established contact with the bishop of Winchester before their arrival in England, and met Archbishop Stephen Langton and Hubert de Burgh soon after they entered the country. As has been stated: 'In contrast to the Franciscans, they [the Dominicans] sought out influential figures, making contact and soliciting their support. Among them were the kingdom's key politicians'.[25] Such a policy would assist greatly in the foundation of the first houses. Jens Röhrkasten considers that the attitude of the Dominicans in thirteenth-century in England was determined and efficient and that they considered it important to make contact with the powerful and important in society.[26]

The king[27]

There are five viable possibilities as founder, the first being King Henry III, who stated that he held the Dominicans 'in special devotion' when he asked the canons of Dunstable to allow the friars to settle there, and said that any help that the canons would give to the Dominicans, Henry would regard as given to himself.[28] From the beginning, all the English kings and queens gave an extraordinary amount of support and financial aid to the Dominicans in England.[29] Henry III's half-brother, Bartholomew, joined the Dominican order.[30] Henry III intervened personally in 1226 when he enquired about a place for the Dominicans in York.[31] In 1230, he granted the Dominicans a house that he owned in Edinburgh. Likewise, in Ireland in 1236 he granted permission for the Dominicans of Waterford to use a vacant site for a church and priory.[32] However, if Henry III was in any way personally involved in the arrival of the Dominicans in Ireland, this fact would be known and indeed reflected in the Dublin Dominican annals. There is no special attitude to the king in Pembridge's annals to substantiate this possibility. The involvement of the king, if at all, could only have been the equivalent of a general nod of approval and, later, royal alms.

Order, pp 259–60.   **25** Röhrkasten, *The mendicant houses of medieval London*, pp 67–8, 344, 381–3.   **26** Ibid., p. 522.   **27** Ibid., 340–79.   **28** Hinnebusch, *Dominican order*, p. 72. **29** Ibid., pp 4, n. 9, 72–3, 458–69. On Henry III's preference for the Dominicans, see Röhrkasten, *The mendicant houses of medieval London*, pp 258, 256–73, 344–8. **30** Röhrkasten, *The mendicant houses of medieval London*, p. 347; Hinnebusch, *Dominican order*, p. 72.   **31** York first recorded notice of Henry III: Hinnebusch, *Early English Friars Preachers*, p. 84.   **32** The priory of St Saviour was founded in 1236 when the citizens of Waterford received permission from Henry III to build a friary for the Dominicans on a vacant spot below the walls, where there was a small tower: *CDI, 1171–1251*, no. 2249, p. 334.

De Burgh[33]

Another possibility worth examining is a de Burgh involvement. Hubert de Burgh was the founder of the Dominicans in London and was buried there in 1243. Hubert was the younger brother of William de Burgh, lord of Connacht, and, incidentally, in 1249, left land in Ireland to the London Dominicans.[34] So there is a connection between Hubert and Ireland, albeit tenuous. But, there is no mention of a de Burgh connection anywhere and Pembridge gives no mention of him either.

Henry of London, archbishop of Dublin (1213–28) and justiciar of Ireland (1213–15, 1221–4)

One theory, proposed by Benedict O'Sullivan, was that Henry of London, the then archbishop, had brought the Dominicans to Dublin.[35] London was both archbishop of Dublin and justiciar of Ireland in the first few months of 1224. His second term as justiciar had coincided with the rebellion of Hugh de Lacy (d. 1242), who arrived in Meath in 1223. In order to defend the land and city of Dublin, Henry even had to borrow funds from the men of Dublin and other cities.[36] He was apparently forced to purchase a truce when de Lacy threatened Dublin in 1224 and shortly after this, in May 1224, he was replaced in office by William (II) Marshal, who arrived in Ireland in June 1224. Henry did not hold formal office in Ireland again.

O'Sullivan's theory is based on two documents in the Christ Church deeds.[37] In *c*.1218, two citizens of Dublin, Audeon Brun and Richard de Bedeford, granted to Holy Trinity (Christ Church Cathedral, Dublin) land near the River Liffey, on the north side of Oxmantown Bridge, as a site for a church to be named St Saviour (fig. 9.1).[38] The name alone, St Saviour (Holy Saviour), does not have any particular significance and was used by many churches. Then in *c*.1219 approval was given for the erection of this chapel near Dublin Bridge with provision being made for the chaplain.[39] There is no record to show whether or not this actually came to fruition. O'Sullivan's

---

33 Buried with the Order of Preachers in London with his wife Margaret, daughter of William king of Scotland and sister of Alexander of Scotland: Hinnebusch, *Early English Friars Preachers*, p. 44.   34 *CDI, 1171–1251*, no. 3012, p. 450; Barker, *Dominican order and convocation*, p. 77.   35 For this theory, see Benedict O'Sullivan, *Medieval Irish Dominican studies*, ed. Hugh Fenning (Dublin, 2009), pp 19–20.   36 A.J. Otway-Ruthven, *A history of medieval Ireland* (London, 1968), pp 90–1; Margaret Murphy, 'Balancing the concerns of church and state: the archbishops of Dublin, 1181–1228' in T.B. Barry, Robin Frame and Katharine Simms (eds), *Colony and frontier in medieval Ireland: essays presented to J.F. Lydon* (London, 1995), pp 49–56.   37 *Christ Church deeds*, ed. M.J. McEnery and Raymond Refaussé (Dublin, 2001), pp 40, 41 (hereafter *CCD*).   38 *CCD*, p. 40, no. 23. Audeon Brun's father, William Brun, also made a money grant to St Mary's, near Dublin, that is to say to the Cistercian abbey on the north of the River Liffey. He was a witness to a deed where he was called son of William Brun: *CSMA*, i, p. 233.   39 *CCD*, p. 41, no. 29.

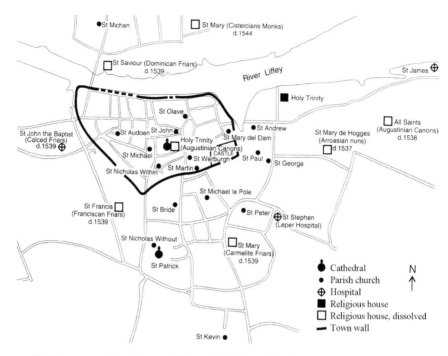

9.1 Dublin, *c.*1300 (after Anngret Simms, 'Origins and early growth' in Joseph Brady and Anngret Simms (eds), *Dublin through space and time* (c.*900–1900*) (Dublin, 2001), pp 15–65 at p. 59 (fig. 15)), with St Saviour's Dominican priory lying north of the Liffey near the bridge to Oxmantown.

suggestion is that Henry of London, five years later, persuaded Holy Trinity (Christ Church) to give the site to the Friars Preachers. There is no evidence to support this interesting supposition and there is no evidence in the Christ Church deeds that it ever happened. One might expect such a transaction to be recorded there.

Indeed, documentary evidence is to the contrary. We can be grateful to Ware for information about Henry of London and his work supporting religious establishments in Dublin during his period as archbishop. Indeed, Ware gives by far the longest entry (until that of John Allen in 1528) to Henry of London.[40] Among other facts, Ware tells us that Henry erected the collegiate church of St Patrick and augmented the revenues of the nunnery of Grace Deiu and that he removed the priory of Holm Patrick from an inconvenient place to a more commodious one. He also gave support to Christ Church Cathedral, where he was buried.[41] Among all the information Ware offers about Henry of London, there is nothing about Henry and the

---

40 Harris, *The whole works of Sir James Ware*, pp 318–20.   **41** Ware, *The antiquities and history of Ireland*, pp 4–5; Harris, *The whole works of Sir James Ware*, p. 319.

Dominicans. It is difficult to believe that Ware would not have mentioned it if Henry had any relationship with the Dominicans. It should be noted again that it was Ware who suggested that Luke de Netterville founded the Dominican house in Drogheda and if Henry of London had been similarly involved in Dublin Ware would have had that information.

Most importantly, if the Dominicans had any reason to be grateful to Henry of London, then a lengthy defamatory tale about him, which was included in the Dominican Dublin annals of John de Pembridge, prior of the Dominicans of Dublin, would not be there. This entry is not in the other Dublin annals of Thomas Case. Pembridge relates that when Henry was made archbishop of Dublin he called all his tenants to come to him and then asked them by what tenure they held their lands of him. The tenants then innocently produced their deeds and Henry ordered the deeds to be burned. Pembridge tells us that the freeholders thereafter called him Scorchvillain.[42] Here, it is important to note that Dominicans recited names of benefactors daily and therefore could not and would not decry a benefactor.[43] Furthermore, the Dublin Dominicans, in common with all the orders, would have a necrology recording the obits of all important benefactors to ensure that the friars prayed for them and we have proof of this from the register of the Dominican house at Athenry and the necrology of the Galway Franciscans. Bearing in mind the great praise bestowed in the annals upon all Dominican benefactors, it is inconceivable that Henry of London was in any way a benefactor of the Dominicans. The conclusion must be that, given the defamatory tale in the Dublin Dominican annals, and the lack of association with the Dominicans, contrasted with the information about Henry of London's work with other religious foundations, Henry of London could not have been involved in the coming of the Dominicans to Dublin.[44]

The citizens of Dublin

A fourth possibility is that the Dublin Dominican priory was founded by the citizens. This is the statement in Hugh Fenning's recently discovered manuscript of 1647.[45] The citizens of Dublin certainly supported the Dominicans and we have plenty of evidence of this from Pembridge's annals, especially in regard to Dublin mayors and in particular John le Decer.[46] Ambrose Coleman in 1902, using a seventeenth-century Chatham manuscript, says that the Dominican convent and church were built by the citizens of Dublin. This is logical; in London, most grants of land came from townspeople. However, the

---

42 *CSMA*, ii, p. 312.   **43** Röhrkasten, *The mendicant houses of medieval London*, pp 144–5. **44** It is also of interest that, 'in the well-documented cases of the foundations of Dominicans and Franciscans, the bishops of London played no role whatsoever': Röhrkasten, *The mendicant houses of medieval London*, p. 302.   **45** Fenning, 'Founders of Irish Dominican friaries', p. 60.   **46** *CSMA*, ii, pp 337, 342, 377.

first grant was made by Hubert de Burgh, arguably the most important man in England during the reign of Henry III.[47] Similarly, in Dublin, because the Dominicans were a new order arriving from England, an initial momentum would be essential and a similar figure of importance would be needed to pave the way.

William Marshal II and the Cistercians

A strong possibility is that William Marshal II was that man, but with Cistercian help. All seventeenth-century historians claimed that the Cistercians were involved in the early establishment of the Friars Preachers in Dublin, and this is certainly possible, considering the early and close relationship between the Cistercians and Dominic. Whatever problems the Cistercians and Dominicans had in later times,[48] it is quite clear that there was closeness in the early period. The site in Dublin was contiguous to the Cistercian abbey of St Mary's on the north side of the Liffey. The statements of O'Heyne, de Burgo and Coleman that the Cistercians gave the land to the Order of Preachers are plausible, especially when one notes that a report in St Mary's cartulary states that the Cistercians also gave land to the Order of Preachers, albeit much later, in the fifteenth century when the monks of Dunbrody gave Portumna to the preachers.[49] The Cistercians would probably not of their own accord have invited the friars, but they would undoubtedly have assisted their coming if asked.

There are many reasons for suggesting that William Marshal II was a person well able to facilitate the establishment of the Order of Preachers in Dublin. One persuasive reason is that by far the longest item in the Dublin annals of Pembridge is the genealogy of the descendants of William Marshal I.[50] On 2 May 1224, William Marshal II became justiciar of Ireland. In April of that year he married Eleanor, the younger sister of Henry III. Eleanor's whole family were particularly strong supporters of the Dominicans; her half-brother was a Dominican and, as we have seen, Henry III favoured the order. When Eleanor died she was buried with them.[51] The Marshal family also supported

---

47 Hinnebusch, *Early English Friars Preachers*, p. 115.   **48** Ibid., p. 98.   **49** *CSMA*, ii, p. xciv. 'The church and abbey first belonged to the Cistercians, but when the magnificent royal monastery of the same order had been erected in 1220 [*recte* 1190] at Knockmoy, a very beautiful place, by Cathal O'Conor, king of Connaught, surnamed the Red Hand, and the monks had been drafted to it from the Cistercian monastery of Boyle and also from that of Galway, this latter house was in a desolate state for about fifty years, possessing only one or two monks. Now, when Athenry Abbey had been built about 1241 [the Cistercians delivered up their Galway house to the fathers of that community], the agreement to that effect being procured about 1249 by Phelim O'Conor, the son and heir of king Cathal ... the original agreement was still to be found in the municipal archives': O'Heyne, *Irish Dominicans*, pp 125–7.   **50** The genealogy covers two of ninety-five pages in the Latin edition of the annals: *CSMA*, ii, pp 312–14.   **51** 'Both the king and his political supporters supported the Dominicans, which may, of course, have been merely coincidental': Röhrkasten, *The mendicant houses of medieval London*, p. 390.

the Dominicans. Gilbert Marshal, earl of Pembroke (third son of William Marshal I), gave eighty oaks and other timber from his woodland to the London priory, a gift that might have been influenced by his relationship with either the king or de Burgh.[52] Two other sons, Richard and William II, were political and close allies of Hubert de Burgh (to 1226) and de Burgh of course was the founder of the Dominicans of London.[53] Ware believes that William II founded the Dominican house in Kilkenny. However, the newly discovered manuscript in Rome states that the founder of Kilkenny Priory was the earl of Pembroke who was killed at the Battle of Curragh with his eighteen knights; this was of course Richard, who succeeded his brother as earl of Pembroke. Pembridge relates that in 1234 Richard died and was buried next to his brother, William, in the choir of the Friars Preachers, 'of whom it is written "of whom under the fosse of Kilkenny the bones remain"'.[54] There are several conflicting claims as to where the members of the Marshal family are buried. The register of Dunbrody claims that William I was buried in New Temple, London, and states that so were sons William II and Gilbert. Isabella, wife of William I, was buried in Tintern, Wales, as were sons Walter and Anselm, while Richard was buried in the Dominican priory, Kilkenny.[55]

William Marshal II crossed to Waterford on 19 June 1224. He got six hundred head of cattle and forty marks from the Cistercians of Mellifont, and two hundred pounds from the Cistercians of Dublin to facilitate the raising of an army.[56] Thus, clearly, William II was in a position to ask the Cistercians to facilitate the Dominicans, if he so wished. The Cistercians would also have been willing to oblige William II because of the strong connection, mentioned above, between Dominic and the Cistercians in these very early years. The land that the Dominicans got for their convent, the site of the present Four Courts, was adjacent to St Mary's Abbey.[57] Ware's notes from St Mary's Cistercian

52 'Gilbert's donation to the Dominicans of Holborn may have been a sign of his loyalty to Hubert de Burgh, because his other religious donations, also abroad, show that he was not particularly drawn to the mendicants': Röhrkasten, *The mendicant houses of medieval London*, p. 391; Hinnebusch, *Early English Friars Preachers*, p. 26. **53** Röhrkasten, *The mendicant houses of medieval London*, p. 522. **54** *CSMA*, ii, p. 315. He was buried on 17 Apr. 1234 with the Franciscans in Kilkenny, according to Roger of Wendover: Fitzmaurice and Little, *Franciscan province of Ireland*, p. 3. The Dominican annalist, Nicholas Trivet, says he was buried with the Friars Preachers, Kilkenny, and the *Liber primus Kilkenniensis* just says that he was buried in Kilkenny: *Liber primus Kilkenniensis: the earliest of the books of the corporation of Kilkenny now extant*, ed. Charles McNeill (Dublin, 1931), p. 62. In 1233, 'Richard, earl Marshal, was killed in battle at Kildare by the Geraldines, who were on the side of the king and acting on his behalf': Williams (ed.), *Clyn*, p. 140. 'One of the worst deeds done in that age': *AC*, p. 49. R.F. Walker, 'The supporters of Richard Marshal, earl of Pembroke, in the rebellion of 1233–1234', *Welsh History Review*, 17 (1994), 41–65. See also Brendan Smith, 'Irish politics, 1220–1245' in Michael Prestwich, Richard Britnell and Robin Frame (eds), *Thirteenth century England VIII* (Woodbridge, 2001), pp 15–19. **55** *CSMA*, ii, pp 142–3. **56** To facilitate the raising of an army: Orpen, *Ireland under the Normans*, iii, p. 42 [2005 ed., p. 302]. **57** Geraldine Stout, 'The topography of St Mary's

abbey annals contain the information that in 1238 the 'church of St Saviour was founded'.[58]

One eighteenth-century historian also believed that Marshal was the principal and first benefactor. This was Mervyn Archdall in his *Monasticon Hibernicum* of 1786. He described the priory as being founded between 1202 and 1218, by William Marshal, the elder, earl of Pembroke, for the health of his soul and that of his wife. Witnesses: Albin, bishop of Ferns, and Hugh, bishop of Ossory'.[59] Now there are several flaws in Archdall's statement. Firstly, the Dominicans did not arrive in Ireland until 1224. Secondly, it obviously cannot be William Marshal the elder, as he died in 1219. Thirdly, the witnesses are a problem; Albin, the Cistercian bishop of Ferns, died in 1223, and the second witness, Hugh, bishop of Ossory, died in 1218. So even though Archdall's claim agrees with the theory of a Marshal involvement, it is not sound.

Notwithstanding that, however, there is support for the role of William Marshal II, when he was the chief justiciar, in the establishment of the Dominicans in Dublin. He was a known supporter of the Dominicans, he was married to the king's sister who was later buried with the Dominicans and whose half-brother was a Dominican. He was in a position to have influence with the Cistercians and, most importantly and most significantly, the Marshal family has the longest entry in Pembridge. This connection between the Cistercians and Dominicans adds force to the likelihood of a Dominican having access to Cistercian annals, and the early section of Pembridge's annals is definitely taken from a Cistercian source as it lists the foundations of all the Cistercian abbeys until Abbeylara in 1212.

Why would the Cistercians have been so obliging? Firstly, the Marshal family were most important patrons of the Cistercian order in Ireland and Wales.[60] Secondly, setting aside the early close relationship, there is also the question of the Dublin suburb in which the Cistercians were situated. On the north side of the Liffey there was only one parish church, St Michan's, compared with the large number of churches on the south side.[61] The Cistercians would have welcomed the Dominicans, whose presence would have enhanced the pastoral care available to residents living on the north side of the Liffey. From the Dominican viewpoint, the site would have been excellent, as on that side of the river there would have been a large enough site to provide

Cistercian abbey and precinct, Dublin' in Seán Duffy (ed.), *Medieval Dublin XII* (Dublin, 2012), pp 138–60.   **58** *CSMA*, ii, p. 289.   **59** Archdall, *Monasticon Hibernicum*, ii, p. 69. **60** In Ireland, Graiguenamanagh (Duiske) and Tintern (de Voto) were founded by William Marshal I, and William Marshal II was particularly generous to Tintern in Wales; from 1219 onwards, he added more lands, especially in 1223–4: David Robinson, *Tintern Abbey* (Cardiff, 1986), p. 12.   **61** Emer Purcell, 'St Michan: cult, saint and church' in John Bradley, Alan Fletcher and Anngret Simms (eds), *Dublin in the medieval world: essays in honour of Howard Clarke* (Dublin, 2009), pp 119–40.

for any subsequent expansion to accommodate, for example, educational needs.[62]

THE DOMINICAN PRIORY IN DUBLIN

The site of the Dominican priory was on the north side of the Liffey close to the Cistercian abbey of St Mary's in the suburb known as *villa Ostmannorum* (Ostmantown/Oxmantown), where, initially, the old Norse element (Ostmen) of Dublin lived. By the time the Dominicans arrived in this suburb, however, men of English origin were also well established in the area. It was an ideal site for the friars because it was in the suburbs, near a gate, near the town wall, and close to a main road. We have several descriptions of the priory, although none from the medieval period. In 1706, the Dominican O'Heyne tells us that

> The abbey is situated on the banks of the river so that when the tide is in ships can come up to its walls. It belonged first to the monks of St Bernard who gave it to the Dominicans in the year 1223 [*recte* 1224] on condition that on Christmas Day every year they should offer a lighted candle to the abbot of St Mary's Abbey, in acknowledgement of the gift.[63]

The detail of the candle at Christmas adds a sense of authenticity to O'Heyne's statement. The question to be asked is how reliable was O'Heyne? Coleman tells us that O'Heyne 'relies not only on the accurate and erudite Ware but also on the French author Allemand, and local traditions whether true or unfounded, and is accordingly full of inaccuracies'.[64] But Coleman is not reliable either. The Dominican Thomas Flynn considers that O'Heyne, while 'not always dependable … is at his best when reminiscing about fellow Dominicans and people he actually knew'.[65] However, in this instance he is merely describing the building. In 1722, Stevens relates that in the city of Dublin

> was a very large and stately monastery of this order, and which is still remaining, but now appropriated to the use of the law, commonly called the Four Courts, … this monastery was one of most ancient of the order, having been founded in the year 1223 (sic). Nor is it needless farther to observe, that it was also one of the richest, as sufficiently appears by the beauty of the structure. It was likewise better situated than any other monastery in Ireland, being in that noble quarter of the city called Oxmantown that is, the town or suburb of the Ostmen, … This

---

62 In London, the Dominicans gave up their first home within the walls and moved to a new site outside the south gate: Hinnebusch, *Early English Friars Preachers*, pp 23–8. 63 O'Heyne, *Irish Dominicans*, pp 25–7.   64 Ibid., p. xxvii.   65 Flynn, *Irish Dominicans*, p. xix.

monastery stood on the bank of the River Liffey so that upon high floods, vessels did and do still come up to the very walls of this house.

He goes on to state that

> Fontana Malvenda (the Dominican historian (1566–1628)) and other authors of this order, mention one thing concerning this house, which I also find in the registers, viz. that this stately house formerly belonged to the Cistercian order but that it was given up to the Dominicans upon condition that they should yearly on Christmas Day offer a lighted taper at the abby of St Mary of the Cistercian order, which was close by it, as an acknowledgement of their holding this monastery, of that abby, which was duly performed yearly on that day.[66]

In 1762, de Burgo agreed that it was founded in Oxmantown in 1224 and that the site was given by Cistercian monks of St Mary's.[67] In 1786, Archdall also described the priory:

> In the Ostmantown, on north bank of river, near the old bridge, and now called King's Inns; it was founded near the great bridge (on the place where stood the chapel of St Saviour) between 1202 and 1218, by William Mareschal, the elder, earl of Pembroke, for the health of his soul and that of his wife. Witnesses Albin, bishop of Ferns and Hugh, bishop of Ossory.[68] This house did first belong to the Cistercians but the Dominicans coming into Ireland in the year 1224, the Cistercians of St Mary's Abbey gave it up to accommodate them on condition that on the feast of the Nativity, yearly, they should offer a lighted taper at the abbey of St Mary as an acknowledgement that this monastery did originally belong to the Cistercian order.[69]

Flynn considers that, although Archdall inevitably relied heavily on Ware, Alemand and Harris, and has many inaccuracies, nevertheless, his work has the value of citing many documentary sources now lost or destroyed.[70] In 1902, Coleman stated that the priory was founded in 1224:

> the first of the Dominican abbeys in Ireland. The fathers in that year leased a site adjoining St Mary's Abbey from the Cistercian monks at a yearly rent of £3, and their convent and church were built by the citizens of Dublin. The site extended along the river bank from the present

66 *Monasticon Hibernicum*, pp 215–16.   **67** Burke, *Hibernia Dominicana*, pp 184, 187.
68 For a problem with this deed, see above.   **69** Archdall, *MonasticonHibernicum*, ii, p. 69.
70 Flynn, *Irish Dominicans*, p. xix.

Church Street to Ormond Bridge. They had a theological school attached to the abbey from the earliest times.[71]

Coleman then appends his source just as 'MS folio vol. in Chetham Library, Manchester, p. 622, written in the early 17th century'. This is in fact 'MS A.6.77, a manuscript volume containing a miscellaneous collection of material relating to Ireland, including a description of Ireland, notes on the Irish peerage, court fees, petitions etc, with much on Irish religious foundations'.[72] This rent of £3 is not mentioned by earlier writers. Information about the building and gardens in 1317 can be found in a petition to the king by the friars when they listed the destruction caused by the action of the city during the Bruce Invasion.[73] At the Dissolution, the Dominican site was only three acres and this is consistent with mendicant practice. The extent made on 12 March 1541 declares that the priory church could be thrown down and the jurors cannot estimate the value of the timber, glass, iron and stones. The other buildings on the site together with the cemetery are contained on three acres and worth nothing. The priory did also have some tenements in the city, particularly in the parish of St Michan, and some land in Co. Meath.[74]

DUBLIN AND THE DOMINICANS

The relationship between the Dominicans and Dublin was good. They were very visible from the city. They were on the north side of the Liffey facing the city, and so everyone coming or going north had to pass them on the road and on the bridge.[75] The city could only gain from their presence and we know from Pembridge that many mayors supported them. The mayor John le Decer looms large in the early days (from 1308) and Kendrick Sherman, whose death is recorded in 1351 as formerly mayor of the city of Dublin, was buried under the campanile of the Friars Preachers of the same city, which campanile he himself erected. He also glazed the window in the chapter choir and roofed the church.[76] It must be said for the purpose of historical truth, however, that like all situations it is the exception that proves the rule; one mayor apparently did not like the Dominican friars.

---

71 Coleman, *Ancient Dominican foundations in Ireland*, p. 23, in O'Heyne, *Irish Dominicans*. **72** I am very grateful to Jane Muskett, archivist at Chetham Library, for this information. **73** *Documents on the affairs of Ireland before the king's council*, ed. G.O. Sayles (Dublin, 1979), p. 87. **74** *Extents of Irish monastic possessions, 1540–41*, ed. N.B. White (Dublin, 1943), pp 53–4. For a discussion about the 'legality' of owning property outside the convent precinct, see Bennett, *The early Dominicans*, pp 176–7. **75** We know that all convents in London were close to a town gate, or near a busy thoroughfare or the river: Röhrkasten, The mendicant houses of medieval London, p. 68. **76** *CSMA*, ii, pp 337, 342, 377, 291.

Robert de Moenes (d. 1324) was mayor of Dublin 1319–20 and his will appears to express his disapproval of the Dominicans. As was the norm, he left a large number of bequests to the religious groups in Dublin. What is of significance is that although he leaves money to the other three mendicant orders (he was buried with the Franciscans), surprisingly, he left nothing to the Dominican order.[77] More significant is the fact that his daughter, Giliana, also ignored the Dominicans in her will in 1348. This appears to indicate a long-running antipathy between the Dominicans and the de Moenes family.[78] A reason for the antagonism between Robert de Moenes and the Dominicans may rest in the years in which Robert was mayor, 1319–20. Robert Bruce was camped at Castleknock in 1316 and the citizens of Dublin feared an imminent attack on the city. Church towers were often used as lookout posts in times of danger and, while Christ Church tower would have the advantage of height to view Castleknock, the view from the Dominican priory could also have been useful. In this time of danger, the position of the priory, outside the walls of the city, was vulnerable and probably dangerous to the city; it was very close to the city and beside the vital Ostmen's Bridge and Ostmen's Gate.[79] Therefore, it could, potentially, have been used by Bruce and his men as a base from which to attack the city.[80] What happened was related by Pembridge in his annals: 'the said mayor [Robert de Nottingham] with the citizens destroyed the church of St Saviour, which is the place of the Friars Preachers and the stones of the same place were transported to build the walls of the city, which was then enlarged in the northern part of the walls upon the quays'.[81] Perhaps the Dominicans were lucky that their whole convent was not destroyed to prevent its use by Bruce and his men. Reading the Dominicans' petition to the king in 1317 asking for restitution, it appears to have been a fairly aggressive destruction of the priory, which included breaking windows, cutting down the trees in the garden and taking corn and other foodstuffs.[82] Bruce did not attack. Pembridge recorded that 'later the king of England ordered the same mayor and community that they should make the convent as before'.[83] This plea from the Dominicans went before the king in 1317.[84] It was de Moenes who was mayor two years later, and he must have been involved in 'making the convent as before'. More significant is that he was bailiff (the administrative

---

77 For examples of Dublin wills where donations were made to the four mendicant orders, see J.T. Gilbert (ed.), *Calendar of ancient records relating to Dublin*, 1 (Dublin, 1889), pp 129, 131 (hereafter *CARD*).   78 J.G. Smyly, 'Old (Latin) deeds in the library of Trinity College', *Hermathena*, 67 (1946), 9. For the daughter's will, see ibid., 69 (1947), 31.   79 *CARD*, pp 103, 106.   80 Marjan de Smet, 'Heavenly quiet and the din of war: *use and abuse of religious buildings for purposes of safety, defence and strategy*' in Paul Trio and Marjan de Smet (eds), *The use and abuse of sacred places in late medieval towns* (Leuven, 2006), pp 11–14, 18.   81 *CSMA*, ii, p. 353.   82 Sayles (ed.), *Documents on the affairs of Ireland before the king's council*, p. 87.   83 *CSMA*, ii, p. 353.   84 Sayles (ed.), *Documents on the affairs of Ireland before the king's council*, p. 87.

position under the mayor) of Dublin in 1313–14, 1315–16, 1316–17, which were crucial years.[85] De Moenes, as the second in command in Dublin during the Bruce crisis, must have also been involved in the original decision in effect to raze the priory. After the threat of the Bruce Invasion had passed, the city underwent great hardship, for the mayor and commonalty asked for exemption from payment of the farm of the city because of the burning of the suburbs during the invasion.[86]

An interesting point of information is that de Moenes' wife, Elena, was the sister of John le Decer (d. 1332), who, although buried with the Franciscans, was a great benefactor of the Dominicans. Apart from doing many good things for the convent of the Friars Preachers of Dublin, Pembridge tells us that he also fed the friars (presumably all of the mendicant orders) each Friday at his table.[87] What is most interesting is that Harris, when discussing the Dublin mayors, tells us that in 1308 this generous magistrate, in a time of great scarcity, raised a vast sum of money, and furnished out three ships to France. When they returned in two months laden with corn, he gave one ship to the lord justice and militia, another to the Dominican and Augustine seminaries, and reserved a third for the exercise of his own hospitality and bounty. At the same time, the prior of Christ Church, being destitute of corn, and having no money to buy it, sent to this worthy mayor a pledge of plate to the value of forty pounds, but he returned the plate and sent the prior a present of twenty barrels of corn. Harris tells us that

> these beneficent actions moved the Dominicans to insert the following prayer in their litany, *Orate pro salute majoris, ballivorum, et communitatis de omni civitate Dubliniensi, optimorum benefactorum hui cordinituo, nunc et in hora mortis* (Pray for the salvation of the mayors, bailiffs and all the community of the city of Dublin now and at the hour of death).[88]

Most importantly, Harris states that this was recorded in the registry of the Dominicans of Dublin.[89] This information does not appear in Ware as published, but Harris had access to Ware's notes and may have found it there. Another explanation is that this registry was still extant in 1766.

There can be no doubt that the Dominican priory was very much part of the city of Dublin, albeit across the bridge in Oxmantown. From the Dominican annals of Pembridge, we get a very strong sense of Dominican involvement

85 Ware, *The antiquities and history of Ireland*, pp 164–5; H.F. Berry, 'Catalogue of the mayors and bailiffs of Dublin city, AD1229–1447' in Howard Clarke, *Medieval Dublin: the living city* (Dublin, 1990), pp 158–9.   **86** Sayles (ed.), *Documents on the affairs of Ireland before the king's council*, pp 86–7; *CARD*, pp 11, 12, 132, 149–51.   **87** This was primarily a penitential, religious, ascetic act, and le Decer would have been fasting too, as it was a Friday. I thank Colmán Ó Clabaigh for this clarification.   **88** Walter Harris, *The history and antiquities of the city of Dublin* (Dublin, 1766), pp 257–9.   **89** Ibid., p. 258.

with the activity of the city. The price of food is mentioned often, and when there was once a shortage of wheat, with the corresponding rise in price, Pembridge related that the bakers who gave a false weight to their bread were caught and punished by being drawn upon hurdles through the streets of the city at horse tails.[90] We know from Pembridge that the Dominican priory was quick to hear any news arriving in Dublin; phrases appear such as 'Nicholas de Balscot came from England with news',[91] 'three weeks after Easter came news to Dublin that …',[92] 'news came to Dublin that the Lord Alexander Bicknor had landed in Youghal'[93] and 'news arrived from England to Ireland that the town of Berwick was captured by the Scots'.[94] The Bruce Invasion is particularly well covered by these annals, clearly fuelled by news constantly arriving in the capital.[95] The annals abound with tales and rumours about Dublin – harsh winters, a frozen River Liffey, burials, problems of high officials who were also Dominican patrons. The site of the priory and the activity of the friars in ministering to the citizens of Dublin ensured their constant close contact and involvement with medieval Dublin. It should always be kept in mind that 'secular authorities used ecclesiastical buildings and lands for non-religious or only half religious purposes'.[96] Religious houses were also used to house visiting dignitaries and meetings and the Dominican priory may well have had more room than most religious houses, situated as it was on north side of the Liffey.[97]

CONCLUSION

The only fact that we can be certain of is that the Dominicans came to Ireland in 1224. I suggest that, unless substantiated by any new medieval evidence, Ware's list should be treated with extreme caution, at least for the dates in the first decade. It is more logical on all grounds to assume that Dublin was the first foundation and accept that Drogheda was also a very early foundation. With regard to founders of the Dublin priory; the Cistercians and citizens have the strongest claim. However, William Marshal II should be considered, at the very least, as a facilitator for the arrival of the Dominicans in 1224. The safest conclusion is that, as long as medieval documentary sources do not provide absolute proof, no possibilities should be ruled out and all early modern sources should be used with great respect, albeit with caution.

---

90 *CSMA*, ii, p. 339. For rules governing bakers in Dublin, see *CARD*, pp 219, 224. **91** *CSMA*, ii, p. 355. **92** Ibid., p. 358. **93** Ibid., p. 359. **94** Ibid., p. 358. **95** Ibid., pp 344–60. **96** Paul Trio, 'Introduction' in Trio and de Smet (eds), *Use and abuse of sacred places*, p. vii. **97** Röhrkasten, 'Secular uses of the mendicant priories of medieval London' *in* Trio and de Smet (eds), *Use and abuse of sacred places*, pp 133–51.

James Yonge and the writing of history in late medieval Dublin

CAOIMHE WHELAN

James Yonge (*c.*1375/80–*c.*1439) was a fifteenth-century Dubliner living and working in the city as a notary, scribe, clerk, translator and writer. We know he was responsible for a number of extant works of prose. He was one of the few named writers in Hiberno-Middle English (HME) – the dialect of English spoken in Ireland in the later Middle Ages – and he also wrote in Latin. Yonge's texts are infused with his sense of identity, his identity as a Dubliner and his identity as a politically minded Anglo-Irishman who knew the importance of history in explaining the past and understanding the present.

His earliest known text, bearing the laborious title *Memoriale super visitatione domini Laurencii Ratholdi militis et baronis Vngarie factum de Purgatorio sancti Patricii in insula Hibernie* ('A record of the visit made by Lord Laurence Rathold, knight and baron of Hungary, to the Purgatory of Saint Patrick on the Island of Ireland'), commonly known as the *Memoriale*, is a Latin account of a journey to the popular pilgrim site, St Patrick's Purgatory in Lough Derg.[1] His second work is an English translation of the *Secreta Secretorum*, which Yonge introduces as 'the book of the gouernaunce of kygis and of pryncis' (henceforth, the *Gouernaunce*).[2] Both of these texts contribute to our knowledge of the history of the English colony in medieval Ireland and examining them can tell us a lot about how history could be perceived and used in the late Middle Ages.

Yonge has also been credited by some scholars with authorship of the English language *Conquest* text – the contemporary translation of *Expugnatio Hibernica* (the Conquest of Ireland) by the twelfth-century historian Giraldus Cambrensis (Gerald of Wales). It is unlikely that Yonge was responsible for this translation: the *Conquest* is written in a very different style from either of Yonge's other works and no medieval source links him with its authorship. It seems that this text has been attributed to Yonge simply because it appears alongside his *Gouernaunce* text in two early manuscripts, but such an observation is hardly conclusive evidence for his authorship.

Many people in the English colony in Ireland would have been familiar with Giraldus Cambrensis' works in either HME or in Latin, which bestowed the

---

1 A new translation and edition of this text is provided in Theresa O'Byrne, 'Dublin's Hoccleve: James Yonge, scribe, author and bureaucrat, and the literary world of late medieval Dublin' (PhD, Notre Dame, 2012), pp 410–64. 2 Robert Steele, *Three prose versions of the Secreta Secretorum* (London, 1898), p. 1.

colony with a record of its history, aimed at reminding them of the great deeds of their ancestors and stressing their link to the crown. It is deeply biased in favour of the newcomers: as Seán Duffy writes, the original twelfth-century work is 'the defence produced by an agent of an invading and conquering army to justify its actions'.[3] For a later colonial audience, the text provided justification of their presence in Ireland.

Yonge's *Gouernaunce*, the focus of this essay, can be read in a similar way, allowing us to see the process of interpretive history at work, this time in the expert hand of a fifteenth-century Dublin writer. Alan Fletcher has noted in an essay in an earlier volume of this series that 'the root activity of all annal and chronicle keeping might be thought to endure in acts of historical memorialization that were also, to more immediately practical effects, acts of consolidation, whether personal, institutional or social.'[4] In this way, history was not confined to the page but could be used to influence the present and help shape the future.

A LATE MEDIEVAL DUBLIN WRITER: JAMES YONGE

James Yonge was proud to claim his allegiance to the city of Dublin and proudly identified himself as a Dubliner in the *Memoriale: Igitur ego Jacobus Yonge notarius imperialis civium et scriptorum minimus civitatis Dublinensis* ('I James Yonge, an imperial notary of the citizens, and least of all of the writers of Dublin').[5] Of course, his claim to be the 'least of all the writers of Dublin' is a traditional humility *topos*, a self-effacing description far from the reality of Yonge's abilities. Yonge was probably born in Dublin (his father can also be located in the city), while much of the extant documentation written by him is concerned with the parishes of St John the Evangelist (of Bothe Street) and St Audeon (Dublin's oldest parish) and it can be assumed that James lived relatively close by. It is likely that Yonge trained as a clerk under the bearer of the seal of the provostship of Dublin, an official in the Dublin municipal administration.[6] This job gave him responsibility for the seal used to authenticate documents when a granter's seal was not well known in order to give a transaction legal authority. Yonge graduated to becoming one of the two or three bearers of the seal of the provostship, an office he probably held for most of his career, and he also may have served as an assistant to the city clerk. His day-job as an imperial notary places him at the centre of the administration of law in the English colony in Ireland. This meant that Yonge worked

3 Seán Duffy, *Ireland in the Middle Ages* (Dublin, 1997), p. 7.   4 Alan Fletcher, 'The annals and chronicles of medieval Dublin: an overview' in Seán Duffy (ed.), *Medieval Dublin VIII* (Dublin, 2008), p. 194.   5 British Library, Royal 10.B.ix, fo. 43v; O'Byrne, 'Dublin's Hoccleve', pp 244–5.   6 See ibid., pp 275–83.

as a legal functionary, specializing in witnessing, drafting and recording legal contracts – sales, charters, wills etc., and on occasion acting as an 'attorney' in property transactions. With literary skills acquired and honed in the course of his job and perhaps access to notable people in the colony, he was well placed to supplement his income by acting as a scribe for hire.

Neither of Yonge's texts is written about Dublin specifically, but Yonge's situation in the capital allows him to provide us with a rare perspective from the hand of a fifteenth-century Dubliner casting his eye over recent events affecting his own life and that of the colony. At times, his location creeps into the depiction of events, giving us a glimpse of the capital in the fifteenth century. An example appears in his 1411 Latin *Memoriale* text. The sole extant manuscript witness of the work is in the late fifteenth-century London, BL Royal MS 10.B ix, recently transcribed and translated by Theresa O'Byrne. In this text, Yonge creates an account of a contemporary event for posterity. He gives us an engaging picture of the citizens of Dublin 'and many powerful men' congregating to hear the tale while the knight waited for a ship, with the citizens clamouring for Yonge to write the account of Laurence's journey (although this may be a literary construct rather than historical reality).

Yonge's works demonstrate an appreciation of the importance of identifying and highlighting the colony's challenges, their capabilities and their loyalty to the crown. This is not surprising, as Yonge was involved in the administration of the English colony and he also worked for one of the most powerful men in Ireland of his period, James Butler, fourth earl of Ormond, the White Earl. Ormond twice held the office of lord lieutenant of Ireland and during his first tenure in 1420, Yonge was appointed to the position of second engrosser of the exchequer.[7] The engrosser was a copyist responsible for keeping accurate accounts of the administration on the great pipe roll. The second engrosser was an assistant to the chief engrosser (and would have been paid about 5*d.* per day when the exchequer was open and £1 for a robe).[8] On 25 April, the day after Yonge was appointed, he nominated a deputy, William Stokenbrick.[9] This was not to be Yonge's only dealing with Ormond; shortly after this, he began work on a translation dedicated to the earl, the aforementioned *Gouernaunce*. This text, one of the few prose translations into HME undertaken in Ireland in the fifteenth century, provides us with a fascinating example of how one Dubliner used the history of the English colony in Ireland to comment on the history and politics of his contemporary sphere in fifteenth-century Ireland.

---

7 *A calendar of Irish chancery letters, c.1244–1509*, ed. Peter Crooks (hereafter *CIRCLE*), PR 8 Henry V, 21; National Archives of Ireland, RC 8/38, pp 104–5. See also Elizabeth Matthew, 'The governing of the Lancastrian lordship of Ireland in the time of James Butler, fourth earl of Ormond, *c.*1450–52' (PhD, Durham, 1994). 8 Philomena Connolly, *Irish exchequer payments, 1270–1446* (Dublin, 1998), p. xxii. 9 *CIRCLE*, PR 8 Henry V, 22;

SECRETA SECRETORUM: JAMES BUTLER AND RECENT HISTORY

The *Gouernaunce* is not a 'history' per say, but a translation of a text of the popular 'mirror for princes' genre – the medieval equivalent of a political self-help book. Niccolo Machiavelli's *il Principe* (*c*.1513) written for *al magnifico Lorenzo di Piero de Medici* (Lorenzo de Medici, 1493–1519), is one of the most famous 'mirror for princes' works from almost a century later. Yonge's original text is based on a thirteenth-century French translation of the *Secreta Secretorum* undertaken by the Dominican, Jofroi of Waterford.[10] Yonge does not credit Jofroi's text as his source but simply tells his patron:

> ... now y here translate to youre souerayne nobilnes [sovereign noble-ness] the boke of arystotle, Prynce of Phylosofors, of the gouernaunce of prynces, ... The wych boke he makyd to his dysciple Alexandre the grete emperoure, conqueroure of al the worlde.[11]

Versions of the *Secreta Secretorum* abound in the Middle Ages in many languages in England and Ireland. The text's claim to be a work by Aristotle imparting advice to his young pupil Alexander the Great was widely believed; however, the text was actually a medieval Arabic forgery. Yonge's patron, James Butler, was esteemed for his learning and patronage of literature and the translation was probably undertaken to celebrate and commemorate his appointment to the position of chief governor of Ireland. Such a work would have pleased Ormond, as he cast himself in the mould of military campaigner in Ireland and, in that regard, it was an appropriate text to present to the earl.

Yonge's work illustrates the understanding of chivalry in the late Middle Ages; he explains that the important 'art' of chivalry was not only ensured by 'dedys of armes', but 'by wysdome and helpe of lawes, and of witt, and wysdome of vndyrstondynge'.[12] When these two are combined, 'in goodnys may the prynce play, and with good men surly walke'.[13]

The text suggests that, in order to rule well, those who govern must be informed how to rule correctly. Yonge's text provides a handbook of governing skills for the earl, including a commentary on the recent past and the contemporary environment that the lieutenant oversaw. The text explains the necessity of understanding the theory behind the practice of governing, declaring that 'Tully the grette clerke [Marcus Tullius Cicero, the Roman

CIRCLE, PR 8 Henry V, 21.   **10** Although much of the discussion is outdated, G.L. Hamilton provides a discussion of the text in 'The sources of the Secret des Secrets of Jofroi de Watreford', *Romantic Review*, 1 (1910), 259–64.   **11** Steele (ed.), *Secreta Secretorum*, lxxiv, p. 122; a modern English translation has been produced by Liz Kerns with an introduction by Elizabeth Matthew, in Kerns (ed.), *The Secret of Secrets (Secreta Secretorum): a modern translation, with introduction, of The governance of princes* (New York, 2008).   **12** Steele (ed.), *Secreta Secretorum*, p. 121.   **13** Ibid.

politician] sayth, than were wel gouernette emperies and kyngdomes whan kynges wer phylosofors, and philosofy regnyd'.[14] Yonge goes on to flatter his patron, noting that

> The whyche thynge, nobil and gracious lorde afor-sayde, haith parcewid the sotilte of youre witte [perceived by the skill of your mind], and the clernys of youre engyn [the clearness of your intelligence], therfor I-chargid some good boke of gouernaunce of prynces out of latyn othyr Frenche in-to youre modyr Englyshe tonge to translate.[15]

The original *Secreta* was not written by Aristotle, but the prospect of pre-senting a version of a text worthy of the great conqueror Alexander captured the imagination of the medieval readership. The earl of Ormond would have appreciated the military parallel between himself and the great Macedonian commander. Well aware of the text's potential to flatter, Yonge freely adapted the prose to his purpose and his patron, advising through historical episodes drawn from antiquity (Alexander's history) and emphasizing the role of the Butler family in Irish history.

In crafting this work, Yonge acts not just as a translator, but as a historian. Just before the index he addresses his patron: 'I writte to youre excellence this boke, entremedelid wyth many good ensamplis of olde stories, and wyth the foure cardynale vertues, and dyuers othyr good matturis, and olde ensamplis and new'.[16] Yonge adds colourful episodes from Irish history to amplify the text's purpose as a handbook for a ruler of Ireland. He incorporates the history of the colony into his prose as gleaned from the twelfth-century works of Giraldus Cambrensis on Ireland and infuses his narrative with accounts of recent heroic deeds of his patron's illustrious family. He also consults the chronicles to provide the lieutenant with the legal justification for the English king's rights to Ireland. At one point, Yonge identifies one of his sources as that written by 'a gret clerke, Richard Cambrensis that makyd the story of the conquest by kynge Henry the Seconde in Irland'. Although he gets the author's first name wrong, the source is undoubtedly the *Expugnatio Hibernica*. Yonge then inserts a very brief account of Diarmait Mac Murchada, king of Lenister, seeking aid from Henry II, who 'rescewid of hym the bonde of subieccioun, and fewtee, and hym toke his letteris of bienvoillaunce wher-by he broght pouer of Englyss-men, Normanes and Walschemen into laynystere'.[17] Giraldus' texts were widely circulated in late medieval Ireland and it is not surprising that Yonge was familiar with the Welsh author's works on Ireland. Yonge's extract follows Giraldus' account closely, but, explaining the resulting invasion, he alters Giraldus' conclusion slightly, indicating a more positive outcome than that which the Welshman claimed. Giraldus says that the

14 Ibid., p. 122.   15 Ibid., p. 121.   16 Ibid., p. 123.   17 Ibid., p. 183.

country was not fully conquered, while Yonge maintains that the land 'was for the more partie I-conquerid'.[18]

We know that there were some *Latin Expugnatio* manuscripts in Dublin; the Cistercian abbey of St Mary's possessed a fourteenth-century copy of the *Expugnatio* (Cambridge University Library Add. 3392) and there were probably many others. Numerous annals, such as the late fourteenth-century work compiled by Thomas Case, drew on the *Expugnatio* or Giraldus' other work, the *Topographia Hiberniae*, while Fletcher has drawn attention to the passage referring to the Bachall Ísu (the staff of St Patrick) drawn from Giraldus' *Topographia*, which is present in the fourteenth-century *Liber Niger* or Black book of Christ Church.[19] Yonge may have been able to access a copy of Giraldus' work through his contacts in Dublin or, indeed, the earl of Ormond may have procured a copy for him.

Giraldus' text provides a justification for the conquest and the English presence in Ireland. However, Yonge claims that he is not relying solely on Giraldus for his knowledge of Irish history. As he tells his patron,

> for-alsmoche, gracious lorde, as I haue now her towchid of the conquest of Irland, I shall now declare yow in partie as y fynde in croncles written, many titles of oure lege lorde the kynge of Englandes ryght to this land of Irland, agaynes t[h]e errourse and haynouse Irysmenes oppynyones, saynge that thay haue bettyr ryght.[20]

The chapter that follows, 'Of the kynges titles to the land of Irland, aftyr the cronyclis', is also, in spite of its claim, mostly based on Giraldus' account.[21] Although Yonge claims the 'chronicles' as a source, it is clear that Giraldus' work is central to relaying the historical rights that he explains. His recourse to the chronicles is perhaps an attempt not to be seen to be relying too heavily on any one source – equally, a comparison of Yonge's list of rights and that of Giraldus and the contemporary English translation of the *Expugnatio* indicates a good deal of switching and some minor additions in Yonge's text.

JAMES BUTLER AND RECENT HISTORY

The text does not confine itself to old history; recent events in which the Ormonds played a part are also recounted. Yonge reminds his patron that 'victory in battail pryncipal is in god' and continues, saying that

---

18 Ibid. 19 Fletcher, 'The annals and chronicles of medieval Dublin', pp 196–7. 20 Steele (ed.), *Secreta Secretorum*, p. 184. 21 Ibid.

the deddis of the nobylle victorius erle, Syr Iamys, yowre gravnde-syre, whych in al his tyme lechury hatid and ther-for god in al his tyme granted hym mervellous victori vp [upon] his enemys wyth fewe pepill, namly vp the morthes, of whyche he slew huge pepill in the red more of athy [red moor of Athy], a litil afore the sone goynge downe, stondynge the sone mervelosly still till the slight was done.[22]

This description of the battle, complete with its miraculous resonance, is probably referring to the victory of James Butler, second earl and justicar of Ireland, over the Meic Murchadha (MacMurroughs) and the Uí Mhórdha (O'Mores) of Laoighis in 1359.[23] Ormond, accompanied by the earls of Kildare and Desmond in this battle, claimed that the Irish were defeated 'through God's providence', just as Yonge was to claim for the second earl and the later victories in which the Ormond family was involved.[24]

The description of the battle in Yonge's text has strong biblical allusions of its own, recalling the great Old Testament military leader Joshua, whose victory in the Aijalon Valley was aided through God's granting of his request for the sun to stand still while his forces completed defeating their enemies.[25] The sun, as a recurring symbol in biblical imagery, stands for the power, law and all-seeing nature of God, its actions here amounting to one of the four great miracles found in the book of Joshua called 'Joshua's long day' or 'the day the sun stood still'. In the biblical chapter, Joshua (whose name means 'God Saves'), is responding to a call for aid to defend and protect the important city of Gibeon against the attack of the Amorite coalition, while the site of the battle, the Aijalon Valley, is an important trade route. The biblical account makes clear that the Israelites were winning the battle but needed more time to rout completely the enemy, just as the HME text suggests is the case with Ormond's forces, implying that the sun stood still until the slaughter of the enemy was complete. Joshua, the successor of the spiritual father Moses, is a practical, resolute military leader, capable of leading his people in battle and confident of the support and aid of God to seize control of the Promised Land. Thus, he was an appropriate and powerful parallel for Ormond as he conducted his battles in Ireland and claimed the right to command such forces and guarantee great victories. Even Yonge's phrase 'he slew huge pepill' recalls the great slaughter perpetuated in Joshua 10.

Continuity, particularly when aligned with genealogy, history and the support of God were important notions in this period; by reminding his patron and other readers of the heroics of Ormond's recent ancestors, Yonge was making a claim for the earl's legitimacy as leader of the colony, not only

22 Ibid., p. 129. 23 Robin Frame, 'The defence of the English Lordship, 1250–1450' in Thomas Bartlett and Keith Jeffery (eds), *A military history of Ireland* (Cambridge, 1996), p. 86. 24 Ibid.; Public Record Office E 101/244/2. 25 Josh 10:12–15.

through his appointment but also through evidence of his family's historical successes. Of course, all good leaders rely on good council and Yonge is not shy in attempting to fill that role, encouraging Ormond to deal harshly with the Irish rebels threatening the safety of Dublin and the colony as a whole, showing the rebels little sympathy:

> Sethyn god and oure kynge haue grauntid you powere, do ye therof execucion in opyn fals enemys, traytouris, and rebelle, trew men quelleris [true men's killers], whan thay fallyth into youre handys, by the thow sharpe eggis of youre swerde.[26]

Such rebellious behaviour, he stresses, must be firmly eradicated to prevent contagion taking hold in the colony:

> For as a sparke of fyre risyth an huge fyre able a realme to brente [burn], so rysyth of the roote of an fals enemy, appert [open] traytoure, othyr rebellis, many wickid wedis sone growynge, that al trewe men in londe sore greuyth. … Therfor, whan thay fallyth into youre handis, raase ham all out of rote, as the good gardyner dothe the nettylle.[27]

Weeds and nettles are abundant in biblical imagery where they grow and take over abandoned, ruined places and cities; their presence here indicates the link between the duty and obligation that administrators have to the king and God to keep the Irish colony under control. Later, Yonge details actions of the White Earl that clearly illustrate that he was diligently rooting out the enemies of the king with force. In some ways, Yonge's text depicts Dublin and its hinterland as 'civilization', while all outside English control seems a wild dangerous land with people threatening the colonists and their way of life with violence and destruction; the earl, as commander of the king's forces, is to the forefront of the defence of the colonists' way of life.

However, Yonge is not solely focused on depicting Ormond and his ancestors as heroes. Along with describing his patron's victories, he is eager to highlight the part that Dublin's citizens played in his successes. Yonge notes the dangers facing the colony and the people of Dublin, providing a list of rebels threatening the colony:

> That is to witte … the brenys [Uí Bhriain, O'Briens] of Thomon, the bourkenys [de Burghs, Burkes] of Connaght and monstre, the morthes of leys [Uí Mhórdha, O'Mores of Leix], the Mcmahens vp the contrey of vriel [Meic Mhathghamhna, MacMahons of Oirghialla], hit more depyr than euer afore brandynge [burning], and O'neyle-boy, Grayfergowse

---

26 Steele (ed.), *Secreta Secretorum*, p. 164.   27 Ibid.

and Vlnestre [Ó Néill of Clann Aodha Buidhe, Carrickfergus and Ulster] atte his owyn wille brandynge and wastynge.[28]

Perhaps in part as a swipe at previous lieutenants who failed to quell the danger, Yonge paints a picture of trouble and fear. In 1421, '[the] clergi of deuelyn [Dublin, were] considerynge the grete myschefe of Irish enemys and rebell were in the land surdynge in acte [i.e., defiling the land]'.[29] With the citizens of Dublin troubled by the incursions of the rebels beyond the walls threatening the peace of the city, the clergy embarked on a campaign of self-empowerment:

> twyes in euery wike in oppyn processyon god prayeden for the good esplaite of the forsayden oure kynge henry, than beynge in Fraunce, and for the forsayd erle his lyeutenaunt of Irland, anent [against] the malice of the forsayden enemys.[30]

By illustrating how the people of Dublin and the clergy felt the need to unite publicly against the Irish enemies pounding against their door, Yonge gives us a brief indication of the sense of danger and community experienced by the citizens at this time. While the Dublin population illustrated their loyalty to the colony and the earl through this display, Yonge is able to illustrate how the campaigns of his patron in fighting the rebels beyond the city walls both affect and are supported by the people of Dublin. Their part is not inconsequential, and Yonge explains that subsequent victories of the earl were the result of the combination of this praying on behalf of the people, God's will and the might of the army:

> [the] erle throgh the grace of god and dewout prayere aforsayd, beynge wyth hym the hoste of deuelyn, alle the moste inly streynthes [inland strengths], p[l]aases, and tounes of leys [Laoighis], wyth moche of hare stode and har cornes [grains], than and aftre eke he braunt and destruyet. And anoone aftyr he rebukid the forsayden breenys and bourkeyns wyth dyuers otheris, and ham to pees reformed.[31]

The earl's force proceeded to rout the enemy. His

> company the same hoste of Deuelyn and many mo … by Doundalke roode and by Mcgenons countre [Mac Aonghusa, McGuinness of Uíbh Eachach or Iveagh], and throgh o'haghuraghtes countree [Uí Anluain, O'Hanlons of Airthir or Orior?], into the moste inli streynthes of Mcmahons contre, thre nyghtes therin I-logid [lodged] he was.[32]

28 Ibid., p. 203.   29 Ibid.   30 Ibid.   31 Ibid., 203–4.   32 Ibid., p. 204.

They then set about destroying Mac Mathghamhna's holdings, his 'stronge newe castell, his townes, his fayre toures, and his stronge p[l]aases into the grownde brake, brande, and destrued, and many of his pepill this erle slowe [slew], and al the remenaunt were scomfited'.[33] By the fourth day, Yonge recalls, the earl's victories ensured that he could ride through the centre of Mac Mathghamhna's land without being attacked.[34]

Yonge again stresses that this victory and other successes were completed in three months through the grace of God, and he highlights that it occurred without the loss of any of the earl's men.[35] Yonge presents the earl's victories during his tenure in charge as a great success: 'many men therin Slayne, And damagelees forto accompte fro thens repayrid, And dyuers othyr proesses did, in the yere that he lyeutenant was'.[36] However, with power comes responsibility and Yonge notes that 'god punyshid hame that chastenet not hare subiectis'.[37] He then goes on to highlight a worrying trend evident in some recent administrators:

> me-thynketh hit apperyth oft-tymes by dyuers Englyshes captaynys o Irland that haue bene and now byth, whos neclygence in non-punyshynge of hare nacionys and subiectes haue destrued ham-selfe, har naciones, and har landis.[38]

For Yonge, this is a truth waiting to be revealed but, 'the names of thes captaynys hit awaylyth nat, ne hit nedyth, and also hit were henyouse and perelos to reherse'.[39] This shadow of 'peril' hanging over those who would make such accusations suggests Yonge is drawing on the contemporary bitter feud between Ormond and supporters of Sir John Talbot, Lord Furnival. Ormond and Talbot were vying with each other for control of the Irish government in this period. Such negative depictions of Talbot (and indeed, by others, of Ormond) were not uncommon in the fifteenth century, when numerous petitions were sent to England arguing for one side or the other.

It is clear that Yonge is not impartial. However, he projects his account as that of a diligent chronicler, dedicated to charting accurately contemporary politics and recent history in a fight against those who desire to keep the truth hidden. Revealing the truth is an important theme in Yonge's work, but he highlights the dangers involved:

> I leue of that matiere … leste y sholde be shente [injured] in this parti, the sothe [truth] forto telle, ffor Salamon in his proverbis sayth, 'verite getyth hatredyn, and good service gettyth frendis'.[40]

---

33 Ibid.   34 Ibid.   35 Ibid.   36 Ibid., p. 205.   37 Ibid., p. 160.   38 Ibid.   39 Ibid., pp 160–1.   40 Ibid.

St Paul's letter to the Galatians to encourage truthfulness is recalled before Yonge paints a dismal picture of the fate of truth in the colony: 'verite in this dayes is myssayd [abused], verite in this dayes is wyth-holde, bonde and prisoner'.[41] In spite of this, he declares that the suppressers of truth will be overcome: '… verite that so now is despied and lytill Settyn of, in tyme comynge hit shall delyuer his louers, and condempne his enemys aftyr the worde of oure Sauyoure …'.[42] Later, Yonge notes that among other things, a good councillor and friend 'sholde bene sothefaste [truthful] in worde and dedd, and lowe throuth abowe al thynge, and hate lesynge [lying]'.[43] He is obviously casting himself in a good light by demanding truth be revealed in his own day. Yonge is not alone among medieval chroniclers calling for truthfulness when discussing politics and history. The *Polychronicon*, a widely read 'world history' in the fourteenth and fifteenth centuries, which draws heavily on Giraldus Cambrensis' *Topographia*, echoes Yonge's sentiments. Its author, the Chester monk, Ranulf Higden (*c.*1280–1364), explains in his preface that, as far as possible in his text, the whole truth shall not be in doubt (*integra pro posse veritas non vacillet*); a little earlier, the historian Gervase of Canterbury (*c.*1141–1210) had gone further, claiming that history should aim to instruct truthfully (*veraciter edocere*).[44] Yonge would surely have approved of his predecessors' statements.

This call for truth was part of Yonge's calculated approach to present Ormond (and Yonge as his councillor) as a purveyor of truth and justice, projecting images of moral strength that their opponents lacked. Yonge's text is steeped in his political environment and his bias against the Talbot faction is clear. Venting such powerful negative rhetoric on such matters of contemporary politics could be dangerous, as Yonge makes clear in his prose. Despite this, he wrote vehemently on these issues, contributing to a body of documentation condemning the Talbot faction. His arguments found a welcome listener in his patron. Unfortunately, Yonge's flowing pro-Ormond prose and anti-Talbot bias probably did not go unnoticed in other less welcoming circles. Ormond was succeeded in the office of lieutenant of Ireland by pro-Talbot officials: Sir Laurence Merbury took office in 1422 after Ormond's term had finished and Archbishop Richard Talbot, brother of John Talbot, in 1423. During that time, possibly shortly after he had completed or was perhaps still writing the *Gouernaunce* text, Yonge was arrested and imprisoned in Trim Castle.

The gaol at Trim was frequently used to hold prisoners (criminals and traitors alike). Conditions were bad and treatment could be harsh, many prisoners died of plague, others starved to death.[45] Yonge's aforementioned

---

41 Ibid., p. 165. **42** Ibid. **43** Ibid. p. 211. **44** *The historical works of Gervase of Canterbury*, ed. and trans. William Stubbs (London, 1879–80), i, pp 87–8. **45** Michael Potterton, *Medieval Trim: history and archaeology* (Dublin, 2005), p. 226.

line, 'Verite in this dayes is wyth-holde, bonde and prisoner', had its physical manifestation when Yonge, so adamant that he is revealing the truth, was captured and imprisoned. Although Yonge does not specifically mention his incarceration in the *Gouernaunce*, a document sent to the constable of Trim Castle on 10 October 1423 indicates that Yonge pleaded to the king that he was kept without trial in great hardship bound in chains (*in ferris in magna duricia*) for nine months in Trim gaol.[46] This letter orders that the constable of Trim send Yonge to Dublin Castle, where he was to complete his incarceration. Yonge's outspoken views and anti-Talbot, pro-Ormond opinions no doubt contributed to his imprisonment. In spite of his harsh treatment in Trim, he returned to writing notorial instruments after his release. It was only when his patron was restored to favour that Yonge received his official pardon – during Ormond's second appointment as lieutenant in 1425; later, in 1428–9, he was in the earl's employ once more, engaged in writing documents.[47]

READING HISTORY IN MEDIEVAL DUBLIN

Was the Talbot faction aware of the text that depicted them in such a negative light? Yonge's original manuscript for Ormond does not survive, but there is a fifteenth-century copy of the text in Bodleian Library, MS Rawlinson B490. That the text was not to everybody's taste is indicated by Trinity College Dublin MS 592. This text is probably a copy of the same original on which Rawlinson B490 was based. But in the TCD manuscript, the copyist breaks off half way through the first folio of Yonge's text, leaving only the English translation of Giraldus' *Expugnatio*. Another partial copy of Yonge's text is found in Lambeth Palace MS 633 and O'Byrne has suggested that certain names on the manuscript indicate that it was circulating in Dublin the late fifteenth and early sixteenth century.[48] It is unclear whether the Talbot faction had seen or knew of the highly critical text, but Yonge's alliance with Ormond was surely attested to and such sympathies would not have endeared him to those who were partial to that faction.

The politically minded translator's experiences of living in the colony were shaped by the city of Dublin in which he lived and worked, providing us with a unique view of one Dubliner's perspective on Irish history and his contemporary political situation. Yonge is doing more than simply translating and updating an old text. His didactic 'mirror of princes' presents the story of Irish history in its fifteenth-century context for the earls of Ormond. This handbook for governance not only highlighted the illustrious history of the Butler dynasty, but noted the importance of history, truth and politics,

46 Ibid., p. 226; *CIRCLE* CR 2 Henry VI, 40.   47 *CIRCLE* PR 3 Henry VI, 45.
48 O'Bryne, 'Dublin's Hoccleve', pp 807–9.

illustrating how a distortion of them could be used to influence the perception of the present and the course of the future.[49] Yonge contrasts exemplary Ormond military leadership with unnamed rival administrators who fail to grasp the unwieldy nettle by the root and risk putting the whole colonial enterprise in jeopardy.

Yonge's experiences of writing contemporary history in Dublin illustrate the dangers involved in commenting on volatile political situations. His passionate defence of Ormond and his critique of the new administrators indicate a loyalty to the White Earl and illustrate Yonge's interest in the administration and the defence of the colony. Such interests point to a sense of community and nationhood within the English colony in Ireland in the late Middle Ages and in Yonge, as he calls himself, the 'least of all the writers in Dublin', one can perhaps detect a civic pride. Yonge's determination to press ahead with the inclusion of barely concealed condemnations of powerful contemporary figures illustrates a courageous resilience to the backlash of producing a history hostile to a powerful political rival. Yonge's *Gouernaunce* illustrates not just the friction between two individual administrators, but the wider chasm between colonial administrators and their supporters, people who resisted the arrival of men who sought to change the way in which things were done in Ireland and open a new chapter in the history of the colony.

---

49 The recent edition of one of the texts dedicated to the tenth earl of Ormond, Thomas Butler (1531–1614), illustrates similar concerns and parallels in a later century: Keith Sidwell and David Edwards (eds), *The Tipperary hero: Dermot O'Meara's Ormonius (1615)* (Turnhout, 2012).

'But what about the earlier city?': John Rocque's *Exact Survey* (1756) as a source for medieval Dublin

JOHN MONTAGUE

ABSTRACT

This is an attempt to assess the extent to which John Rocque's mid-eighteenth-century map of Dublin can be used as a source for understanding the medieval city: to the extent that medieval fabric survived in the early modern city, or the degree to which this record of its eighteenth-century topography reflected what had gone before; and to what degree and how reliably such remnants of the 'earlier' city were recorded on Rocque's extraordinary map. Some attempts will be made to identify specific lines on the map that represented – sometimes inadvertently – elements of medieval archaeology. Generally, particularly with regard to the city walls, lines on the map were delineated as property boundaries, or as elements of the built city, and were in no way identified by the map-maker as archaeology. A short introduction to John Rocque, his work prior to the creation of the Dublin map, and some remarks on his practice as a mapmaker, are considered as a way into understanding the nature, if not reliability, of the map that he made of this city.

INTRODUCTION

This is not the first essay in which Rocque's 1756 Dublin map (fig. 11.1) has been considered in the round as a source for understanding the archaeological topography of medieval Dublin.[1] While Rocque's *Exact Survey* is used continuously by archaeologists and historians of Dublin as evidence for discrete areas or individual plots in the city, there is also a small number of essays in which Rocque's record overall has been considered more directly. In 1979, Anngret Simms carried out a broad morphological analysis of the developing town plan of the medieval city using Rocque's map as her basis.[2] More recently, Linzi Simpson inquired into the longevity of medieval property alignments by comparing those recovered in excavations at the corner of South Great George's Street and Stephen Street Lower to the eighteenth-century

1 *An exact survey of the city and suburbs of Dublin in which is expres'd the ground plot of all publick buildings, dwelling houses, ware houses, stables, courts, yards &c. by John Rocque, chorographer to their royal highnesses the late & present prince of Wales* ([Dublin], 1756). 2 Anngret Simms, 'Medieval Dublin: a topographical analysis', *Irish Geography*, 12 (1979),

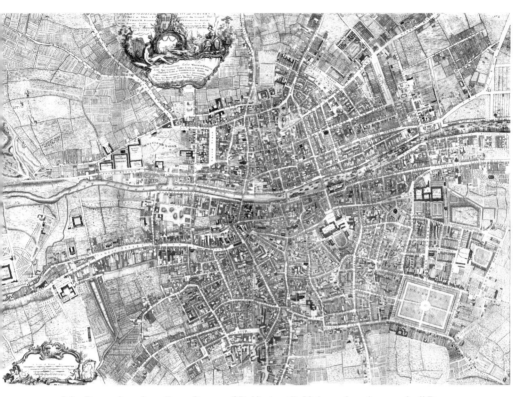

11.1 John Rocque's 4-sheet *Exact Survey of Dublin* (1756). Unless otherwise stated, all Rocque images are reproduced from a map in Trinity College Dublin Library, with the permission of the Board of Trinity College. This copy of the map consists of four sheets representing various states of Rocque's plan made after its first publication in 1756, which include changes to the map on sheets 2 and 3, representing changes to the city dating to as late as 1762 and 1769 respectively.

boundaries represented on Rocque's map.[3] The author's previous researches on Rocque have concentrated largely on his principal Dublin map as a record of the mid-eighteenth-century city.[4] Consideration was given to the nature of Rocque's record, how valid or accurate it was, and, if in some places it erred, what the nature of the error was, and how an understanding of these qualities and shortcomings might help us in our use of the map as an historical source. This was founded on new research into Rocque's previous career as a mapmaker and topographical engraver, with particular emphasis on an inquiry into the nature of his work practices, especially in so much as they might pour

25–41. **3** Linzi Simpson, 'John Rocque's map of Dublin (1756): a modern source for medieval property boundaries' in Seán Duffy (ed.), *Medieval Dublin VII* (Dublin, 2006), pp 113–51. **4** John Montague, 'John Rocque and the making of the 1756 *Exact Survey of*

light on his intentions and ambitions when he arrived to make a map of a city, as he did to Dublin in 1754. Any conclusions in this regard should also prove useful to us in our consideration of Rocque's map as a source for the fabric and appearance of the medieval city. Also, it goes without saying that more of the medieval city survived in Rocque's day, and we will want to know how Rocque recorded it, if at all.

Consequently, the first part of this essay is a summary of some findings regarding the nature of Rocque's Dublin map, which have been rehearsed elsewhere, albeit with a different (historically later) focus in mind.[5] The lessons may be usefully applied in any interpretation that follows of Rocque's mapping of medieval Dublin. The second portion of the essay concerns itself with some aspects of the medieval city as Rocque may or may not have recorded them, and on any new insights regarding medieval Dublin – at least in so far as remnants of it had survived until 1756 – that may yet be garnered from this oft-considered source.

MAPPING DUBLIN

Although no contemporary medieval Dublin maps survive, Dublin is reasonably well served by historic maps. John Speed's 1610 map is the earliest surviving map image of the city (fig. 11.2).[6] It stands up well to scrutiny, and its early date – probably based on a survey made *c.*1605[7] – allows for a capture of what are essentially still the outlines of the medieval city, not only of its walled enclosure, but also of the new suburbs, and their dissolved monastic origins.

The post-medieval development of the city was well advanced by the time Dublin was recorded in such detail again by Bernard de Gomme in his manuscript map of 1673 (fig. 11.3).[8] Besides the outline of a citadel at Ringsend, which was never built, de Gomme's plan delineates the surviving city walls with their mural towers and gates, the layout of Dublin Castle with rough plans of some of its buildings, the early plan of Trinity College, built on the dissolved medieval monastery of All Hallows, the new public spaces of Smithfield and St Stephen's Green, and the field system south of St Thomas Court, which soon afterwards was laid out by the earl of Meath as a new industrial quarter. Like Speed, de Gomme showed some buildings from a

Dublin' (PhD, TCD, 2009).   **5** Colm Lennon and John Montague, *John Rocque's Dublin: a guide to the Georgian city* (Dublin, 2010).   **6** John Speed, map of Dublin, from 'the countie of Leinster with the citie of Dublin described' (1610) in *The theatre of the empire of Great Britaine* (London, 1611–12).   **7** J.H. Andrews, 'The oldest map of Dublin', *PRIA*, 83C (1983), 205–37 at 107–10. Andrews' article also includes, at pp 205–7, a discussion of the evidence for earlier, no longer surviving, maps of Dublin.   **8** Sir Bernard de Gomme, 'The citty and svbvrbs of Dvblin: from Kilmainham to Rings-End, werein [*sic*] the rivers, streets, lanes, allys, churches, gates &c. are exactly described 15th No: 1673' (London, National Maritime Museum, P/49 (11)).

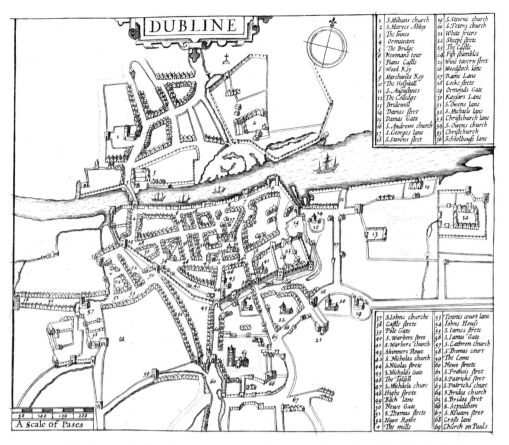

11.2 John Speed, 'Dubline' from 'the countie of Leinster with the citie of Dublin described' (1610) in *The theatre of the empire of Great Britaine* (London, 1611–12).

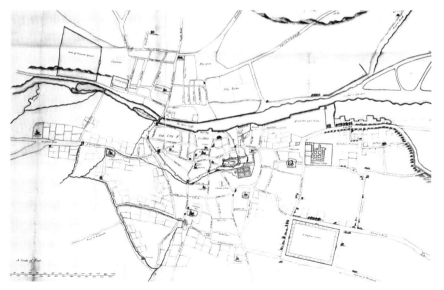

11.3 Bernard de Gomme, 'The city and suburbs of Dublin' (1673). Courtesy of the National Maritime Museum, London.

bird's-eye point of view, but we should be cautious about concluding anything about house densities or architectural types from either map. Thomas Phillips, who worked with de Gomme on his 1673 map, also made a manuscript map of Dublin and its environs in 1685.⁹ This was a smaller-scale map, with a larger coverage, and consequently the city portion is portrayed in less detail, although developments since de Gomme's map – such as three new Liffey bridges, the Royal Hospital at Kilmainham, and the gridded suburbs of the Jervis estate – now appear.¹⁰

Some fifty-five years after de Gomme, we come to the very significant, but sometimes crudely drawn, map of Dublin published by Charles Brooking in 1728 (fig. 11.4).¹¹ Here, within the map at least, instead of a more traditional bird's-eye view, the map is planiform, being what contemporaries referred to as ichnographic.¹² The ichnographic approach had great potential for measurable accuracy, but was partly limited in Brooking by the fact that he records only the city block, rather than the footprints of individual buildings. This was in truth fairly much the universal approach at the time. Brooking's map is augmented by a series of invaluable framed illustrations of public buildings, churches and other important civic structures.

Rocque's 1756 map of Dublin is in another league. This is a house-by-house plan, which purported at least to record every building, whether public or domestic, including their stables and yards.¹³ An examination of the map shows that Rocque included outhouses, back-yard industrial buildings, warehouses, hidden churches and dissenter meeting houses, as well as the domestic, commercial and public buildings that fronted onto the more important city thoroughfares (fig. 11.5). This is a remarkable thing, in that such a house-by-house city plan was the first such map in the whole of Rocque's corpus of works up until that point. Such copious and insistent detail was very much outside his own practice before then – and for the most part outside the practice of his contemporaries.¹⁴

9 'An exact survey of the citty of Dublin and part of the harbour. Anno 1685' (British Library Maps K.Top.53.3.2).   10 See Colm Lennon, *Dublin Part II, 1610 to 1756. Irish Historic Towns Atlas*, 19 (Dublin, 2008), p. 3.   11 *A map of the city and suburbs of Dublin and also the archbishop and earl of Meaths liberties with the bounds of the parish. Drawn from an actual survey. Made by Charles Brooking* (London, 1728); see also J.H. Andrews, '"Mean pyratical practices": the case of Charles Brooking', *Irish Georgian Society Quarterly Bulletin*, 23 (1980), 33–41.   12 See J.A. Pinto, 'Origins and development of the ichnographical city plan', *Journal of the Society of Architectural Historians*, 35:1 (1976), 35–50.   13 The map title includes the following text: 'An exact survey of the city and suburbs of Dublin in which is express'd the ground plot of all public buildings, dwelling houses, stables, courts, yards &c. …'.   14 An earlier precedent is John Ogilby's *Large and accurate map of the city of London*, published in 1676, although Ogilby's map records only the outline plans of properties – i.e. their curtilage perimeters – rather than, as Rocque would do in the *Exact Survey*, the plan of each building contained within each property. See John Montague, 'John Ogilby's map of London (Fag. portfolio XV, no. 1)', in W.E. Vaughan (ed.), *The Old Library, Trinity College Dublin, 1712–2012* (Dublin, 2012), pp 72–6.

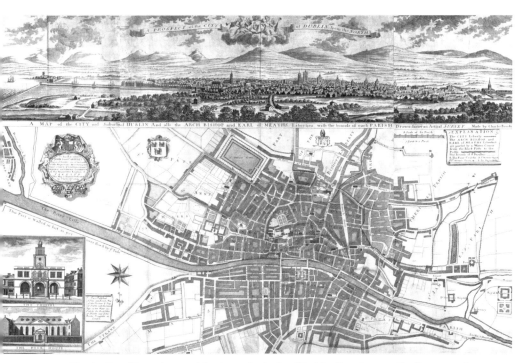

11.4 Charles Brooking, *A map of the city and suburbs of Dublin* (London, 1728). Courtesy of the Royal Irish Academy.

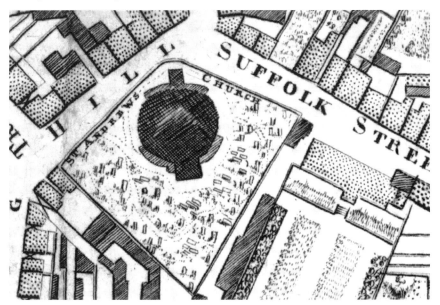

11.5 St Andrew's Church, Suffolk Street, Dublin, as depicted on Rocque's *Exact Survey* (1756).

JOHN ROCQUE

There is little documentary evidence left – besides his over one hundred published maps – from which to reconstruct Rocque's life.[15] In terms of evidence from Rocque's own hand regarding his professional activities, we have two letters sent to a nephew (see below), and two sent to London's Royal Society of Arts, in 1759, applying unsuccessfully for bursaries for the production of county maps of Berkshire, Oxfordshire and Buckinghamshire, which he was undertaking at this time.[16] Rocque died reasonably young, in 1762. He was approximately 57. Although he married twice, he had no children.[17] His second wife, Mary Ann Rocque (née Scalé), was his business partner, and indeed kept the business afloat for a number of years after Rocque died.[18]

John Rocque was a Huguenot – a French Calvinist refugee – who may have been born in London, or the south of France, or even in Geneva, sometime around 1704 or 1705. There is not enough evidence to say with certainty.[19] We know, for example that his brother Bartholomew had spent time in Geneva at the beginning of the eighteenth century, but was in London from as early as 1724.[20] Geneva was one of the principal havens for refugee Huguenots during the seventeenth and eighteenth centuries. Bartholomew was a renowned horticultural innovator.[21] Neither he nor John was a garden or landscape designer, as some have proposed without evidence.[22] Rocque was a craftsman, principally an engraver, who specialized in topographical and decorative

15 John Varley, 'John Rocque, the map-maker, and his Huguenot associations', *Proceedings of the Huguenot Society of London*, 17:4 (1942–7), 457–61; idem, 'John Rocque: engraver, surveyor, cartographer and map-seller', *Imago Mundi*, 5 (1948), 83–91; Henry Wheatley, 'Rocque's plan of London, 1746', *London Topographical Record*, 9 (1914), 15–28; Hugh Phillips, 'John Rocque's career', *London Topographical Record*, 20 (1952), 9–25; John Montague, 'John Rocque and the *Exact Survey* of Dublin' in Lennon and Montague, *John Rocque's Dublin*, pp ix–xiv; Laurence Worms and Ashley Baynton-Williams, *British map engravers: a dictionary of engravers, lithographers and their principal employers to 1850* (London, 2011), pp 559–63.   16 London, Royal Society of Arts, RSA PR.AR/103/10/146.   17 Varley 'John Rocque, engraver', 85.   18 Ibid., 86.   19 Two of Rocque's brothers, Claude and Bartholomew, were in Geneva in the 1720s: see Friedrich Walter, 'Zur Levensgeschichte des Kupferstechers: B. Rocque (de la Rocque)', *Mannheimer Geschichtsblatter*, 21:7/8 (July/Aug. 1920), 99–105. For more on this, see Montague, 'John Rocque' (PhD), pp 24–6. 20 Sir James Caldwell, referring to a conversation with Bartholomew Rocque, who told him in 1764 that he reckoned that he had been in England then for forty years: 'A letter to the Dublin Society, from Sir James Caldwell, Baronet, Fellow of the Royal Society; giving an account of the culture and quality of several kinds of grass lately discovered. Volume V', *Museum Rusticum et Commerciale: or select papers on agriculture commerce arts and manufactures drawn from experience and communicated by gentlemen engaged in these pursuits* (London, 1765), pp 13–22 at p. 14.   21 Caldwell, 'A letter', p. 19; Bartholomew Rocque, *A practical treatise of cultivating lucern* (London, 1761).   22 Renzo Dubbini, *Geography of the gaze*, trans. L.G. Cochrane (Chicago and London, 2002), pp 42–3; Paul Laxton, 'Rocque, John (1704?–62)', *Dictionary of national biography, missing persons*, ed. C.S. Nicholls (Oxford, 1993), pp 563–64; hinted at by Varley, 'John Rocque, engraver', 83–4.

image-making, before he became involved in large-scale town and county mapping. Rocque cut his teeth by creating published images of aristocratic estates – his first being of Richmond in 1734.[23] Although many of his earliest works were these published estate surveys, Rocque is also listed in a number of decorative pattern books, simply as the engraver. One example is a book of ornaments by the artist Gaetano Brunetti, which Rocque engraved with Henry Fletcher in 1736.[24] Rocque was an important early purveyor of the rococo style.[25] His rococo cartouches – the decorated frames around his map labels – came to play an important part in all of his estate map publications, and these characteristic designs remain a signature feature in his later more complex town and county works, including on the four-sheet Dublin map. It is likely that Rocque engraved all of the cartouches himself. Such fine rocaille work is difficult to execute, and in all of his published works the same confident hand can be discerned in this particular detail. Most of the rest of the engraving was farmed out among his assistants, and in the manner of a medieval artist's workshop, a discernible house (or Rocque) style was maintained. In the case of the Dublin map, Andrew Dury's signature – 'A. Dury Sculpt'[26] – appears in the bottom right corner of the south-east map sheet (No. 3); as noted, Rocque was most likely responsible for the rocaille work on the cartouche; another artist may have been responsible for the putti and other figures it contained, and apprentices or some other assistants were probably responsible for the copious stippling and symbolic marks that appear across the surface of the map.

Rocque's most famous map production was the 24-sheet map of London, which was published almost a decade prior to the Dublin map, in 1747.[27] In 1738, despite his lack of experience in the field of cartography at this scale, Rocque was invited to get involved as surveyor in the Royal Society project to map the city of London.[28] The eventual map took some eight years to produce. It was through Royal Society men such as its secretary, Peter Davall, who had published on the subject of French surveying and cartographic techniques, that Rocque learnt, or at least refined his knowledge of, the mathematically

23 John Rocque, *Plan of the house, gardens, park & hermitage of their majesties, at Richmond; and of their R.H. the prince of Wales, and the princess royal at Kew* (London, 1734); for a near complete list of all of Rocque's published works, see www.mapforum.com/05/rocqlist.htm [accessed 10 June 2013], which supersedes an earlier list in Varley, 'John Rocque, engraver', 89–91. 24 John Rocque and Henry Fletcher, *Sixty different sorts of ornaments invented by Gaetano Brunetti, Italian painter* (London, 1736). 25 Michael Snodin and Elspeth Moncrieff (eds), *Rococo: art and design in Hogarth's England* (London, 1984), cat. B11, p. 38; Christine Casey, 'Gaetano Brunetti', *GPA Irish Arts Review Yearbook* (1988), 244–5; Joseph McDonnell, 'The influence of the French rococo print in Ireland in the eighteenth century', *Bulletin of the Irish Georgian Society*, 36 (1994), 63–74. 26 Meaning that it was engraved by A. Dury. 27 *A plan of the cities of London and Westminster, and borough of Southwark ... from an actual survey, taken by John Rocque, land-surveyor and engraved by John Pine* (London, 1746 [1747]). 28 Ralph Hyde, 'The making of John Rocque's map' in *The A to Z of Georgian London: facsimile of John Rocque's 1746 map of London* (Lympne

involved craft of town and large-extent county surveying.[29] These were triangulated maps. The broadest armature of the city was worked out firstly by measuring a long straight base-line, and afterwards establishing the location and distance of all other salient points by building up a series of triangles whose angles are known. By means of trigonometry, then, the exact location of these signal points can be established to a very high level of accuracy. Details of individual streets, and back lanes and houses in between, were measured on the ground, by means of what was called a street traverse, and these detailed measurements were reconciled with the overall superstructure of the city worked out by trigonometry. The 1746 map of London, however, records the extent of city blocks and public buildings only. It does not include an attempt at a graphical census of every single building, as would its less famous Dublin successor.

JOHN ROCQUE IN DUBLIN

There are two poignant letters written by John Rocque to his nephew, dating to 1753, the year before Rocque came to Dublin.[30] Rocque's nephew, like his brother, was also called Bartholomew, and was an engraver and horticultural entrepreneur based in Mannheim.[31] In the 1753 letters, Rocque spoke of his need to tie up very quickly his business and pass it on to someone he could trust.[32] Despite his worries – we do not know what the nature of his disquiet

Castle, Kent, 1981), pp v–viii at p. v.   **29** A number of statements, one of which suggested that large parts of the London map had to be redrafted in order to fix errors, and later ones that corroborated the overall scientific technique carried out by the surveyors, were made by Royal Society members, Martin Folkes and Peter Davall, during the production of the London map. These were reproduced by John Pine and John Tinney, the eventual publishers of Rocque's London map, in the *Alphabetical index of the streets, squares, lanes, alleys &c. contained in the plan of the cities of London and Westminster, and the borough of Southwark* (London, 1755). See discussion of this, and the role of Peter Davall in scientifically underpinning the survey, in Montague, 'John Rocque' (PhD), pp 119–21, 127–37.   **30** Mannheim, Gesellschaft der Freunde Mannheims und der ehemaligen Kurpfalz, MS. 'Letter from John Rocque to Bartholomew Rocque', 11 May and 2 Oct. 1753. **31** Walter, 'B. Rocque', pp 100–2.   **32** 'Letter from John Rocque', 11 May 1753, '... car j'ai été et suis encore malheureux par les étrangers que j'emploie qui sont actuellement dix tant dessinateur que graveurs, j'avais d'autant plus de besoin au presant d'une personne de confiance en ce que je ne suis pas en état de faire ce que je fais joint au que je me propose avec l'aide de Dieu de quitter tout commerce lorsque les [entreprises]que j'ai en main seront finies ce qui me tiendra encore quelques années ...', translated to English: 'I have been and am still unhappy with the foreigners/strangers I employ. There are ten of them at the moment, both draughtsmen and engravers. I really need somebody in whom I have confidence, because at the moment I am not able to complete my present work in addition to future proposals. It is my intention, with the help of God, to cease all business when my present projects are completed. This will take at least a few more years'.

was – Rocque's nephew could not be prevailed upon to come to London. Rocque, forced to continue in business without the familial help he sought, came to Dublin to seek out new enterprise and business opportunities. There is no evidence that he was invited, despite his own formulaic claims to that effect in his early advertisements.[33] The only patronage he received was through subscriptions,[34] through in-shop map sales,[35] and through the small grant of twenty guineas given to him by Dublin Corporation after the map was already completed.[36] In order to drum up subscriptions, Rocque made a series of advertisements in the Dublin press, announcing his arrival to the city and his intentions to create a map on the same scale as his own London map, and in the same format; that is, block by block.[37] However, Roger Kendrick, the Dublin city surveyor, having got wind of Rocque's intentions, proposed in the press that he would produce a similar map. By means of a series of tit-for-tat map advertisements made by the two Dublin and London mapmakers, Rocque's intentions were inadvertently forced, and he eventually advertised that he would create a house-by-house survey, the first ever taken of Dublin, and the first Rocque had carried out until that time.[38]

As already noted, Rocque employed a workshop, which assisted him, not only in the engraving, but in the surveying of the map, which partly explains the speed with which he produced it. Astonishingly, the first Indian-ink mock-ups of his new Dublin map appeared within two months of Rocque's first arrival in the city[39] – although it would be another two years before the final

33 'Sollicited by many of the nobility and gentry of this kingdom to survey and publish by subscription, a map of the capital in all respects like those of London, Paris &c.', from broadsheet advertisement, published 5 Sept. 1754. Proof copy in TCD OO.a.59, no. 1B, and reproduced in Paul Ferguson (ed.), *The A to Z of Georgian Dublin* (Lympne Castle, Kent, 1998), p. iv. Earlier, in the *Dublin Journal*, 27 Aug. 1754, we hear that 'the celebrated Mr Rocque (chorographer to his royal highness the prince of Wales) … is now employed (by proper authority) in making the same of this metropolis, in order to lay it down on the same scale'. However, there is no evidence of any commission by gentry or parliamentary or other corporate body. 34 'Subscriptions [for the *Exact Survey*] are t[aken in] by all the booksellers in Dublin, and by their correspondents abroad, and by the said John Rocque, at his lodgings at the Golden Heart opposite Crane-lane in Dame-Street …', *Dublin Journal*, 10 Sept. 1754; see *A list of subscribers to this work*, which appears on the verso of the separately published title page to the *Exact Survey*, copies of which can be found at TCD OO.a.58, and in the King's Inns Library, *inter alia*. 35 Rocque published a number of catalogues of all of his works that he had with him for sale in his shops, firstly at Crane Lane, and afterwards at Bachelors Walk. See, for example, TCD OO.a.59, 1A & 1B. 36 J.T. Gilbert (ed.), *Calendar of ancient records of Dublin* (19 vols, Dublin, 1889–1944) (hereafter *CARD*), x, p. 252, 21 Jan. 1757. 37 *Dublin Journal*, 27 Aug., 5 & 10 Sep., 26 Oct., 23 Nov. 1754. 38 This point is dealt with in more detail in Montague, 'John Rocque' (PhD), pp 202–18, which is founded on the list of publications in J.H. Andrews, 'The French school of Dublin land surveyors', *Irish Geography*, 45 (1964–68), 275–92 at 278. 39 The announcement that Rocque was in a position to display his first mock-up of the map as '[it] will be when engraved' appeared in the *Dublin Journal*, 26 Oct. 1756. Rocque's arrival in the city was announced by him in the *Dublin Journal* on 27 Aug. 1756.

engraved map itself would be published.[40] The mock-ups, which Rocque claimed would be in the 'same Manner as they will be when engraved', were displayed in Rocque's shops, first in Crane Lane, and later on Bachelors Walk, where he made them available to critical review.[41] The engraving on the copper plates could be changed regularly, subject to suggestions from residents and, as time went by, to material changes to the fabric of the city itself. During the six years he spent living in Dublin, Rocque produced the *Exact Survey*, arguably his greatest map, and a host of others to complete what had been an incredibly productive career.[42]

JOHN ROCQUE'S *EXACT SURVEY* – A CRITICAL REVIEW

So how did Rocque do? How exact is the *Exact Survey*? Results are mixed. Rocque's attention to detail on a micro-level is at times extremely careful and potentially enormously revealing. For example, Rocque has coded the map by means of stippled and hatched symbols corresponding to building function, which retains enormous potential as a source for the pattern of contemporary society as represented by its building stock. Stipples represented domestic buildings, and diagonal hatching represented outbuildings, warehouses and workshops. A cross-hatch was the code for public buildings, which, along with Church of Ireland churches, were usually labelled with their title (fig. 11.6). Catholic churches and dissenter meeting houses were also recorded, and Rocque's graphical depiction of their muted relationship to the public sphere is telling.[43] The main parish and sometime metropolitan Roman Catholic church of St Mary's, for example, was discreetly hidden behind a terrace of modest houses on Liffey Street.[44]

Rocque's focus can be precise and revealing. A case in point is Peter Landré's market garden on the east side of St Stephen's Green, where a French type of hôtel-entre-cour-et-jardin arrangement is depicted with great graphical care – a care no doubt related to the fact that Landré was a Huguenot horticulturalist whom Rocque most likely knew personally.[45] Rocque also knew the Putlands, and the internal ground plan of John Putland's house on Great

40 *Dublin Journal*, 13 Nov. 1756.   41 *Dublin Journal*, 26 Oct. 1756.   42 Other maps produced by Rocque while in Ireland include the four-sheet *Survey of the city, harbour, bay and environs of Dublin* (1757), a four-sheet *Actual survey of the county of Dublin* (1760), a *Survey of the city of Kilkenny* (1758), a *Survey of the city and suburbs of Cork* (1759), a county map of Armagh (1760), which included town plans of Armagh city and Newry, and his *Map of the kingdom of Ireland* (n.d., *c.*1760), based on Henry Pratt's *Tabula Hiberniae Novissima* (1708). Rocque also produced during this time, an eight-volume manuscript survey of the earl of Kildare's estates.   43 See Kenneth Ferguson, 'Rocque's map and the history of nonconformity in Dublin: a search for meeting houses', *Dublin Historical Record*, 58:2 (autumn 2005), 129–65.   44 Lennon and Montague, *John Rocque's Dublin*, pp 18–19. 45 Ibid., pp 44–5.

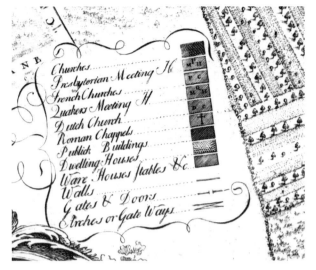

11.6 Legend of map symbols on Rocque's *Exact Survey* (1756).

Britain Street, is – along with that of the Parliament House – one of only two such internal plans recorded on the map.[46] The microscopic nature of Rocque's record can also be found in his transcription in plan form of the bollards along Sackville Mall.[47] Indeed, a little ambiguously, his dots to the rear of the Custom House represent the colonnade there, which was caught in truncated fashion in the drawing of the 'Shoe Boy' in Hugh Douglas Hamilton's 'Cries of Dublin' of 1760. These were the Piazzas of Essex Street.[48] An early notice for them is in Denton's account of his trip to Dublin in the 1690s, in which he refers to them as cloisters.[49]

Rocque, however, could be equally offhand, showing a lack of fidelity to detail at times, particularly, as Bill Frazer has suggested, in areas towards the periphery of the town, such as in the earl of Meath's liberties.[50] A comparison to any of Sherrard's manuscript maps, made for the Wide Streets Commissioners from the 1780s to the 1830s, shows Rocque to be more than a little off-hand in his counting of houses in some terraces and in assigning their correct lengths, or even their proportions to each other.[51] Rocque's record of

46 Ibid., pp 12–13. **47** Ibid., pp 26–7. **48** John Montague, 'A shopping arcade in eighteenth-century Dublin: John Rocque and the Essex Street "piazzas"', *Irish Architectural and Decorative Studies*, 10 (2007), 224–45; Lennon and Montague, *John Rocque's Dublin*, pp 22–3. **49** A.J.L. Winchester and Mary Wane (eds), *Thomas Denton: a perambulation of Cumberland, 1687–1688, including descriptions of Westmorland, the Isle of Man and Ireland* (Woodbridge, 2003), p. 531. **50** Bill Frazer, 'Cracking Rocque?', *Archaeology Ireland*, 18:2 (2004), 10–14. **51** Thomas Sherrard, surveyor to the Wide Streets Commissioners (WSC), completed a house-by-house manuscript map of Dublin in 1791, on an enormous scale (80 feet to 1 inch), which has tragically not survived. A small portion of one of these maps – the area around Christ Church and Wood Quay – was redrawn and published in the *Irish Builder*, 33 (1891), 165. However, many other smaller maps on paper by Sherrard, no doubt sometimes based on the larger now-lost vellum map, survive among the collection of Wide

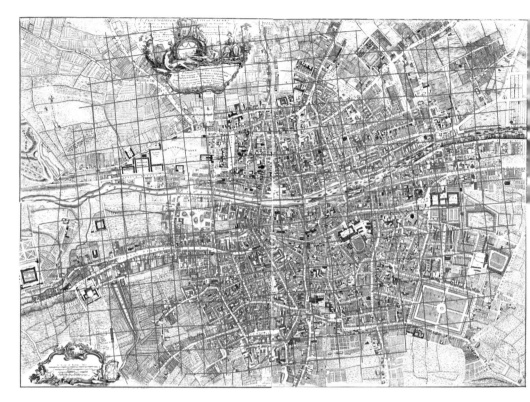

11.7 Distortion grid, created using MapAnalyst software, showing the degree of error or distortion between Rocque's *Exact Survey* (1756) and the earliest Ordnance Survey map of Dublin, surveyed in 1837.

house returns – the type of early modern cabinet projections at the back of so many of Dublin's houses – is very mixed. We cannot always rely on him to be correct about what side of the house these might have been on, or whether they were even there. The reason for this has to do with the independent and commercial nature of Rocque's enterprise – he was not assisted or given licence by the city or the government to ask to see the rear-sides of the properties he measured, nor was he in any way equipped financially to invest time in such a thankless if not impossible architectural survey. Where Rocque excelled was in his measurement and depiction of the shapes of the open (or negative) space of the streets themselves.

Most surprising of all, perhaps, is the startling degree of accuracy of Rocque's overall record of the city as a whole. By pairing location points on an

Streets Commissioners' maps in Dublin City Library and Archives (DCLA), and these can be profitably compared to Rocque's house plans, albeit with the proviso that Sherrard's plans were produced at least two to three decades after Rocque's Dublin map was published.

old map, such as Rocque's, to a GIS-referenced modern map, in this case the 1837 Ordnance Survey map of Dublin, the author, using MapAnalyst, a computer software application,[52] created a grid that demonstrates the distortion on the older map relative to the control map (fig. 11.7). The resulting distortion grid represents in two dimensions the degree, nature and general location of error. Overall, the MapAnalyst results are a graphic affirmation of Rocque's overarching record.[53]

THE MEDIEVAL CITY ON ROCQUE

But what of the medieval city? Straight away, we must understand that Rocque was neither an antiquarian nor an architectural draughtsman. A quick look at his depiction of the Parliament House, designed by Edward Lovett Pearce in the late 1720s, the premier building of the city, and easily accessible then as now, shows the limits of either his ability to record individual buildings, or his ambitions. Crucially, Rocque or his surveyors wrongly counted the depth of the projecting portico, recording it as four columns deep when it is, and was then, only two.[54] Those with a professional or even an amateur interest in architecture would have looked very carefully for such telling details of the plan of this innovative building. Such anomalies in Rocque's record of individual buildings crop up quite regularly, which must give us caution when we use Rocque as our only source for establishing the exact footprint of buildings that have disappeared or for which we have no more dependable visual record.

Christ Church Cathedral, whose overall footprint by the eighteenth century encompassed a muddled conglomerate of medieval and early modern accretions, but was nevertheless the principal church in the city, faired hardly better in Rocque's account (fig. 11.8). One must consider only the transepts, which are not placed opposite each other as they should have been. We can only speculate, as with the Parliament House, not just how Rocque got this so wrong, but why he was so little concerned with it, despite the editorial input of the public over the six years he was in the city. It might be allowed that this was not a freestanding building, as it became following its extensive transformation by G.E. Street in the 1870s, but was surrounded by later additions, including the then Four Courts, which was founded on its medieval claustral ranges.[55]

---

52 http://mapanalyst.org, accessed 10 June 2013; Bernhard Jenny, 'MapAnalyst: a digital tool for the analysis of the planimetric accuracy of historical maps', *e-Permetron*, 1:3 (summer 2006), 239–45.   **53** Further details on the carrying out of this software trial can be found in Montague, 'John Rocque' (PhD), pp 307–13.   **54** Lennon and Montague, *John Rocque's Dublin*, pp 34–5.   **55** Roger Stalley, 'The architecture of the cathedral and priory buildings, 1250–1530' in Kenneth Milne (ed.), *Christ Church Cathedral, Dublin: a history* (Dublin, 2000), pp 95–129 at pp 112–13.

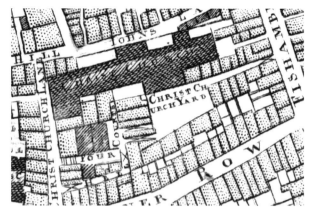

11.8 Christ Church
Cathedral, Dublin, as
depicted on Rocque's
Exact Survey (1756).

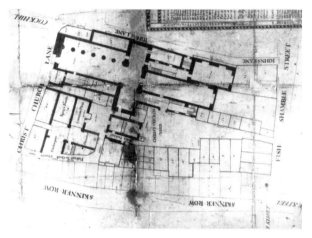

11.9 Thomas Reading,
plan of Christ Church
Cathedral. Reproduced
from Colm Lennon,
*Dublin Part II, 1610 to
1756. Irish Historic Towns
Atlas*, 19 (Dublin, 2008).
© Courtesy of the
Representative Church
Body Library.

However, a much more reliable graphical account of how all of this was arranged appears on Reading's, almost contemporary, 1761 plan (fig. 11.9).[56]

Indeed, Rocque was capable of much better. His plans of Kilkenny (fig. 11.10) and Armagh (fig. 11.11) cathedrals are both faithful antiquarian accounts of these churches, which compare favourably with later more dependable records of the same buildings.[57] Even in Dublin, Rocque could prepare a better ecclesiastical ground record. His delineation of St Patrick's Cathedral (fig. 11.12), while naïve in comparison to Kendrick's careful and proprietorial plan (fig. 11.13),[58] is nevertheless a much more insightful and

56 'Map of the liberty of Christ Church' (1764) by Thomas Reading: Dublin, Representative Church Body Library MS.   57 These cathedral plans appear in *A topographical map of the county of Armagh, to which is anex'd the plans of Newry and Armagh by Iohn Rocque* (1760) and *A survey of the city of Kilkenny by John Rocque corrographer to his royal highness the prince of Wales* (1758).   58 Roger Kendrick, 'The liberty of St Patrick's Catherdral [*sic*], Dublin', as copied in 1883, Marsh's Library.

11.10 Detail of Kilkenny
Cathedral taken from
John Rocque, *A survey of
the city of Kilkenny*
(1758). TCD OO.a.60.
Courtesy of the Board of
Trinity College Dublin.

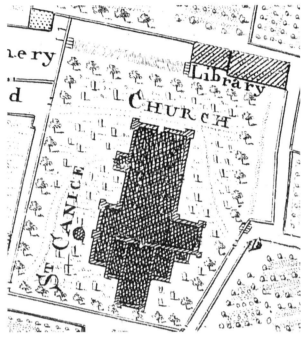

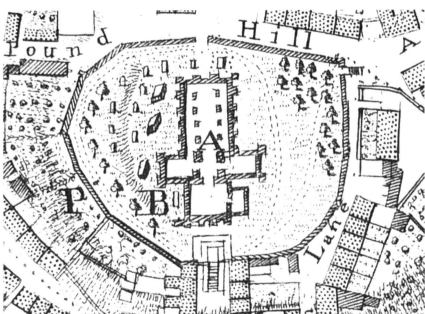

11.11 Detail of Armagh Cathedral taken from John Rocque, *A topographical map of the county of Armagh, to which is Anex'd the plans of Newry and Armagh* (1760). TCD OO.a.60. Courtesy of the Board of Trinity College Dublin.

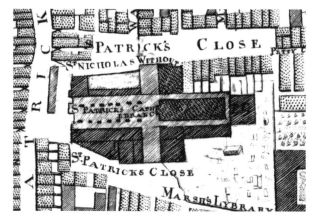

11.12 St Patrick's
Cathedral, as shown on
Rocque's *Exact Survey*
(1756).

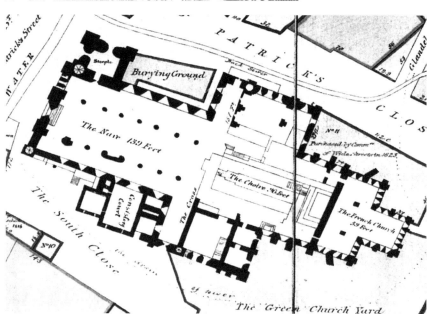

11.13 Roger Kendrick, plan of St Patrick's Cathedral (1754). Reproduced with the
permission of the Governors and Guardians of Marsh's Library, Dublin.

accurate record of that medieval cathedral as it appeared at that time, than the
one he had made of Christ Church. Although Rocque's was not a conventional
type of interior plan, some sense is given to the cathedral's interior
arrangement. The seven nave piers are represented correctly; some broad hints
are given of the division into separate chambers of the north transept; and of
the accumulation of consistory court and other buildings set around the south
transept; and the choir and lady chapel, which is labelled, as FC (French
Chapel). Indeed, the latter appears to be a possible explanation for the extent

of the detail in this depiction in comparison to that of Christ Church, as it is quite probable that this was the church that Rocque attended each Sunday while he lived in the city. The degree of implied detail, including a representation of the main elements of the internal plan, is quite telling, no matter how gauche their depiction.

City walls

Other above-ground archaeology had survived to the 1750s, not least the medieval city walls, built, extended or consolidated from the late eleventh to the fourteenth century, of which, some significant portions survive at Ship Street Little, Lamb Alley, Power's Square, Cook Street and Wood Quay at the Civic Offices.[59] Generally, to the extent that he did so, Rocque recorded the walls as lines representing property boundaries – as no doubt they were perceived by contemporaries – without any suggestion of their significance as archaeology.

It may seem redundant to attempt to trace out on Rocque lines representing the city wall whose positions have been established more reliably on modern maps as a result of knowledge gleaned from archaeological investigation, particularly when the positioning and measurement of individual structures – walls around houses, or walls that establish the limits of curtilage – were not always so precisely recorded by him in the first place. However, if lines can be identified on the Rocque map that represented elements of the city walls, understanding may be gained firstly of what remained or was accessible of the medieval walls in the middle of the eighteenth century, and secondly and more crucially, of how such a divisional structure played a part in creating the pattern of urban topography in the early modern period and since.

A number of important studies have been carried out in which attempts were made to recreate the circuit of the city walls based on graphically superimposing lines on later maps, most notably by Howard Clarke,[60] Claire Walsh[61] and Margaret Gowen.[62] All are based on a combination of historical evidence for the circuit of the wall – John Perrot's 1585 survey[63] and the Speed (1610) and de Gomme (1673) maps, being the principal sources – and

59 Linzi Simpson, 'The archaeological remains of Viking and medieval Dublin: a research framework' (unpublished report submitted to Dublin City Council and Heritage Council (Irish National Strategic Archaeological Research), 2010), p. 26; Margaret Gowen (ed.), *Conservation plan: Dublin city walls and defences* (Dublin, 2004), pp 3–9; Linzi Simpson, 'Fifty years a-digging: a synthesis of medieval archaeological investigations in Dublin city and suburbs' in Seán Duffy (ed.), *Medieval Dublin XI* (Dublin, 2011), pp 9–112 at pp 58–64. **60** H.B. Clarke, *Dublin, c.840–c.1540: the medieval town in the modern city* (Dublin, 1973, new ed., 2003). **61** Claire Walsh, 'Dublin's southern town defences, tenth to fourteenth centuries: the evidence from Ross Road' in Seán Duffy (ed.), *Medieval Dublin II* (Dublin, 2001), pp 88–127 at p. 90. **62** Gowen, *Conservation plan*, fig. 1; reproduced in Simpson, 'Archaeological remains', fig. 22. **63** State Papers Ireland, 63/121/73, reproduced in full in H.B. Clarke, *Dublin Part I, to 1610, Irish Historic Towns Atlas, 11* (Dublin, 2002), pp 32–3.

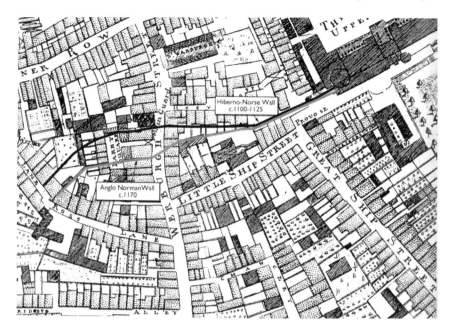

11.14 After Simpson's suggested depiction of the lines of the two walls at Werburgh Street: Linzi Simpson, 'The medieval city wall and the southern line of Dublin's defences: excavations at 14–16 Werburgh Street' in Seán Duffy (ed.), *Medieval Dublin VIII* (Dublin, 2008), pp 150–77 at p. 158.

archaeological evidence for what is extant: either still upstanding, or found through excavation. An exercise to choose which lines on a particular map – Rocque's in this instance – represent the city wall is a slightly different one. For example, in her important reassessment of the two lines of the city wall from Ship Street to St Nicholas Gate – based on the discovery that the original southerly defences of *c*.1100–25 were rebuilt some 10–15m further south sometime after 1170[64] – Simpson has drawn a pair of lines on the Rocque map suggesting what line the wall was likely to have followed along that stretch of map (fig. 11.14). She is careful not to speculate which lines on Rocque record portions of the wall, which were either extant, or recognized as such by him in the *Exact Survey*, although such an exercise was carried out in the Dublin City Council Conservation Plan of the City Walls, edited by Gowen (fig. 11.15).[65] Some portions of the line of the wall on Rocque, as suggested by Gowen, may be open to further inquiry. Also, Gowen's marked-up Rocque map follows for the most part the likely line of the wall only.

64 Walsh, 'Dublin's southern town defences', pp 88–127; Linzi Simpson, 'The medieval city wall and the southern line of Dublin's defences: excavations at 14–16 Werburgh Street' in Seán Duffy (ed.), *Medieval Dublin VIII* (Dublin, 2008), pp 150–77. 65 Gowen, *Conservation plan*, fig. 6.

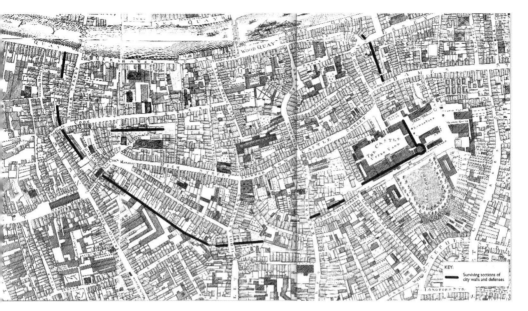

11.15 After Gowen's suggested depiction of the circuit of the city walls: Margaret Gowen (ed.), *Conservation plan: Dublin city walls and defences* (Dublin, 2004).

It might be possible still to interrogate Rocque's map a little further regarding the series of mural towers, gateways and other wall appurtenances, which either could or should have survived around 1756 when the map was published. Upkeep of the walls after the mid-seventeenth century ceased to be a priority, and portions were actively demolished from the 1680s onwards.[66] Nevertheless, there remains a good deal of evidence concerning the parts of the city walls that should have survived in Rocque's day.[67]

Dublin Castle   Rocque's record of surviving medieval elements in Dublin Castle, comprising the south-eastern corner of the walled enclosure of the city, and what was later developed as the Upper Yard of an extended complex from the late seventeenth century onwards, appears fairly adequate (fig. 11.16). A 1673 plan, of the southern range of the castle,[68] suggests that the outer wall on

66 Lennon, *Dublin Part II*, pp 1–2.   **67** See list of towers, turrets and gates, based in part on Lord Deputy John Perrot's survey of 1685, in Patrick Healy, 'The town walls of Dublin' in Elgie Gillespie (ed.), *The liberties of Dublin* (Dublin, 1973), pp 16–23; with further documentary details on these in Lennon, *Dublin Part II*, pp 1–2, 24–6; and Avril Thomas, *The walled towns of Ireland* (2 vols, Dublin, 1992), ii, pp 79–93.   **68** Ann Lynch and Conleth Manning, 'Excavations at Dublin Castle, 1985–7' in Seán Duffy (ed.), *Medieval Dublin II* (Dublin, 2001), pp 169–204 at p. 177; see also J.B. Maguire, 'Seventeenth-century plans of Dublin Castle', *JRSAI*, 104 (1974), 5–14; Edward McParland, *Public architecture in Ireland, 1680–1760* (New Haven and London, 2001), p. 92.

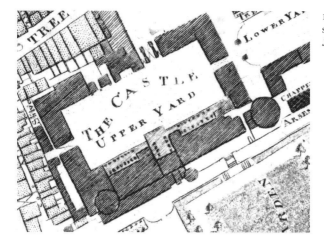

11.16 Dublin Castle, as shown on Rocque's *Exact Survey* (1756).

this side of the medieval fortress was canted northwards from the middle tower. The parts on either side of the middle tower on Rocque, however, are shown on axis with each other. Yet, this side of the castle had been extensively remodelled, over a period of approximately eighty years, following the fire of 1684,[69] and Rocque's assessment is corroborated by the Ordnance Survey.[70] The surviving round medieval structures of the Record Tower on the southeast corner of the castle enclosure and of the Bermingham Tower on the southwest corner are both shown. A small octagonal turret, which is still extant, but is a later replacement for the medieval middle tower, is also shown.

Ship Street   Further west, an important stretch of the wall survives today in Little Ship Street, and Gowen has suggested the location of the line of the wall on Rocque by a pair of lines set directly behind some houses on the north side of the street (fig. 11.17).[71] One element that at first appears to be missing from Rocque, and that we might expect to see, is Stanihurst's Tower, also known as Cole's Bastion.[72] This is a five-sided bastion, faced with later snecked masonry, with a vertical join between this and the roughly coursed masonry of the earlier wall.

There is reason to believe that the line of the wall should be represented on Rocque further back from the line of the street. For one thing, the lines shown on Gowen are set to the south of a small body of water shown on the map, which is one of a number of places where the River Poddle is represented above ground.[73] The city wall was to the north of the Poddle, which in places

69 McParland, *Public architecture*, pp 91–113.   **70** Ordnance Survey, City of Dublin map, 1:1056, Sheet 21, 1838–47.   **71** Gowen, *Conservation plan*, fig. 6.   **72** Healy, 'Town walls', p. 18; Lennon, *Dublin Part II*, p. 25; Thomas, *Walled towns*, ii, p. 80.   **73** Some other places where Rocque has shown parts of the Poddle above ground are the west side of Pimlico; on the south side of the linen tenters fields at the rear of Weavers Square and Mill Street; at the rear of houses on New Row; and at the back of houses on 'Marrow Bone Lane'.

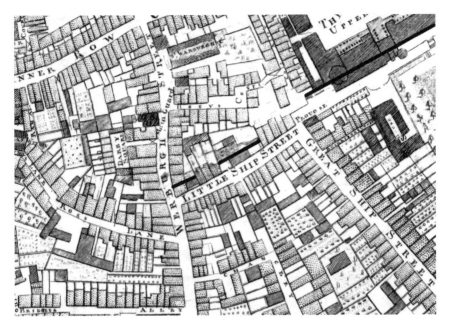

11.17 After Gowen's suggested depiction of the section of wall at Ship Street: Gowen (ed.), *Conservation plan.*

acted as an external moat to it. However, Simpson, as noted above, and based on her excavation at 14–16 Werburgh Street, has suggested a pair of lines for the Anglo-Norman Wall of *c.*1170 and for the earlier Hiberno-Norse wall of *c.*1100–25, stretching from Ross Lane on the south-west to a point to the rear of some houses on Little Ship Street on the north-east, where the lines of the two walls converge (fig. 11.14).[74] The extant wall at Ship Street, which she has now established represents the Anglo-Norman wall, is placed further back again on the Rocque map than on Gowen's proposal, or indeed than merely directly north of the small portion of the exposed Poddle. This trajectory is partly based on our knowledge of parish boundaries as recorded, *inter alia*, by the Ordnance Survey, and, more importantly, on the excavation, which revealed that the line of the wall cut through the southern part of Darby Square. Bringing the line of the wall on the eighteenth-century map as it crosses Darby Square eastwards, as Simpson does, allows us to suggest that one of the more northerly lines on Rocque represents the Anglo-Norman wall behind Ship Street.

However, as already noted, a complete trajectory (represented by an unbroken line) suggesting the position of the historical circuit of the wall in this position, is noted on Simpson's diagram (fig. 11.14), which represents

74 Simpson, 'The medieval city wall at 14–16 Werburgh Street', pp 158–9.

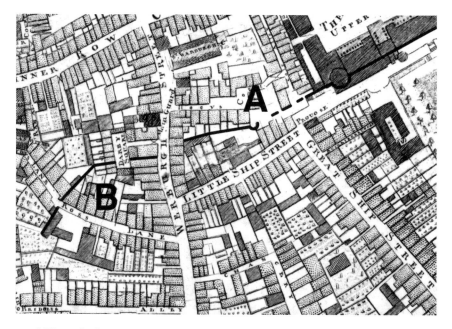

11.18 The author's suggested depiction of the lines on Rocque representing the city wall at Werburgh Street and Ship Street.

more than what merely survived or was shown on Rocque. When such lines are picked out instead (fig. 11.18A), a small semi-circular shape at the eastern end of the proposed circuit also comes into view, and may represent Rocque's plan of the apparently missing Cole's Bastion. Taking the measure from here, a number of other very tentative lines to the east of this again, as far as Bermingham Tower, may be suggested as other small extant stretches of the wall at this time.

Werburgh Street to St Nicholas Gate   It is difficult to find any sign of the trajectory of the wall between Werburgh Street and Nicholas Street in the street pattern on Rocque's map in this area. The post-medieval development of the zone involved the introduction of a new street – comprising Kennedy's Lane and Ross Lane – which ran in a curving diagonal from the north-west to the south-east, contrary to the line of the wall that ran from the north-east to the south-west. In this way, the early modern street alignment appears to have crossed the line of the walls in an X-wise fashion.[75] As noted, excavations by Walsh at Ross Road, and by Simpson at Werburgh Street, revealed evidence of two stretches of medieval wall, dating to *c.*1100–25 and *c.*1170 respectively, the second running south of the first, resulting in a considerable expansion of the

75 The later Ross Road is aligned differently again, in an east–west direction.

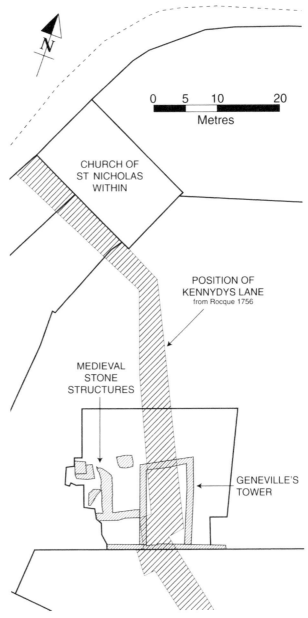

11.19 After Walsh's depiction of Kennedy's Lane: Claire Walsh, 'Dublin's southern town defences, tenth to fourteenth centuries: the evidence from Ross Road' in Seán Duffy (ed.), *Medieval Dublin II* (Dublin, 2001), pp 88–127 at p. 90.

earlier city (fig. 11.14). Walsh also found substantial remains of Genevel's (Geneville's) Tower here,[76] and she has traced the likely position of Kennedy's Lane as shown on Rocque, relative to the found medieval structures of the wall and the tower (fig. 11.19).[77] Comparing this to the footprints of buildings on

76 Walsh, 'Dublin's southern town defences', pp 112–16.   **77** Ibid., fig. 11.

Rocque, none of his lines definitively suggest the survival of these medieval remains to 1756. Nevertheless, on the basis of these findings, and using for guidance the parish boundaries as delineated on early Ordnance Survey maps, which were in turn founded on ancient property divisions created by the wall itself, Simpson's figure (fig. 11.14) makes a plausible suggestion for the line of the wall in this area. Again, one could instead pick out only the lines representing boundary divisions on Rocque that might have represented extant elements of the circuit at that time (fig. 11.18B).

St Nicholas Gate   How the exact location of St Nicholas Gate is recorded on Rocque is also open to argument. The gate itself does not appear to have survived in 1756. Paddy Healy noted a corporation rental of 1763, stating that a Robert Rochford was paying £4 per annum for 'building over St Nicholas' Gate',[78] the expression, perhaps implying that houses were built over, or on top of, the site of the original structure – that is, that the gate had been demolished in order that new buildings be put in its place. Establishing the location of the wall to the east and directly to the west of the gate, by means of Rocque, and consequently where Nicholas Gate exactly might have been, is challenging. However, a pattern of houses, including a pair of lanes, marked by Rocque's usual X-mark to indicate a vault, on either side of the 'N' of Nicholas Street, seems a more likely location for the earlier gate structure than that marked in a more northerly position on the Gowen-annotated Rocque map (fig. 11.20). This pinch point in the major road itself is fairly telling, and may be compared to those at St James' Gate and New Gate (discussed below). Indeed, the long stretch of wall to the rear of Back Lane, which is clearly delineated on Rocque, seems to turn southwards and then, after about 30m, it turns at an obtuse angle to the east, to accommodate this more likely location for the then recently demolished gate (fig. 11.21). The record of the parish boundaries on early Ordnance Survey maps also corroborates this southerly swelling to the area enclosed by the wall.[79] It is confirmed by the parish boundary symbol on Brooking's 1728 map, which turns southwards as far as a similar pinch point, which on Brooking, Rocque and on the Ordnance Survey is just north of a block of houses called Draper's Court at the junction of Bride Alley. The southerly turn to the portion of wall that survives at Power's Square[80] also seems to corroborate this positioning of the pattern for St Nicholas Gate on the Rocque map. This pattern – representing a bunching together of houses at Nicholas Street – is given added meaning then by its associated medieval antecedence, their being houses built around (or on top of) the original structure of the southerly portal to the medieval city.

---

78 Healy, 'Town walls', p. 19.   **79** Ordnance Survey map of City of Dublin, 1:1,056, Sheet 20, surveyed 1838–47, published 1847.   **80** Linzi Simpson, 'Fifty years', pp 62–3.

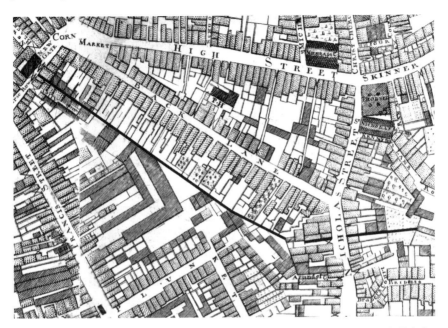

11.20 After Gowen's suggested depiction of the section of wall at Back Lane and Nicholas Gate: Gowen (ed.), *Conservation plan*.

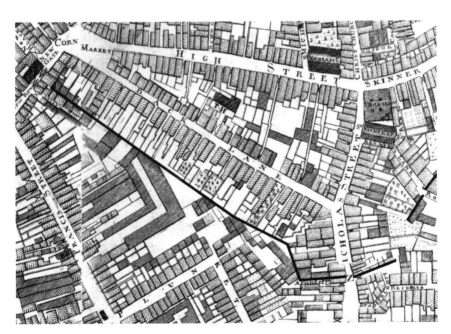

11.21 The author's suggested depiction of the lines on Rocque representing the city wall at Back Lane and Nicholas Gate.

Back Lane   On Rocque's map, a very long section of surviving medieval wall is depicted as the rear wall to the properties on the south side of Back Lane (fig. 11.21). Small sections of this wall survive at Lamb Alley[81] and to the rear of properties in Power's Square. In a similar way to the southward swelling of the city wall at St Nicholas Gate, one of the most characteristic aspects of Rocque's depiction of the long stretch of surviving wall to the rear of Back Lane is the degree to which it clearly separates quite distinct urban patterns, which is suggestive of the exclusive or sectional nature of such an urban feature.[82]

Newgate   The circuit of the wall continued north-westwards along the rear of Back Lane to the important Newgate, which was between the early eighteenth-century Corn Market House (to the south and outside the walls), which market was recorded in plan on Rocque and in elevation in Brooking,[83] and the street called Corn Market (to the north and inside the walls), the location of the grain market in the Middle Ages (fig. 11.22). The earliest documentary reference to the 'New West gate' is in 1177. The gate was to have been augmented by the addition of towers in the mid-thirteenth century, and these were rebuilt and repaired in the fourteenth and fifteenth centuries.[84] Newgate led from the city to the important ancient highway of the Slige Mhór, and the suburb around St Thomas' Abbey, the street itself becoming Thomas Street. There are references to the Newgate being used as a gaol from the late thirteenth century, and it continued in that function until 1780.[85]

The gatehouse is known to have had large circular towers at its corners, which were in a 'rotten' state by 1732.[86] Some portion of the towers survived until at least 1932.[87] Charles McNeill, in a paper given in 1916, describes how part of the curved wall of the south-western tower had been recovered the previous year. It was preserved *in situ* by the city engineer, M.J. Buckley, after a house was demolished that sat over a passage between Lamb Alley and Cut Purse Row, the narrow street leading to Newgate from Thomas Street: 'It now stands apart, in plan rather more than quarter of a circle, about 8 feet high, and on its inner side it shows the holes into which the ends of the stone steps were fitted'.[88] Photographs of the interior and exterior of the recovered quadrant of the tower were shown by McNeill.[89] He also reproduced a plan, made by Austin Cooper in 1782 (fig. 11.23), which indicated how, at this date at least, remnants of three of the four round corner towers survived. However, all

81 Tim Coughlan, 'The Anglo-Norman houses of Dublin: evidence from Back Lane' in Seán Duffy (ed.), *Medieval Dublin I* (Dublin, 2000), pp 203–33 at p. 209.   82 See also Simms, 'Medieval Dublin', p. 35.   83 Lennon and Montague, *John Rocque's Dublin*, pp 68–9. 84 Clarke, *Dublin Part I*, p. 21.   85 Healy, 'Town walls', p. 19.   86 Lennon, *Dublin Part II*, pp 2, 25.   87 Gowen, *Conservation plan*, p. 12.   88 Charles McNeill, 'New Gate, Dublin', *JRSAI*, 11:2 (Dec. 1921), 152–65 at 152.   89 McNeill, 'New Gate', pl. xxiv.

11.22 Newgate as shown on Rocque's *Exact Survey* (1756).

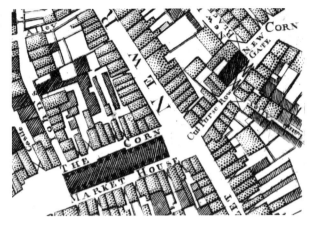

11.23 Newgate plan, as depicted by Austin Cooper in his diary of 1782, and as reproduced in Charles McNeill, 'New Gate, Dublin', *JRSAI*, 11:2 (Dec. 1921), 152–65, fig. 3.

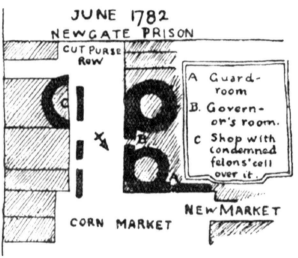

of them, like the tower recovered in the house demolished in 1915, were somehow enclosed within later dwelling houses and so not evident from the exterior of the buildings, or in their footprints.[90] Rocque labelled a densely hatched rectangular building as 'New Gate' and, based on the Cooper plan, we should not be surprised that no corner turrets are in evidence. The pair of X-marks on Rocque, on axis with the line of the street, and set beside the shaded rectangular building, indicate that there was a passage here which is in keeping with an arched gateway that was in some way intact as such at that time.

Brown's Castle   The city wall continued in a north-western direction to the rear of houses on the eastern side of New Row (now Upper St Augustine Street). Gowen identified a strong continuous stretch of back wall to a number

90 Ibid., fig. 3.

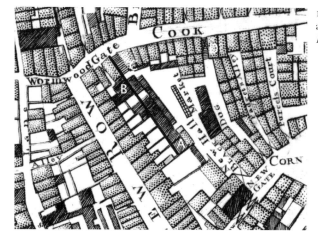

11.24 Wormwood Gate, as shown on Rocque's *Exact Survey* (1756).

of houses on the east side of New Row that is the likely line of the city wall (fig. 11.15, 11.24A). Somewhere along this portion of the wall was Brown's Castle, which was also referred to as Fitzsimon's Tower and, according to Colm Lennon, was possibly used as a mass house in the early seventeenth century.[91] Significantly, this mural tower was recorded in Francis Grose's *Antiquities* in 1791[92] and, like Newgate, it appears to have had corner turrets, albeit, in this case, with square rather than circular plans. Despite its depiction over three decades later by Grose, disappointingly, at least at first glance, no such building appears to be depicted on Rocque (fig. 11.24). There is a single building, which is diagonally hatched, has a stepped plan, and is accessed down an alley (with the familiar X representing an arch-entry) from Wormwood Gate (fig. 11.24B). At a pinch, and considering Rocque's sometimes casual shorthand for the plans of individual buildings, this *might* be Rocque's representation of what survived of Brown's Castle. If so, it lies against, but apparently outside, the city wall. It is interesting to note that what might be mistaken as hatching lines, to the east of the two dwelling houses on 'Worm Wood Gate' that give onto the lane in question, are in fact a set of steps shown by Rocque directly inside the medieval wall (fig. 11.24C), and plausibly of medieval origins, giving access up the steep hill to the area of New Hall Market, also labelled here as 'Black Dog'.[93]

Brown's Castle to St Audoen's Arch   The original, *c.*1100–25 city wall turned eastwards at approximately this point, and was retained even after later extensions of the circuit were made northwards as far as the river (fig. 11.15). A number of medieval mural buildings should have been visible in 1756.

91 Lennon, *Dublin Part II*, p. 25.   **92** Healy, 'Town walls', p. 20.   **93** Lennon, *Dublin Part II*, p. 30.

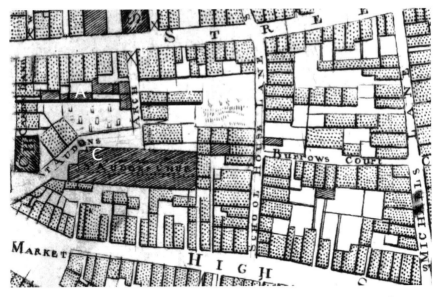

11.25 St Audoen's wall, arch and church, as shown on Rocque's *Exact Survey* (1756).

However, the exact position of the line of this wall is not obviously delineated by Rocque, only the long terraces of houses on the south side of Cook Street. We may assume, as the Gowen Conservation Plan map annotations do, that the line is set back considerably to the rear of these houses on Rocque, forming the northern perimeter of the graveyard of St Audoen's Church, which is the location of the extant wall (fig. 11.25A).

Before getting to St Audoen's, another set of steps should be noted on the map just below the K in Cook Street, over which an X-mark indicating a passage through a building was inscribed (fig. 11.24D). These steps, like those described at Wormwood Gate nearby, also gave access to the enclosed space of the Black Dog Market, by way of an arch. The line of the city wall at this point may be tentatively placed directly south of the highest (most southerly) step. Perhaps this is the location of a postern gate. Alternatively, the passage might indicate (as we shall see below regarding an archway through a terrace of houses to the south of Audoen's Arch) the route from the street to a postern gate, possibly even that of Fagan's Tower, which appears on de Gomme, and was recorded by Perrot as giving access to a passageway linking Cornmarket to Cook Street, and was recorded as still standing in 1788.[94]

Further east, a mural gateway giving access from Cook Street to the graveyard and church of St Audoen's, survived intact until the 1880s, when it was altered, albeit retained until the present day.[95] The archway is both

94 Healy, 'Town walls', p. 22.   95 Gowen, *Conservation plan*, p. 12.

indicated (using the usual X-mark), and labelled as 'ST AUDONS ARCH' on Rocque. However, the X is placed between houses directly onto Cook Street (fig. 11.25B), rather than further south and further up the hill, as it appears on the first edition Ordnance Survey map,[96] and as it survives to this day. Perhaps there was also a passageway through the terrace of houses at this time, but the X-mark is not the location of the archway through the medieval wall. Furthermore, the line of the medieval wall on Rocque does not obviously continue beyond the line recording the northern perimeter of the graveyard – although there are many boundary walls about which one could speculate – despite the fact that a substantial section of the city wall is recorded here on later Ordnance Survey maps.[97]

Fyan's Castle If, instead of turning eastwards at Brown's Castle, we continued northwards towards the river, and then eastwards as far as Isolde's Tower and Essex Street, there are still one or two remaining associated buildings that we might expect to appear on the 1756 map. Of these, a number of structures appear on a plan copied in 1755 by the Wide Streets Commissioners, of a map made in 1721 (fig. 11.26).[98] The first of these mural buildings, moving from west to east, is Fyan's Castle, which was also sometimes known as Proudfoot's Castle, was recorded on the Wide Streets Commissioners map as Profot's Castle, and is the last building (or building plot) on Blind Quay (Exchange Street) at the foot of Fishamble Street (fig. 11.26A). 'Fian's Castle' was mentioned by the City Assembly in 1752,[99] when they stated that no coals or salt measures were to be delivered by the 'craner of this city', except under direction of the mayor, between Fiann's Castle and Ormond (O'Donovan Rossa) Bridge. A *c.*1870 photograph of two houses at the end of this terrace is reproduced by Peter Pearson (fig. 11.27).[1] The houses face westwards, rather than north or south to the quay or to Exchange Street. They are gabled buildings, probably with cruciform roofs, and are likely to date to the first quarter of the eighteenth century, rather than to after 1752 – although gabled, or the more elaborate so-called 'Dutch Billy', houses were being built as late as the 1740s, at least, in Molesworth Street[2] – when the castle is referred to by the City Assembly. Rocque's map seems more in keeping with the evidence of the gabled buildings that survived into the late nineteenth century at least. His plan – which sits awkwardly in this place across the divide between his sheets 2 and 3 – nevertheless clearly delineates two dwelling houses facing westwards (fig. 11.28). This suggests that when

---

96 Mary McMahon (ed.), *St Audoen's Church, Cornmarket, Dublin: archaeology and architecture* (Dublin, 2006), p. 8. **97** Simpson, 'Archaeological remains', fig. 62. **98** Dublin City Library and Archives, WSC/Maps/654; reproduced in Lennon, *Dublin Part II.* **99** *CARD,* x, p. 20. **1** Peter Pearson, *The heart of Dublin: resurgence of an historic city* (Dublin, 2000), p. 246. **2** Robin Usher, *Dawson, Molesworth and Kildare Streets, D2: a*

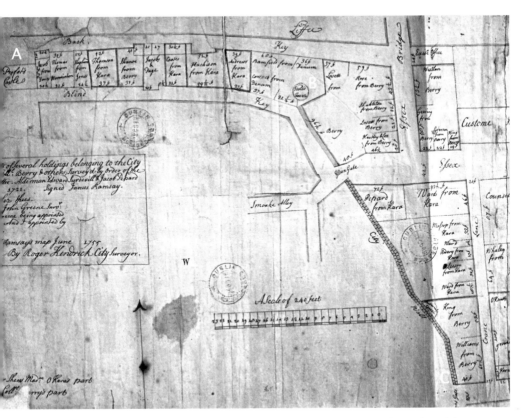

11.26 Profot's (Proudfoot's) or Fyan's Castle, at A; Isolde's Tower, at B; and a section of the city wall between two points both marked C, on a Wide Streets Commissioners map of 'ground plots of several holdings belonging to the city of Dublin ...', WSC/Maps/654. Courtesy of Dublin City Library and Archives.

referencing Fyan's Castle, the City Assembly was speaking toponymically rather than topographically, referring to a place then current in living memory, rather than to a surviving medieval building.

Isolde's Tower Nor does Isolde's Tower appear on Rocque, although we are much less likely to expect that it would have. While this was until recently buried within the cellars of buildings,[3] and quite patently was archaeology, rather than in any way a possible property boundary of the type Rocque was almost exclusively interested in, it is worth noting that this round building *was* nonetheless recorded – in the form of a dotted line – in the Wide Streets Commissioners plan of 1721/55 (fig. 11.26B). In the same way, a large section

study of the past, a vision for the future (Dublin, 2008), pp 72–4.   3 Linzi Simpson, *Excavations at Isolde's Tower, Dublin* (Dublin, 1994).

11.27 Photograph, *c.*1870, of two houses on the junction of Essex Quay and Blind Quay at the bottom of Fishamble Street. From a photograph formerly in the possession of Larry O'Connor of Mason Photographers. Reproduced from Peter Pearson, *The heart of Dublin: resurgence of an historic city* (Dublin, 2000), p. 246.

of the city wall is identified as such on this map running diagonally from north-west to south-east, from a house that juts out slightly near the south-eastern corner of Essex Gate (the street), as far as Dame Street, approximately 14m west of Crane Lane (fig. 11.26C). The location of this wall is not at all in keeping with the pattern of houses as recorded on Rocque, and yet is consistent with the diagonal property divisions recorded on this map and on other Wide Streets Commissioners maps,[4] and with sections of the wall that were recovered during excavations.[5] These different facts are difficult to reconcile. The property divisions on the Wide Streets Commissioners map seem to run contrary to the physical pattern of walls and houses in this patch of land, as recorded by Rocque. Nevertheless, it is the city wall, perhaps buried at basement level beneath what Rocque could see, that was still dictating the patterns of ownership. Rocque's depiction of boundaries always represents

4 DCLA, WSC/Maps/493.   5 Georgina Scally, 'The earthen banks and walled defences of Dublin's north-east corner' in Seán Duffy (ed.), *Medieval Dublin III* (Dublin, 2002), pp 11–33.

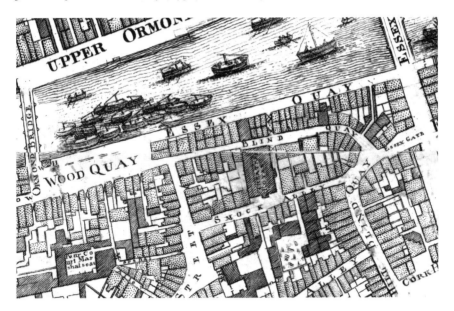

11.28 Two houses at the location of Fyan's Castle, Essex Quay, as shown on Rocque's *Exact Survey* (1756). Harry Margary facsimile of an early (1756) state of Rocque's *Exact Survey*. Reproduced from Paul Ferguson (ed.), *The A to Z of Georgian Dublin* (Lympne Castle, Kent, 1998).

clearly visible physical ones. His is neither a cadastral map (representing property divisions), nor an archaeological map. The patterns of how the above-ground footprints of buildings were actually aligned are nevertheless crucial evidence, despite not matching up to a sometimes contrary pattern of ownership. Based on the Wide Streets Commissioners map, a possible trajectory of the underground wall on Rocque can be made (fig. 11.29C).

Bysse's Tower   One other building, mistakenly named as 'Butivant's [Buttavant's] Tower', but actually Bysse's Tower,[6] is also delineated on the 1721/55 Wide Streets Commissioners' map (fig. 11.26D). Healy notes that this building was demolished in 1763 for the opening up of Parliament Street.[7] There is nothing, again, marked out as 'castle' or 'tower' or 'archaeology' on Rocque. However, the closest possible building is marked PH, which Paul Ferguson identifies as Printing House (fig. 11.29D);[8] that is, the premises of Faulkner's *Dublin Journal*. One can only speculate about the possibility that this newspaper, in which Rocque regularly advertised, was located in old Bysse's Tower, or alternatively, that the printing house contained fabric of the earlier tower, as the houses at Newgate did, as shown on Cooper's map.

6 Lennon, *Dublin Part II*, p. 25.   7 Healy, 'Town walls', p. 21.   8 Ferguson, *A to Z*, p. 65.

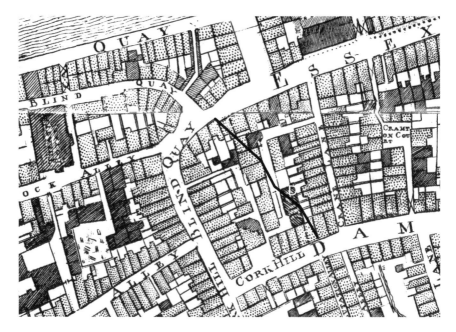

11.29 The author's depiction of the suggested line of the city wall on Rocque between Blind Quay and Dame Street, following the line of the wall (between the two letters C) recorded on WSC/Maps/654 (fig. 11.26, above). Harry Margary facsimile of an early (*c*.1756) state of Rocque's *Exact Survey*. Reproduced from Ferguson (ed.), *The A to Z* (1998).

Monastic enclosures

One of the great hopes sometimes invested in Rocque's Dublin map is that we might be able to discover in the pattern of his street plan the layout of some of the dissolved monasteries upon whose grounds the suburbs north, south, east and west of the walled city were founded. Some, such as Stuart Kinsella[9] and Michael O'Neill[10] separately at Christ Church, Seán Duffy and Linzi Simpson at St Augustine's friary at Cecilia Street in Temple Bar,[11] and Mary McMahon at St Saviour's Dominican priory, under the present Four Courts,[12] have tried to find some traces of the monastic precincts in the street plan described by Rocque, without a great deal of certainty.

9 Stuart Kinsella, 'Mapping Christ Church Cathedral, Dublin, *c*.1028–1608: an examination of the western cloister' in John Bradley, A.J. Fletcher and Anngret Simms (eds), *Dublin in the medieval world: studies in honour of Howard B. Clarke* (Dublin, 2009), pp 143–67. 10 Michael O'Neill, 'Christ Church Cathedral as a blueprint for other Augustinian buildings in Ireland' in Bradley et al. (eds), *Dublin in the medieval world*, pp 168–87. 11 Seán Duffy and Linzi Simpson, 'The hermits of St Augustine in medieval Dublin: their history and archaeology' in Bradley et al. (eds), *Dublin in the medieval world*, pp 300–30. 12 Mary McMahon, 'Archaeological excavations at the site of the Four Courts Extension, Inns Quay, Dublin', *PRIA*, 88C (1988), 271–319.

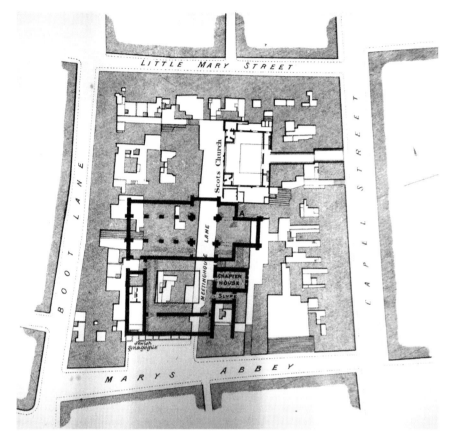

11.30 Reconstruction of the monastic enclosure of St Mary's Abbey by Thomas Drew in Thomas Drew, 'Problematical plan of the buildings which formed old St Mary's Abbey, Dublin' in *Remains of St Mary's Abbey, Dublin: their explorations and researches, AD1886* (Dublin, 1887), opposite p. 4.

St Mary's Abbey   One of the most tantalizing prospects is the possibility of discovering what remains of the great St Mary's Cistercian abbey – founded as a daughter house of the Benedictine abbey of Savigny in 1139, but united with the Cistercians in 1147[13] – within the pattern of the street network north of the Liffey, planned and built in the late seventeenth century by Sir Humphrey Jervis and Sir Richard Reynell.[14] While Purcell has made a close study of the broader precinct of the abbey, and made some topographical connections between the contemporary documentary and later cartographical evidence, the

13 Aubrey Gwynn and R.N. Hadcock, *Medieval religious houses: Ireland* (Dublin, 1970), p. 130; Roger Stalley, *The Cistercian monasteries of Ireland* (London and New Haven, 1987), p. 244.   14 Lennon and Montague, *John Rocque's Dublin*, pp 14–15.

complex of abbey buildings themselves – church and claustral ranges –
remains elusive.[15] As early as 1886, albeit using the Ordnance Survey rather
than Rocque, Thomas Drew made an attempt to establish the exact location of
the church and claustral ranges (fig. 11.30).[16] A cloister garth (tenuously
corresponding with the street plan) measuring approximately 18m square
(approx. 60 ft) was suggested. If the cloister aisles are included, the length of
the square increases to 27m (90 ft). As the wealthiest Cistercian monastery in
Ireland[17] – at least at the time of the Dissolution – one might expect to find
something a little larger, perhaps in the order of 30m square (100 ft) for
dimensions of the cloister garth alone. Roger Stalley attempted,[18] like Drew, to
superimpose known plans of Cistercian houses on the early Ordnance Survey
plan, and reports some success with the plan of Dunbrody Abbey, Co.
Wexford, one of the largest Cistercian houses, whose cloister garth measured
internally approximately 27m square (90 ft).[19]

It is equally difficult to establish a correspondence between the known plans
of other Irish Cistercian houses and the pattern of extant buildings in this
location in 1756, as outlined by Rocque (fig. 11.31). Remarkably, the twelfth-
century chapter house, and the adjacent passageway (or slype), both survive.
These are buried within a terrace of warehouse buildings on the east side of
Meeting House Lane. The lane runs north from the street labelled on Rocque
as 'Marys Abby [sic]' towards the square-planned Abbey Presbyterian church,
which was built *c*.1703.[20] Any hopes that the promising-looking square-shaped
enclosure within which the early eighteenth-century Presbyterian church was
built (fig. 11.31A) might represent the remains of a cloister garth – it measures
approximately 90 ft square on Rocque – are dashed by the position of the
extant chapter house. Although it is not indicated on Rocque, we know from
the Ordnance Survey maps that the chapter house is approximately 30m (100
ft) further south, down the laneway (fig. 11.32), and consequently could not
form, as all chapter houses do, part of the eastern range of a cloister, if it were
located at the Presbyterian church. In the same way, the rectangular bite out of
the southern part of the block (fig. 11.31B) appears at first to be too far to the
south of the location of the chapter house to be part of an earlier cloister.
However, if we were simply to take out four stippled houses and their rear
gardens directly north of this indent, we are presented with a very plausible

15 Emer Purcell, 'Land-use in medieval Oxmantown' in Seán Duffy (ed.), *Medieval Dublin
IV* (Dublin, 2003), pp 193–228 at pp 203–11; and see now, Geraldine Stout, 'The
topography of St Mary's Cistercian abbey and precinct, Dublin' in Seán Duffy (ed.),
Medieval Dublin XII (Dublin, 2012), pp 138–60, which appeared too late for consideration
here.   **16** Thomas Drew, 'Problematical plan of the buildings which formed old St Mary's
Abbey, Dublin' in *Remains of St Mary's Abbey, Dublin: their explorations and researches,
AD1886* (Dublin, 1887), opposite p. 4.   **17** Stalley, *Cistercian monasteries*, p. 244.   **18** Pers.
comm.   **19** Stalley, *Cistercian monasteries*, fig. 20.   **20** S.C. Smyrl, *Dictionary of Dublin
dissent: Dublin's protestant dissenting meeting houses, 1660–1920* (Dublin, 2009), pp 28–32.

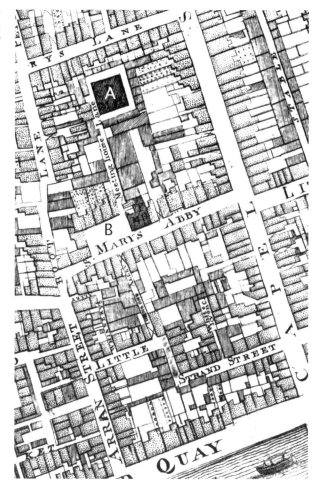

location for the cloister garth and alleys (fig. 11.33A), which measures precisely half an inch on Rocque, or 100 ft on the ground. The latter represents the full dimensions of the cloister enclosure (garth and aisles), and does not differ greatly from Drew's 90 feet, and is only a little bit smaller than Dunbrody's *c.*34m (113 ft) for garth and aisles. Such an interpretation of the buildings as represented on Rocque in turn suggests the possibility that the long, diagonally shaded, building north of the gardens of these houses (fig. 11.33B), may have contained (on its northern side) the southern wall of the nave of the church. The bite-sized gap at the south of this block might then represent the position, if not the actual dimensions, of the refectory (fig. 11.33C), which in Cistercian abbeys is always in the range opposite to the church, usually, and in this case, to the south. The chapter house, whose exact location on Rocque cannot be established with certainty, may be placed at fig. 11.33D.

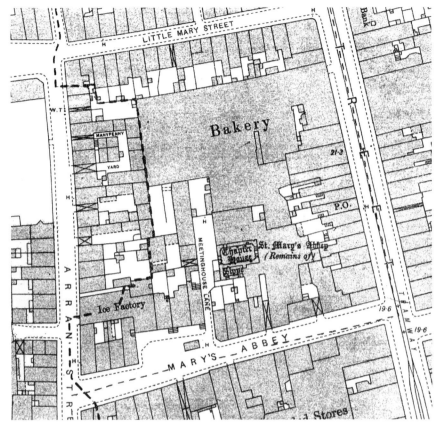

11.32 St Mary's Abbey, as shown on the Ordnance Survey map of Dublin, 1–1056, sheet 18:57 (1908–9).

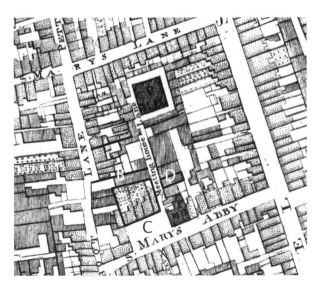

11.33 Possible locations of: the cloister garth and alleys at A; the south wall of the church at B; the refectory at C; and of the extant chapter house at D, of St Mary's Abbey, as shown on Rocque's *Exact Survey* (1756).

11.34 St Sepulchre's
Palace complex as
shown on Rocque's
Exact Survey (1756).

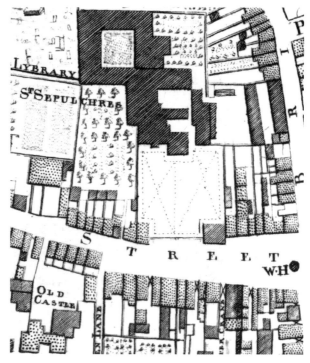

The palace of St Sepulchre At St Sepulchre's, a good deal of the original medieval fabric of the twelfth-century bishop's palace has also been recovered.[21] Rocque's plan of the incomplete enclosure is suggestive, and confirms its location, as the more southerly, and incomplete of the two joined enclosures in the eighteenth-century city (fig. 11.34). So does the surviving building, and more recent town plans, which means that no new information, over and above that to be found in later maps and in the extant buildings, can be gleaned from the 1756 map in this regard. As noted by Simpson,[22] Rocque recorded an 'Old Castle' on the opposite side of Kevin's Street (just west of Cabbage Garden Lane), but there is no suggestion that this was in any way related to the episcopal palace complex.

The priory of All Hallows Simpson has also had some success at Trinity College, where excavation, combined with interpretation of the Hatfield and Thomas Dineley drawings, and other evidence, suggest that in 1756 something survived of the north range of the original medieval cloister upon which the

---

21 Danielle O'Donovan, 'English patron, English building? The importance of St Sepulchre's archiepiscopal palace, Dublin' in Seán Duffy (ed.), *Medieval Dublin IV* (Dublin, 2003), pp 253–78; Simpson, 'Fifty years', pp 78–9. 22 Simpson, 'Archaeological remains', p. 294. 23 Linzi Simpson, 'The priory of All Hallows and Trinity College

later college quadrangle was founded. This confirms that the fully enclosed quadrangular plan south of the then chapel, as represented on Rocque, was associated with, if not entirely coterminus with, the earlier monastic enclosure.[23]

St Thomas' Abbey   Walsh, at St Thomas' Abbey, found a portion of the south wall of the monastic church.[24] But this fragment as yet provides no convincing starting point from which a putative monastic enclosure might in part at least match Rocque's topography, although the general layout of the precinct has been overlaid by Walsh on a series of maps including Rocque's.[25] All of this is not to say that the representation by Rocque of the street pattern in the area is flawed. Great destruction and robbing out of monastic masonry took place and some new street patterns must have emerged. We will know better, perhaps, if excavations at St Thomas' Abbey are advanced.

The hospital of St John the Baptist   Another monastic house that disappeared under later buildings is the hospital of St John the Baptist (Fratres Cruciferi), founded before 1188 by Ailred Palmer, just outside (west) of Newgate, on the north side of Thomas Street.[26] The site is now occupied by the National College of Art and Design (formerly the John's Lane distillery), and the great Pugin and Ashlin designed Catholic church of SS Augustine and John, begun in 1860 and completed by William Hague in 1895.[27] Excavations in 1995 found burials from the medieval cemetery and a mill-race to the north of the site of the present art college, but no medieval monastic buildings.[28] The precinct of the abbey was defined by Thomas Street to the south, the city wall to the east, Croker's Lane (Mullinahack) to the north and some fields on the west.[29] However, McNeill also suggested that the precinct was defined by the boundary lines between the parish of St James and that of St Audoen,[30] which, according to the Ordnance Survey maps, reaches further north to a laneway not named on Rocque, approximately 90m north of Mullinahack. This possibly extended precinct encompasses a convent, labelled as 'Nunry', which

Dublin: recent archaeological discoveries' in Seán Duffy (ed.), *Medieval Dublin III* (Dublin, 2002), pp 195–236; see also her essay in the present volume.   **24** Claire Walsh, 'Archaeological excavations at the abbey of St Thomas the Martyr, Dublin' in Seán Duffy (ed.), *Medieval Dublin I* (Dublin, 2000), pp 185–202, fig. 1.   **25** Walsh, 'Archaeological excavations at the abbey of St Thomas', figs 2–4.   **26** Grace O'Keeffe, 'The hospital of St John the Baptist in medieval Dublin: functions and maintenance' in Seán Duffy (ed.), *Medieval Dublin IX* (Dublin, 2009), pp 166–82; Gwynn and Hadcock, *Medieval religious houses*, p. 212; Simpson 'Fifty years', p. 86.   **27** Dictionary of Irish Architecture (www.dia.ie), accessed 6 June 2013. **28** Simpson, 'Archaeological remains', p. 29, referring to Linzi Simpson, 'Excavations at the National College of Art and Design, Dublin 2. Licence 95E045 (unpublished report submitted to the former Dúchas now National Monuments and Architectural Protection Division, and the National Museum in May 1996).   **29** Charles McNeill, 'Hospital of S. John without the New Gate, Dublin', *JRSAI*, 15:1 (1990), 58–64 at 59–60.   **30** McNeill, 'Hospital of S. John', p. 60.

11.35 Convent or
'Nunry', north of
Mullinahack, as shown
on Rocque's *Exact
Survey* (1756).

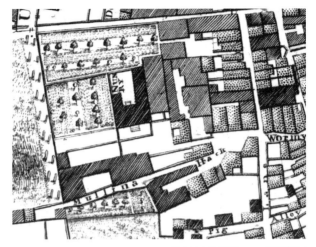

11.36 'Iohns Castle' in
the location of the
former Hospital
(Priory) of St John the
Baptist, Thomas Street,
as shown on Rocque's
Exact Survey (1756).

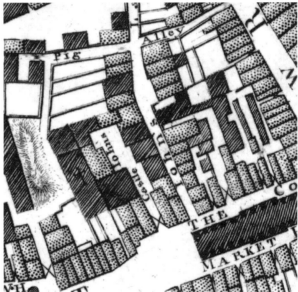

is shown by Rocque to have been set within cultivated grounds (fig. 11.35). Little is known about this convent, but it may be an institutional, if not a physical, survival from the medieval hospital.[31]

Nothing resembling the usual complex of church and cloister of this monastic hospital suggests itself in Rocque's plan (fig. 11.36). A Catholic church, built in 1748,[32] whose long rectangular plan is oriented north–south, is distinguished on Rocque by a simple cross symbol. The church has been built

31 The hospital was only finally closed in 1666: Lennon, *Dublin Part II*, p. 33.   32 Pearson, *Heart of Dublin*, pp 196–7.

11.37 St John's Tower, Thomas Street, as depicted by Gabriel Beranger. Royal Irish Academy, 3C30, no. 78.

to adjoin a square building that Rocque identifies as John's Castle ('Iohns Castle'). This is no doubt the same building as Beranger recorded in his *c.*1780 drawing[33] of St John's Tower, 'taken from a waste ground in the rear which affords the best view' (fig. 11.37).[34] This has all the appearance of a medieval church tower. The contemporary record states that 'the church was thrown down' at the Dissolution but, in contradictory fashion, that the whole site, including 'church, belfry and cemetery', was granted to farm to Edmund Redman in 1539.[35] It is probable that the tower depicted by Beranger and

33 Peter Harbison, *William Burton Conyngham and his circle of antiquarian artists* (New Haven and London, 2012), cat. 99.   **34** Royal Irish Academy, MS 3C30, 78; a separate note in Beranger's hand, in the margin of the drawing, states that the tower was 'taken down in 1800'.   **35** N.B. White (ed.), *Extents of Irish monastic possessions, 1540–1, from manuscripts in the Public Record Office, London* (Dublin, 1943), pp 55–6.

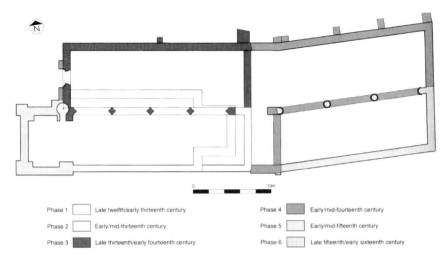

11.38 Schematic plan of St Audoen's Church from Mary McMahon (ed.), *St Audoen's church, Cornmarket, Dublin: archaeology and architecture* (Dublin, 2006).

Rocque represented the belfry in question. However, we cannot say from which angle Beranger recorded this image, or whether the modest single-storey pantile-roofed building in front of it represents the eighteenth-century church, as it may do. A number of substantial coursed masonry walls are also shown. It is possible that these were remnants of walls of the original monastic enclosure. One of these, on the right foreground, is buttressed by timber trusses against an adjoining building, perhaps suggesting a precocious example of the conservation of medieval fabric.

Churches
St Audoen's On a smaller scale, at the level of individual church buildings, there is one church in the city, St Audoen's, of which a great deal of medieval fabric still survives. We are quite clear about how the building was aligned in Rocque's time, as well as now. This is where the very quickly sketched, and sometimes slightly careless, aspect of the *Exact Survey* can come into play (fig. 11.25C). Subtleties of alignment, as captured in Mary McMahon's recent work on the church (fig. 11.38),[36] such as the canted portion of the later medieval eastern extensions, are completely overlooked by Rocque. The crowded nature of the abutting properties is some excuse for his not getting the survey right. But this suggests a reluctance on his part to overly scrutinize the backlands, and confirms to us again a lack of antiquarian curiosity in the execution and engraved rendering of the Dublin map at least, if not in the original surveying upon which this was based.

36 McMahon, *St Audoen's*, fig. 7.1.

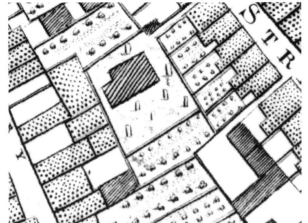

11.39 St Michael le Pole Church as shown on Rocque's *Exact Survey* (1756).

St Michael le Pole   Nor is Rocque at first encouraging in helping us to establish, or to at least corroborate what has been found in excavations,[37] regarding the nature of the tower of the possible twelfth-century St Michael le Pole's Church, located west of Great Ship Street (fig. 11.39). Two surviving drawings, one by an anonymous artist, dated to 1751,[38] and a well-known image by Beranger of 1766,[39] show a round tower associated with the building. However, both are ambiguous regarding the exact nature of the relationship of the tower to the building: whether it was attached, or somehow incorporated within the plan of the church, as foundations uncovered on site during excavations carried out in the 1980s seem to suggest.[40] The Beranger drawing could be interpreted to suggest that the tower was set behind the church, being either engaged to, or freestanding of, it. Close inspection suggests that bite-shaped indents depicted by the artist are his way of showing that the tower came up through the roof, and was thus built within the body of the plan of the church. This seems to be confirmed, if we are to believe it, by what must be a copy of Beranger's image in an album of drawings of 'antiquarian doorways, windows and towers from Irish scenes' (fig. 11.40).[41] In this later drawing (made in the 1840s), a smoother junction is drawn, showing more clearly the tower emerging from the roof. Of course, this drawing was made after the tower had been dismantled, although the medieval church building appears to have survived longer, being recorded as a school house on later maps. But the anonymous artist of these drawings demonstrated a breath of interest, if not expertise, in other buildings of a similar nature, including, among other drawings in the album, one of Dromiskin, Co. Louth, which at that time

37 Margaret Gowen, 'Excavations at the site of the church and tower of St Michael le Pole, Dublin' in Seán Duffy (ed.), *Medieval Dublin II* (Dublin, 2001), pp 13–52.   **38** Reproduced in Clarke, *Dublin Part I*, p. 16.   **39** Harbison, *William Burton Conyngham*, cat. 100.   **40** Gowen, 'Excavations at St Michael le Pole', pp 39–40.   **41** National Library of Ireland, MS TX2047.

11.40 St Michael le Pole Church, as depicted in an anonymous 'Sketchbook of antiquarian doorways, windows and towers from Irish scenes' (NLI TX 2047). Courtesy of the National Library of Ireland.

11.41 'Killossy [Killashee] Church', Co. Kildare, as depicted in NLI TX 2047. Courtesy of the National Library of Ireland.

involved an almost freestanding tower, attached to a small vernacular thatched cottage. More interesting in regard to the Dublin example is the drawing of a tower at 'Killossy [Killashee], Co. Kildare', in which a round tower emerged from a two-storey gabled square-planned tower, which was in turn attached to the gable of what must previously have been the nave of a church, but was by then reduced to a small blunted cottage building (fig. 11.41). While Rocque's map image of the St Michael le Pole church plan is not terribly illuminating, it is nevertheless likely to be an accurate enough summary of the footprint of the building, in which indeed the round tower was enclosed among walls, and hence not legible at this level.

St Michael's, High Street　　Rocque also recorded the outline of St Michael's Church, High Street, with its cemetery directly to the north (fig. 11.42). The church was to the south-west of Christ Church Cathedral, in the location of the present Synod Hall, constructed in the 1870s by G.E. Street. However, the church had been rebuilt in 1670, and only the fifteenth-century tower was preserved, as it is still.[42] Rocque's map is perhaps useful in indicating the possible footprint of the earlier building, although if we are to go by his recording of St Audoen's we might content ourselves with its inclusion and broad positioning, and not overly rely on Rocque's map in this case for its exact extent, shape or orientation.

Other churches　　Although St Bridget's Church (*c.*AD1000) is one of the earliest foundations in the city, the church that is illustrated on Rocque had been rebuilt by William Robinson in 1683–5.[43] We cannot say with any certainty what relationship Robinson's building, as recorded on Rocque and on later maps – St Bridget's was not demolished until the building of the Iveagh Trust flats in the late nineteenth century[44] – had with its medieval predecessor. The graveyard is also illustrated on Rocque's map, and some sense of how it and the church related to the street can be seen. Many other medieval churches were also rebuilt in the seventeenth century, and unless we can be certain that the same footprint was used in the subsequent build, Rocque's map is not much help in establishing the nature or extent of the earlier building. St John's was rebuilt in 1681, St Michan's in 1686, St Catherine's extended in 1696, St Nicholas Within and St James', in 1707, St Kevin's rebuilt in 1717 and St Werburgh's *c.*1719. St Peter's and St Stephen's churches had both been demolished before the eighteenth century.[45]

---

42 Simpson, 'Archaeological remains', p. 197.　　**43** TCD MS 1476; British Library MS Eg 1772 f 120; Irish Architectural Archive, Edward McParland files, Acc. 2008/44, Index Cards, 'Dublin, St Bride's Church'.　　**44** Simpson, 'Archaeological remains', p. 146. **45** Lennon, *Dublin Part II*, pp 22–3.

11.42 St Michael's
Church, High Street, as
shown on Rocque's
Exact Survey
(1756).

11.43 Thomas Street
burgage plots as
shown on Rocque's
Exact Survey
(1756).

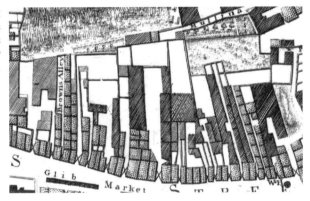

Street network

Whatever of Rocque's sometimes uneven record of individual buildings, it must be emphasized just how important his map is as a record of the city streets, their complex geometrical shapes and interrelationships. These early modern streets, as depicted on Rocque, are replete with evidence as to the spatial format of the former medieval city. Certain excavations, such as Simpson's in South Great George's Street at the corner of Stephen Street, have found that the early medieval street pattern and house alignments match very closely to the pattern, if not the exact boundaries, on Rocque.[46] The permanency of curtilage across the centuries is not unexpected. The characteristic burgage-plot pattern to be found in the long rectangular plots at the north side of Thomas Street as far as Mullinahack, for example, is a telling survival in the eighteenth-century plan of early Anglo-Norman commercial

46 Simpson, 'John Rocque's map: a modern source', pp 149–50.

11.44 Aungier Street enclosure as shown on Rocque's *Exact Survey* (1756).

expansion west of the newly developing city in the late twelfth century
(fig. 11.43). However, without excavation confirmation, we can only speculate
wisely about which house plots delineated on Rocque are likely to represent
exact medieval origins. The street patterns are altogether sounder. Kinks,
swellings, turns, openings, back lanes and alleys are convincingly captured on
Rocque's *Exact Survey*, and if the surviving eighteenth-century boundaries at
that time matched the earlier medieval ones, as so many did, then Rocque must
surely have got these right in the main. Although surviving in the modern
topography, and so to be found on modern maps, it is the crispness and clarity
of its pattern of negative space on Rocque which makes the plausible
ecclesiastical oval of Aungier Street stand out so clearly (fig. 11.44).[47]

47 H.B. Clarke, 'The topographical development of early medieval Dublin', *JRSAI*, 107
(1977), 29–51.

Based on a comparison between Lennon's and Clarke's two volumes of the Irish Historic Towns Atlas volumes on Dublin, there are up to one hundred streets or laneways listed on Rocque that have a history prior to 1610 at least.[48] In her 1979 'topographical analysis', Anngret Simms,[49] nodding to M.R.G. Conzen,[50] has very subtly combed through Rocque for clues to the shapes of the earlier city, much of which informs the debate and growing understanding of that city among archaeologists and historians since then.

CONCLUSION

Thus, while Rocque might fail in recording some individual buildings accurately, he has mastered the pattern of the city, to a level of interlocking complexity never before seen for Dublin, or possibly for any other city. Also, as in the case of the surviving belfry of the hospital of St John the Baptist, or the sets of steps leading from Cook Street up a steep hill and through the city wall, or the precise nature of the contrasting building patterns on either side of the city walls at Back Lane, and at the portal at St Nicholas Gate, Rocque's is nevertheless a kind of fabric census, despite the omissions. If we allow that the detail is more reliable as part of a larger matrix of shapes and topographical relationships, than for the exact form of any single element, then Rocque's map, however stretched and distorted, captured the very pattern of this modern city. To the extent that the medieval city survived within eighteenth-century Dublin, then that medieval Dublin may be recovered on Rocque.

---

48 Clarke, *Dublin Part I*, pp 12–16; Lennon, *Dublin Part II*, pp 10–22. **49** Simms, 'Medieval Dublin'. **50** M.R.G. Conzen, 'The use of town plans in the study of urban history' in H.J. Dyos (ed.), *The study of urban history* (London, 1968), pp 113–30.

The priory of All Hallows and the Old College: archaeological investigations in Front Square, Trinity College Dublin[1]

LINZI SIMPSON

INTRODUCTION

The paths

In the summer of 2011, a network of wheelchair-accessible paths was laid at the western end of Trinity College Dublin, stretching from Front Gate in the west, as far east as the Old Library and Library Square (figs 12.1–12.3, 12.15, 12.19, 12.21, 12.26, 12.28; Simpson 2011). The paths were designed to sit flush with the existing surface and this required the removal of the cobbles along their route, for which planning permission was granted (Planning ref. 2269/08) (fig. 12.4). The cobbled surface was not an original feature as such, having been relaid in the late 1970s on a mass concrete base. Some of the new paths were laid directly on this concrete foundation and therefore did not require the removal of the concrete or any further excavation. However, other paths did require deeper excavation to accommodate a network of plastic conduits designed to house fibre-optic cables, which will service the west end of the college in the future. As these additional works necessitated excavation to an average depth of 60cm, this was carried out under archaeological supervision by the writer under licence (03E0152 ext.), as part of the general college policy of monitoring all excavations within the grounds.

The archaeological site of Trinity College

The western end of Trinity College has long been identified as an archaeological 'hot-spot' for two reasons (fig. 12.5). Firstly, it is the known location of the medieval priory of All Hallows. Secondly, it is also the site of 'Queen Elizabeth's College of the Holy and Undivided Trinity, near Dublin', founded in 1592.[2] The Old College quadrangle is known to have been located

1 I would like to thank the contractor, Mark Flynn, and his team (Tommy, Joe and Myles) of Michael Duffy & Sons Construction Ltd, who greatly facilitated the archaeological monitoring programme and provided additional help during the exposure of walls and other features. The writer also acknowledges the help and guidance of the staff of the Director of Buildings Office, Trinity College Dublin.   2 A previous essay by the writer, which appeared in Seán Duffy (ed.), *Medieval Dublin III* (Dublin, 2002), pp 197–236, details the history of both institutions and should be read in conjunction with this essay. See also Budd 2001 for detailed information about the Old College.

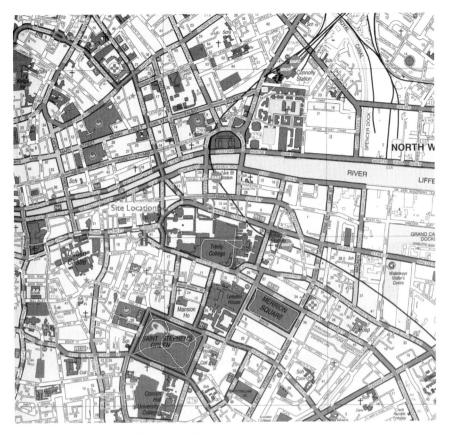

12.1 Site location: Trinity College, Dublin.

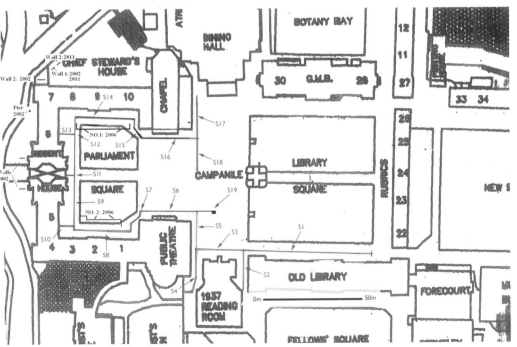

12.2 SECTIONS 1–18.

12.3 Front Square, from the south-east.

12.4 General works.

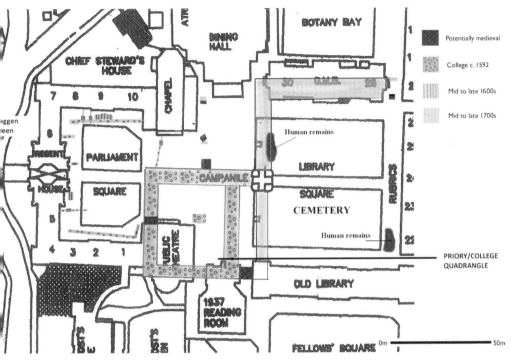

12.5 Summary of findings.

in the eastern half of Front Square, the north-east corner of the quadrangle marked roughly by the Campanile or bell-tower. This site may also have been the location of the monastic quadrangle, the documentary sources inferring the reuse of certain priory buildings in the construction of the college, particularly the steeple of the church in the north-east corner of the north range, appearing in the cartographic sources of the college as an octagonal tower (Budd 2001, 38–42).

The Old College quadrangle, recorded on various maps of Dublin (figs 12.6–12.7, 12.9–12.11, 12.13–12.14), remained at the core of the college complex until the mid-eighteenth century, when ambitious plans to open up the western college frontage and create sweeping open spaces resulted in the gradual demolition of what had come before (see McParland 1978). The result was the creation of the monumental vista of the Front Square we know today. What had previously been the Parliament Square (the eastern end of Front Square), was already annotated 'Old Square' on Rocque's map in 1756 (fig. 12.13), despite the fact that the original Old College quadrangle was still partially intact, a testimony to the complicated and convoluted building history of the college from the sixteenth century onwards.

The only clue to the college's past life as a monastic house and the location of the quadrangle is to be found in Library Square, where excavations for services in 2002 along the western edge (east of the campanile) exposed the remains of five medieval skeletons, approximately 1m below present ground level, with additional disarticulated remains in the south-east corner, close to the Old Library (fig. 12.14). These must be the mortal remains of canons of the priory of All Hallows buried in their cemetery, on the eastern side of the monastic quadrangle (Simpson 2002, 229–33).

Summary findings

The construction of the paths in Front Square developed into a major archaeological watching-brief, which produced very significant findings, high-lighting the importance of Front Square as a large archaeological site, not only in terms of the heritage of the college itself but also the wider city of Dublin (fig. 12.15). The most impressive finds were the significant foundations of both the twelfth-century monastic priory and the original brick college quadrangle, dated *c.*1592, positioned, in some instances, just 30cm below the modern cobbled surface (fig. 12.5). The presence of these foundations finally allows us to fix the position of the Old College with some degree of accuracy within the modern university landscape, as first suggested by the cartographic sources. Most importantly, the west range was found to be possibly medieval, con-firming that the priory and Old College site are likely to be one and the same.

Discoveries were not confined to the priory/Old College quadrangle. The sustained building activity from the early seventeenth century onwards, which saw the erection of various ranges to the north and north-west of the quadrangle, could also be traced in the trenches as far west as the present western frontage of the college (fig. 12.5). These presented as a myriad of structures including walls, drains and brick surfaces, along with various pits and dump layers, all of which revealed the extent of the 'Great Court' in the sixteenth and seventeenth centuries. The dump layers are particularly interesting as they represent the refuse from the college inhabitants themselves and contain a wealth of artefactual material dating from the late sixteenth and seventeenth centuries.

The massive demolition project began with the reconstruction and refurbishment of the western frontage in the second half of the eighteenth century, hand-in-hand with a building programme, the aim of which was to expand Parliament Square, enclosing it with a new east range (which was never built) to form a monumental square flanked by suitably impressive buildings. This could only be achieved by sweeping away all that had gone before, including the quadrangle core of the Old College, which was still partially in position in 1756. This ambitious project was carried out gradually but persistently, and eventually involved the complete demolition of the Old College quadrangle and the later north-west range along with other buildings, including the west range of Library Square. This demolition was carried out in conjunction with a general infilling programme at this end of the college, which involved raising the ground level right across the college. The infill was deepest towards the western frontage (1.1m) in what had formerly been the riverbed of the Steine, but also extending southwards to include the Provost's Garden, where it was a similar depth. This material, a mixture of demolition debris and domestic refuse, has left a distinct and massive archaeological footprint that is identifiable all across the college (including College Park), which has the potential to provide information, not only about buildings and the building materials used from the twelfth century onwards but also about the college's inhabitants, from the ceramics, glass, faunal remains and other household detritus they threw out as rubbish.

The construction project
The new paths extend around Front Square, along the southern side of the Library Square (to the north of the Old Library) and into Fellows Square on the south, their geometric pattern designed to reduce the impact on the symmetry of the college buildings (fig. 12.2). The works entailed the removal of a 2.5m-wide strip of cobbles to an initial depth of 20cm, down onto the concrete base, which formed the foundation for the cobbles when they were relaid in the 1970s by ANCO (forerunners of FÁS). This concrete varied in depth from 20 to 40cm, but the strategy was to leave it *in situ* where a fibre-optic service trench was not required, if the concrete was deemed robust enough to support the new paths. The works were carried out under Mark Flynn of Michael Duffy & Sons Ltd, who were responsible for the excavation of the service trenches and the laying of the new paths.

Where trenches were required, these were generally narrow (between 70 and 80cm) and were excavated mechanically through the concrete base, in the centre of the trench to a depth of 60cm. A series of manholes was also constructed at various junctions, usually measuring 1m square by 90cm in depth.

BRIEF HISTORICAL BACKGROUND

The priory of All Hallows
Trinity College stands on the site of the medieval priory of All Hallows, in the eastern suburb of the Hiberno-Norse walled town. Founded by the infamous king of Leinster Diarmait Mac Murchada (Dermot McMurrough) in 1166, it pre-dated the Anglo-Norman invasion of Ireland by just three years. The priory was positioned in the strategic eastern suburb of the medieval city (figs 12.2, 12.13, 12.15), known as the Hoggen Green, which appears to have been the most important space outside the fortress in both the Viking and Hiberno-Norse periods and was a focal point for the pre-Anglo-Norman inhabitants of Dublin, its importance heightened by the fact that there was a main landing stage on the River Liffey at a place called the 'Long stone' of the Steine somewhere close to Pearse Street Garda Station to the north of the modern college (Simpson 2002, 201).

The Anglo-Norman takeover

In 1170 the Anglo-Normans took Dublin after landing at the Steine and expelling the ruling Hiberno-Norse dynasty after a bloody battle. The priory of All Hallows, founded by the very man responsible for the invasion, survived this takeover and a period of increased prosperity and expansion followed. The house, which followed the Augustinian rule, appears to have enjoyed royal favour, receiving a substantial amount of property after the invasion, as did other houses in Dublin. The monastic complex occupied a large site and, at the time of the Dissolution of the monasteries in the sixteenth century, its property at Dublin included twelve acres of meadow, nine acres of pasture and seven orchards, all probably in the general vicinity. Additional lands held and controlled by the canons amounted to 2,267 acres, a considerable holding by any standards (Simpson 2002, 203).

The College of the Holy and Undivided Trinity, near Dublin

The priory of All Hallows was dissolved in 1538, but the sources suggest that the precinct continued to be occupied and the complex was certainly not demolished and plundered at this time, the fate of some of the other monasteries in Dublin. This is likely to be because the priory was granted to the mayor and commonalty of Dublin, rather than an individual, and the buildings were considered valuable assets. This is confirmed in the sources: in 1570, there is a reference to the 'wester stone house' with a vault (north of the quadrangle), the steeple, the cloister, the vestry, the Great Bawn (precursor of Parliament Square), a tower over the gate adjoining Hoggen Green (precursor of Front Gate) along with various gardens and orchards (Budd 2001, 31).

On 21 July 1592, the corporation granted this valuable site to Adam Loftus, archbishop of Dublin, for a university, which was subsequently called 'Queen Elizabeth's College of the Holy and Undivided Trinity, near Dublin'. Work began soon after on the new construction, the plan of which survives as a painting held in the home of the marquess of Salisbury at Hatfield in Hertfordshire (fig. 12.6). This depicts an elegant new quadrangle, faced in stone in the exterior and brick in the interior with a courtyard on the western side, facing the city (for the history, see Simpson 2002, 201–7). The college was subsequently built along the lines of the Hatfield plan in *c.*1592, evolving slowly into the complete quadrangle as the south range had still not been completed two years later. Nearly fifty years later, in *c.*1640, work had begun on a new quadrangle, to be modelled on the old one but located to the north-west, in the western bawn.

A second vigorous building programme was initiated in the 1680s, which involved rebuilding some of the main buildings of the quadrangle including the hall and chapel, and the development of the western frontage along with plans for a new Front Gate in 1699. The focus at this end of the college was

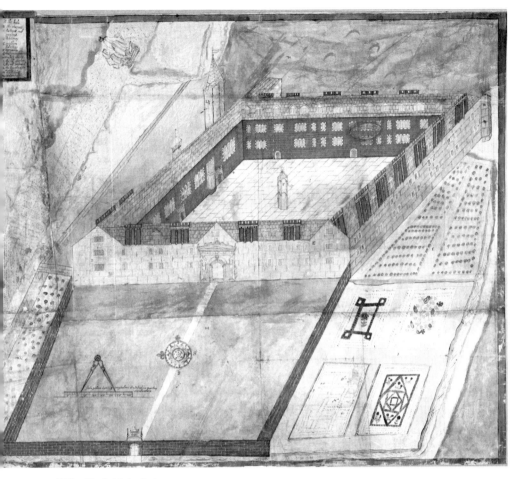

12.6 The Hatfield depiction, *c*.1592.

reflective of the fact that it formed the grand main entrance, facing onto the city, as had the medieval priory before it. Regent House or Front Gate opened onto College Green and Dame Street, the latter of which was a major thoroughfare connecting the college with the city from earliest times.

Expansion was always a priority for the college authorities, who engaged in persistent lobbying, not just of successful former scholars but also of the government of the day. This began to pay off in the early eighteenth century, when sums of money were made available to finance works on the development of Parliament Square and especially the reconstruction of the western frontage. The result was the impressive and iconic Front Square, which emerged in the mid-eighteenth century, the newly created space in sharp contrast to the congested complex of old and decaying buildings it replaced.

As with all such works in the pre-machine era, however, the transformation was not as complete as one might expect, as the demolished remains were simply spread over the below-ground foundations and subsequently cobbled.

Hatfield, c.1592 (fig. 12.6)
The earliest representation of the college is the colour perspective view, now in Hatfield, dated *c*.1592, although this is thought to represent a plan rather than an actual depiction as the literary sources record that the south range had not been built by this date. It is a beautiful illustration of the college, depicting an elegant quadrangle of attractive bright red/orange in the interior with a cut stone grey (limestone?) exterior. The extensive use of brick in the new college is very evident and this is one of the earliest examples in Dublin, its extensive usage confirmed by the description of the college by William Travers (provost between 1594 and 1598) in which he tells us that the

> college was a quadrant of brick three storeys high and on every side within the court it is 120 feet broad, the west side which is of chambers and the north side wherein are the chapell, hall, buttery and kitchen, are orderly finished. The other two sides are only walles saving some little begginninge of chambers which fore want of further means is yet unperfect (Mahaffy 1904, 82–6).

The view is taken from the west, looking towards the main entrance in the west range, and the college is flanked by formal gardens to the south and the River Liffey to north. The major feature is evidently the quadrangle, with a large courtyard to the front (west) and this can be compared directly to the later Thomas Dineley depiction of 1681 (fig. 12.10).

The east range   The position of the east range of the college was identified during the investigations and there is a good view of it in the Hatfield plan. This range was built *de novo* and is two storeys with twelve dormers windows. It appears to be divided into five blocks, judging by the five brick chimney stacks on the roof set on the exterior edge (Dineley depicts six: fig. 12.10). The northern two have seven chimneys apiece, while the remaining three are rendered differently, with perhaps only five chimneys. The pitch of the roof is very steep and the windows are long and narrow, in groups of three and four and singletons. Access is through two narrow round-headed inset doorways at ground-floor level, but with no corresponding windows at that level. The later Dineley depiction suggests that there is a third doorway at the southern end, just out of view.

The north range   The north range is thought to have incorporated earlier monastic buildings, the hall at the western end and the church at the eastern, the latter denoted by the belfry. The belfry is rectangular but free-standing and the projection eastwards beyond the east range must be the nave, as it is built of stone and is wider than the brick buildings, with a less steeply pitched roof. The position of the east range must have been influenced by the fact that the church was in this location and perhaps by the necessity of avoiding a chancel or transept. The tower is shown as narrow and rectangular, with a crenellated parapet and is probably a fifteenth-century addition to the church, as was common at this time. It is not clear from this depiction whether or not the church is attached to the college quadrangle at all.

The interior of the range is brick-faced and very similar to the east range but with some differences. There is only one level of windows shown and no dormer windows, while the two doorways also differ, having elaborate and ornate door surrounds. The eastern window is flanked on the west by what might be a projecting semi-hexagonal window. This may be connected to a projecting smaller tower or spire on the northern side of the roof, which projects beyond the roof line, similar to the belfry tower, although the Dineley depiction places this feature further west over the western doorway (fig. 12.10). These features may be associated with the dining hall known to have been at this end of the north range. The western end of the range is similar to the east range and has two chimney stacks set closely together.

The west range   The west range was the main frontage of the college and the investigations suggest that part of this might have been reused from the monastic period. The exterior is of stone and there are two gables on either end, both of which have three sets of windows. The range has four chimney stacks and a hint of dormer windows (confirmed in the Dineley depiction, fig. 12.10), but the main feature is an elaborate gate with an ornate surround (arched with a prominent key-stone), which is centrally placed in the range. This led into a substantial front courtyard, which is surrounded by a brick precinct wall. A smaller gate within the precinct wall provides access to Hoggen Green and the road (Dame Street) that led to the city. There are formal gardens lying to the south of the main front courtyard, with what appears to be the Steine river, orientated north–south. This river originally ran just past the priory but had evidently been culverted by this date.

The south range   The south range is similar to the west range – two storeys with similar windows and with dormer windows in the attic. There are seven tall chimney stacks, however, and a curious external semi-octagonal projecting tower at the eastern end. This tower was evidently accessible, as there are two staggered windows, but the function is difficult to determine. Its presence may

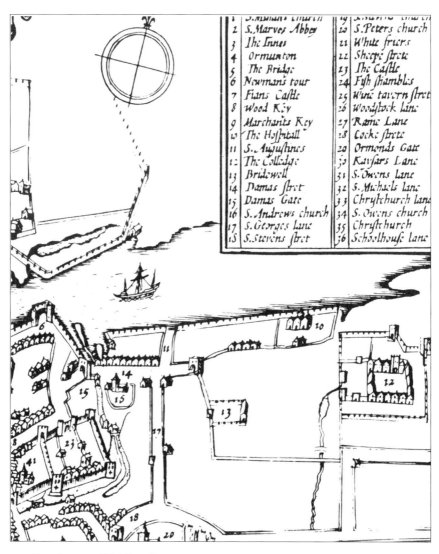

1 S. Miahans church
2 S. Marves Abbey
3 The Innes
4 Ormunton
5 The Bridge
6 Newmans tour
7 Fians Castle
8 Wood Key
9 Marchants Key
10 The Hospitall
11 S. Augustines
12 The Colledge
13 Bridewell
14 Damas street
15 Damas Gate
16 S. Andrews church
17 S. Georges Lane
18 S. Stevens street
19 S.Isuri's chuch
20 S. Peters church
21 White friers
22 Sheepe strete
23 The Castle
24 Fish shambles
25 Wine tavern street
26 Woodstock Lane
27 Rame Lane
28 Cocke strete
29 Ormonds Gate
30 Kaisars Lane
31 S. Owens Lane
32 S. Michaels Lane
33 Chrystchurch Lane
34 S. Owens church
35 Chrystchurch
36 Schoolhouse Lane

12.7 Speed's map of Dublin, 1610.

suggest that part of this end of the range also incorporated earlier buildings, the anomalies indicative of an earlier build.

Speed, 1610 (fig. 12.7)
Speed's map of Dublin, dated 1610, also depicts the college and the quadrangle set within a walled precinct and various features can be identified, which correlate with both Dineley (fig. 12.10) and Hatfield (fig. 12.6), suggesting a certain degree of local knowledge. The gables of the south range are visible, as

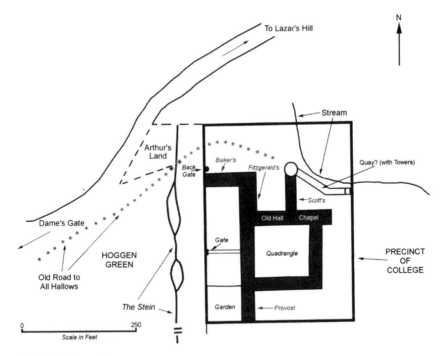

12.8 Mc Carthy, *c.*1640.

are the doorways and two storeys in the north range. The tower is also shown, as part of the north range and with a doorway. There is what appears to be the gable end of a structure orientated north–south (a chancel or transept) with a high roof (the nave?) running east–west behind it. There is, however, no indication that the north range extends beyond the east range, as depicted in Hatfield (*c.*1592) (fig. 12.10) and Bernard de Gomme (1673) (fig. 12.9).

Another feature to note is the Steine river and what appears to be a pond (a millpond?) outside the western precinct wall. This is also depicted on Hatfield (fig. 12.6), although the pond is positioned further south. On Speed, the river flows into the college via what is now Front Gate and then promptly disappears, although this is not shown on Hatfield, perhaps reflecting an intention to culvert it, which was duly carried out. The main gate is also flanked by two large rectangular buildings, one on either side. Also of note is the fact that the main college quadrangle is within a much larger precinct likely to correspond with the boundaries of the medieval priory, with a separate walled bawn in the north-west corner of the college, perhaps the one referred to as the 'western bawn' in the documentary sources.

The northern precinct wall was a major structure that contained at least two square towers in the north-eastern corner (probably to the north-east of Botany

Bay), but these are not depicted in subsequent sources, although they are likely to have been medieval. The tower or belfry can be seen in the north range along with a walled bawn on the western side, which formed the main frontage of the college, as it does today.

Expansion *c*.1640 (fig. 12.8)   A general expansion of the precinct began in *c*.1640 when the college authorities decided to expand and build a new quadrangle to the north-west of the main 'Great Court'. They were mindful of the architectural heritage of the college even at this early date, and the new buildings were to have stone facing to the exterior and brick to the interior, in keeping with the style of the old quadrangle (McParland 2001, 143). A new range, orientated north–south, was added just north of the steeple tower and this was called the 'Scott's building' (possibly incorporating a medieval 'building with the vault' in this location), while the west range of the quadrangle was extended at the northern end – the new build known as 'Fitzgerald's'. A corresponding additional range was also added onto the southern end of the west range (Mc Carthy n.d., 6).

The main focus, however, was the construction of a new range, and partial funding for this scheme was received in 1638 when George Baker died, leaving £500 for the 'building of a new quadrangle' (ibid.). Work began on a new north range (orientated east–west) known as the 'Baker buildings', which, with the FitzGerald building, created the beginnings of the new quadrangle lying to the north-west of the original quadrangle (the northern end of Parliament Square) (Simpson 2002, 223). The result was the beginnings of the formation of the western frontage, at the northern end.

De Gomme, 1678 (fig. 12.9)

The expansion can be seen on the de Gomme's map of 1678, which shows the new developments including the Baker, Fitzgerald and Scott buildings, the latter shown attached onto the steeple on the northern side. The main entrance at the western end of the north range is shown and the two blocks at the eastern end of the north range, the chapel, are significantly wider than the rest. The projection eastwards of the north range beyond the line of the east range is also evident and the internal courtyard is divided into four quadrants, as it is in the later Dineley drawing (fig. 12.10).

The extended western frontage at the southern end (towards what would later be the Provost's House) is something of a puzzle, although it may be represented by the large gable depicted by Dineley in 1681 (fig. 12.10). Alternatively, it may have been a short-lived development. To the west, the western court does not look very big, relative to the quadrangle, and a very simple western frontage is depicted with no buildings or discernible gate tower, the main entrance defined simply by two parallel walls, flanking the main path to the large entrance into the old quadrangle.

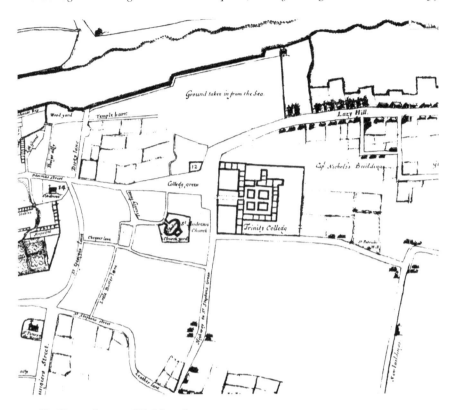

12.9 De Gomme's map of Dublin, 1673.

This important map also charts the major changes in the topography caused by the active reclamation along the northern boundary where the land is denoted as 'taken in from the sea'. The earlier precinct wall and towers of Speed's map (fig. 12.7) are gone and the boundary or precinct now appears much smaller. The land to the east of the college is laid out in fields.

Dineley, 1681 (fig. 12.10)
The Dineley depiction, executed three years later, indicates considerable new development; viewed from the west, this also provides considerable information about the original college quadrangle on the eve of a big building programme, which saw considerable expansion of the college precinct under two provosts, March and Humphries (McParland 2001, 144). The Dineley details correlate well with Hatfield, the ranges laid out around a central courtyard divided by paths and with the steeple in the north range very much in evidence. The general style of Hatfield is confirmed: solid buildings, three storeys in height with dormer windows and pointed gables in the west range. The east range has three round-headed entrances from the courtyard, with six

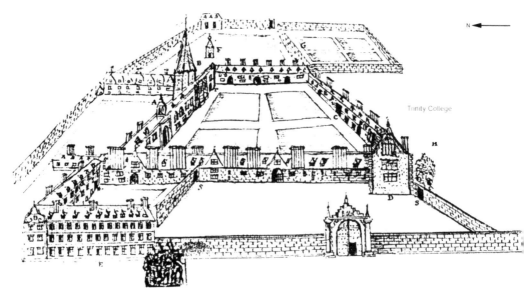

12.10 Dineley's sketch, 1681.

large chimney stacks and ten dormer windows with rectangular windows at
ground- and first-floor levels.

The south range is similar, but the north range is very different. The
octagonal tower is shown as integrated into the north range but on the
northern side, and therefore not fronting onto the courtyard as shown in Speed
(fig. 12.7). In addition, there is an attempt to present a projecting element of a
structure (with windows?) perhaps related to the church and corresponding to
the projection shown on Speed in the earlier map, which may have been part of
the church, perhaps a transept or chancel? The Dineley drawing also shows an
entrance into the courtyard on the eastern side, also depicted on de Gomme
with what appears to be a bell-tower or chimney, and this may be connected
with the hall and/or kitchen mentioned in the sources. A similar type of
structure can be identified in the Hatfield depiction (see above). The southern
end of the west range is also interesting, as this is portrayed as a substantial
gable, projecting from the main range, which is not represented on anything
gone before. This three-storeyed building is shown as dotted rather than being
of stylized block like the precinct wall, while the quoin stones are depicted as
rectangular blocks. It also has a large four-light window at the upper storeys.

The expansion of the college on the western side is also charted, giving flesh
to the buildings depicted by de Gomme (fig. 12.9). The buildings of the new
north-west range comprising the Baker's buildings, Radcliffe and Alexander
buildings are all shown in great detail but appear to be mislocated: presumably
the north range was further north than depicted, as portrayed on de Gomme.

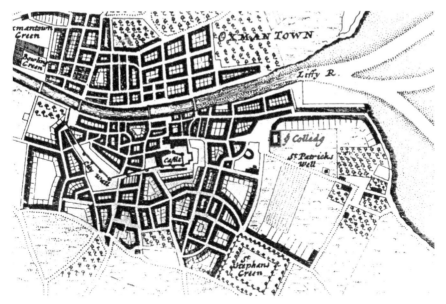

12.11 Pratt's map of Dublin, 1708.

But the detail it provides about the new north-west ranges is interesting. The north range consists of a tall austere three-storey building with dormers and what appears to be a curvilinear gable at the western end, similar to the Dutch gabled houses being built elsewhere in Dublin at this date. This range is relatively small, as it is only serviced by three chimney stacks. The new western frontage is a very striking building, as it is formed by a similar tall building, twelve bays wide, which is three storeys also and has dormer windows. Four chimney stacks service this building. The remainder of the western frontage is denoted by a well-built precinct wall and very ornate gate in the middle. Dineley also shows the beginnings of a third quadrangle, directly north of the old quadrangle and also depicted on de Gomme (fig. 12.9). This consists of two north–south ranges, built onto the northern side of the old quadrangle. The range at the western end (a continuation of the west range of the old quadrangle) must be a mistake, as this should be the continuation of the north-west range as depicted by de Gomme. It is shown as a small one-storey range with dormer windows and serviced by two chimney stacks, not extending as far as the northern precinct wall, while the east range is a far more substantial affair, showing a two-storeyed range with seven dormer windows and three narrow chimneys.

Dineley also depicts good detail of what was happening at the eastern end of the college on ground that was probably reclaimed from slob-land. The northern boundary wall has a diagonal orientation, which presumably reflects the similar orientation on the precinct wall depicted on Speed, dating from

1610, and in fact the rather squat building with two windows in the north-east corner may be the remains of the tower depicted on Speed also. The enclosed area must contain the medieval cemetery of the priory known to be located here and there is a pump-house or a well marked in the middle. A new walled area lies to the south and this was laid out in quadrants; evidently a garden.

Pratt, 1708 (fig. 12.11)

The documentary sources suggest that, by the late 1690s, another building programme was underway, which included laying plans for the greatest challenge to date, the creation of an imposing western front. The new gatehouse, the jewel in the crown, was measured in 1699 after a gift of money was received from Sir Michael Boyle, archbishop of Armagh (McParland 2001, 145). The hall was also repaired, the chapel having been extended and repaired previously in the 1680s. By the late 1690s, the north-west quadrangle was well developed and the gatehouse was in position (fig. 12.12). Curiously, Henry Pratt's highly stylized map of 1708 depicts the college quadrangle fronting directly onto Hoggen Green, with no evidence of the western bawn (fig. 12.11). While evidently inaccurate, this map does show the development of house plots along the northern boundary of the college, evidence of the rapid building programme in this area first recorded by de Gomme. Pratt also records the precinct of the college as it was then, with considerable land enclosed on the western side.

Developments by the mid-eighteenth century   By the early to mid-eighteenth century, there were great changes. The great library, one of the finest buildings in the college, finally opened in 1732 after a long building programme, from the conception of the project in 1684 and the laying of the foundations in 1712. Richard Castle's bell tower was also constructed in 1741 at what was originally the north-west corner of the quadrangle. Library Square, the east range of which (known as the Rubrics) was started in 1699, had the northern and west ranges added by *c.*1723, to be completed by the new library in 1732 (McParland 2001, 147). There was also a new dining hall in 1747, albeit generally unstable and eventually rebuilt by Hugh Darley twenty years later.

   Of the proposed new western frontage, there was little mention until the 1750s when monies were received from government to complete the project (McParland 2001, 161). Work began on the north range, and the original plan was to enclose Parliament Square to the east with a new range. Instead, the complete opposite was carried out and the decision was taken to create a new monumental space (Front Square) fronting onto the city. This, of course, involved the demolition of the congested Old College quadrangle and ancillary structures in what must have been a controversial but ambitious scheme. This

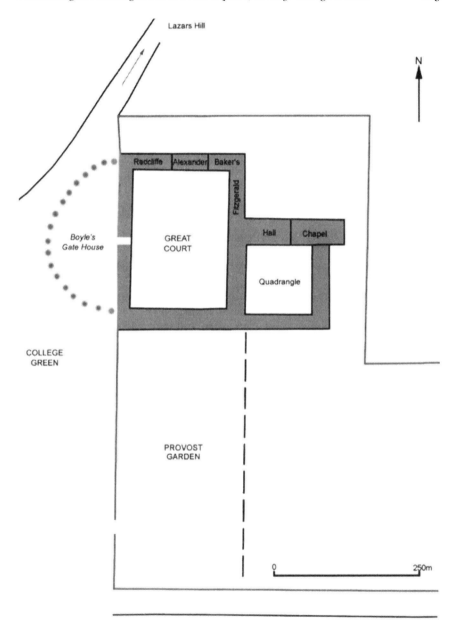

12.12 Mc Carthy, *c.*1697.

involved the demolition, not only of the college quadrangle, including the chapel and hall, but also Richard Castle's bell tower (1741–91), which had been built, badly as it turned out, at the north-west corner of the Old College

12.13 Rocque's map of Dublin, 1756.

quadrangle. The new space was created slowly, gobbling up all that had gone before including the west range of Library Square, but the result was the creation of the wide open majestic square now known as Front Square, the peace and tranquillity of which contrasts so dramatically with the bustling city, on entering through Front Gate (Regent House).

Rocque, 1756 (fig. 12.13)

As mentioned above, the period between Pratt in 1708 (fig. 12.11) and Rocque saw rapid expansion (McParland 1978, 2–9). The most obvious changes since Pratt depicted on Rocque's map, dated 1756, are the completed western 'Great Court', with the south and west ranges (but annotated, ironically, 'Old Square' by this date), and the completion of Library Square. Most importantly, this map provides a glimpse of the Old College quadrangle in tandem with the

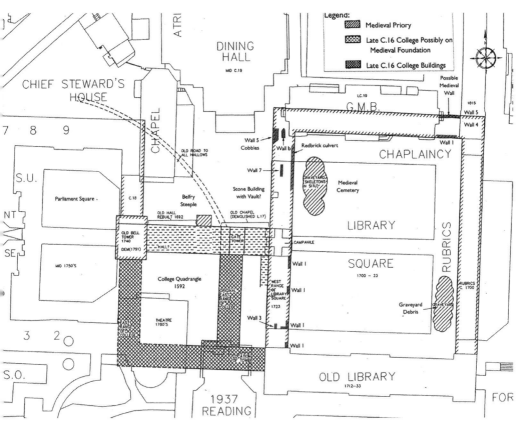

12.14 Findings from previous investigations (Simpson 2002).

newer buildings that would eventually replace it (fig. 12.14). By this date, the quadrangle had seen considerable alteration, namely the demolition of the iconic steeple only to be replaced, albeit further west, with Richard Castle's bell-tower, and the construction of the Public Theatre (Examination Hall).

But the original Old College quadrangle still dominates Rocque, clearly identifiable within all the new developments, the south range much wider than the others. It should also be noted that the west range was wider than the east range, perhaps related to the fact that this side may have incorporated earlier remains, as suggested in the monitoring programme (Wall 7: SECTION 7: figs 12.22, 12.26, 12.28: Wall 6: SECTION 6; fig. 12.20). The last stage was the demolition of the east range of Library Square, which created one sweeping vista on entry into the college via Front Gate, the view uninterrupted as far eastwards as the Rubrics. The symmetry involved in the new building, East Chapel and the Public Theatre, greatly enhanced this view, which was crowned by the Campanile. This radical new layout, however, which involved so much destruction, did owe something to the past of the college, the bell-tower marking the north-east corner of the original Old College and probably the priory of All Hallows, while Library Square defined the latter's cemetery.

THE MONITORING PROGRAMME

The trenches are arranged into sections in this essay (figs 12.2, 12.15, 12.19, 12.21, 12.26, 12.28: SECTIONS 1–18), and these generally run from east to west, from the Old Library to Front Gate and around East Chapel (easting 715962: northing 734108) (fig. 12.1). However, while they are presented in sequence for reasons of clarity, they were excavated at different times and the information reassembled. The first trenches (SECTION 1) extended along the northern side of the Old Library heading east, past the 1937 Reading Room (SECTIONS 2, 3, 4, 5), and the Public Theatre (SECTION 6, 7), Houses 1–5 (SECTIONS 8, 9, 10), past Front Gate (SECTION 11), Houses 6 and 7 (SECTIONS 12, 13), Houses 8, 9 and 10 (SECTIONS 14, 15), around the chapel (SECTION 16, 17) and across Front Square (SECTION 18). The other paths did not require ducts and were not excavated, the existing concrete bases being left *in situ*.

The general policy of 'preservation *in situ*' was adopted during the entire project, and the vast majority of the features were protected and left in position unless stated otherwise. However, investigations were generally limited to the development depth although some archaeological investigations were carried out in specific locations (Wall 7: SECTION 7, for instance), where the contractor's tight programme allowed it.

SECTION 1 (fig. 12.15)

This trench was located in the southern end of Library Square and was orientated east–west, running parallel to the Old Library and perpendicular to the Rubrics (1699). Previous investigations in this area established that Library Square was originally the graveyard attached to the medieval priory and that the size of the square was probably dictated by the size and position of this original cemetery (Simpson 2002, 229–30). As previously mentioned, the works in 1998 exposed the remains of human skeletal material in the south-east corner of Library Square, very close to the trench under discussion and lying approximately 1m below present ground level. To the north-west, the remains of five skeletons were found *in situ*, establishing that this represented a burial ground (fig. 12.14). The works under discussion, however, in SECTION 1, did not expose any burials, probably because the excavation was limited in depth to 60cm. However, brown undisturbed organic humic clay, identified as cemetery fill previously, was located just below the existing cobble bed. This suggests that human burials may survive in situ in this location, but at a lower level.

Library Square: west range: *c.*1700 (Walls 1, 2)   The foundations of the west wall of the west range of Library Square were located in the trench at the western end, and these were the same walls that were located in the monitoring programme in 1998 that lay further north, where they were found to stand to

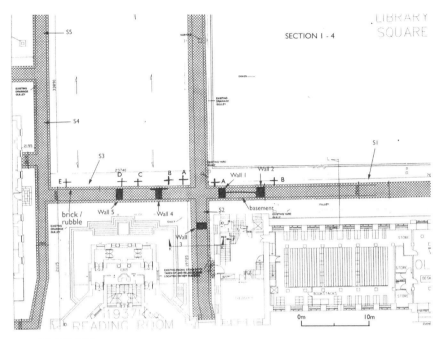

12.15 SECTIONS 1–4.

approximately 40cm (fig. 12.14: Simpson 2002, 231). Wall 1 was the eastern wall and this was a heavy and solidly built masonry wall, orientated north–south, which was 45cm below present ground level and measured 80cm in width by at least 25cm in height (fig. 12.16). It was constructed of limestone blocks, averaging 30 by 40cm, and was bonded with a distinctive white concrete-like mortar (with no visible inclusions) with a strongly mortared rubble core.

Wall 2 lay 6.2m west of Wall 1 and was almost identical in construction, measuring 78cm in width by at least 35cm in height. This wall also contained one fragment of dark red brick within its core, at the northern end.

Conclusion of SECTION 1   The discovery of the foundations was not unexpected in this location, and they are likely to be the continuation of the sections of wall uncovered in an investigation in 1998 (Simpson 2002). These were identified at the time as the walls of the east range of Library Square, *c*.1723, and this does appear to be the case, as the walls that were positively identified as Old College walls (Walls 4, 5) were very different in style and type (see SECTION 3 below). Rocque's map of 1756 depicts the Old College quadrangle and Library Square with a narrow and somewhat unsatisfactory blind passageway between, both obviously the result of the organic develop-ment of the college buildings at this time (fig. 12.13). The archaeological monitoring programme suggests that the east range of the college was built anew in *c.*1592, the foundations being of limestone, but the walls proper of distinctive early handmade brick. What is somewhat disappointing is that the walls of the west range of Library Square do not appear (on the limited investigations) to contain earlier medieval elements, despite the fact that this range is likely to have been on the alignment of the original west range of the priory, of which there was no trace. This finding was perhaps only to be expected, as the west range is noticeably narrower than the western and north range. But, in general, the lack of features found in the archaeological monitoring programme in such a long trench was somewhat surprising, perhaps to be explained by the fact that the cemetery was never built on.

SECTION 2 (fig. 12.15)
This trench was orientated north–south, extending from the western end of SECTION 1 and running between the east wall of the 1937 Reading Room and the western end of the Old Library. The very truncated remains of a wall (Wall 3), orientated east–west, were found and identified as possibly the north wall of the south range of the Old College.

Wall 3: south range?   A very truncated east–west masonry wall was identified in SECTION 3, lying 46cm to the south-west of Wall 2 (SECTION 1). It lay directly beneath the modern concrete bedding at 35cm below present ground and was sealed by loose demolition rubble and clay deposits. The orientation and location suggest that it is related to the south range of the quadrangle, but it projects across the passageway depicted on Rocque, which is a puzzle (fig. 12.13). The wall was in a very bad state, as the western end had been almost completely removed by services. The eastern end did survive, however, establishing that it originally measured 1.05m in width and was thus wider than Walls 1 and 2 in Library Square to the north. The wall survived for just 85cm in length (east–west) and was at least 25cm in height at the north-western end of the wall, with just 15cm of remains intact at the southern end. It was solidly built of roughly cut limestone blocks, with no core and bonded with a white/grey mortar, containing flecks of lime, differing from Walls 1 and 2 of Library Square. There was no indication of brick in either the build or the mortar.

Conclusion of SECTION 2   The width of the wall of 1.05m suggests that it may be relatively early in the sequence of buildings, perhaps even medieval, although this was impossible to determine given the truncated remains. Its function is also difficult to establish. The wall projects beyond the west range of the Old College, but lines up perfectly with the alignment of the northern wall of the south range, suggesting that it may originally have been part of this structure. A description by Provost Travers in the late sixteenth century,

12.16 SECTION 1, Wall 1, from the south.

however, implies that the college south range was not completed in his time, suggesting the wholesale demolition of the priory south range. But there may have been an earlier influence in the new build, suggested by the fact that, in Rocque's map of 1756, the south range is considerably wider than the others, implying a different building sequence. Perhaps Wall 3 was demolished to help create the passage between the Old College and Library Square. Alternatively, this wall may represent part of an enigmatic turret/tower shown on Dineley's sketch of 1681 (fig. 12.10) and Byron's 'view across the college', dated *c*.1753 (not illustrated: see Simpson 2002, fig. 166, 227).

SECTION 3 (fig. 12.15)
This trench was orientated east–west and ran parallel to the front of the 1937 Reading Room, between the Old Library and the Public Theatre. The remains of two walls, Wall 4 and Wall 5 (SECTION 3), were located in front of the 1937 Reading Room, and these can be identified as the southern end of the east range of the *c*.1592 Old College (figs 12.17–12.18). Two main layers were identified between the walls: a pure brick construction level, related to the college and probably dated to *c*.1592, and a rubble deposit of brick and limestone, probably related to the demolition of the quadrangle in the mid- to late eighteenth century.

Wall 4 (east wall of east range of the Old College) (fig. 12.15)   The
remains of a north–south brick-and-limestone wall (Wall 4) were identified at
the eastern end of the trench, lying 46cm below present ground level and
surviving to 55cm in depth (figs 12.17–12.18). This was immediately identified
as the east wall of the east range of the Old College by the distinctive early
brick used in the build, and the trench was deepened to 1.2m on the eastern
side to expose the full wall footing. The upper portion or wall proper was 75cm
in width by 12cm in height, on a base or foundation 1m in width by 43cm in
height. The foundation was composed of two courses of roughly cut limestone
blocks, measuring, on average, 40 by 30cm, and was roughly faced. It was
strongly mortared, however, with a distinctive hard off-white/yellow mortar,
which contained small black grit and occasional charcoal fragments (1–2mm in
diameter).

The wall was founded directly on natural yellow stony clay, identified as
natural ground in this location, the stones averaging between 4 and 8cm in
diameter. The remains of a foundation trench for the wall were also identified,
the eastern face built into the wall of the trench resulting in a very rough facing
on that side. The wall proper was a combination of brick and stone, but it had a
band of brick facing, in stretcher style and measuring 10cm in width, along the
northern side, which was three courses in depth. This brick, possibly the
earliest identified in Dublin to date, was bright orange/red and was very pure,
containing no inclusions or impurities of any sort. The early date was
suggested by the irregular sizes and the fact that it was clearly handmade, with
impressions of grass on some bricks, where they had been laid out to dry. In
general, the bricks were large, averaging 23 by 10cm wide by 6cm in depth.
This section of brick facing had distinctive wide pointing and was mortared
with a creamy sandy coarse mortar, with lime inclusions, slightly different to
that used in the foundation.

A door?   The location of the brick facing along the northern side of the wall
may suggest that there was a doorway in this location, the brick build
representing a southern jamb, a theory that is supported by Rocque's map of
the college quadrangle in 1756. This depicts an entrance into the courtyard in
roughly this location (fig. 12.13). This suggestion is supported to some extent
by the presence of an east–west wall, which abutted the jamb directly but
consisted of two only mortared bricks in the stretcher style. This flimsy wall
was sitting on a loose deposit of brick demolition and rubble fill, but both the
brick type and the mortar used were identical to those of Wall 4 (fig. 12.17).

Wall 5: West wall of east range of the college   A similar wall, Wall 5, was
located 5.7m to the west of Wall 4 and this was the corresponding west wall of
the east range, suggesting an external width for the east range of approximately

12.17 SECTION 3,
Wall 5, from the south.

12.18 SECTION 3,
Walls 5 and 4,
from the west.

7.4m, which is matched in Rocque's map (figs 12.13, 12.18). The top of this wall lay 50cm below present ground level, but it was slightly wider than Wall 4, measuring 90cm in width by 55cm in height. The foundation was also of limestone, but the main wall was clearly of brick as a single course survived, identifiable as the early brick mentioned above. The foundation level was constructed of solid limestone block, which was roughly hewn and varied from 30 by 20cm, to 15 by 5cm to 20 by 6cm. It was tightly coursed and roughly faced and was mortared with hard white/yellow mortar with inclusions of small grit and occasional charcoal fleck, identical to Wall 4. The single brick course was, as mentioned above, identical to that used in Wall 4 but a noticeably better quality brick was used along the eastern face, which would originally have faced into the courtyard. As with Wall 4, this brick was a distinctive handmade pure bright orange/red brick, but it had a badly degraded or 'melted' appearance, apart from on the eastern side, where the individual bricks could still be identified, orientated east–west. In this location, the joints were very large, measuring between 1.8 and 2mm in width.

Investigative trenches, Wall 4 and Wall 5   Two trenches were excavated, the first on the western side of Wall 4 (40cm wide by 1.05m deep), the second on the eastern side of Wall 5 (40cm wide by 1.48m deep). A deposit of rubble fill ran between the two walls for a depth of between 10 and 40cm, and this could be identified as demolition rubble from the *c.*1592 structure, evidently demolished in the mid- to late eighteenth century and then collapsed over the old foundations. This differed in type to a pure crushed or decomposed brick layer, which was identified on the eastern side of Wall 5 and appeared to mark either the late sixteenth-century construction level of the brick build or a brick surface.

Conclusion of SECTION 3   This section of trench identified the east range of the Old College, *c.*1592, which was a very important development, as it confirmed the location of the college quadrangle, now anchored in the modern architectural landscape by the known location of the east range. This range was found to measure almost 7.4m in width externally and 5.7m internally and was composed of bright red brick walls sitting on limestone foundations. The two walls located, Walls 4 and 5, were very similar in type and can be identified as early by the use of handmade brick, as described above. The eastern wall had what might be an entrance, flanked by an internal east–west wall, and this may represent the access route suggested by Rocque's map of 1756 (fig. 12.14). The west range was also identified further west (Walls 6, 7: SECTIONS 6, 7).

The account of the college by Travers was also verified during this work: the measurement given of 120ft for the court converts to 36.5m, which correlates almost exactly with the distance between the wall of the west range (Wall 6:

SECTION 6) and the west wall of the east range (Wall 5: SECTION 5), as recorded during the archaeological monitoring programme. In general, the monitoring established that the quadrangle is likely to have measured 50m in width externally, with the ranges measuring between 7.4 and 8m in width externally by between 5.3 and 5.7m internally.

SECTION 4 *(fig. 12.15)*

This section was T-shaped: the northern section orientated north–south (along the western side of the 1937 Reading Room), with a second section orientated east–west at the southern end, widened into a manhole at the far southern end. This trench established the presence of an organic archaeological deposit at 70cm below present ground level, which was left *in situ* and not excavated. This earlier layer was sealed and infilled by domestic refuse, probably dating to the late eighteenth century, which was used to build up the ground in this location.

Conclusion of SECTION 4   An archaeological horizon was identified in this location lying just south of the south range of the Old College and this comprised organic material containing domestic refuse probably dated to the sixteenth/seventeenth century. This area was always within the college precinct as suggested in the de Gomme map of 1673 (fig. 12.9). But the Hatfield depiction of *c.*1592 (fig. 12.6), although thought to have been a plan rather than an actual representation, maps this area as formal gardens attached to the Old College. Presumably these gardens were fertilized by spreading organic waste and/or domestic household rubbish, perhaps the origin of the organic deposit.

SECTION 5 *(fig. 12.15)*

This trench ran north–south along the eastern side of the Public Theatre (Examination Hall), but was not monitored. The cobbles were removed to reveal a mixed rubble and clay deposit, which was identified as an infill rather than *in situ* deposits. In previous investigations, these deposits were found to be 1.8m in depth, and had been used to infill and build up the ground (*Excavations* 2004, 0593).

SECTION 6 *(fig. 12.19)*

This trench was orientated east–west and extended across the Public Theatre but was wider than the other trenches, measuring 1.8m in width. This trench traversed the supposed site of the west range of the Old College and, happily, this was confirmed when the foundations of a solid wall (Wall 6) were identified as the east wall of the west range (fig. 12.20). Only the top of the foundation of Wall 6 was exposed, as the trench was not deep in this location and it was sealed by early brick demolition deposits, presumably associated with the demolition of the west range in the eighteenth century. Other features of this section include the remains of a brick surface and drain and these formed part of the original courtyard of the Old College. After the general demolition of the eighteenth and early nineteenth century, this new space was cobbled and two sections of this surface were found in the trench, presumably the first cobbled surface of Front Square.

The courtyard brick surface   The remains of a brick surface were identified at the eastern end of the trench, which would have been almost centrally placed within the Old College courtyard. The surface, lying at 60cm below present ground level, was composed of soft brick deposits, 15cm in depth, which clearly formed a surface or a bedding for a surface as the impressions of brick could be identified, laid side by side. Interestingly, both the Hatfield and the Dineley depictions suggest that this area was paved. Most importantly, the brick, although rotted down, can be positively identified as the same sixteenth-century brick used in the east range of the college, linking both features to the Old College (Walls 4, 5: SECTION 3). The surface was identified over a distance of at least 2m east–west by 1.88m wide and was rising slightly to the west. A similar deposit was identified at the western end of the trench, between Wall 6 and Wall 7 (SECTION 7: see below).

The courtyard drain   The courtyard was evidently well constructed, as a brick drain, of a similar early date, was located in the middle of the trench orientated north-west/south-east and lying 45cm below present ground level. It measured internally 38cm in width by 33cm height and the walls stood to four courses. The roof was relatively intact and was composed of limestone flags, roughly placed over the drain, the largest of which measured 60 by 40cm. The brick used was the early brick, measuring an average of 23cm by 65mm. Full and half bricks were used throughout the drain. In addition, the structure was mortared copiously with a yellow crumbly lime mortar, similar to the mortar found in the Old College walls, and the jointing was very wide. On excavation, the base of the drain was found to be lined with rectangular tight-fitting thin limestone flags (3mm in thickness), which were shattered but intact. These were sealed by a pure dark grey silt deposit, which produced no artefacts. The drain was evidently repaired at some time, as there was an additional later coursing along the eastern side, which extended above the height of the roof slabs. After recording, the capstone was replaced and the drain was left in situ.

Wall 6: East wall of west range (figs 12.19–12.20)   The remains of a substantial limestone wall (Wall 6) were located at the western end of the trench, orientated north–south, and the location suggests that it is the east wall of the west range. The width of the wall, 1.1m, appears to confirm this and a

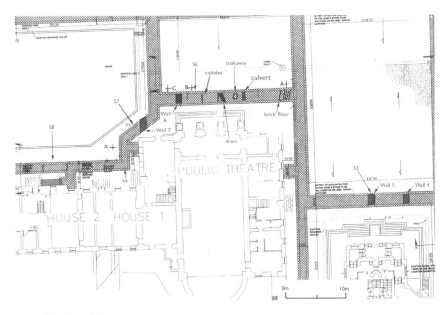

12.19 SECTION 6.

12.20 SECTION 6, Wall 6, from the north-west.

small excavation at the eastern side revealed that the wall was constructed of large decaying limestone (average 40 by 42cm), while the core was composed of smaller irregular-shaped limestone (10 by 12cm and 8cm in diameter), strongly mortared. The latter yellow mortar was very distinctive and used copiously, comprising a gritty and sandy mortar mix, which contained visible lime flecks. Interestingly, the remains of a layer of plaster were identified on the western face (internal side), which was 20mm in depth and was an off-white/yellow, similar to the mortar used in the wall.

The wall was sealed on the eastern side by a distinctive band of bright red rubble, 20cm in depth, and this is likely to be the remains of the demolished brick wall of the quadrangle, although no brick was identified in the limestone foundation of Wall 6. This was a feature noted elsewhere, where a band of crushed brick sealed a limestone wall foundation beneath. However, it is difficult to establish whether Wall 6 was a brick wall with limestone foundations or whether it was a reused medieval limestone wall, as suggested by a width of over 1m. In the late sixteenth-century description by Travers, we are told that the north and west ranges were completed at the time of writing (1594–6), suggesting that they reused existing priory buildings, including Wall 6. This may be supported by the fact that the west wall of the range (Wall 7), in SECTION 7, is probably a medieval wall, confirming some reuse of priory buildings on the western side of the quadrangle (figs 12.22–12.23).

Brick surface   A spread of brick was identified on the western side of Wall 6, lying 60cm below present ground level and extending for 2.45m in length, east–west. It was at least 30cm in depth and was a substantial deposit, extending slightly over Wall 6 in the eastern section. This deposit was similar to the red brick layer sealing Wall 6, but had mixed mortar throughout and was more compacted. However, it was predominantly composed of sixteenth-century brick and therefore is likely to have been associated with the Old College quadrangle and its demolition. It can be paralleled with a similar deposit found further west in SECTION 7 (see below), which was also confined to within the west range.

Later culvert and soak-away   Several later features were also identified within the trench, the largest being a culvert orientated north–south that was exposed for 70cm within the trench. It was arched and measured externally 60cm in width and was built of brick, an assorted orange but predominantly a narrow red brick, measuring 23 by 8cm. The entire culvert was heavily mortared with a very cement-like light yellow mortar, and some of the bricks had yellow render attached, suggesting reuse. The culvert was sealed by dark grey clay, which contained stones, slates, animal bone and oyster shells along with nineteenth-century pottery. This feature was left intact and the ducts were laid over it. The remains of a post-medieval soak-away were also identified, measuring 1.3m in width by at least 60cm in depth, and this was filled with a mix of mortar, brick and stone. It was sealed when the entire area was cobbled, sometime after the mid-eighteenth century, using distinctive oval limestones, set upright.

Later cobbled surface   A section of cobbles was found sealing Wall 6 (thought to be a medieval or Old College wall (Wall 6: see below)), suggesting that the surface post-dates the great clearances of the eighteenth century. This surface lay 55cm below present ground level and survived for 2.2m in length east–west, truncated at the western end. It was composed of limestones of various sizes, some as large as 10 and 20cm in diameter, but also smaller stones measuring 4 by 3cm. The stones were rounded and square and were set on edge, extending into the ground for an average of 30cm in depth. They were bedded in grey silty clay and continued westwards, where they could be traced in the section. Further west, the surface was bedded in a brown organic layer. A second stretch, a continuation of this surface, was exposed further west, extending for a distance of 4.8m (east–west), lying 40cm below present ground level. They were composed of rounded and oval limestone, measuring between 8 and 12cm in diameter and were set in a brown organic layer, which sealed a deposit of mortar (not excavated).

Conclusion of SECTION 6 (fig. 12.19)   This section of the works confirmed the location of the west range of the Old College by the identification of the eastern wall (Wall 6) (fig. 12.20). This was a substantial wall, but, unfortunately, it was not fully exposed as it lay beneath the depth required for excavation and could not be investigated fully as there were live services in the area. The width of the wall attests to its antiquity and it may be related to the priory of All Hallows, reused, as previously discussed, as part of the college complex in *c.*1592. Other features related to the Old College were also found, including the brick surface within the courtyard and the brick and stone drain, which formed part of the drainage system. The brick surface at the eastern end of the trench is particularly interesting, as this is a common feature that extends right across Front Square, stretching from outside House 7, at the western end, to SECTION 6. In SECTION 6, the surface is within the central courtyard of the quadrangle, an indication that it was paved (albeit in brick, or perhaps the brick was a bedding), as shown in the Hatfield depiction (fig. 12.6). The early drain was also part of a much larger system that is likely to have extended across the entire area, the orientation of north-west–south-east being at variance with the college quadrangle.

The section also produced evidence of the demolition of the west range, represented by a band of rubble that sealed the demolished remains and raised

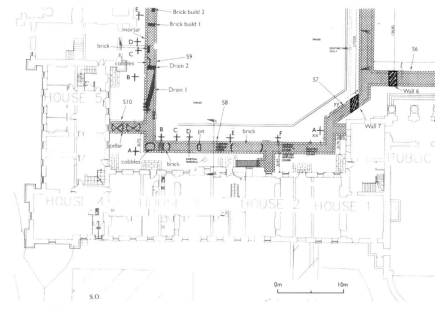

12.21 SECTIONS 7–9.

the ground level in the area by approximately 20cm. This end was then cobbled, the surface bedded in the demolition deposits, which sealed the Old College walls. The cobbles were evidently laid as part of the creation of the Front Square, representing the first cobbled surface of the new space. The cobbles were replaced again when the entire square was sealed by rubble infill deposits, which measure at least 40cm in depth, raising the ground level to the current level of cobbling (although these were relaid in the 1970s). A series of drains and culverts were laid at this time through these infill layers.

SECTION 7 (fig. 12.21)
This trench extended along the west wall of the Public Theatre (Examination Hall), but was at an angle, orientated north-east–south-west. It was excavated as a continuation of SECTION 8 (see below) and traversed the presumed location of the west range, specifically the west wall, which was subsequently found and identified (Wall 7; figs 12.22–12.23). On excavation, however, the suspicion was that it was a medieval wall, very different from the limestone and brick walls (Walls 3, 4) of the east range. SECTION 7 was excavated in two sections: XX the southern end and YY the northern end.

Wall 7: West wall of west range   Wall 7 was located in the central area of the trench, lying 40cm below present ground level and orientated north–south. It was visually different from the Old College brick walls (Walls 4, 5: SECTION 3)

12.22 SECTION 7, Wall 7, from the east.

12.23 SECTION 7, Wall 7, overhead.

and was clearly very substantial, measuring 1.3m in width (east–west) (figs 12.22–12.23). A limited exploratory excavation was carried out down the eastern side of the wall, which revealed that the wall extended to 70cm in depth and was a fine solid wall, built of large limestone blocks and bonded with a yellow gritty mortar, which contained visible charcoal and lime flecks. The size and form immediately suggested that it was medieval and therefore related to the priory of All Hallows. Its location, within the footprint of the college quadrangle, however, suggests that it was reused by the builders of the Old College, perhaps in the early days of the college.

In general, the wall construction was superior to the Old College walls (Wall 4 and Wall 5: SECTION 3), the block size ranging from 44 by 17cm to 35 by 27cm. These blocks, however, were neatly cut and tightly jointed in contrast to the Old College walls, which were more roughly hewn. A total of four courses were identified on the western side, the upper two well-faced and representing the wall proper, while the lower two were probably foundation courses within a trench. The upper section was well faced and had a rubble core of smaller stones, strongly mortared. One fragment of early brick was identified in the western external face of the wall, but is likely to have represented repair. There was no brick within the wall proper. The lower two courses were composed of longer and more rectangular blocks that were more roughly hewn than the upper courses and displayed evidence of clay bonding, as well as mortar. A projecting offset was identified on this side, which measured 22cm in width by 34cm in depth. After demolition, the wall was sealed by a layer of hard compact green clay, 6cm in depth, and black silt, 8cm in depth, the combination of which produced a cementatious seal over the wall, which was difficult to remove. A small section of the core of the wall, 18cm in height, had to be removed as part of the works, to facilitate the construction of the paths. After this, the wall was lined with a breathable membrane and the western trench filled with loose stone.

The eastern side: south section   The exploratory trench, down the eastern face, was excavated to 90cm in depth, and this exposed a mortar and rubble layer at the base, which was at least 30cm in depth and was clearly earlier than, and presumably associated with the construction of, the wall. This deposit was composed of dark grey cement-like mortar, which contained lumps of lime, charcoal and shell, along with small limestone fragments, but, critically, no brick at all. It was sealed by dark green sticky clay, 15cm in depth, which produced two small sherds of medieval ceramic pottery identified as Dublin wheel-thrown ware, along with shell and charcoal fragments. The wall was founded on this infill clay deposit and there were faint traces of a foundation trench, the edges of which were defined by a thin layer of charcoal, 3cm in depth, perhaps representing a burning event. This deposit also extended over part of the offset, suggesting that it had been thrown back into the trench, after the foundation was constructed. The foundation trench and green clay were sealed by a black silt deposit, 17cm in depth, while the remainder of the deposits consisted of seven identifiable bands of mixed mortar and limestone deposits, butting up against the face of the wall, containing lumps of redeposited yellow clay but no brick. There was evidence of a cut on this side, however, which suggests that the top of the wall might have been re-exposed at some date, perhaps if it was reused in the Old College phase.

The west section   The western side of the wall was also exposed and a similar stratigraphy was found, but with less clay and more rubble. Unlike the eastern side within the quadrangle, however, the natural ground was exposed at 60cm below present ground level and found to be composed of coarse grey gravel rather than clays.

Brick deposit   A distinctive deposit of pure early brick clay, 10cm in depth, was located between 40 and 55cm below present ground level at the southern end of the SECTION 7, and this was traced further west in SECTION 8 (see below). It had also been identified in SECTION 6 to the east, at the eastern end of the trench. This distinctive deposit, which was a feature in and around Front Square, may be the remains of some sort of brick precinct wall or surface, the bright red clay presumably the residue of rotted-out brick. The clay was sealed by a spread of cinders, 16cm in depth, and a layer of white mortar representing an infill layer dated to the eighteenth century. The general infill and demolition deposit dated to the eighteenth century and noted elsewhere was also located in SECTION 7, where it was found to be 60cm in depth.

Conclusion of SECTION 7 (fig. 12.21)   Wall 7 is likely to represent the west wall of the west range, the companion wall to Wall 6 in SECTION 6 (see above). The position and size correlate with the known location of the quadrangle, the measurements suggesting that, like the east range (Walls 4, 5: SECTION 6), the west range measured 7.4m in width externally by 5.3m in width internally. However, this wall was different to the other walls, most obviously wider and of a superior quality of build, as detailed above, and, as a result, may have been earlier, perhaps related to the priory of All Hallows. Corroborating this, the wall was founded on clay that produced medieval pottery (although this may have been residual). The remains of the brick clay deposit at the southern end of the trench are likely to relate to a very similar deposit that continued further west (SECTION 8), and this may have marked the line of a brick precinct wall or a brick surface. The dump of eighteenth-century cinders in the southern end of the trench suggests that domestic refuse was used to infill the ground in this location along with demolition debris, in the eighteenth century.

SECTION 8 (fig. 12.21)

This trench was orientated east–west and extended parallel to Houses 1, 2 and 3, a continuation of SECTION 7 at the eastern side (widened for a manhole at the western end). A section of early cobbling was identified at the western end, but the predominant feature was a consistent deposit of early brick clay, similar to that found further east in SECTION 7 (see above). The brick deposit of SECTION 8, however, extended the full length of the trench and may have represented a decayed precinct wall of the Old College, such as that shown on the Hatfield depiction (fig. 12.10). It may also have represented the brick debris from the construction of additional ranges to the north and west of the Old College from the late sixteenth century onwards.

Cobbled surface   A surface of cobbles, possibly late sixteenth century in date, was identified at the western end of the trench (in the area widened for a manhole) and this measured at least 1.5m east–west, lying 70cm below present ground level but truncated on the eastern side (fig. 12.24). This surface was composed of angular rather than oval limestone cobbles, which were generally laid east–west but, unlike previous surfaces found, were spaced widely apart. In general, they included large and small stones, varying from 8 to 25cm in diameter, but the bulk were predominantly 15cm in diameter. At the western end, this surface was set in bright yellow boulder clay, over a thin dark grey silt layer, but at the eastern end the bedding deposit was black silty clay. The latter contained shell and small fragments of animal bone, but, unfortunately, no finds were recovered. The cobbles were removed in antiquity and replaced at the eastern end with a brick surface, 10cm in depth, which was very badly decayed but had traces of mortar or render along the top, lying at 70cm below present ground level. It was composed of fragments of brick, averaging between 8 and 12cm in diameter, which were very compressed and which appear to have replaced the cobbles, truncating them and partially sealing them at this end of the trench.

Spread of brick   The second significant feature of SECTION 8, as mentioned above, was the consistent layer of bright red brick clay that lay between 45 and 50cm below present ground and extended east–west for a distance of at least 32m, sealing the cobbles and surface beneath them. It sat on a dark brown silty clay deposit, which contained brick fragments, shell, mortar and charcoal but no finds. The deposit varied in depth from 10 to 20cm, but did contain some half bricks and impressions of brick, suggesting that it may originally have been some sort of a brick structure, although an actual build pattern was hard to decipher. A concentrated spread, measuring 5.2m east–west and between 18 and 25cm in depth, was noted at the western end of the trench and this produced one fragment of mottled-ware pottery from the

12.24 SECTION 8, Cobbles, from the west.

upper levels, suggesting a date in the seventeenth/eighteenth century for its demolition. This deposit could not be traced northwards along SECTION 9, but this is probably because the ground in this location was disturbed by later constructions, including a stone drain and a possible cellar (see below).

Monitoring in 2006 (no. 2: 2006: fig. 12.2)   A trench 8m to the north of SECTION 8 and also orientated east–west (running along the grass verge of the green on this side) was monitored in 2006 and this was excavated to a greater depth – 90cm (Simpson 2006a). At 90cm, dark brown loose clay was found, 35cm in depth, which contained red brick fragments, mortar and charcoal, presumably associated with the Old College. This was sealed by a crushed brick demolition deposit, similar to that found in SECTION 8 but far less substantial, in places measuring less than 7cm in depth, while at the western end it was 40cm in depth. A number of clay layers sealed the brick, suggesting that this area was built up in clay rather than demolition debris during the late seventeenth and early eighteenth century. What was notable, however, was that the brick layer found in this trench consisted of brick rubble as opposed to brick clay, suggestive of demolition of some sort of structure, possibly a precinct wall. Also of note was the identification of a trampled surface or old ground level approximately 1m below present ground level. The deposits also suggest a fall in the ground level from south to north.

Later features: the pit and infill   The brick clay was sealed by dark grey silty clay, which contained shell, mortar and eighteenth-century brick and was at least 15cm in depth. This was highly organic and was probably originally refuse from the college, mixed with natural river silt, perhaps related to the Steine river somewhere in the vicinity. The remains of a pit were found at the western end of the trench, lying 28cm below present ground level, and this measured 30cm in width (east–west) by 20cm in depth, extending across the full width of the trench at 50cm (north–south). It was filled with eighteenth-century brick and mortar deposit, but was cut into the riverine gravels mentioned above, in this location composed of dark grey silt deposit, which contained highly organic material, as well as charcoal, coal, mortar and brick. A spread of cinders to the east of the pit, lying at a similar level and extending for 80cm in length (east–west) by 25cm in depth, was also representative of college domestic refuse, used to infill the ground in the college in the eighteenth century.

Conclusion of SECTION 8 (fig. 12.21)   SECTION 8 was a very long trench but produced surprisingly few features. The earliest was evidently the cobbled surface at the eastern end, which, lying at 70cm below present ground level, is quite likely to be late sixteenth century and contemporary with the Old College. The surface was succeeded by a brick surface at a similar level, also related to the Old College, although only a small section survived. The dominant feature of this trench, however, was the spread of early brick along the entire length, all the more significant as an identical deposit was noted on the other side of the square, in SECTION 14, suggesting that it extended right across Parliament Square. In addition to this, previous works, outside House 5, established that it measured at least 40cm in depth. It may, as suggested above, represent some sort of rotted-out precinct wall or even the 'construction area' of the Old College, if not for the original quadrangle for the other brick ranges built on this side of the college from the late sixteenth century onwards.

SECTION 9 (fig. 12.21)

This trench extended northwards from SECTION 8 (outside House 4) as far as Regent House (or Front Gate, as it is commonly known). The sixteenth-century stone surface and the brick clay layer found in SECTION 8 did not continue immediately northwards, but there was evidence of considerable construction in this area, along with infilling in the eighteenth/nineteenth century, which may have removed them. A small patch did survive further north, however, halfway along the trench, making it likely that both features originally did extend further northwards but had been removed. The most significant feature of this section was probably the foundations of a brick building, which was located just south of Front Gate and can probably be dated to the mid-seventeenth century. It is not clear what this was originally, but it may have been part of a brick western frontage *c.*1640, perhaps even associated with the western gate of the college but clearly pre-dating the expansion of the western frontage in the 1690s to the current line. Cobbles to the north of this building are likely to have been contemporary, perhaps part of an entrance feature. The trench also produced a brick drain, dated to the sixteenth century and evidently part of the Old College drain, along with a second major drain, probably eighteenth century in date.

Drain 1   A major French drain, probably eighteenth century, dominated the southern end of the trench and this was orientated north-east/south-west, the exposed section measuring a distance of 7.9m before continuing beyond the eastern side of the trench on the north. It was deep, the top lying 70cm below present ground level and, as a result, it was exposed along the very base of the trench only and was therefore left *in situ*. As the drain was low, only the capping stones of limestone flags were exposed, fifteen in total, and these were found to be thin, square dark grey slabs measuring, on average, between 34 and 42cm square by 2cm in depth. This drain was partially rebuilt or repaired at the northern end, as the capstones had been replaced by large roughly hewn limestone, in contrast to the southern end. These larger capstones measured, on average, 50 by 40cm, with one capstone measuring 70 by 30cm. Although examination was limited as the drain was so deep, the mortar was identified as a cementatious dark grey mortar with lime inclusions (1cm). Through a gap in the capstones at the northern end, it was evident that it had been infilled with mixed silt layers, dark green and grey, which contained brick and slates. The drain was cut through mixed demolition layers, which had mortar, charcoal and loose friable yellow mortar (similar to medieval mortar) and was sealed by a layer of dark grey silty clay containing brick fleck and occasional mortar. At the northern end, the drain intersected with a second east–west drain (Drain 2: see below) and the junction was slightly damaged previously, exposing the drain beneath and the join. Examination revealed that Drain 2 was earlier and that Drain 1 had been built into it, the rough joint being liberally mortared with a hard white/grey cement-like mortar, which had a pronounced and heavy lime fleck similar to the mortar of Drain 1. The west side of the wall of Drain 1 was also visible at this junction and this was composed of sharp orange brick, measuring 22 by 12cm, which had a distinctive yellow render.

Drain 2   The second earlier drain, Drain 2, as mentioned above, was orientated east–west and was deeper, lying 75cm below present ground level. On inspection of the join, it was clear that Drain 2 measured 25cm square internally and that the side walls were composed of small limestone blocks interspersed with bright red brick, the early brick used elsewhere in the Old

College. When Drain 1 was broken through Drain 2, the north wall of Drain 2 was rebuilt in that location and the more modern eighteenth-century brick, which was orange, can be clearly identified. Drain 2 was also filled with black silt to a depth of 18cm, revealing a stone-flagged floor, composed of limestone rectangular slabs, averaging 30cm square. The drain was mortared with a grey/white mortar and was left in situ during the works.

Cobbles 1   A large patch of cobbling, sealed by a brick layer, was exposed just north of Drain 2, lying 55cm below present ground level, and this surface is likely to be associated with the Old College and possibly even part of the cobbles located at the southern end of SECTION 8, such was the similarity between the surfaces. The cobbles were composed of rounded, angular and irregular-shaped small stone, measuring, on average, between 8 and 10cm in diameter. There were also several brick fragments. The surviving section measured 1.4m north–south by at least 50cm in width, but it was truncated along the eastern side of the trench, probably by a modern service trench. The actual stones were generally orientated east–west and were sealed by a layer of early brick clay, 10cm in depth, in an identical sequence to the surface found further south in SECTION 8. A black silt layer had built up in and around the cobbles. A second surface sealed part of the cobbles, but only traces of this survived *in situ*. This surface was a thin layer of dark redeposited yellow clay, which was 2cm in depth but appeared to be a trampled surface, set over the cobbles and the black silt deposit, which had accumulated over them.

Brick build 1   One of the most important findings was a brick structure, almost completely demolished, which was found at the northern end of SECTION 9, just south of Front Gate. This foundation extended for at least 4.8m north–south and lay 60cm below present ground level. At the southern end, it survived as an east–west build of brick, one brick wide (16cm), which was at least two courses and appeared to be retaining a rough foundation of loose brick to the north, measuring 3.3m north–south. The brick was a mix and probably dated to the mid- to late seventeenth century, the sources suggesting it pre-dated the 1690s. Some of it was pinkish and generally irregular in size, varying from 22 by 10 by 6cm to 22 by 15 by 7cm, but all was handmade, and bonded with yellow mortar, which contained flecks of limestone and charcoal. The remainder was the distinctive red early brick of the Old College, which had probably been reused in this location. Other brick had a distinctive purple tinge, being very heavy, containing various inclusions of grit and stone. The area immediately north of the foundation was marked by a rough mix of this rubble and brick combination, which was compressed and heavily mortared and may have formed some sort of foundation.

12.25 SECTION 9, Brick build 2, from the south.

Brick build 2   Confirmation that this was originally some sort of structure was received when a north–south brick wall was identified 2.3m north of the east–west wall in the eastern section of the trench, extending for at least 75cm (figs 12.25, 12.26). This wall was also severely truncated, but was very similar to Brick Build 1, surviving to only one course and mortared with an identical mix. It was also one brick thick, measuring approximately 15cm in width, and was within a similar compressed brick deposit. The structure was sealed by a layer of mortar, measuring 17cm in depth, which also sealed a set of cobbles further north (see below).

Cobbles 2   The remains of a cobbled surface were located immediately north of the brick structure and this surface is likely to be associated with it, as it abutted the build neatly on the eastern side. This patch lay 60cm below present ground level and extended for 1.2m (north–south) along the eastern side of the trench, before extending across the full width of the trench (48cm) at the northern end (fig. 12.25). The surface was composed of rounded and oval cobbles, averaging 6cm in diameter, which were set in a dark grey silty layer, but had been removed along the south-western side. They were set neatly together, forming a tight and neat surface and were of a better quality than those found further south (Cobbles 1). The surface was sealed by a black fill, composed of silty clay mixed with brick rubble.

Later features   A general layer of brick could be identified along the western section of the trench, sealing the earlier foundations and measuring approximately 22cm in depth, dating to the eighteenth century. This appeared to be a demolition layer probably caused by the same activity that truncated the cobbles further south (Cobbles 1). In the area of the brick build, this had a greater dry mortar component, with at least one identifiable band of crushed mortar, which was 10cm in depth, sealing the foundation directly along with the cobbles to the north (Cobbles 2). After the demolitions, the ground was infilled as part of a general infilling programme in and around Front Square. This presented as dark grey clay, mixed with rubble, brick and mortar and approximately 30cm in depth, which produced one sherd of eighteenth-century tin-glazed earthenware.

Conclusion of SECTION 9 (figs 12.21, 12.26)   SECTION 9 extended across the western extent of the original 'Great Bawn' associated with the Old college and this was confirmed during the investigations in this area by the identification of part of the early drainage and at least one cobbled surface (1) at the southern end of the trench. While this end was dominated by a large stone drain, which is likely to be eighteenth/nineteenth century, it was tied into the pre-existing drainage system in a remarkable continuity of usage. This location of the drain is also significant as it is likely to be associated with the Western Gate of the college, the main entrance to the college at this time.

The second significant find was the remains of a brick structure that can probably be dated to the mid-seventeenth century and lay just south of Regent House (Front Gate). Although only a small section lay within the trench, this foundation may have formed part of an earlier brick western frontage demolished when the boundary was pushed further west in the 1690s. The position of brick, so close to Front Gate, might even suggest that it was part of the original Old College gate at this side rather than the main west range. This is also suggested by the lack of structures further north, in SECTION 12 (see below). The cobbles to the north of the build may support the latter notion and may be all that survives of a path extending through the gate.

The inclusion of at least one drain built in the late sixteenth century should not come as a surprise, as the documentary sources suggest that there were buildings in this location, associated with the priory, even before the college was established. In 1570, well after the priory had been dissolved, the sources record the 'wester stone house by the great Bawn, the Vestry, cloister and little garden within the precinct and the tower over the gate adjoining Hoggen Green' (Simpson 2002, 218). The main features, even at that date, then, were the precinct and monastic buildings, and Front Square known as the Great Bawn. The last reference to the gate, called 'the gatehouse of Alhallows', dates to 1576, when it was in disrepair after it was plundered for stone (Simpson

2002, 218). It must have been repaired, probably in brick, as it was not replaced until the late seventeenth century, when the Boyle gatehouse was built. The orientation and position of the drain (Drain 2) is interesting, as it almost lines up with what would have been the original gate into the quadrangle, as shown by the Hatfield depiction. It may have followed the line of the path to this main gate, on the northern side.

SECTION 10 (fig. 12.21)
This trench was located between Houses 4 and 5 and was 6.8m in length, orientated east–west. It located the remains of some sort of cellar, to which there is no access, the top of which lies 60cm below present ground level. This structure had a double-arched roof, which was sealed initially by a layer of mortar and then with redeposited yellow/orange gravel deposit mixed with boulder clay, 30cm in depth. Efforts to locate a cellar entrance from the basement of House 5 were not successful, and it is possible that the cellar was earlier. The redeposited boulder clay that sealed the mortar deposit was hard and dark yellow, containing lenses of bright yellow clay and occasional brick and animal bone. It was sealed by a rough rubble deposit, which contained blackware pottery, dating to the eighteenth/nineteenth century.

Conclusion of SECTION 10 (fig. 12.21) The nature and extent of the potential structure/cellar found in SECTION 10 could not be clarified, as it lay beneath the required depth and there were fears of damage if further investigations were carried out.

SECTION 11 (fig. 12.26)
This trench was orientated north–south and extended across Front Gate, measuring 6.6m in length and positioned approximately east 3.35m from Front Gate. However, this section produced very little information, as there was a concentration of services that disturbed the ground to at least 1m in depth, removing any earlier features including the cobbles (Cobbles 2) associated with the brick build (Brick Build 2) in SECTION 9 (fig. 12.25). At the very base of the trench, however, 1.1m below present ground level, a coarse riverine gravel was located that may have been related to the Steine river, which is now culverted under Parliament Square.

SECTION 12 (fig. 12.26)
This trench was orientated north–south and extended from Regent House (Front Gate) as far as House 8. It not did produce many features, but did reveal the remains of brick deposits, associated with the Old College, and also sandstone fragments, probably originally the residue of stone-working on site, perhaps as part of the original western frontage. A substantial brick wall was

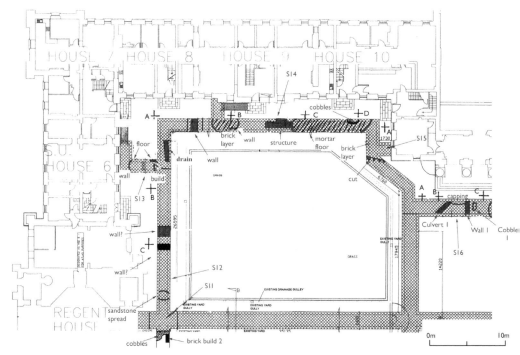

12.26 SECTIONS 11–16.

found just north of Regent House, and this may relate to an earlier brick western frontage or earlier gatehouse. Other features included a nineteenth-century French drain and wall.

Sandstone deposit   A distinctive spread of sandstone and mortar was identified at the southern end of the trench, just north of Front Gate, lying 80cm below present ground level and extending for 82cm, north-south. This deposit was predominantly composed of sandstone fragments but also contained rounded pebbles, building debris and limestone fragments, within a coarse yellow mortar. The origin of the sandstone is not known, although this type of stone was used extensively in medieval buildings, albeit found in a later context in this case. The fine light yellow sandstone fragments were not cut, but were irregular in shape, representing waste and measuring, on average, 15 to 20cm in diameter. It should be noted that sandstone fragments very similar to this were located during monitoring in the Chief Steward's Garden (to the north of the north range of Parliament Square) and outside Front Gate, at the College Green frontage (Simpson 2002a).

Brick wall, *c.*1592?   A concentration of brick clay was found at the southern end of the trench, north of the concentration of sandstone fragments, and this was bright red, the type of brick used in the Old College, dated to *c.*1592. This clay lay 40cm below present ground level and measured 1.3m in width, the southern end terminating in a straight line with fragments of brick found within the clay. This spread is similar to the spread of brick clay found sealing the limestone foundations of Wall 5 in SECTION 3, identified as an Old College wall, and may seal similar foundations. This location is interesting, as it suggests that this possible wall marks the northern precinct brick wall of the western court, shown on the Hatfield depiction (fig. 12.10).

Brick wall, seventeenth-century A spread of slightly later handmade seventeenth-century orange brick was also located 1m south of this possible wall, lying at 55cm below present ground level. This deposit was very concentrated, measuring 95cm in length north–south by at least 20cm in depth, and it may be all that survives of a wall, probably orientated north–south.

Later features: French drain and mortar spread The remains of a French land-drain were located at the northern end of the trench, orientated north-west–south-east and extending for 3.6m. The drain measured internally 30cm in width by 15cm in depth and the side walls were constructed of limestone but also contained a heavy dark red brick, mortared with a hard white/grey mortar. The drain was filled with pure black silt and was capped with large limestone flags measuring, on average, 65 by 32cm, one of which was yellow sandstone, possibly indicative of reuse. This feature is likely to date to the eighteenth/nineteenth century. A spread of sandy mortar was identified at the northern end of the trench, north of the drain, and this extended for 1m east–west. At least 20cm in depth, it was a very mixed deposit containing limestone fragments, pebbles and brick along with shells, animal bones and oyster shells.

Conclusion of SECTION 12 (fig. 12.26) This stretch of trench confirms the presence of features related to the Old College in the form of at least one wall, possibly two. The width of the potential wall, at 1.3m, suggests that it was a substantial feature, while the east–west orientation raises the possibility that it may be related to the original northern precinct wall, as shown on the Hatfield depiction (fig. 12.10). The collection of sandstone fragments at the southern end of the trench is certainly of interest, especially as they have been found previously at this end of college, in the Chief Stewart's Garden (to the rear (north) of Houses 7 and 8, and outside (west) Front Gate in the small enclosed green (Simpson 2002a). They may, as previously mentioned, have been from the original brick western frontage and are clearly fragments only, suggesting that they were worked on site, the left-over debris after rough-out blocks were converted into mouldings. The later features include a French drain and mortar spread, the drain reflective of the general problem of drainage at this end of the college, probably related to the presence of the Steine river, which is culverted in this location.

SECTION 13 (fig. 12.26)
This trench was orientated east–west, extending to House 6 and designed to tie in to existing services. The trench located the remains of an early surface or structure, which is likely to have been associated with the Old College, dated *c*.1592.

Surface/floor The excavation of the trench revealed a hard surface comprised of the early bright red/orange brick, brick dust and mortar lying 52cm below present ground level and related to the Old College. This surface extended for at least 5.3m (east–west) and, on excavation, the impressions of brick, laid flat, were discernible, confirming that this type of brick dust layer was possibly originally some sort of a build. The floor was damaged at the western end, but can be traced in the northern section of the trench where it was found to be 5cm in depth. A sherd of pottery was found in the upper levels and identified as painted pearlware, dated to the late eighteenth century, confirming an eighteenth-century date for the general demolition in this area.

Limestone build? The remains of a possible limestone build were identified at the eastern end of the trench, orientated east–west and located along the northern side of the trench, but clearly very truncated, as it only measured 30cm in length by 14cm in width. It lay 34cm below present ground level and was composed of limestone block and mortar. Although only a small section survived, it is likely to be later in date than the brick surface but pre-dates the current western frontage.

Conclusion of SECTION 13 (fig. 12.26) Excavation of SECTION 13 revealed the remains of a significant brick surface or floor that was presumably related to either the original Old College or the development of the north-west quadrangle in the 1640s. The brick was the early type used in the main quadrangle and may be related to the earliest phase of the college, suggesting that brick was produced on the college site, although there was no evidence of brick clamps. The position of the possible building is interesting, as it lies slightly north of the projected line of the north quadrangle. This may give credence to the Dineley view (fig. 12.10), which suggests that the north-west quadrangle only projected northwards slightly, although this is contradicted by the de Gomme view (1678), which shows the new range further north (fig. 12.9). The remains of the limestone wall, although very truncated, suggest that there was other building activity in this location, but very little survived.

SECTION 14 (fig. 12.26)
This trench was orientated east–west and ran parallel to Houses 8 and 9. It produced significant evidence of construction at this side of the college,

including a consistent deposit of early red brick likely to be associated with the Old College. In addition, the foundations of a red brick structure, probably part of the Baker building, constructed in the mid-seventeenth century, were also found, associated with a mortar floor. The excavation of the trench also revealed a large ditch or pit, probably late seventeenth or early eighteenth century, at the northern end, which extended southwards into SECTION 15.

Brick spread   A consistent deposit of early brick clay/dust, which was very pure and concentrated, was found along the length of the trench, lying 50cm below present ground level and corresponding to a similar deposit in SECTION 8, running parallel on the southern side of Front Square. The deposit suggests red brick construction in this location also, perhaps a precinct wall as suggested for SECTION 8, although the spread of the brick clay appears considerable and does extend further south where similar deposits were found during monitoring in 2006 (see below).

Brick deposit 1 (wall?)   The remains of a brick wall, orientated north–south and located at the western end of the trench, were suggested by the presence of a concentrated deposit of bright red chips of early brick, lying 56cm below present ground level. This spread measured 1.8m in width by at least 30cm in depth (not excavated) and had vertical edges at the east and west end. The deposit contained half bricks that had not rotted out, with faint traces of a build. It was sealed by a layer of mortar and rubble, 7cm in depth, and a layer of organic material, which produced a sherd of glazed and decorated eighteenth-century pottery.

Brick layer (and east-west wall)   The remains of what might have been a second early wall, although orientated east–west, were located in the southern section of the trench, lying 3.4m to the east of the north–south wall and probably associated with it. This consisted of three bricks, extending for just 30cm, which were jointed and mortared but were badly disturbed. This small section of build was associated with a large rubble deposit of early brick, which lay 57cm below present ground level, extended for 3.1m (east–west) and was least 10cm in depth (not excavated).

Large brick structure   The remains of a large brick structure were found lying to the east at 56cm below present ground level, and this appeared, by the type of brick used, to be slightly later than the Old College walls, perhaps dating to the mid-seventeenth century (fig. 12.27). On removal of the demolition/infill layers sealing the structure, an east–west brick wall, at least two courses in height (not excavated), was identified in the centre of the trench, which measured 40cm in width and extended for at least 3.6m,

12.27 SECTION 14, Brick build, from the west.

terminating at the eastern end in a straight joint. The brick was handmade and bright red, but it differed slightly from the Old College brick as it included a superior dull orange brick, which was slightly larger, measuring 22 by 11 by 5cm. In addition, the build was very heavily mortared with hard white mortar and had distinctive wide pointing.

The wall petered out at the eastern end, where a mortar floor was exposed, composed of yellowish mortar, suggesting that the east–west wall represented the interior of a building (see below). A larger north–south wall was identified abutting the northern face of the east–west wall, almost centrally placed, and this extended beyond the northern section. This was massive, faced on both sides and measuring 90cm in width, suggesting that it was a very substantial build. This north–south section was also two courses and had been demolished to a similar level, the entire remains sealed by mixed bands of white crumbly mortar, rubble and charcoal, the demolished remains of the structure.

Mortar floor/surface As mentioned previously, the brick build was associated with a mortar floor that abutted it at the eastern end and this was very extensive, lying between 60cm (west) and 45cm (east) below present ground level. The surface was composed of a light grey soft mortar, 20cm in depth (which sounded hollow), and was an extensive spread, the western end surviving in a stretch that measured 4m east–west. However, it could be traced a further 8m east in both sections of the trench, suggesting a total length of 12m east–west. At the western end, the surface was at the required depth and, as a result, was left *in situ*, but further east the surface was slightly higher and was removed, revealing cobbles beneath at 60cm below present ground level (see below). The entire surface was sealed by two distinct deposits, limestone rubble (which did not have much brick) and a band of black charcoal, 30cm in depth.

Monitoring 2006 (no. 1: 2006) (fig. 12.2)   A trench was monitored in 2006 running parallel to SECTION 14, but lying approximately 4.2m south along the edge of the green and measuring 60cm in width by between 80 and 115cm in depth (Simpson 2006). The western end produced the distinctive early brick deposits, lying 60cm below present ground level and extending to at least 50cm in depth. The deposit mostly consisted of fragments of red/orange brick, but this was mixed in with limestone fragments with mortar attached along with some plaster, indicative of demolition material. A possible original ground level, formed from a clay beaten surface, lay at 1.1m in depth, below present ground level.

Cobbles   On removal of the mortar floor at the eastern end, a patch of cobbles was identified along the northern side of the trench, lying 60cm below present ground level. These consisted of large oval and rounded cobbles, laid generally north-east–south-west, and their general depth suggests that they are relatively early, in addition to the fact that they predated the mortar floor of the building. The cobbles only survived in a very small patch measuring 1m east–west by 60cm wide, and varied in size, measuring between 4 and 12cm in diameter. These were similar in type to other cobbled surfaces found during various site-works at this end of the college, which suggests some sort of a cobbled open area in this location prior to the laying out of Parliament Square. The cobbled surface was sealed by a layer of compact rubble, 12cm in depth, which was very hard and produced no finds but contained charcoal and shell.

Later features: the rubbish pit   A manhole was constructed at the western end of the trench and this revealed a large cut or pit, lying 47cm below the present ground level and measuring 1m north–south, but it extended further south as it was traced in SECTION 15. It was filled with dark black consistent and compressed organic layers, which contained fragments of off-white mortar, orange brick, shells and cinders (see below).

Conclusion of SECTION 14 (fig. 12.26)   The excavation of SECTION 14 produced significant information about the northern side of the 'Wester bawn' in the sixteenth and seventeenth centuries, suggesting the presence of brick structures and other features in accordance with the cartographic and documentary sources, confirmation that the early development of the college was occurring to the north-west of the original college quadrangle. The early brick spread was much in evidence along the north side of Parliament Square and it must have formed part of the early precinct, which was developed quickly, as evidenced by the Baker buildings, which were under construction by 1638 (Simpson 2002, 223). There were also buildings in this location from the monastic period and it is likely that these buildings were used in the early years, most likely supplemented by the additional brick buildings for which evidence was found during the monitoring programme. Vast quantities of brick were purchased by the college to repair existing buildings (Budd 2001, 51).

The sources indicate that the Great Bawn was eventually divided into smaller areas and by 1640 not only were the Baker buildings under construction along the northern boundary but so too was the Fitzgerald block along the north-eastern side (Simpson 2002, 214). In 1670, however, it was decided to refurbish the western frontage of the college and part of the Baker building was demolished at this time, presumably the western end (ibid., 223). By the late seventeenth century, the building activity was concentrating on enlarging the 'Great Court', now Parliament Square, resulting in the construction of the Radcliffe buildings adjoining the Alexander building (fig. 12.12). The most significant effect of this was that the western frontage, probably just a precinct wall in the central area at this date, was moved westwards and this must have involved demolition of the brick buildings already constructed. The southern side of the square was relatively undeveloped at this date and was not completed until the late 1690s (Mc Carthy n.d., 8).

The new western frontage involved the infilling of the ground in Parliament Square to almost 1m, and this was done with domestic refuse and brick demolition debris, a common deposit used in Dublin to infill at this time. This demolition deposit sealed all that had gone and formed the bedding for cobbles. This significant deposit is identifiable right across Front Square, deepening towards the west, as there was a fall in ground, towards Front Gate where the Steine river and generally low-lying marshy ground was located. The general levels of infill observed suggest that the priory of All Hallows had been situated on a prominence surrounded on at least three sides (east, west and north) by generally low-lying ground.

SECTION 15 (fig. 12.26)
This trench was orientated north–south, running parallel to the west wall of the chapel and outside House 10. It turned south-east at the southern end.

Brick layer   At the northern end of the trench, a brick layer was exposed at 62cm below present ground level, and this was a hard and compact crushed brick deposit, possibly a trampled surface, truncated at the southern end by a later cut (see below). This brick layer also contained pebbles and mortar, and may have marked the location of a wall, although this was difficult to establish. The deposit was certainly related to the seventeenth-century brick walls and mortar floor located further west in SECTION 14, suggested by the type of brick, which included an orange brick but also early brick associated with the Old College. However, a third type of brick was also found within this deposit and this had a distinctive pinkish hue, suggesting that the differences in colour were caused by the overlying deposits.

Later features: the rubbish pit, infill and truncation   The continuation of the pit identified in SECTION 14 was also found in SECTION 15, the top lying 30cm below present ground level and extending for 3.7m. As in SECTION 14, the infill was a dark brown highly organic layer, which had a purple tinge and produced a number of pottery sherds, datable to the late seventeenth and eighteenth century. A significant amount of cinders and charcoal could be identified within the deposit, suggesting that it represents domestic refuse, presumably emanating from the college and dumped in pits in and around the square, as found elsewhere. The feature was truncated by a second larger cut at the southern end (see below). At 5.80m south of the pit, both it and the earlier brick layer beneath were abruptly cut by a second larger pit or truncation, which was infilled with a loose mortar and rubble fill. This contained slate and stone and was identical to the infill deposit identified outside House 7 in SECTION 14. This cut extended for the remainder of the trench, over 4.5m in length north–south by at least 55cm in depth.

Conclusion of SECTION 15 (fig. 12.26)   The layer of brick identified at the northern end of SECTION 15 is most likely to be related to the structure to the north-west identified in SECTION 14. However, this brick layer was founded on a mixed limestone which appears to be a demolition deposit (but with no brick), suggesting a sequence of buildings and demolitions in this area. This may be the result of the demolition of some sort of stone house that was not built of brick and was earlier than the foundation of the college, possible related to the priory. One monastic building, 'the wester stone house', was somewhere at the western end of college, as was the gate tower of the priory, fronting onto Dame Street. However, only a small section of this deposit was examined.

The brick clays, the bright orange/red and the brick with a pinkish hue must be related to the various ranges constructed in this area from the 1640s, traces of which were found in SECTION 14. The organic layer that sealed the clays was distinctive and appeared to represent refuse, a type of mixed deposit that is so often found in pre-Georgian cellars, which were sometimes infilled with the domestic waste from the house itself. The cut or truncation at the southern end may have been for a service of some description, although the southern extent was not exposed. It measured at least 1m in length, north–south and was evidently a significant feature.

SECTION 16 (figs 12.26, 12.28)

The trench was orientated east–west and extended past the chapel, continuing from SECTION 15 at the western end. In general, this trench exposed the remains of an early brick culvert, probably associated with the college and part of that early first drainage complex also found in SECTION 4 and pre-eighteenth-century cobbles. Other features included a surface of brick and mortar and the remains of a wall that pre-dated the construction of the chapel (1798). Dumps of seventeenth-century domestic refuse were found at the eastern end of the trench, having been used as general infill.

Culvert 1 (*c*.1592?) (fig. 12.26)   The remains of a brick culvert were exposed at the western end of the trench and this was orientated north-east–south-west. It was a very substantial build. The exterior of the drain was exposed through a hole in the roof and from this it was evident that it measured internally 40cm wide by 42cm in height, standing four courses. The roof was formed by large uncut limestone cappings, at least one of which measured 30 by 40 by 15cm. The pointing was very distinctive and the joints were particularly wide, bonded with a hard yellowish mortar containing stone and grit inclusions. The southern end of the culvert was fully exposed where it had been damaged, and at this end the half bricks could be examined *in situ*, where they were found to measure, in general, 18 by 8 by 5cm, but were generally irregularly sized. Most significantly, the brick can be identified as the early bright red brick of the Old College walls, suggesting that the drain forms part of an early drainage system, as identified in SECTION 4 (see above). The orientation of the drain, north-east–south-west, suggests an early orientation associated with the Old College, although this area lay outside the quadrangle to the north, according to the Hatfield depiction. This early orientation, however, is also reflected in a drain in SECTION 16 and a wall in SECTION 17 (see below).

Spread/capping   A mix of brick, limestone and concrete-like cement extended from the eastern side of the culvert mentioned above, a distance of 2m, and this appeared to represent some sort of sealing deposit or capping, which sealed the east wall of Culvert 1 at the western end. It lay 35cm below present ground level and was composed of a mix of small limestone, 14cm in diameter, and half brick, all mixed with a substantial deposit of off-white pure mortar, which was difficult to remove. At the eastern end, when part of this deposit was removed, the remains of a brick, north–south wall were exposed (see below).

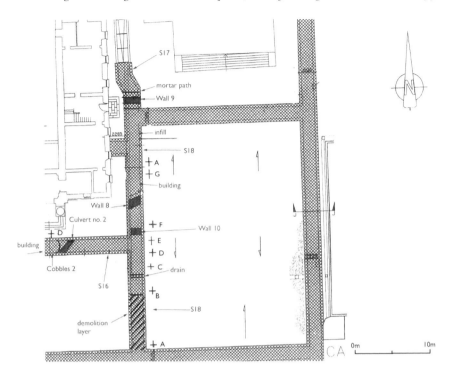

12.28 SECTIONS 16–18.

Wall 1   A small north–south wall was located on the eastern side of the drain, lying 32cm below present ground level, but sealed within a hard concrete mix, which was difficult to remove. It originally measured 44cm in width and stood 16cm in height, composed of a mix of hard concrete-like mortar and mixed brick fragments, along with fragments of slate. There was no discernible face and it was mortared with concrete-like mortar throughout. The stone used in the wall was smaller than in the culvert, measuring, on average, 10 by 15cm, and including a mix of brick. The mortar was a cementatious dark grey mortar with grit inclusions. Although difficult to date, this wall was small and formed a foundation rather than a major structural wall and, judging by the brick, is eighteenth century. While it may relate to a service, it is likely to be earlier than the chapel steps built in 1798 (designed by William Chambers) and is perhaps connected with the northern end of the west range of the 'Old Square' depicted by Rocque (fig. 12.13).

Cobbles 1   A small section of cobbling was identified almost centrally within the trench and lying 40cm below present ground level. The patch measured only 47cm north–south by 30cm wide and it was composed of long oval limestone cobbles, measuring, on average 15 by 5cm, set vertically but loosely in a dark brown/black silty clay mix. The stones were generally orientated east–west and evidently formed a surface, but these were possibly earlier than Wall 1 as they were at a lower level. They certainly suggest that the area north of the old quadrangle was cobbled in the late seventeenth/early eighteenth century.

Yellow mortar deposit   A mortar deposit was identified in the northern section of the trench, east of the cobbles, and this measured 90cm in length (east–west) by 20cm in depth. This deposit was extensive, composed of light yellow crumbly mortar, 20cm in depth, which extended as far east as a second section of cobbling (Cobbles 2), almost linking the two features.

Cobbles 2 (fig. 12.28)   The second stretch of cobbling was far more extensive and lay further west, at a similar level to Cobbles 1, between 38 and 45cm below present ground level, the yellow mortar described above abutting it on the western side. The cobbles extended eastwards for a distance of at least 6.3m, suggesting a substantial surface but possibly not part of Cobbles 1, as they were better laid and composed of larger stones. These cobbles were also oval limestone, and set vertically into a dark grey silt, which contained cinders, limestone fragments and mortar but far more securely and packed more tightly. The stones were also different, of varying sizes, ranging from massive rounded boulders, between 22 by 15cm and 17 by 10cm, to smaller cobbles measuring between 10 by 5cm and 8 by 5cm in diameter at the eastern end. They were set closely and neatly together and formed a major compacted surface, probably late sixteenth to seventeenth century in date.

The brick and mortar surface   Cobbles 2 were sealed by a thin layer of dark grey silt at the eastern extremity, 8cm in depth, which formed the bedding for a second surface, of which only a small section survived. This second surface, which extended for only 1.8m at the eastern of the cobbles, was a solid cementatious yellow mortar, while at the western end it was composed of bright red brick dust and measured 11cm in depth, sealing the cobbles directly. The brick layer on top of the cobbles was a feature of some of the cobbled surfaces elsewhere (SECTIONS 6, 8), where they were thought to be an early feature, suggesting that the cobbles were augmented in some way by brick (perhaps by the addition of brick paths?). The mortar and brick surface was formed on dark grey silt, as mentioned above, which contained small stones and flecks of brick, but no finds. The silt deposit was laid deliberately, perhaps as a bedding for the surface, as it sealed a layer of rubble composed of small limestone, averaging 20cm in diameter, below which was a layer of soft yellow mortar, with very little brick.

A brick surface   The remains of a distinct brick surface or floor were identified extending over a distance of 4.3m and lying approximately 25cm below present ground level, only 5cm in depth. This surface sealed Cobbles 2 and the mortar and brick floor, and suggests the presence of an additional brick floor with a very distinctive dip in the middle. It contained one fragment of mottled glass and a fragment of Frechen, which can be dated to the late sixteenth or early seventeenth century and must have been associated with an earlier structure in this location, although this is difficult to place on the cartographic sources.

Culvert 2   A second large drain or culvert was exposed at the eastern end of the trench and this was still active, carrying water. It was constructed of solid limestone and contained no brick and was orientated north-east–south-west, similar to Culvert 1, which is likely to be sixteenth century. Access was difficult, but the culvert was at least 60cm in width by 50cm in height. It was clearly a substantial structure. It has been in use for a considerable time as it contains silt deposits along the base, which contained modern debris. The culvert truncated the cobbles and is thus later, although the orientation reflects the orientation of Culvert 1 to the west, which was built of early brick. A set of modern services, including sewer and heating pipes, was located along the western side of Culvert 2 in a concrete casing measuring 1.1m in width. On the western side of the culvert, the upper deposit was a dark silty clay layer, with animal bone, mortar fragments, shell and one sherd of eighteenth-century pottery. This end of the trench was not excavated, as the old sewer was converted into a manhole.

Domestic refuse   A spread of dark brown clay, including lenses of sand and containing animal bone, was located at the eastern end of the trench, and this sealed a mixed clay and stone deposit, which contained stone and slate. This appeared to be dumped domestic refuse, rich in finds of shell and animal bone, but producing little pottery apart from one sherd of brown ware, seventeenth-century in date. This material appears to have been used to infill the ground and was similar in type to the organic deposit at the southern end of Trench 15.

Natural ground   Midway along the trench, natural clay was exposed, lying 60cm below present ground level. This was dark brown/yellow clay with some stone inclusions. At the eastern end, yellow sticky boulder clay was located 80cm below present ground level.

Later feature: rubble deposit 1   A major demolition layer, composed of a mixed mortar deposit, containing brick and charcoal, was exposed at the western end of the trench, extending for just less than 5m. At the western end, the top of the rubbles lies 48cm below present ground level, but it humps up, rising to the east and, at its highest point, is just 24cm below present ground level. The deposit is composed of heavy dark orange brick, half bricks and limestone fragments, suggestive of a major demolition phase. This is sealed by layers of organic refuse, sand and mortar.

Conclusion of SECTION 16 (fig. 12.28)   SECTION 16 provided good information about the development of the college outside the Old College quadrangle. The small culvert (Culvert 1) at the western end of the trench may be related to the Old College phase (*c.*1592) and was similar to that found in SECTION 6. The second large culvert (Culvert 2) at the eastern end was also potentially early, possibly reflected in the orientation (north-east–south-west), but also in the fact that it was constructed entirely of limestone with no brick and was evidently a major drainage feature.

The major cobbled surface at the western of the trench (Cobbles 2) is likely to have been seventeenth century and therefore forms part of the general developments, as depicted in the Dineley sketch of 1681 (fig. 12.10), most notably the addition of a new east range directly north of the old quadrangle, perhaps even associated with the Scott buildings, built by 1640 to the east (fig. 12.8). This new courtyard was evidently cobbled by this time. The distinctive brick surface over the cobbles (Cobbles 2) is also interesting as this is a feature found in SECTION 6 and 8 and is suggestive of either demolition of early brick structures or augmentation by additional brick surfaces. The mortar spread and wall are difficult to identify or date in such a small trench, but appear, by date, to be relatively late in the sequence, lying only 32cm from present ground level. They are clearly a rough foundation. The mix of brick suggests a date later than the seventeenth-century brick structure found further west in SECTION 14 and it may have been associated with drainage works, which were removed. The other significant information gleaned from this section of trench is that boulder clay lies between 60 and 80cm below present ground level.

SECTION 17 (fig. 12.28)
This trench was at the northern end of SECTION 18, extending northwards, parallel to the chapel (1798) but extending for less than 10m. The excavation identified the truncated remains of what may have been a solid medieval wall, orientated east–west, and infill deposits of rubble and refuse deposits, dated to the late seventeenth and early eighteenth century. Traces of an east–west path, perhaps associated with the chapel or its forerunner, were also found, north of the possible medieval wall. The eighteenth-century cobbled surface found elsewhere in Front Square was also exposed.

Possible medieval wall (Wall 9)   The major feature in this section, as mentioned above, was the foundation of a substantial limestone wall, orientated east–west, the top of which lay 72cm below present ground level.

This wall may be medieval and measured at least 1.05m in width, and possibly wider, as its southern face appeared to have been robbed out. It was composed of large roughly cut limestone blocks, measuring, on average, 30 by 40cm, and was strongly mortared with an off-white/yellow mortar, similar to the possible medieval wall further south, Wall 8 (SECTION 18). Only the lower two courses of the wall survived, standing to just 18cm. It was mortared right the way through, with no rubble core. This was clearly a foundation, as it was built within a wall trench cut into the natural clays.

Cobbles A small patch of cobbles was identified immediately north of the possible medieval wall (Wall 9), 60cm below present ground level. It extended east–west for only 1.5m east–west, but had clearly been severely truncated at either end. The limestone cobbles were generally oblong and rounded and were set upright within a brown silty organic deposit, similar to other cobbles found in and around Front Square. This surface is likely to represent the first cobbled surface after the great demolitions of the eighteenth century.

A mortar path The remains of a mortar path, orientated east–west, sealed the cobbles, its construction probably preserving the cobbles beneath. This path lay 60cm below present ground level and was 1m in width, the lowest level being defined by a layer of crumbly yellow mortar, 7cm in depth. This was sealed by hard orange gravel, 17cm in depth, which had a deep iron-panned staining resulting in a very distinctive bright orange colour. On examination, this was found to be a very compacted surface with a distinctive humped profile, the top of which was only 40cm below present ground level. An edging of stones was identified along the southern side (eastern end), composed of a series of limestone blocks, measuring, on average, 30 by 25cm and set close together. The orientation of the path did line up with a door in the east wall of the chapel (1798), suggesting that it was an original access route.

Later features: dumped infill deposits A series of infill deposits was identified at the northern end of the trench, which contained rounded stones, oyster shell and purple slate, likely to have been domestic refuse from the college. A total of five deposits were identified, measuring between 7 and 17cm in depth. These were evidence of a consistent dumping campaign in this location. The lowest deposit consisted of a rubble layer, containing brick, which was sealed by a layer of mixed clay containing lumps of brick, large animal bones and off-white crumbly mortar. This was overlain by a similar mixed clay containing bricks and clay with distinctive large fragments of charcoal. The upper layer consisted of brown clay, with stone lenses along with gritty lenses containing charcoal and brick. The lowest level produced a tiny

fragment of thin glazed brown pottery, which was dated to the seventeenth/
eighteenth century.

Conclusion of SECTION 17 (fig. 12.28)   The large wall (Wall 9) was
probably medieval, lying some distance to the north of the main monastic
quadrangle, but was very truncated and only the top was exposed, making
speculation difficult. However, the documentary sources do record a stone
building with a vault in the general vicinity, an indication that there were stone
buildings outside the main quadrangle of the priory (Simpson 2002, 217–18).
In addition, while this wall may have been medieval, it could also have been a
foundation associated with the early development of the college, as Walls 4 and
5 in SECTION 3 did have limestone foundations and an early block, known as
Fitzgerald's, was built in *c*.1640 (fig. 12.8) in this location. This block is also
depicted on Gomme's map of 1673 (fig. 12.9).

It should be noted that previous archaeological investigations to the west of
SECTION 17, along the site of the west range of Library Square, also located
limestone walls, one of which (Wall 5: fig. 12.14), while badly damaged, was
also large, measuring 90cm in width by 50cm in height (three courses high)
(Simpson 2002a). It was constructed of limestone blocks and extended for at
least 7.5m, north–south, along the line of the projected west range of Library
Square. This wall, however, was significantly larger than the other walls
associated with the west range of Library Square (Walls 1, 3, 7) and may have
been earlier.

Wall 9 was evidently demolished by the time the cobbles were laid, and this
may have been an early surface associated with the pre-demolition phase of
Front Square, although only a small patch survived. The iron-panned-stained
gravel deposit, which was edged in stone, is likely to have been a pathway, and
this may have been relatively late as it corresponded to a door in the east wall
of the chapel, constructed in 1798. The northern end of the trench revealed
deep layers of organic infill, composed of domestic refuse, the legacy of the
general infill project at this end of the college.

SECTION 18 (fig. 12.28)
This trench was orientated north–south and was located at the eastern end of
SECTION 16, extending southwards to the middle of Front Square. The most
significant find was an extensive limestone rubble deposit at the southern end,
which may have been related to the demolition of the belfry or spire of the Old
College, thought to have formed the steeple of the medieval church of the
priory. The tower was reused in the Old College phase, when it was converted
into an octagonal steeple as depicted in the Dineley drawing of 1681 (fig.
12.10), and it was repaired between 1610 and 1620 (Simpson 2002, 215). The
remains of a possible medieval wall (Wall 8) were also found, and this was

12.29 SECTION 18, tower rubble from south-west.

orientated north-east–south-west, also suggestive of an earlier orientation, first identified to the west and reflected in the Old College drainage system (Culverts 1, 2, SECTION 16). The remains of an early brick wall or surface, probably associated with the Old College, were also found.

Demolished belfry/steeple? A deep deposit of limestone rubble was identified at the southern end of the trench, and this was clearly a demolition deposit and composed wholly of fragments of mortar and limestone, the latter averaging 20cm in diameter (fig. 12.29). The mortar was a loose dry lime mortar, off-white but containing small grit inclusions with no evidence of any brick. The spread extended for almost 6m from the southern end of the trench, but, most strikingly, there was vertical interface between the demolition deposit and the clay layers that had accumulated to the north, presumably against the face of a wall now gone. This interface was at least 40cm in depth, but was not bottomed in this location. The clays that had accumulated on the northern side consisted of layers of deposits, the basal one of which contained early brick, suggesting that this was an early feature. The position, as mentioned above, suggests that it represents the remains of the bell tower of the monastic church of the priory of All Hallows, outside the Old College quadrangle.

Possible medieval wall (Wall 8)   The remains of a wall were located in the centre of the trench, 68cm below present ground level, and this was similar to the medieval wall, Wall 7 in SECTION 7 (fig. 12.30). It was a substantial wall, but, significantly, the structure was orientated north-east–south-west, and therefore correlated with the orientation of Culverts 1 and 2 in SECTION 16, an orientation not reflected in the various cartographic and pictorial sources but possibly related to the priory. The wall was substantial, originally measuring 1.2m in width, but was badly damaged, standing only one course high. The facing on either side had also been robbed out, suggesting that it was originally at least another 60cm in width, giving a total width of close to 2m. It was constructed of large limestone blocks, measuring, on average, 30 by 40cm, and was very heavily mortared with a fine beige silty lime mortar, containing visible inclusions of both lime and charcoal. Localized excavation revealed that the wall was founded on a dump of large limestones, which formed a foundation, composed of irregular limestone, measuring, on average, 15cm in diameter. This foundation was heavily mortared with hard grey/off-white mortar.

A possible building?   The northern side of the wall was incorporated within a later building at some date, and this was suggested by the remains of a brick floor, lying 70cm below present ground level, and sealed by seventeenth-century clays. This floor extended for at least 80cm, north–south, and was 3cm in depth, the remains suggesting that it comprised rotted floor tiles, as one fragment survived. This thin plain tile, the fragment of which measured 8 by 6cm, had a dark red fabric and was glazed green on the upper surface. The floor was laid on a layer of mixed dark brown clay, which contained early brick fragments along with dark red brick and shell.

Brick wall/surface (Wall 10)   A spread of compressed brick clay was identified between the possible belfry demolition deposits and the possible medieval wall (Wall 8), and this lay 60cm below present ground level. It measured 1.1m north–south by 60cm in width (the trench was widened at this point for a manhole) and was of early brick, similar to the brick used elsewhere in the Old College. The rotten brick layer was 25cm in depth and was very pure, suggesting that it represents either a wall or a surface or even some sort of construction level. It was on a distinctive mixed dark green clay deposit, which contained stone and large animal bones and was at least 90cm in depth, excavated in this location for the manhole. This clay also contained fragments of yellow sandstone, similar to that found further west, in and around Front Gate.

Limestone wall? *(not illustrated)*   The remains of a very rough limestone build, composed of small limestone, were identified just south of Wall 10 lying at 42cm below present ground level and this may be all that survives of a very truncated wall, orientated east–west, although this was impossible to ascertain.

12.30 SECTION 18, Wall 8, from the south.

The remains were fragmentary in the extreme and consisted of a small concentration of stone, measuring collectively 31cm wide by 20cm deep. However, the stones, which measured 10 by 12cm, were mortared with a grey mortar containing lime inclusions, similar to the possible medieval wall, Wall 8 (see above), suggesting that it represents a much robbed-out build. The wall was sitting on a yellow clay layer, acting as a foundation, and was sealed by a mixed dumped deposit that contained blackware pottery, datable to the eighteenth and nineteenth centuries.

Later features: drain and vitrified cinders The remains of an east–west drain were identified at the southern end of the trench, which was located just beneath the cobbles and bedding and this was probably contemporary with the laying out of Front Square in the mid-eighteenth century. It had been exposed previously when the capping was removed, probably when the modern cobbles were relaid in the 1970s. The drain measured internally 42cm in width by 22cm in height and the side walls were built of limestone blocks, averaging 14 by 25cm. Sections of the roof capping did survive, where they were found to be of thin dark grey slate, while the base was of green slate. The entire structure was mortared with an off-white coarse mortar, with inclusions of grit and charcoal, and the base was composed of green slate. It was almost completely blocked by a pure black silt deposit, which contained fragments of early brick, slate and charcoal but no ceramics. Unfortunately, the drain had to be removed as part of the works as it was less than 20cm below present ground level. A spread of black cinders was identified north of the drain and these deposits were vitrified and, as a result, were very hard and compact, resembling a hardened surface, although this was impossible to ascertain. In total, the spread measured 1.5m in length north–south and was 13cm in depth, containing inclusions of dark grey clay, brick fragments, purple slate, stone and bone fragments, the latter suggesting that it represents cellar refuse, dumped to infill the ground as elsewhere in this area.

Natural ground   Bright orange boulder clay was identified at the southern end of the trench, lying at 60cm below present ground level.

Conclusion of SECTION 18 (fig. 12.28)   The most significant finding of SECTION 18 was the possible remains of the demolished belfry or steeple at the southern end of the trench, marked by a deep and distinctive deposit of limestone rubble (fig. 12.29). The belfry was at the western end of the church, which formed part of the north range, on the eastern side. This medieval building is likely to have survived and formed part of the Old College complex, still connected to the chapel at this end (demolished in the late seventeenth century) (Budd 2001, 52). The location of a possible limestone structure in this location was suggested by a vertical interface between the mortar remains and the early brick and clay deposits that accumulated against the north face of the building and measured 40cm in depth. If the position of the original north range of both the priory and the Old College is correct, as it is likely to be, based on Rocque (1756) (fig. 12.13), the belfry/steeple measured almost 6m north–south and was located not quite on the corner of the quadrangle, as suggested in the cartographic and pictorial sources.

This steeple is the only monastic building that can be identified in the Old College having survived the Dissolution of the monasteries, appearing in the Hatfield depiction (fig. 12.6), de Gomme's map of 1678 (fig. 12.9) and Dineley's sketch of 1681 (fig. 12.10). In addition, the sources record a steeple, which was in a bad state of repair in 1571 (before the college was founded), and again in 1600 and 1610, when it was repaired, making it likely that it was the same structure (Simpson 2002, 215).

The second significant finding was the location of what is likely to be a medieval wall (Wall 8) composed of large limestone blocks but very badly truncated, the facing apparently robbed out on the northern side. This wall contained no brick and was similar in type and mortar to Wall 7 across the Square in SECTION 7, suggesting a substantial build, but outside the original main quadrangle. If the wall is medieval, the north-east–south-west orientation must also be significant, reflecting an orientation now lost, but preserved in the lines of the later culverts (1, 2) identified in SECTION 16. There was at least one medieval building in this location in 1538, recorded as a stone building with a vault and garden, on the north side of All Hallows (Simpson 2002, 218). This possible medieval wall was later incorporated within a building lying to the north, which in turn was demolished in the late seventeenth/early eighteenth century. It is difficult to establish what this building might have been, but there may be a hint on the de Gomme map (1673) in the projection in the north range, eastern end, which represents the steeple and what may be another building on the northern side (fig. 12.8). This might have been Scott's building, which was just north of the steeple (fig. 12.8).

The remains of the east–west early brick spread (Wall 10) may be all that survives of some sort of a brick wall in this location, perhaps an outer precinct wall associated with the Old College. It might have been associated with the very truncated limestone build to the south, which was possibly a wall, although this was impossible to establish on the limited area of excavation. The cinder deposit is easier to identify and is likely to represent infill, presumably dating to the early eighteenth century, while the drain can be associated with a cobbled surface, which preceded the modern one and was probably also mid- to late eighteenth century.

SECTION 19 (fig. 12.2)

An additional section was opened up on 8 November 2011, which consisted of a 1m-square pit excavated to form a foundation for a Christmas tree (fig. 12.2) (erected that year for the first time), along with a service trench connecting into SECTION 6. This located the foundations of the west wall of the east range, confirming the position of the quadrangle. The trench was expanded in this location to avoid the wall foundation.

West wall of the east range   The remains of a very truncated north–south limestone wall were located lying just 35cm below present ground level, and this is likely to be the west wall of the east range, previously exposed in SECTION 3 (Wall 5). The position of the wall, however, suggests that the quadrangle was orientated slightly north-west–south-east rather than true north–south, an orientation reflected in Rocque's map of 1756 (fig. 12.13). Unfortunately, the wall was found to be much damaged on the western side and, as a result, measured only approximately 75cm in width. It stood at least 43cm in depth, but the base was not exposed as it was below the required level. A total of four courses survived, and the wall was tightly coursed, the blocks varying in size from long and narrow (60 by 10cm) to almost square (30 by 25cm). There was a very distinctive demolition deposit of early brick across the wall, a feature of Walls 4 and 5 (SECTION 3) further south, and this presumably represented the upstanding brick section of the wall, demolished over the foundations in the mid- to late eighteenth century.

The mortar of the wall in general was a creamy white with charcoal flecks, and the entire structure was very heavily mortared, similar to Walls 4 and 5, at the southern end of the east range. However, a second mortar type was identified at the very base of the wall at the northern end, where it was very yellow, gritty and friable, suggesting that this end of the wall was earlier, despite the fact that, at the southern end, Walls 4 and 5 had no earlier elements. However, an organic layer that abutted the east face of the wall (north end) at this low level did not produce any brick, suggesting a possible medieval date for the lower foundations.

The brick build   The remains of a skim wall or build of brick were identified extending along the east face of the wall for at least 45cm in length north–south, and this was composed of a single width of handmade orange brick (15cm in width), not the early brick of the Old College but rather that identified elsewhere as seventeenth century (SECTIONS 12, 14, 15, 16). It did not extend further north originally, as there were organic deposits in situ along the east face of the wall at the northern end, but was clearly related to the wall. This build was just 13cm from the east face of the wall and was within a cut that measured 30cm in width, the gap between it and the wall filled with loose rubble. The structure was very heavily mortared with a light yellow mortar, and the brick was the very distinctive, bright orange and measuring 22 by 10 by 6.5cm; thus, it was larger than the very early brick found in demolition rubble sealing the wall and the earlier investigations and dated to *c.*1592. This may have represented some sort of brick lining built up against the wall within the east range. It was sealed when the wall was demolished in the eighteenth century.

East side of wall   The trench was repositioned eastwards to avoid the wall and this exposed, at 1m below present ground level, a sticky brown organic clay layer, which contained shell and animal bone, but no finds or evidence of any brick, raising the possibility that it is a medieval deposit. This layer, which was at least 10cm in depth, abutted the east face of the wall at the northern end, where a yellow mortar was also noted, coating the wall face. The organic layer was sealed on the southern side by a thick deposit of grey sticky clay, 40cm in depth, which contained numerous stones, some as large as 6cm in diameter, along with cockle shell fragments and animal bone and cinders, but little else. The grey clay was then sealed by two layers of rubble, the first a crushed rubble layer mostly composed of mortar, the second a coarser bright red brick, the early brick of the college. The final deposit was a spread of highly organic material, evidently dumped domestic refuse, which extended the full length of the pit, over the wall and along the trench at the western side.

This deposit was noted elsewhere in the college and represents a deliberate attempt to infill the ground with refuse, which included cinders, animal bone, grit and stones.

CONCLUSIONS

The archaeological monitoring programme at Trinity College has proved very fruitful in providing new and tangible evidence of the archaeological potential of Front Square, which is known to contain the sites of two Recorded Monuments (RMP), the medieval priory of All Hallows and the Old College of *c*.1592. It is now known that the great demolitions from the mid-eighteenth century onwards, which saw the removal of the Old College and culminated in the monumental Front Square we see today, did not sweep away all that went before, as the footprints of the older buildings survive, sealed beneath a thin layer of infill material and lying between 30 and 60cm below present ground level. While the investigations were very limited in scope, in regard to the width and general depth of the trenches, they did extend right across Front Square, from Library Square in the east as far west as Front Gate, providing comprehensive cover across the area of interest.

It has frequently been hypothesized that the site of the monastic range of All Hallows and the quadrangle of the Old College were one and the same, and, based on this new evidence, that now seems proven. The investigations have also confirmed the presence of at least four possible medieval walls (Walls 3, 7, 8, 9) and perhaps the foundations of the belfry or steeple – an inkling of what potential exists for the discovery of further significant foundations related to the medieval priory.

The positive identification of the east and west ranges of the Old College, and possibly part of the south range, was also a significant finding, as was the identification of what is probably one of the earliest uses of brick in Dublin. The account of the Old College given by Provost Travers in the immediate aftermath of its foundation was also verified during this work: the measurement he gives of 120 feet for the internal width of the court converts to 36.5m, which correlates with the distance between the west wall of the west range (Wall 6: SECTION 6) and the west wall of the east range (Wall 5: SECTION 5). This suggests that the quadrangle measured 52.25m in width externally (with the ranges measuring *c*.8m in width externally by 5.3m internally).

The information unearthed was not confined to the Old College quadrangle, as early features were also exposed to the west, suggesting that the 'western bawn' formed part of the Old College precinct from the very beginning, as one might suspect, since it was the main frontage of the college. The subsequent evolution and north-westward development of the college was also charted during the monitoring programme, a large number of post-Old College features being found in almost every trench, documenting the rapid building development programme from the mid-seventeenth century onwards. This includes evidence of the new north-west range identified in SECTION 14 on the northern side of Parliament Square, where the documentary sources record that development began in the 1640s, along with the foundations of a large brick structure just south of Front Gate, which may have represented the earlier gatehouse in this location (before the frontage of the college was moved westwards in the 1690s). Even negative evidence was supported: there was an almost complete lack of buildings along the southern side of Parliament Square, in accordance with the documentary evidence charting its slightly later development. There were also hints of additional buildings just south of the present chapel, which are something of a puzzle but attest to development outside the old quadrangle in the mid- to late seventeenth century.

The final phase of development was a demolition programme and general infill, which can be traced across the western end of the college, stretching from the Campanile to Front Gate, as far south as the Provost's Garden. This is a significant layer in its own right, as it represents domestic waste, presumably from the college, used as an infill layer in some areas. It is full of artefactual and faunal material relating to the college in the mid-eighteenth century and earlier. Thus, the demolitions of the eighteenth century, while clearly very destructive above ground, also helped preserve a detailed and complex sequence of archaeological layers below ground, which document the history of the college from the medieval period to the present day.

BIBLIOGRAPHY

Bennett, Isabel 1987–present *Excavations: summary accounts of archaeological excavations in Ireland*. Dublin (also available online at www.excavations.ie).
Budd R., 1996 'The priory of All Hallows and the archaeology of Trinity College Dublin' (BA dissertation, TCD).
Budd, R., 2001 *The platforme of an universitie: All Hallows Priory to Trinity College Dublin*. Dublin.
McParland, E. 1978 'The buildings of Trinity College Dublin: part I, II and III', *Country Life*, 99:4114.
McParland, E. 2001 *'Public architecture in Ireland, 1680–1970*. London and New Haven.
Mc Carthy, D.P., n.d. 'Trinity College Dublin: layout in the seventeenth century' (unpublished typescript).
Mahaffy, J.P. 1904 *The particular book of Trinity College Dublin*. London.
Simpson L. 2002 'The priory of all Hallows and Trinity College Dublin: recent discoveries'. In S. Duffy (ed.), *Medieval Dublin III*, 195–236. Dublin.
Simpson, L. 2002a 'Archaeological monitoring of a pipe trench at College Green, Trinity College Dublin' (unpublished report lodged with the Department of the Environment, Heritage and Local Government and the National Museum of Ireland, 26 November 2002).

Simpson, L. 2006 'Archaeological monitoring of a service trench at the northern end of Parliament Square' (Front Square), Trinity College Dublin, Dublin 2' (unpublished report lodged with the Department of the Environment, Heritage and Local Government and the National Museum of Ireland, 7 April 2006).

Simpson, L. 2006a 'Archaeological monitoring of a service trench at the southern end of Parliament Square' (Front Square), Trinity College Dublin, Dublin 2' (unpublished report lodged with the Department of the Environment, Heritage and Local Government and the National Museum of Ireland, 12 October 2006).

Simpson, L. 2011 'Archaeological monitoring works of wheelchair accessible paths in Front Square and Old Library building, Trinity College, Dublin 2' (unpublished report lodged with the Department of the Environment, Heritage and Local Government and the National Museum of Ireland on 28 Nov. 2011).

APPENDIX 12.1

(see figs 12.15, 12.19, 12.21, 12.26, 12.28 for positions)

SECTION 1: STRAT. AA

0.00m–0.20m	Modern cobbles
0.20m–0.40m	Concrete slab
0.40m–0.42m	Bedding for concrete
0.45m–0.58m	Demolition layers including brick, limestone, cobbles and stones
0.58m–0.65m	Brown clay with charcoal flecks, fragments of mortar and brick

SECTION 2: STRAT. AA

0.00m–0.20m	Cobbles
0.20m–0.40m	Concrete bedding
0.40m–0.58m	Demolition layers including brick and mortar, likely to date to the eighteenth century

SECTION 3: STRAT. AA

0.00m–0.22m	Concrete bedding
0.22m–0.38m	Dark organic layer with lenses of charcoal and a distinctive layer of white mortar with red brick mixed through. This deposit also included very small fragments of brick and timber
0.38m–0.60m	Dark-grey sticky clay, with charcoal flecks and numerous animal bones along with purple slate

SECTION 3: STRAT. DD

0.00m–0.10m	Cobbles
0.10m–0.18m	Concrete bedding
0.18m–0.38m	Mixed grey fill containing loose cobbles brick and mortar (eighteenth-century demolition?)
0.38m–0.64m	Brick rubble, loose and dry, the brick thought to be sixteenth century
0.68m–0.76m	Dark grey soil with sandy clay and the occasional fragment of mortar
0.76m–0.98m	Similar dark grey soil with stones but visibly more mortar and grey slate. The mortar fragments are the same as the mortar used in the wall
0.98m–1.0m	Dark grey clay, a natural deposit

1.08m–1.34m   Large rounded boulders a natural deposit, measuring, on average 0.12m
               by 0.06m
1.46m   Light grey boulder clay

SECTION 4: STRAT. AA
0.00m–0.26m   Cobbles and concrete bedding
0.00m–0.60m   Dark brown organic stony clay deposit, loose and friable and containing
               charcoal, brick, some animal bone and small sherds of glass, eighteenth
               century
0.65m–0.70m   Fine gravel with some stone
0.70m–1.00m   Brown organic material (not excavated)

SECTION 6: STRAT. AA
0.00m–0.22m   Concrete bedding
0.22m–0.38m   Dark organic layer with lenses of charcoal and a distinctive layer of white
               mortar with red brick mixed through. Included very small fragments of
               brick and timber
0.38m–0.60m   Dark-grey sticky clay, with charcoal flecks and numerous animal bones
               along with purple slate
0.60m   Brick surface. Likely to be some sort of construction level or surface lying
               outside the west range but within the central courtyard

SECTION 7: STRAT. AA
0.00m–0.20m   Cobbles and bedding
0.15m–0.40m   General black/brown silty clay with bricks and general demolition
               material suggestive of infill
0.40m–0.65m   Pure red brick clay deposit, with small fragments of brick, only 20mm in
               diameter

SECTION 8: STRAT. AA
0.00m–0.40m   Modern cobbles and bedding
0.40m–0.46m   Sticky black/grey clay with early red brick fragments, assorted limestone
               and dark yellow gritty mortar
0.46m–0.70m   Almost pure early brick deposit, which contains actual fragments and
               chips early red brick, identified as part of the original college quadrangle
0. 70m   A layer of cobbles

SECTION 9: STRAT. AA
0.00m–0.38m   Cobbles and bedding
0.30m–0.65m   Mixed demolition layers containing early brick, mortar, charcoal and
               limestone. This deposit produced blackware ceramic, suggesting that it
               can be dated from the eighteenth to the nineteenth century. This
               demolition deposit indicates that this area is disturbed and, as a result, the
               brick layer and cobbles located just south in SECTION 8 were removed

SECTION 10: STRAT. AA
0.00m–0.35m   Cobbles and bedding
0.35m–0.40m   Mixed layer of clay and rubble with many pure red brick and fragments of
               limestone. This deposit produced blackware pottery

0.40m–0.60m   Hard stony clay, which was very cement-like. It was dark green, with small angular stones, containing brick and occasional animal bone

SECTION 11: STRAT. AA
0.00m–0.30m   Limestone setts and bedding
0.30m–0.65m   Infilled ground associated with the water main, which was identified in this trench, encased in concrete and very close to the surface. This old main appeared to be leaking
0.65m   A very coarse gravel and stone deposit, rounded stones, on average 50mm in diameter and set within an orange boulder clay, possibly natural ground

SECTION 12: STRAT. BB
0.10m–0.20m   Cobbles
0.20m–0.20m   Concrete
0.30m–0.60m   Mixed rubble deposit and clay deposit containing brick fragments and charcoal, similar to the deposit at the northern end of the trench but with less brick

SECTION 13: STRAT. AA
0.00m–0.18m   Cobbles and bedding
0.18m–0.28m   Concrete and light grey mortar
0.28m–0.50m   Mixed clay with brick, charcoal along with slate and fragments of dark purple slate
0.50m–0.57m   Dark band of organic material containing stones and charcoal flecks
0.57m–0.67m   Pure off-white creamy mortar, loose and friable with bright red fleck of early brick. Possibly an early deposit

SECTION 14: STRAT. AA
0.00m–0.28m   Cobbles and bedding
0.28m–0.50m   Mixed clay with brick, charcoal, purple slate, fragments of brick
0.50m–0.57m   Dark band of organic material, dark brown
0.57m–0.67m   Pure off-white creamy mortar, loose and friable, with brick red fleck. An early brick deposit

SECTION 15: STRAT. AA
0.10m–0.18m   Cobbles and bedding
0.18m–0.50m   Hard concrete and pebbles
0.50m–0.62m   Mixed loose purplish cellar fill with brick, slate (purple and grey), charcoal along with oyster shell measuring 3.80m north–south. Two sherds of tin-glazed earthenware were recovered along with a sherd of gravel tempered ware, seventeenth and eighteent centuries
0.62m   Brick clay deposit, as found elsewhere in association with the Old College. Hard and compact and had occasional pebbles and stone but appeared to be a tramped surface

SECTION 16: STRAT. AA
0.00m–0.14m   Cobbles and bedding
0.14m–0.24m   Hard concrete layer with small rounded limestone pebbles

0.24m–0.32m	Dark brown organic cellar fill, loose, friable, containing charcoal, coal, brick fragments (pure orange brick), animal bone fragments, small stones and purple slate. All the fragments were very small, suggesting that this material represented disturbed domestic waste, which had been moved around
0.32m–0.34m	A thin layer or lens of pure yellow sandstone
0.34m–0.48m	Dark brown clay, containing stones and some charcoal along with occasional brick fragments
0.48m–0.65m	Mixed loose mortar, off-white with pronounced charcoal and brick flecks

SECTION 17: STRAT. AA

0.00m–0.35m	Cobbles and bedding
0.35m–0.70m	Mixed rubble and demolition deposit, mostly consisting of light beige mortar but containing other demolition debris, including brick, limestone and slate. At the northern end, a vertical edge or cut was identified, extending for at least 0.40m in depth, suggesting the presence of a building in this location. This may have been the tower thought to have been positioned in this location
0.70m	Very sandy clay

SECTION 18: STRAT. AA

0.00m–0.22m	Cobbles and bedding
0.22m–0.70m	Dark brown consistent humic cellar fill containing animal bone, some large, along with dark red brick, slate and shell

Architecture for archaeology and urban context: the Ship Street–Werburgh Street Framework Plan

NIALL McCULLOUGH

McCullough Mulvin Architects were commissioned by the Heritage Department of Dublin City Council to prepare an architectural and urban design Framework Plan for the Ship Street–Werburgh Street area of Dublin in 2007. The Framework Plan came about as a part of the overall study of the Dublin City Walls Conservation Plan prepared by Margaret Gowen and Co. Ltd. While the study area focused on the strongly defined section of walls at Ship Street, the scope was gradually extended to cover a substantial section of the medieval city and suburbs, eventually stretching from George's Street to Patrick Street and from Christchurch Place to St Patrick's Cathedral – a relatively cohesive urban zone that subsequently became known as the 'Cathedral Quarter'. The project was a collaborative one, with the full engagement and support of the Heritage Department in particular (fig. 13.1).

The medieval city and its cathedrals are vividly imprinted in the public imagination; the area between them – Ship Street, Bride Street, Chancery Lane, Golden Lane, Peter Street – has been effectively eradicated from memory through the progressive destruction of its urban fabric. Relatively intact until the mid-twentieth century, existing buildings were subsequently demolished, with poorly conceived rebuilding taking place in the 1980s and 1990s, leaving little but its (widened) streets and topography as a memory. Denuded of meaning and recognition above ground, it endured as a grey and nameless quarter between the Central Business District and the Liberties.

The practice approached this work with a strong interest in the city, its history and, in particular, its archaeology, concerned to find a way to display archaeology in the context of new development and to determine methods by which the history of the city could be harnessed in an appropriate way to give depth, meaning and memory to contemporary architecture. It appeared to us that this had never been done in Dublin and that Dublin was in particular need of this approach – a piece-by-piece study of place leading to small, radical changes rather than a simplistic stock modernist analysis resulting in apparently innovative but in fact inappropriate and, in the end, arid solutions.

The study provided an opportunity to explore new possibilities in the fraught relationship between architecture, urban design and archaeology – an exchange littered with disenchantment and unsatisfactory solutions on both sides. While both disciplines are materially linked through built fabric

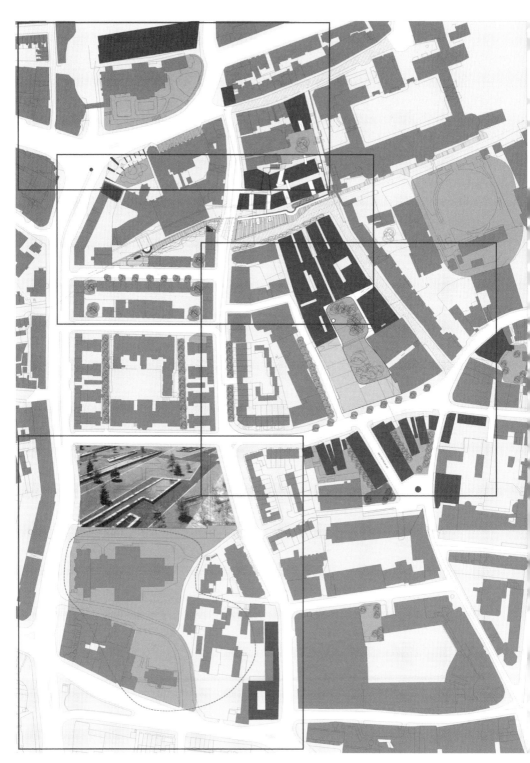

13.1 General plan of Ship Street–Werburgh Street Framework Plan area between the Liberties and the modern centre of Dublin defined by Ship Street, Christchurch Place, Patrick Street and Kevin Street; it is character-ized by a network of strongly defined north–south streets and a herringbone of smaller east–west ones. Dark hatch shows proposed new interventions into the urban fabric. There are four main areas – Christchurch Place, Ship Street Square, Ship Street/Golden Lane and St Patrick's Park; these are picked out in more detail in the following illustrations.

(necessary construction and destruction doggedly following one another through time) and both use the same language (a unique obsession with layering and levels, grids, the plan, section and the relationship between artefacts in space) these are approximations – perhaps inevitable in stepping from the forensic analysis of material remains to the subjective arrangement of the same materials to make life work – and which can, on occasion, be art. There are so many potential overlaps and so many gaps, not least the lack of an overall vision drawn from site reports across Dublin, the academically risky but fruitful linkage of urban plans exploring the aggregation of the city – what did you see from your door, orientation, space between buildings.

In practical terms, traditional European city plans carry a clear imprint of what lies beneath in a palimpsest of layers; the city plan is probably the greatest artefact of all physical remains, representative of continuity, the basis of particular character – and success in surviving antique origins. Excavated cities (such as Pompeii) are, of necessity, failed entities. Even zealots probably agree that this layered world where history coexists with daily life, enduring in buildings that may themselves be ancient, provides the richest nature of urban experience. Archaeology takes a probing role, recorded, exposed in sections, adding to the levels of memory and imagination. The history of it is the history of all of it.

So how to go about remaking what has vanished, dealing with the destruction of Dublin's urban frame over the last half-century, the legacy of low-energy thinking about the city? Destruction has had dividends for archaeology, but at a price we all pay; the medieval city cannot be treated as an open archaeological park or as a site for poor development denying time and place. Streets have to be rebuilt, but how, and how to absorb their meaning into new work, a practice signally missing from most current developments?

Single works of architecture offer some clues, though first there must be a belief that contemporary design is capable of bearing ideas about history without becoming a ludicrous pastiche. This can happen, but it is more allusive than direct, to do with site, increment, materials, the way a building juts over a street rather than a formal stylistic response. It becomes more interesting when architecture combines old and new; how do you measure new fabric against an old form? It is not scientific, rather like painting a picture; what do you leave and take out? Do you circumscribe or radically adjust the old building? It is more interesting again in buildings made to deal specifically with archaeology; should remains be exposed or covered up; how much should the architecture adjust to it? There are potentially huge linkages, architecture working with archaeology, using imagination to develop vigorous and sustainable designs with adventurous structures and new technology. Ireland is very poorly served in this work, though the radical engagement of new with old is a consistent theme of good European architecture.

These ideas were brought to bear on the Ship Street–Werburgh Street Framework Plan at a strategic and a detailed level. The first actions were to survey topography, upstanding buildings and the archaeological record, noting the city wall – the largest single medieval artefact in Dublin – as a dividing line between 'inside' and 'outside', a marker of different histories, plot lines, section and architecture. Its line through the city at this point is shadowed by the Poddle; Ship Street is as much the line of the river as the wall. Maps and images were studied to explore the evolved history of Tudor, Caroline and Georgian streets and spaces – the most particular aspect of this period the way the area on both sides of the wall had been overbuilt, creating a dense network of alleys and courts against the medieval defences. This evolution is well known to archaeologists; Speed's map of 1610 shows the line relatively clearly with space inside and out; Rocque's 1756 map reveals it at its densest; clearances gradually revealing the monument into the twentieth century. All of these had a right to be represented or considered in a new plan.

The first Framework Plan proposal was not about physical change, but about breathing some life into the identity of the quarter to reclaim its damaged memory; a map was drawn setting out and 'naming' all of the vanished monuments, spaces and well-known buildings that had once stood there. The second was to take a radical approach to the treatment of existing fabric; the plan proposed that every existing building of any age would be conserved and given some form of protection, with plenty of space left for intelligent innovation. Thirdly, it was proposed that the essential street lines, which encapsulated the area's embedded memory, would also be regarded as of value, lines rebuilt with clear and innovative contemporary architecture paying some regard (but not slavish emulation) to the grain and plot of the city.

Strategically, the quarter had to be reintegrated into the city and developed to support the amenity of modern urban life; to achieve this, a network of new routes and public spaces was proposed. The Dublin City Walls Conservation Plan had already proposed a public route around the walls, advocating a hierarchy of response, firstly the maintenance and repair of the wall, then an enhancement of its context, and finally the linkage of the sections by a new route that would allow a coherent understanding of them. Running from Dublin Castle through to Ross Road, the Ship Street section of the walls were clearly an important part of the whole; the plan set out a new public space in front of it; other routes fanned out into existing streets and through new lanes and courtyards, linking a network of civic spaces that would generate an overall hierarchy and legibility for the plan (fig. 13.2). Some of these spaces were existing – the green spaces at Christ Church, Dublin Castle Gardens and St Patrick's Park – and had to be knitted in; others were new – Ship Street, another around the site of St Michael le Pole and a third behind Whitefriar Street. Proposals for investing in old street-lines generated an interesting

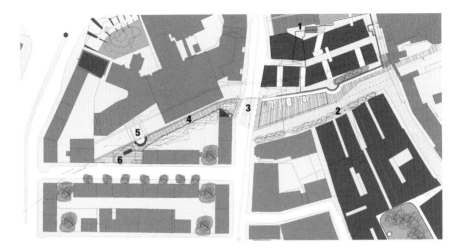

13.2 Ship Street Square and wall route to Genevel's Tower and Ross Road: (1) new development on old plots, Werburgh Street/Hoey's Court; new walk along the top of the wall; (2) Ship Street Square; (3) infill building with ground floor arch leading to Ross Road; (4) Walk along external side of wall; (5) Genevel's Tower; (6) new tower at Ross Road.

debate on Golden Lane, where the plan analysis found that building set-backs created since the 1950s were a massive overprovision; whole sections of new city could be reconstructed on them without loss of reasonable circulation.

It was clear that approaches to dealing with the city walls in the Framework Plan area would have wider implications for the way they would be dealt with in other areas of the city. The plan was proscriptive in terms of the character, material and height of any new development in the quarter; to be successful in such circumstances, architecture would be specified to a greater degree than was traditional in Dublin. However, it also had to be open to new ideas and other solutions.

Ship Street was doubly important, as it combined the most accessible section of city wall with the potential for the best urban space. Standing at the corner of Ship Streets Little and Great, it forms a dramatic line running from the castle to St Werburgh's Gate; there is a strong sectional difference between inside and outside (fig. 13.2). The architecture of the space was established in stages; the first action would be to properly excavate and conserve the wall and then to provide a proper context for it. Despite a strong interest in the accretive nature of the seventeenth- and eighteenth-century city, it was considered appropriate in this case to remove the small amount of later fabric in front of it to expose its full length. Professional excavation and conservation on the moat side would reveal more of the wall and bring out its detail; the conserved artefact would be displayed against a finely made stone surface angled downwards to accommodate (and accentuate) the increased height. The

13.3 View of city wall, Ship Street.

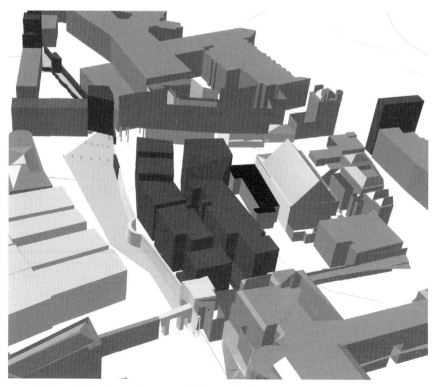

13.4 3D view of Ship Street Square and adjacent development.

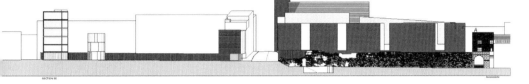

13.5 Elevation of city wall and Werburgh Street at Ship Street Square.

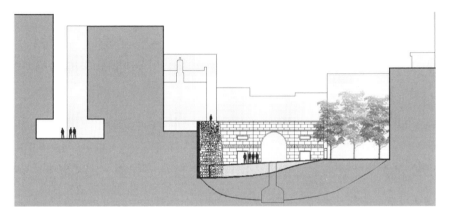

13.6 Section of Ship Street Square.

13.7 Perspective of Ship Street Square.

13.8 View of Ross Road.

new square also marked the line of the Poddle in its paving and enclosed a new subterranean Poddle listening room and viewing chamber below ground (figs 13.3, 13.4, 13.5, 13.6, 13.7).

Within the walls, the plan of Werburgh Street was studied, exploring its original form as an elongated square around the baroque church façade; the Framework Plan suggested that new buildings on the empty site around Hoey's Court would project further into the street than the present line, recreating a sense of enclosure, but also be set back from the line of the city walls to create an accessible public wall-walk. Subject to a critical analysis of architectural quality (and carefully specified as framed on light piled foundations), new buildings were to be contemporary in character, formed on east-west plots, based generally on the morphological formation of Hoey's Court, and open up views and access to St Werburgh's churchyard. The architecture envisaged a brick building with a very open ground-floor level; this rose through a solid base to a series of individual blocks above it; this arrangement unashamedly emphasized the towering difference between inside and outside the walls, creating a dramatic architectural background to the new square.

The public route was extended from St Werburgh's Gate to Ross Road, the design approach changing in response to the fact that the city wall here was a property line with a narrow strip of land outside it; the excavated base of Genevel's Tower lay in a chamber about midway along. A new building was proposed for the gap site in Werburgh Street. Starting here, the line of the city wall was marked by a Cortene steel and wattle surface, its top level approximating to the height that the buried wall would have been, had it survived.

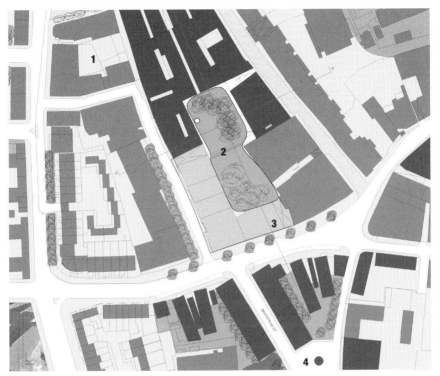

13.9 Ship Street and Golden Lane: (1) development on Ship Street; (2) courtyard garden St Michael le Pole; (3) Golden Lane, new housing on old streetline; (4) Whitefriar Square.

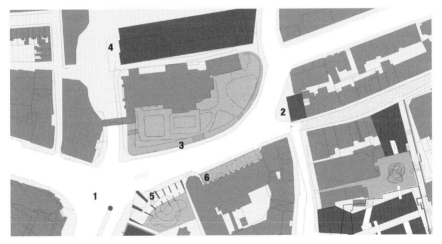

13.10 Christchurch Place (plan), remaking a coherent urban space around the cathedral: (1) new monument on traffic island; (2) new book-end building at east end; (3) Christchurch Museum and Visitor Centre with grass roof built below line of railings; (4) Museum of Dublin; (5) new public building, access to Peace Garden behind; (6) additional infill to hotel to original streetline.

Genevel's Tower was celebrated by a tower-like projection giving convenient public access; the route ended at Ross Road with modern residential tower structures marking the other end of a demonstration scheme designed to extend – with time – all the way around the walls of Dublin (fig. 13.8).

Illustrations survive of the round tower that formerly stood in the church of St Michael le Pole; its location on Ship Street was known, as the foundations had been part-excavated – familiar to archaeologists, but less so to fellow citizens. There was limited development on the site (in 2007); the Framework Plan proposed that any new project should include a singular public space near the site of the church, a circular outdoor room lined in wattle or timber. Given St Michael's original position outside the walls, the space was green in character and open to the south and the sun, its planting incorporating some memory of it being 'outside' the walls or in the country. It also contained a contemporary sculpture – an austere steel cylinder of considerable height invoking some memory of the round tower without emulating its detail. This approach, using carefully integrated contemporary form to dig deep for meaning, is potentially rewarding in creating urban landscapes; the tower created a significant monument in the city that, in the context of the Framework Plan, would be visible from the city walls, reestablishing their taut physical and cultural relationship (fig. 13.9).

Working in Christchurch Place was very different (fig. 13.10). It still existed in outline; it had been subject to significant evolution over time – there was the work by the Wide Streets Commissioners and G.E. Street's dramatic Victorian alterations to the cathedral; it also remained, in some way, the ceremonial heart of the city, close to hearts and minds. Random demolitions had removed the urban context of the monuments, leaving them rawly exposed in the middle of busy roads and inappropriate green spaces. The Framework Plan proposed that Christ Church's legibility would be improved by a new urban context of quality around it, the monument seen – as before – over the roofs and against the walls of 'ordinary' buildings. In making proposals, there was a strong awareness of the contentious nature of the space given its history and the emotive context of the Wood Quay debate. This ended, unsatisfactorily, with the Civic Offices framing a view of the cathedral across a green sward, the monument reduced to a picturesque object rather than a titanic form soaring over a medieval density of streets.

The layout required an acceptance of evolution; it was not a reconstruction of inconvenient medieval streets, but a recognition of the intelligent intentions of the Wide Streets Commissioners and, later, Street's work to create a dramatic space for an (increasingly) dramatic monument. Much of the value relied on an absolute requirement for high-quality architecture, a view taken that low standards of design were too easily accepted in Dublin and that better contemporary work could be specified for special areas of interest. This

13.11 Perspective of Christchurch Place.

resulted in stated standards for heights, materials and building increment, discouraging single large-scale developments in lieu of a series of smaller interventions, and placing strict controls on foundation design and basements. Achieved in other European contexts, there was no absolute reason why it would not work in Dublin. Single building proposals were considered in terms of their dramatic potential to complete existing urban vistas.

Four interventions were projected to initiate a new enclosure, generally (but not absolutely) aligned on earlier street plans. The first was a brick tower on the vacant site at the junction of Castle Street and Skinners Row. This corner was of particular resonance in the history of the city, perhaps its first crossroads, the site of the last timber building in Dublin, and deserved particular attention. Substantially open at ground floor, the new structure formed a relationship with the modern brick building on the opposite corner and closed the vistas down Christchurch Place and Werburgh Street (figs 13.11, 13.12).

The second intervention was a new corner building on and over the Peace Garden, incorporating the remains of the church of St Nicholas Within behind it. Arcaded at ground-floor level, this incorporated rather than removed the garden; given that this was the site of the tholsel, a public use was suggested. St Nicholas Within was to be re-roofed and serve as an information

13.12 Book-end building, Christchurch Place.

centre for the quarter. As elsewhere, the response was an architecture attuned to place and history without being pastiche, incorporating and building on rather than removing and excluding. The scheme did not take on the massive traffic junction at Patrick Street, leaving the re-civilianization of that zone for another phase of recovery; it did, however, initiate the re-focusing of Christchurch Place as a coherent urban space (fig. 13.13).

A third initiative placed a single-storey grass-roofed sliver of rooms against the retaining wall separating the cathedral from Christchurch Place; this form – practically invisible – was proposed as a potential Cathedral Visitor Centre, discreet glazing opening onto old stonework. The fourth set out a new Museum of Dublin on John's Lane north of the cathedral, where a terrace of low houses stood until around forty years ago. This proposal had multiple implications, not least the extant graveyard of St John's Church. The architecture worked to resolve this, form pushed into shape by particular circumstance; it became a contemporary form, with an evolved roof structure raised over an open ground floor to protect new excavations. The intention was, in part, to initiate a debate about the re-habitation of the Civic Offices, urban fabric or open green space, returning the cathedral to its original context or accepting the twentieth-century diminution of density as a necessary progression.

13.13 View of new public building, Christchurch Place.

Further South, Golden Lane was 'narrowed' (as opposed to the universal 'widening' of recent decades); the Framework Plan put forward an idea for a phased redevelopment of the housing here on a different, denser plan. This intervention also started to redefine the edge of the 'monastic oval' and shaped a new public space on Whitefriar Street at the site of one of Dublin's eighteenth-century Methodist meeting houses. A new building project was located precisely on its footprint, taking on any eighteenth-century foundations as a given discipline.

St Sepulchre's Palace, and St Patrick's Cathedral and Park were also the focus of study, giving some support to their very particular origins and urban evolution (fig. 13.14). Unlike Christ Church, the status of St Patrick's as a free-standing monument with the fortified palace beside it had some ancient validity, despite extensive – and haphazard – development around them in the

13.14 St Patrick's and St Sepulchre's: (1) St Patrick's Park; new layout; (2) new green context for St Patrick's; (3) St Sepulchre's Museum.

seventeenth and eighteenth centuries. The park was a success in bringing green space to a very dense quarter and returning some sense of this original context. Until the 1950s and 1960s, however, park and cathedral were set in a close network of streets that gave them 'meaning' as open space and monument; these had been pointlessly dissipated – especially the intense space of Cross Poddle to the south. The Framework Plan here responded, not by building substantial new structures, but by emphasizing open space, greenery and old linkages. It made the simple statement that the deanery, palace and cathedral might work in a more integrated way by recreating the open space of the close between them, the existing tarmac road relaid as a green route. St Sepulchre's was designated as an accessible public cultural building in the plan, sharpening the focus on its future role as one of the great monuments of Dublin.

In the end, the framework produced a series of mini-plans and inter-ventions based on a detailed examination of place rather than an approach supporting total redevelopment; there was an overall strategy but it was a flexible policy of working with the grain to make memorable new places. The new architecture created spaces and linkages and was sustained by a commitment to the retention and refurbishment of existing fabric and to a new public realm of quality paving, signage and utilities. It was important that the architecture of new buildings would be contemporary in expression and that their quality would derive from design, the use of good materials, mixed functions, life at ground-floor level and the proper increment of development. While the resolution was tied to the particular issues of the city, it was a universally applicable attempt to knit archaeology, urban design and history into a weave that would sustain a twenty-first-century search for new and original urban life.

* * *

It is worth some analysis of what has occurred since the plan was completed and passed by Dublin City Council. One immediate impact was to halt suggestions for a new development on part of the Ship Street public space, but other results were slow. In one way, despite its small increment, the plan was a product of expansionary times; the finance to support both conservation and new work of quality has evaporated. Development did occur after its incorporation, with some notice taken of general aspects of the plan, but without any detailed reference to heights, densities or materials; it was used in the relatively unspecific way that all framework plans tend to operate, without recourse to the detailed specifications required to deliver real quality. Old fabric continued to be removed. In truth, the inclusive nature of the planning required to deliver this kind of small-boned change is very difficult to deliver in early twenty-first-century Dublin, faced by the increment of profitable development, complex landownership patterns, legal assault and private property legislation, uneven Protected Structures implementation and low general expectations of high quality and good results. It is possibly useful to ask the question the other way: if you wished to achieve something along these lines, what would have to change? Some of the answer would lie in convincing a wider constituency of the value of the result, and the work required to achieve it – a matter of clear, agreed aims and dogged consistency. While some of the ideas may lie fallow for a time, efforts continue to try and bring the new public space in front of the Ship Street wall into being. Revealing this monument would have a strong and lasting impact, establishing the city walls as one of the key structures in the city plan. If executed, it would perhaps stand as the city's first great urban achievement of the new century.